T0375064

DUMBARTON OAKS
MEDIEVAL LIBRARY

Daniel Donoghue, General Editor

JEWEL OF THE SOUL

VOLUME I

HONORIUS AUGUSTODUNENSIS

DOML 79

DUMBARTON OAKS MEDIEVAL LIBRARY

Daniel Donoghue, General Editor
Danuta Shanzer, Medieval Latin Editor

Jan M. Ziolkowski, Founding Editor

Medieval Latin Editorial Board
Julia Barrow
Thomas F. X. Noble
Daniel Nodes
Michael Roberts

Medieval Latin Advisory Board
Walter Berschin
Ralph Hexter
Mayke de Jong
José Martínez Gázquez
Kurt Smolak
Francesco Stella
Jean-Yves Tilliette

Jewel of the Soul

VOLUME I
HONORIUS AUGUSTODUNENSIS

Edited and Translated by

ZACHARY THOMAS
and
GERHARD EGER

DUMBARTON OAKS
MEDIEVAL LIBRARY

HARVARD UNIVERSITY PRESS
CAMBRIDGE, MASSACHUSETTS
LONDON, ENGLAND
2023

Copyright © 2023 by the President and Fellows of Harvard College

ALL RIGHTS RESERVED

Printed in the United States of America

First Printing

Library of Congress Cataloging-in-Publication Data available from the Library of Congress at https://lccn.loc.gov/2022038059

ISBN 978-0-674-29081-5 (cloth : alk. paper)

Contents

Introduction   vii

DEDICATORY LETTERS   2

PREFACE   6

BOOK 1   10

BOOK 2   430

Abbreviations   559
Note on the Text   561
Notes to the Text   565
Notes to the Translation   569

Introduction

Honorius Augustodunensis's *Gemma animae,* or *Jewel of the Soul,* stands out among the treatises of the pre-Scholastic blossoming of commentary on the Franco-Roman liturgical rite. Building on the work of Amalar of Metz (775–850), who wrote during the formative stage of this rite, the *Jewel* is a liturgical encyclopedia, a rhymed-prose *summa* that explains the sacred mysteries of the Latin Church for clerics. It was read and imitated widely in the twelfth and thirteenth centuries as the major authority on the liturgy, only superseded by William Durand's *Rationale divinorum officiorum* (1291–1292), a work deeply indebted to it.

LIFE AND WORKS

The fame of the *Jewel*'s author—a priest, monk, and hermit active in southern Germany and Austria—did not, unfortunately, leave sufficient clues for a biography of his life in any traditional sense. Modern accounts conflict and, given the lack of solid ground, ring either overconfident or discouragingly negative. In the end, the clearest windows into Honorius's person remain his works, which reveal a consistent vision of spiritual realities that he labored passionately to convey in the service of Church reform.

Evidence from his early writings suggests Honorius may have begun an ecclesiastical career at Canterbury in England, learning at the feet of the saintly archbishop Anselm (r. 1093–1109) and collecting materials for his own oeuvre. Early in life, he published his *Elucidarium,* an exceptionally successful catechism soon translated into many languages, and likely his *Offendiculum,* a tract on clerical celibacy. Leaving England sometime after Anselm's death (1109/10), he eventually settled in another dynamic center of the Gregorian reform, the imperial city of Regensburg, where he completed the majority of his works.[1]

In a late composition, *De luminaribus Ecclesiae,* Honorius styles himself *Augustodunensis ecclesiae presbyter et scholasticus,* which should mean "priest and schoolmaster of the church of Autun."[2] Evidence tying him to that city, however, is equivocal.[3] Valerie Flint has taken the designation to refer to Regensburg's *Alte Kapelle,* where, she argues, Honorius lived as a canon and teacher under the patronage of bishops Hartwig (r. 1105–1126) and Cuno (r. 1126–1133).[4] *De luminaribus* lists twenty-one works by Honorius, probably in chronological order. They form a broad teaching library, featuring an encyclopedia of cosmology and geography *(Imago mundi),* a chronicle of world history *(Summa totius),* liturgical works and sermons, and commentaries on the Psalms and the Song of Songs, of which he was especially proud. A handful of polemical writings agitated, in the context of the Gregorian reform, for a pastoral role for monks, and his *Summa gloria* took an extreme line on papal supremacy during the Investiture Controversy, a conflict between the emperor and the pope over primacy in Church affairs.

Honorius's writings reveal him to be a gifted teacher and

preacher, an encyclopedist, an Augustinian Neoplatonist, and one of his century's few students of Eriugena and, through him, of Dionysius the Areopagite.[5] In some cases, the thrust of his literary labors — frequently expressed in dedicatory letters — was to create teaching materials and accessible summaries of clerical culture for religious houses with limited access to books. Steering clear of novelty and speculation, he aimed to compile and order knowledge, but he did so with trademark genius for lively, dramatic expression that won acclaim across Europe. In other works, such as the commentaries on the Psalms and the Song of Songs, Honorius made bold new syntheses and constructed a highly alluring cosmic vision.

Around 1133, according to Flint, Honorius took the Benedictine habit and spent the rest of his life as a solitary, at Weih Sankt Peter in Regensburg or Lambach Abbey in Austria, passing to his reward around 1140.[6] Beyond the grave, Honorius the recluse and teacher wags his finger at modern students' immoderate curiosity about his identity, urging us to look past his person to that vision of glory and cosmic harmony for which his labors were meant only as a means of transport.

SCRIPTURE AND ALLEGORY

Honorius's liturgical writings include his *Sigillum beatae Mariae,* a short commentary on the office of the Assumption; his *Speculum Ecclesiae,* a widely received cycle of sermons; his *Sacramentarium,* a pithy discussion of liturgical topics; and the *Jewel of the Soul,* a full-length commentary on the Mass, Office, and liturgical year.

The genre of liturgical commentary to which the *Jewel* belongs has its roots in early Christian biblical typology. Christ's life was seen as a recapitulation of the foundational events and persons of Jewish history: he is a new Adam who founded a renewed people, and a new Moses who gave God's law on a mountain (Matthew 5–7) and commanded the waters (Mark 4). His death was a Passover sacrifice, liberating souls from the devil's dominion and settling them in a new paradise, the Church. Christ is therefore the antitype, the reality behind the types or shadows of the Old Testament.[7]

Typology allowed Christian sages to read the entirety of scripture as the record of God's mysterious dealings with humanity from the world's creation and to unfold the sundry ways his saving work was prefigured in its narratives and prophecies. They drew on Hellenistic literary theory to create a hermeneutic based on three mystical or spiritual senses beyond the literal meaning.[8] Simply put, all scripture could simultaneously report a historical event (the literal or historical sense), point to mysteries in the New Testament (the allegorical or typological sense), speak to the present life of an individual soul (the moral or tropological sense), and represent heavenly or eternal realities (the anagogical or eschatological sense). Thus, Noah's wooden ark is at once Christ upon the wood of the Cross, battered by the storm of God's penalty for our sins, the sole means of salvation (allegorically); the individual soul afloat amid a sea of temptation, yearning for her final port of rest (morally); and the Church, containing all the faithful and bearing them safely across the flood of the world to the port of heaven (anagogically).[9]

The ensemble of these senses was called allegorical interpretation. But how far could this four-tiered reading be ap-

plied? Did *every* detail of scripture conceal a manifold Christian mystery? Augustine offered one stable, flexible "rule of charity": any interpretation is legitimate if it builds up the Christian Church in charity, provided it does not contradict the faith.[10]

Patristic and Carolingian Commentaries

The earliest liturgical commentators used allegory to interpret the ancient Christian rites, especially those connected with Easter and baptism.[11] Theodore of Mopsuestia (d. 428) and Narsai (d. 502) went further, applying the spiritual senses to specific ritual actions. Among the Latins, Ambrose (d. 397) and Isidore (d. 636) wrote influential liturgical treatises that contain many allegorical themes,[12] while the *Expositio* of the Gallican Mass (early eighth century) explains certain rituals allegorically. This method, however, remained inchoate in the West in the early Middle Ages.

Charlemagne's importation of the Roman rite across the Alps injected new energy into liturgical exegesis. Handbooks were needed to train clergy and explain the new books. Moreover, as the foreign rite melded with the local rites of the Empire, allegory became a convenient tool to arbitrate ritual preferences. The ninth century, therefore, witnessed an explosion of *expositiones missae*, short and often anonymous treatises that explain the Mass and baptismal rituals, mixing literal and allegorical approaches.[13] Major Carolingian authors such as Alcuin, Rabanus Maurus, and Walafrid Strabo made contributions, but it was Amalar of Metz who first applied the fourfold method in full in his *Liber officialis*, claiming to have uncovered the whole narrative of salvation

history and Christian doctrine behind the liturgical symbols and actions.[14] Though he portrayed it as a revelation, he was really building on traditional mystagogical foundations.[15]

Amalar's allegorical method was not welcomed everywhere. Agobard and Florus of Lyons fiercely attacked it and in their own treatises favored a historical approach that stuck more closely to patristic precedents. Despite this criticism, the Amalarian approach soon predominated.

Revival of Liturgical Commentary

Commentary on the liturgy waned after Amalar. Even as the Franco-Roman rite developed rapidly, its geographical horizons expanded, and need for clerical education grew, new reflective scholarship on the liturgy ceded place to eclectic compilations and anthologies.[16] By 1100, however, the winds had shifted. Gregorian reformers of the previous century had initiated a struggle over the nature of religious authority, pushing for the reconstruction of religious experience based on the ideal of Gospel sources, the primitive Church, and Roman authority. In this context, Honorius's liturgical work may profitably be viewed as part of an international effort by contemporary compilers of the *Glossa ordinaria,* concordances of canon law, and early *summae,* to reform Christian life faithfully through a rational process *(ratio),* in order to bring it into full harmony *(concordia)* with the authority of sacred texts and Roman precedent *(auctoritas).*[17] The ensemble of writings produced on the liturgy in this period employed a mix of allegorical and canonical-historical methods designed to establish the legitimacy of liturgical customs in the face of the new scrutiny visited upon the post-Carolingian Church. Allegory *(allegoria)* was central to

their project, since sound mystical reasons could justify a departure from precedent, as could history *(historia)*, since conformity with approved models and sacred precedents was highly coveted.

In the eleventh century, Berno of Reichenau (d. 1048) and Bonizo of Sutri (d. ca. 1095) pioneered an account of ritual customs based on the New Testament and papal decrees as recorded in the *Liber pontificalis* and collections of canon law.[18] As the Investiture Controversy intensified, Bernold of Constance extended the historical-canonical approach while advocating close adherence to Roman practice in his *Micrologus de ecclesiasticis observationibus* (ca. 1085–1110), a work that set the standard for the Roman rite in the Empire and beyond.[19] Once polemics between papacy and empire wound down, allegory came back to the fore in works like Rupert of Deutz's *De divinis officiis,* dedicated to Bishop Cuno, and Ivo of Chartres's (d. 1115) sermons, which seek Old Testament precedents for Christian rituals.

The demand for liturgical commentaries that swept Europe during the twelfth century and brought Rupert's treatise to Regensburg also drove a certain "company" of unidentified canons "on campaign" in the area of Regensburg to request a volume from Honorius (*Jewel,* Dedictory Letter 1). By 1140 he had probably put the last touches on his watershed contribution to this renaissance.[21]

SUMMARY

The title *Jewel of the Soul* leads us directly into the world of allegory with a trope that makes a notable appearance in Honorius's later commentary on the Song of Songs, where the precious stones of the beloved's necklace stand for scrip-

ture verses, or the doctrine that beautifies the soul.[21] Similarly, the heavenly Jerusalem is "a rare jewel" whose foundations, the saints, flash like precious stones.[22] Morally, a just person emerges from the fiery pressures of tribulation as a flashing gem to adorn the walls of heaven (see *Jewel* 1.141). In the allegorical optic, therefore, the divine services are Christ's dower for the Christian soul, an interior castle, a mystical foretaste of the heavenly Jerusalem.[23]

The first book contains the Mass commentary and three other treatises: on the church building, on the ministers, and on sacred vestments. The Mass commentary has three parts. The first is an allegorical commentary on the seven "offices," or parts of the Mass. The ritual alternates in an Augustinian dialectic between acts of Christ (the head) and the Church (his body), each part also recalling an event in the Old Testament. The rite commented on is a solemn pontifical Mass as celebrated in twelfth-century German cathedrals, though viewed through the lens of more ancient texts in the tradition of the *Ordines Romani.*

The first office (1.3–12) is the bishop's entrance, prayer, and seating on his throne, which represents Christ's royal entry into the cosmos (1.6.2), Passion (1.7.2), and enthronement in heaven (1.7.3), and recalls how Moses delivered the Jews from Egypt. The second office (1.13–18), covering the reading of the Epistle and intercalary chants, displays the work of the apostles who "thundered forth scripture in the world" after Christ's ascension (1.13), and recalls Miriam's victory song. The third office (1.19–25), which is Christ's preaching, comprises the Gospel reading, sermon, and recitation of the Creed. It was prefigured by Moses when he received and taught the tablets of the Law. The fourth (1.26–

43) describes an offertory procession, which Honorius exploits to introduce a compendium of ascetic theology (1.29–30); the people of Israel prefigured it when they gave offerings for the Tabernacle's construction. The fifth office (1.44–59), whose type is the Israelites' battle with Amalek, covers the consecratory prayers of the Roman Canon. Couched as an account of the twenty-three signs of the cross made over the offerings (1.50–56), these chapters reveal a theology of history as the story of humanity's redemption in successive ages. The sixth office is the pontifical blessing (1.60), presented as a summation of the biblical promises and blessings that are fulfilled in the Eucharist. The seventh office (1.61–67), including the final blessing and Postcommunion, shows Christ's Resurrection and Ascension when he gave peace to the whole world, just as Joshua distributed the spoils of conquest to the children of Israel.

The next part is a miscellany of allegories drawn from sacred scripture. Chapters 1.68–71 treat processions, likening them to the Hebrews' victorious march to the Promised Land. In 1.72–79 and 81, Honorius reads the Mass as a lively stage fight. Finally, chapters 1.86–121 give a more literal commentary, joining the tradition of the Carolingian *expositiones missae* with contemporary interest in canon law and concluding with questions on ritual practice.

The treatise on the church building (1.122–71) describes ecclesiastical architecture and decor (1.122–49) and then goes through the consecration ritual (1.150–71). The church fabric and decoration symbolize the "spiritual edifice" of believers (1 Corinthians 3:9–11, 16–17) and form an image of the cosmos (1.124, 139). The consecration shows Christ's nuptial coupling with his Church (1.149) in the presence of

the angels and saints, and is also a *mise-en-scène* of the soul's interior wedding to Christ (1.159). The treatise on ministers (1.172–97) introduces them in hierarchical order (1.172–89), then their rites of ordination and tonsure (1.190–97), stressing continuity between the Christian and Mosaic priesthood. The treatise on sacred vestments (1.198–243), the longest written in the Middle Ages, describes vestments proper to each sacred order and includes the earliest surviving discussion of several episcopal vestments.[24] This section also touches on ecclesiology, laying out the powers of archbishops, patriarchs, and popes.[25]

Book 2 turns to the Divine Office. If the Mass reenacts Christ's life and death, the Office, with its weekly Psalter and cycle of Old Testament readings arranged by Jerome (2.17), plunges readers into a sacred history spanning the six ages, wherein the soul recovers, celebrates, and internalizes the voices of those who have served God in justice. At Sunday Matins each nocturn corresponds to the watch duty of certain patriarchs: the psalms of the first nocturn, for example, are sung by Abel, Enos, Enoch, and Lamech (2.2). By another allegory, the Divine Office depicts the work of just men in Christ's vineyard through successive ages of the world (2.18–26). Honorius draws his exegesis of Lauds (2.31–53) from a constellation of scriptural allusions revolving around the *Benedictus* canticle that concludes Lauds. He gives a sparing glance at Vespers in 2.62 but does not submit each psalm to detailed analysis. As one who lived between the canonry, observing the Roman office, and the monastery, which followed Saint Benedict's arrangement, Honorius is keen to reveal the harmony of the two forms of the office, discovering an identical allegorical scheme in both psalm orderings (2.28–30, 65–68).

Book 3 treats the major feasts of the Christian year. Beginning with the Epiphany cycle, he gives reasons for the feast's institution and examines each Sunday's salient responsories and antiphons (3.1–5). The Paschal cycle takes up the rest of the book, with special attention to the catechumenate (3.53–69) and the baptismal ceremonies of Holy Week (3.110–16). Chapters 136 to 147 take up the Rogation litanies, Ascension, the Pentecost Vigil, and the ordinations on Ember Saturday (3.150–56), rounding off the temporal cycle with brief remarks on the post-Pentecost season (3.157–59). Scattered notes on a few saints' feasts reveal no clear design, and may be unfinished (3.160–69).

Book 4 is Honorius's original attempt to account for all Sundays of the year, including the Sundays after Pentecost, within a single allegorical scheme.[26] If the Mass and annual feasts celebrated the earthly life of Christ (the head), the Sundays *per annum* follow the paths of his body, the Church, in its millennial pilgrimage toward heaven. Honorius sets out to show how Jerome and Gregory ordered the liturgical cycle as a continuous pageant portraying the journey of God's people through six ages of exile *(peregrinatio)*, sustained along the way by God's consolation *(consolatio)*, from creation to the present day.

The readings and responsories at Matins *(historiae)* form the basis of an exposition of the liturgical year in three cycles. The propers of each Sunday office perform parallel episodes from the Old and New Testaments. In each case, the latter is shown to follow the former's pattern. The readings of the first cycle, from Septuagesima to Pentecost (4.2–42), represent various exiles and returns of God's people to the Promised Land, up to the establishment of the monarchy; each is shown to correspond to a Christian mystery, culmi-

nating in the gift of the Holy Spirit (4.42). The second cycle sings the story of the Jewish kingdom and the Christian Church. On the first Sunday after the Octave of Pentecost, Saul hounds David (4.43) and Christians are "oppressed by infidels, heretics, or bad Catholics" (4.44). By the sixth Sunday (4.55), Solomon is crowned and Constantine rules over the Christian people (4.56). On the nineteenth Sunday, *Salus populi,* King Cyrus frees the Jews (4.86) and Charlemagne "transfers the Roman Empire to Germany" (4.87). The last Sunday points to the end times, when Nebuchadnezzar, a symbol of Antichrist, appears in the reading of Judith. Finally, the Christmas-Epiphany cycle celebrates the world's expectation of Christ's birth and his manifestation through miracles (4.99–115). The book concludes with notes on the Office of the Dead and a collection of rubrics (4.116–18). An ornate peroration commends the *Jewel* to the company of canons, here recast as "daughters of Jerusalem."

SOURCES FOR THE *JEWEL*

The *Jewel* takes inherited patristic themes and types of Carolingian commentary and tailors them to suit the new methods and perspectives of the twelfth century. Literal and allegorical currents *(allegoria)* from Isidore, pseudo-Alcuin, and Amalar blend with a more recent historical-canonical stream *(historia)* emanating from Berno and Bernold, both authors from the southern Imperial sphere in vogue at Regensburg. Key themes plucked from Honorius's sermons and other works link the liturgy with other aspects of medieval culture—including theology, art, and science.

Honorius draws widely from Amalar's works—especially

the *Liber de ordine antiphonarii, Eclogae,* and *Liber officialis.* In Book 1, Honorius uses Amalar's themes and imagery to craft a more lively, flowing, and systematic Mass commentary, which he intersperses with notes from *Micrologus,* Isidore, and Rabanus Maurus. Minor Amalarian works were also consulted,[27] but the historical-canonical sections (1.86–90, 112–21) are gleaned from the South German tradition of Berno, Bonizo, and Bernold. The treatise on the church building may be more original, but it draws key notions from Honorius's own sermon *De dedicatione* and Bede's *De tabernaculo,* while the treatise on the dedication of a church merely streamlines the Carolingian *Quid significent duodecim candelae* to heighten its dramatic and narrative effect and highlight nuptial and Christological allegories.[28]

Book 2 reorganizes themes and material from *Liber officialis* 4 while accenting anagogical and astrological elements. Book 3 borrows from Amalar, pseudo-Alcuin, Bede, and others' treatises on the liturgical year.[29] Book 4's effort to transcribe the harmony of the Sunday offices is inspired by Berno's tentative steps in this direction in his *De quibusdam rebus pertinentibus ad missae officium libellus.* Honorius goes much further, unveiling a comprehensive musical score linking all Sundays, which thus become individual movements of a grander symphony.[30] The book marks a major contribution to the contemporary trend of concordist exegesis and may have inspired Joachim of Fiori.[31] The book also engages with *Micrologus*'s ritual prescriptions, concluding with a digest of its rubrics for the liturgical year (4.117), but avoids its polemical tone and accommodates departures from its rigid prescriptions. Finally, the liturgy of Regensburg shows through most clearly in this book, reminding us that Hono-

rius's liturgical works "should be considered as an integral part of the Regensburg liturgical landscape."[32]

INFLUENCE

The *Jewel*'s popularity is indicated by its survival in over seventy manuscripts. It was copied mainly in the scriptoria of the Empire, particularly in southern Germany, where large excerpts were also translated into German as part of the *Lucidarius* (1190–1195), an encyclopedia for laymen, and incorporated into the twelfth-century Ritual of Augsburg.[33] Many were owned by monastic houses that espoused the Gorze-Fruttuarian reform dear to Honorius and his patrons, and by regular canonical houses.[34] His work was soon taken up as the chief source for Sicard of Cremona's *Mitrale* (ca. 1180), written in Paris or Mainz, which later influenced Innocent III.[35]

Outside the Empire, over a dozen manuscripts survive in France and England, and a handful even in central Italy. Robert Paululus in his *De caeremoniis* (ca. 1175–1185) and John Beleth in his *Summa de ecclesiasticis officiis* (1160–1164) did Honorius the honor of extensive borrowing, and Rudolf of Liebegg used him in his popular versified handbook *Pastorale novellum* (1323–1325).[36] Catalogs show that copies of the *Jewel* circulated especially in Augustinian and Benedictine houses in England, where Gerald of Wales lifted passages regarding Church officials for his *De principis instructione*.[37] The fact that only seven of the known manuscripts date to later than the thirteenth century points to the *Jewel*'s eclipse by William Durand's *Rationale divinorum officiorum*, which nevertheless follows in the channel cut by Honorius's

wedding of *allegoria* and *historia*.[38] Its critical apparatus reveals ample borrowing from the *Jewel*. Still, as late as 1397, Radulph of Rivo makes the *Micrologus* and *Jewel* the twin pillars of his Mass commentary in *Liber de canonum observantia,* adding little more than cross-references to Gratian's decretals.[39]

Allegorical commentary was beloved of clergy and laity alike, as attested by thousands of sermons and devotional treatises and expressed in the vivid mimetic piety of layfolk such as Elisabeth of Spalbeek (1246–1304).[40] The *Jewel* supplied material for the *Hortus deliciarum,* an illuminated encyclopedia for the instruction of female religious, and fed a wider taste for allegorical art that, beyond liturgy and exegesis, found less sober expression in the next century in *The Romance of the Rose* and mystery plays.[41] Allegorical commentary on the liturgy deeply informed the styles and interpretations of architecture, sculpture, and other media.[42] In this light, Honorius's commentary may be seen as a fusion of biblical exposition and budding dramatic or even narrative forms of medieval piety.

After a long eclipse, symbolic reading of scripture and liturgy now elicits popular interest once again.[43] Recent scholarship has displayed new appreciation for the presence and power of allegory in many literary genres throughout Christian history.[44] This edition is meant to contribute to the growing consensus that allegorical commentary—as expressed so vividly and ingeniously in the *Jewel*—remains an invaluable window into the medieval world view and a key for unlocking the mysteries of Christian worship and art forms. Honorius shows us how the liturgy was actually experienced by clerics and laymen.

We strive to offer a readable, graceful English version. We could not imitate Honorius's rhyming prose but have tried to preserve his syntax and elements of style, such as alliteration and puns. Honorius writes in rhymed prose, as in the following example:

Agmen in castris aeterni Regis excubans, sub impetu vitiorum undique irruentium desudans, idoneo instructori armorum, laureari in triumpho victorum.

A company on campaign with the army of the eternal King, straining under the assault of the vices that charge against us from all sides, to a skilled instructor in the arts of war: may you wear the laurel crown in the triumphal parade of victors.

Honorius's artful valediction has been rendered in English rhymed prose as a sample of what the Latin text may have sounded like to twelfth-century audiences. Notes elucidate major themes of theology and exegesis and the most important biblical and patristic sources, explain liturgical peculiarities, and point to parallel themes in Honorius's other works, but much remains to be uncovered by a critical edition. Scripture quotations are from the Douay-Rheims translation, modified as needed.

We thank our editors, Daniel Nodes and Danuta Shanzer, and all those whose encouragement and expertise made this work possible, especially Shen Yichen, along with James Monti, Susan Boynton, David Hiley, Gregory DiPippo, Pat-

rick Owens, Julia Schneider, Margot Fassler, Peter Jeffrey, Yitzhak Hen, and our mystagogue Justin Stover, who initiated us into allegory at the Pro Civitate Dei conference by the azure coasts of Provence.

NOTES

1 See Valerie Flint's account, the fruit of lifelong study: "Honorius Augustodunensis of Regensburg," in *Authors of the Middle Ages,* ed. Patrick Geary, Constant Mews, and Valerie Flint (Aldershot, 1995), vol. 2, pp. 89–183. The theory of Irish origin, defended most ably by Marie-Odile Garrigues in her article "Qui était Honorius Augustodunensis?," *Angelicum* 50, no. 1 (1973): 20–49, also merits consideration, as do far more agnostic accounts by Robert Crouse in "*De Neocosmo:* A Critical Edition of the Text with Introduction and Notes" (PhD diss., Harvard University, 1970), and Walter Hannam in "The *Ineuitabile* of Honorius Augustodunensis: A Study in the Textures of Early Twelfth-Century Augustinianisms" (PhD diss., Boston College, 2013).

2 *De luminaribus Ecclesiae* 14.7 (PL 172:232–34).

3 Although Flint rejects any connection to Autun, Garrigues proposes that he was ordained there ("Qui était," 27–29).

4 Flint, "Honorius Augustodunensis of Regensburg." The *Alte Kapelle* was an imperial chapel built on a hill in the city center, hence *Augustodunensis* would mean church "of imperial height," from *augustus* (imperial) and *dun* (hill). Honorius mentions Regensburg in *Imago mundi* and may have written books for the city's religious communities.

5 The precise extent of Eriugena's influence on Honorius is hotly debated. See Robert Crouse, "Disciple of Anselm?," in *Analecta Anselmiana,* ed. Helmut Kohlenberger (Frankfurt, 1975): 137; Crouse, "*Hic sensilis mundus:* Calcidius and Eriugena in Honorius Augustodunensis," in *From Athens to Chartres: Neoplatonism and Medieval Thought,* ed. H. J. Westra (Leiden, 1992), 283–88; Paolo Lucentini, *Platonismo medievale: Contributi per la storia dell'eriugenismo* (Florence, 1980): 56–75; and Hannam, "The *Ineuitabile* of Honorius Augustodunensis," 144–96.

6 See Flint, "Honorius Augustodunensis of Regensburg," 128. She rejects

the earlier suggestion by Josef Endres that Honorius was still active as late as 1153.

7 Typology appears already in the New Testament in Romans 5:14, 1 Corinthians 10:1–5, 1 Corinthians 15, 1 Peter 3:19, Colossians 2:16–17, and John 7:37–38.

8 On the rise of the spiritual senses from Hellenistic allegory, see Jaroslav Brož, "From Allegory to the Four Senses of Scripture: Hermeneutics of the Church Fathers and of the Christian Middle Ages," in *Philosophical Hermeneutics and Biblical Exegesis,* ed. Petr Pokorný and Jan Roskovec (Tübingen, 2002), 301–9.

9 Amalar defines these four senses in his *Liber officialis* 1.19.6. The most authoritative treatment of the four senses is Henri de Lubac, *Medieval Exegesis: The Four Senses of Scripture,* trans. Mark Sebanc and E. M. Macierowski, 3 vols. (Grand Rapids, 1998–2009).

10 See *De doctrina Christiana* 1.36.

11 Saint Cyril of Jerusalem's *Mystagogical Catecheses* (ca. 370s), Maximus the Confessor's *Mystagogy* (ca. 640), and especially Dionysius the Areopagite's *On the Ecclesial Hierarchies* focus on the symbolism of cultic acts and sacred spaces. On liturgical commentators from patristic to medieval times, see Roger E. Reynolds, "Liturgy, Treatises on," in *Dictionary of the Middle Ages,* ed. Joseph Strayer (New York, 1982–1989), vol. 7, pp. 624–33.

12 See Ambrose, *De mysteriis* and *De sacramentis,* and Isidore, *De ecclesiasticis officiis* and *Etymologiae* 6–7.

13 For studies of these texts, see Cyrille Vogel, *Medieval Liturgy: An Introduction to the Sources* (Washington, DC, 1986), and Thomas J. Heffernan and E. Ann Matter, eds., *The Liturgy of the Medieval Church* (Kalamazoo, MI, 2001).

14 See Amalar of Metz, *Liber officialis,* ed. and trans. Eric Knibbs, *On the Liturgy,* 2 vols., Dumbarton Oaks Medieval Library 35 and 36 (Cambridge, MA, 2014), and the thorough work of David Diosi, *Amalarius Fortunatus in der Trierer Tradition* (Münster, 2006).

15 Amalar, *Liber officialis* Pref. 2.

16 On liturgical literature and practice in the Ottonian Church, see Henry Parkes, ed., *Making Liturgy in the Ottonian Church* (Cambridge, 2015), and Reynolds, "Liturgy, Treatises on," 629.

17 On Honorius's role in this movement, see Valeria de Fraja, "*Ratio* e *auctoritas* nella liturgia," in *Prédication et liturgie au Moyen Âge,* ed. Nicole

Bériou and Franco Morenzoni (Turnhout, 2008), 163–81. On liturgy and canon law, see Roger E. Reynolds, *Law and Liturgy in the Latin Church* (Brookfield, VT, 1969).

18 See *Berno Augiensis Tractatus liturgici,* ed. Henry Parkes, CCCM 297 (Turnhout, 2019).

19 The *Micrologus* can be found in *PL* 151:978–1021. See Daniel Taylor, "Bernold of Constance, Canonist and Liturgist of the Gregorian Reform" (PhD diss., University of Toronto, 1995).

20 Marie-Odile Garrigues summarizes attempts to date the *Jewel* in "L'œuvre d'Honorius Augustodunensis: Inventaire critique," *Abhandlungen der Braunschweigischen Wissenschaftlichen Gesellschaft* 38 (1986): 91.

21 "Her necklace is interior understanding, marked by various notions as by precious stones" (*PL* 172:376); "They deck you with their doctrine as with a necklace" (*PL* 172:462); "For faith graces and defends a soul as a necklace graces and protects the breast" (*PL* 172:465). See also *PL* 172:368, 376. Christ himself is the "priceless necklace" in Honorius's *Sigillum beatae Mariae* (*PL* 172:513).

22 See Revelation 21:11, 19. Compare *Jewel* 4.64.

23 For the services as dower, see Honorius, *Expositio in Cantica Canticorum* (*PL* 172:370), where necklaces are the "praises" Christ heaps on his spouse.

24 Joseph Braun, *Die liturgische Gewandung im Occident und Orient: Nach Ursprung und Entwicklung, Verwendung und Symbolik* (Freiburg im Breisgau, 1907), 9.

25 On the understudied role of liturgical commentators in the Investiture Controversy, see Roger E. Reynolds, "Liturgical Scholarship at the Time of the Investiture Controversy," *Harvard Theological Review* 71, nos. 1–2 (1978): 109–24.

26 Amalar reads Lenten and Advent offices allegorically (Book 1 and chapters 3.40–43, 4.30–34). On Honorius and Berno, see Daniel Sheerin, "Interpreting Scripture in and through Liturgy," in *Jewish Biblical Interpretation and Cultural Exchange: Comparative Exegesis in Context,* ed. Natalie Dohrmann (Philadelphia, 2008), 172–81.

27 Such as Amalar's *Canonis missae interpretatio,* ed. John Hannsens, *Amalarii opera omnia liturgica,* vol. 1, *Introductio; Opera minora,* Studi e testi 138 (Vatican City, 1948), 284–338.

28 The treatise *Quid significent* has been edited by Cyrille Vogel and Reinhard Elze in *Le pontifical Romano-Germanique du dixième siècle,* vol. 1, *Le texte,*

Studi e testi 226 (Vatican City, 1963), 90–121. English translation by Brian Repsher in *The Rite of Church Dedication in the Early Medieval Era* (Lewiston, NY, 1998), 171–93.

29 Valerie Flint has sourced much of this book in "The Career of Honorius Augustodunensis," *Revue bénédictine* 82 (1972): 63–86.

30 See Berno of Reichenau, *Libellus de quibusdam rebus ad missae officium pertinentibus* 5–6, and note to *Jewel* 4.1.

31 See Marjorie Reeves, "The Originality and Influence of Joachim of Fiore," *Traditio* 36 (1980): 269–316. For a background on concordist exegesis, see Bernard McGinn, "The Concordist Imagination," in *Revealed Wisdom: Studies in Apocalyptic in Honour of Christopher Rowland,* ed. John Ashton (Leiden, 2014), 217–31.

32 Viatcheslav Kartsovnik, "Honorius Augustodunensis of Regensburg, Liturgical Tropes, and a Sequence by Notker Balbulus," in *Hortus troporum: Florilegium in honorem Gunillae Iversen,* ed. Alexander Andrée and Erika Kihlman (Stockholm, 2008), 117.

33 Munich, Bayerische Staatsbibliothek, Clm 226. For discussion, see Josef Endres, "Ein Augsburger Rituale des dreizehnten Jahrhunderts," *Theologisch-praktische Monats-Schrift* 13 (1903): 636–40.

34 See Flint, "Honorius Augustodunensis of Regensburg," 118–25.

35 See *Sicardi Cremonensis episcopi Mitralis de officiis,* ed. Gábor Sarback and Lorenz Weinrich, CCCM 228 (Turnhout, 2008).

36 See Robert Paulus, *De caeremoniis, sacramentis, officiis et observationibus,* in PL 177:381–456; *Iohannis Beleth Summa de ecclesiasticis officiis,* ed. Heribert Douteil, CCCM 41 (Turnhout, 1976); and *Rudolfi de Liebegg Pastorale novellum,* ed. A. P. Orbán, CCCM 55 (Turnhout, 1982).

37 On the presence of the *Jewel* in English medieval catalogs, see seven entries in Richard Sharpe, *List of Identifications,* Corpus of British Medieval Library Catalogues (London, 1993), 400.

38 See *Guillelmi Duranti Rationale divinorum officiorum,* ed. Anselme Davril and Timothy Thibodeau, 3 vols., CCCM 140 (Turnhout, 1995–2000).

39 The *Liber de canonum observantia* has been edited by Leo Cunibert Mohlberg, *Radulph de Rivo, der letzte Vertreter der altrömischen Liturgie,* vol. 2, *Texte,* Recueil de travaux 42 (Louvain, 1915), 34–156.

40 The most extensive discussion of the allegorical tradition is Adolf Franz, *Die Messe im deutschen Mittelalter* (Darmstadt, 1963), especially 333–740, but

important dissertations by Douglas Mosely, Mary Schaefer, and Ronald Zawilla remain unpublished. For Elisabeth of Spalbeek, see Jesse Njus, "What Did It Mean to Act in the Middle Ages?," *Theatre Journal* 63, no. 1 (March 2011): 1–21.

41 On the *Hortus deliciarum,* see Fiona J. Griffiths, *The Garden of Delights: Reform and Renaissance for Women in the Twelfth Century* (Philadelphia, 2011), and Otto Gillen, *Ikonographische Studien zum "Hortus deliciarum" der Herrad von Landsberg,* Kuntswissenschaftliche Studien 9 (Berlin, 1931), 66–69. On the dramatic potential of the liturgical act, see Richard McCall, *Do This: Liturgy as Performance* (Notre Dame, IN, 2007), 41–77.

42 On the role of liturgical commentary in the genesis of art forms and interpretations, see Margot Fassler, "Liturgy and Sacred History in the Twelfth-Century Tympana at Chartres," *Art Bulletin* 75, no. 3 (1993): 499–520.

43 A discussion of modern authors' assessments of the commentary tradition may be found in David Frank Wright, "A Medieval Commentary on the Mass" (PhD diss., University of Notre Dame, 1977), 5–43.

44 See especially Frances Young, *Biblical Exegesis and the Formation of Christian Culture* (Ada, MI, 2002); Paul Blowers and Peter Martens, eds., *Oxford Handbook of Early Christian Biblical Interpretation* (Oxford, 2019); Rita Copeland, ed., *Cambridge Companion to Allegory* (Cambridge, 2010); Ignacio Carbajosa, *Faith: The Fount of Exegesis* (Ignatius Press, 2013); and a modern commentary on the Mass, James W. Jackson, *Nothing Superfluous: An Explanation of the Symbolism of the Rite of St. Gregory the Great* (Lincoln, NE, 2016).

JEWEL OF THE SOUL

DEDICATORY LETTERS

Fratres solitario

Agmen in castris aeterni Regis excubans, sub impetu vitiorum undique irruentium desudans, idoneo instructori armorum, laureari in triumpho victorum. Divinorum sacramenta officiorum scire volentibus, sed partim penuria librorum partim multimodorum occupatione negotiorum minime valentibus, rogamus te ut quemadmodum in multis aliis ita et in hoc negotio nobis velis stilo prodesse, quatenus memoriam tui omnium orationibus liceat iugiter interesse.

Responsio solitarii

Postquam Christo favente pelagus scripturae prospero cursu in *Summa totius* transcucurri, atque naufragosam cymbam per syrtes et piratas multo sudore evectam vix ad optatum litus appuli, rursus habitatores Sion me in fluctus cogitationum retruditis, et nec vires recolligere nec navis armamenta sinitis reficere. Dicitis enim nunc esse tempus laborandi, postea requiescendi, nunc tempus seminandi, postmodum fructus percipiendi. Hac spe coactus sum onus vires meas excedens subire, petens vos orationibus me ad

DEDICATORY LETTERS

The Brethren to the Solitary

A company on campaign with the army of the eternal King, straining under the assault of the vices that charge against us from all sides, to a skilled instructor in the arts of war: may you wear the laurel crown in the triumphal parade of victors. Wishing to understand the mysteries of the divine services, but unable to do so, owing partly to scarcity of books and partly to the demands of our manifold duties, we ask that you deign to lend your quill in this matter, as you have in so many others, so that you may be remembered unceasingly in the prayers of all men.

The Solitary's Response

After making a fortunate run across literature's open main with my *Summa totius* — Christ smiled upon me — scarcely have I put my parlous craft into the long-desired shore, saved at great pains from the hazardous reefs and pirates, when you denizens of Zion thrust me back out again into the tempest of deliberations, allowing time neither to recover my strength nor to repair my ship's tackle. The time for toil, you say, is in this life, and rest is for the coming age; now is the time to sow, then to gather in the fruits. By this hope I am compelled to take on a load that exceeds my strength; I ask you to speed me along my way with your

iter expedire, quatenus pondere peccatorum deposito ad desideratum portum quietis liceat fixa anchora pervenire. Vestra itaque iussione funes verborum a portu otii solvo, quassatam naviculam stili procellis meditationum impello, vela sententiarum distendens vento Spiritus sancti committo. Ipse autem secundum cursum tribuat, qui nutu mare ventosque tranquillat.

prayers, so that having discharged the burden of my sins, I may arrive at the longed-for port of rest, and there cast my anchor. At your bidding, then, I loose the hawsers of my words from the harbor of leisure, drive the battered ship of my quill out into the squalls of invention, and, unfurling the sails of my commentary, I entrust them to the wind of the Holy Spirit. May he who soothes the sea and winds at his pleasure grant me a happy voyage.

PREFACE

INCIPIT PRAEFATIO LIBRI

Plerosque vesania captos—piget me mente considerare—
quos non pudet abominanda poetarum figmenta ac captiosa
philosophorum argumenta summo conamine indagare,
quae mentem a Deo abstractam vitiorum nexibus insolubili-
ter solent innodare, religionem autem Christianae profes-
sionis penitus ignorare, per quam animae liceat perenniter
cum Deo regnare. Cum sit summae dementiae iura tyranni
velle scire, et edicta imperatoris nescire, atque ea quae cottidie necessario facias non intelligere. Porro quid confert animae pugna Hectoris, vel disputatio Platonis, aut carmina
Maronis, vel neniae Nasonis, qui nunc cum consimilibus
strident in carcere infernalis Babylonis, sub truci imperio
Plutonis?

2   Dei autem Sapientia maxima gloria hunc cumulat, qui
prophetarum et apostolorum facta et scripta investigando
iugiter ruminat, quos nunc in caelestis Ierusalem palatio
cum rege gloriae exultare nemo dubitat. Sapientium namque iudicio tantum differt a non intelligente intelligens,
quantum a caeco videns. Qui enim non intelligit quae agit,

Most people are so thoroughly mad—it pains me to consider it in my mind—that they are not ashamed to pore with great energy over the poets' detestable confections and the frivolous arguments of philosophers, which shackle the mind they draw away from God in inescapable bonds of vice, while at the same time being completely ignorant of the Christian way of life, through which the soul can reign with God in eternity. For it is a deluded man indeed who wishes to understand the laws of a tyrant, but not the edicts of the emperor, nor to understand the things one is obliged to do daily. How does the soul benefit from the battles of Hector, the disputations of Plato, the poems of Maro, or the nonsense of Naso, who now shriek along with others like them in the prison of the infernal Babylon under Pluto's brutal sway?

On the other hand, God's Wisdom heaps great glory on 2 him who ruminates ceaselessly upon the deeds and writings of the prophets and apostles, who even now exult with the King of glory in the courts of the heavenly Jerusalem, as no one doubts. In the judgment of wise men, a man of understanding differs from a man without understanding as much as the seeing from the blind. For he who does not

est ut caecus qui nescit quo vadat, et ut Tantalus in mediis undis siti deperit. Et licet simplicitas fidelium Deo nostro placeat, tamen intelligentiam sapientum quantum lucem prae tenebris approbat. Ob hanc causam ut iussistis libellum de divinis officiis edidi, cui nomen *Gemma animae* indidi, quia videlicet veluti aurum gemma ornatur, sic anima divino officio decoratur.

understand what he is doing is like a blind man who knows not where he is going, and perishes of thirst, like Tantalus, in the midst of the sea. And though the simplicity of the faithful is pleasing to our God, nevertheless he approves the wise man's understanding as much as he prefers light to darkness. For this reason, I have written, as you bade me, a little book on the divine services, to which I have given the name *Jewel of the Soul*. For you see, just as gold is adorned by a jewel, so the soul is made lovely by the divine services.

I

Incipit *Gemma animae*

In primis igitur de Missa per quam nobis vita redditur, et de ecclesia in qua agitur, et de ministris per quos celebratur videamus. Deinde de reliquis horis, quae sunt debitum nostrae servitutis edisseramus. Tertio de sollemnitatibus totius anni dicamus. Quarto de concordia officiorum rite subiungamus.

2

De Missa

Missa a quattuor causis nomen accepit, duabus a legatione, et duabus a missione. "Missa" quippe dicitur legatio, quia in eius officio nobis legatio Christi repraesentatur, qua pro humano genere Patris legatione fungebatur. Item Missa legatio dicitur, quia in ea sacerdos pro Ecclesia ad Deum

I

Here Begins the *Jewel of the Soul*

In the first place, therefore, let us see about the Mass by which we are restored to life, and about the church in which it is performed, and about the ministers by whom it is celebrated. Next let us treat the other liturgical hours, which are the dues of our servitude. Let us speak thirdly about the feasts of the whole year. In the fourth place, let us provide a fitting conclusion about the concordance of the offices.

2

On the Mass

The Mass takes its name from four legal causes: two from the concept of legation, and two from the concept of formal dismissal. "Mass" means legation because this service reenacts the legation Christ undertook, at the Father's behest, on behalf of the human race. The Mass is also a legation because in it the priest performs a legation to our Lord on the

legatione fungitur. A missione "Missa" dicitur, quia populus qui quasi ad iudicium convenit peracta causa a iudice dimittitur. Item a missione dicitur, quia populi conventus qui ad Vesperam et ad Matutinam quasi iure tenetur celebrato sacrificio dimittitur.

3

De primo officio

Missa autem in septem officia distinguitur, in quorum primo Christi legatio agitur, quam Moyses praefigurasse cognoscitur, qui deus gentilium, papa sacerdotum, rex populorum legitur. A Deo namque *deus Pharaonis,* propheta Aaron sacerdotis, dux populi constituitur. Hic legatione Dei in Aegyptum fungitur, a senioribus et populo suscipitur, populum dispersum congregat, Aegyptum signis perdomat. Oppressos a tyranno de dura servitute liberans, de Aegypto educit, in terram repromissionis inducit.

2 Sic Christus, Deus deorum, sacerdos sacerdotum, rex regum, legatione Patris in mundum fungitur. Ab angelis et pastoribus pastorum Ecclesiae typum gerentibus excipitur. Qui

Church's behalf. The word "Mass" also comes from the concept of dismissal because the people assemble, as it were for a trial, and are dismissed by the judge once the case has been resolved. "Mass" also derives from dismissal because the congregation, who are obliged as a rule to be present for Vespers and Lauds, are dismissed once the sacrifice has been celebrated.

3

On the First Office

Now, the Mass is divided into seven offices. The first enacts Christ's legation, which was prefigured by Moses, the man who was the god of all nations, pope of all priests, and king of all peoples. For God appoints him *god of Pharaoh*, prophet of the priest Aaron and leader of the people. He performs God's legation in Egypt, is received by the elders and the people, gathers the dispersed people, and utterly subdues Egypt through miracles. Freeing those who were oppressed by the tyrant from their harsh servitude, he leads them out from Egypt and brings them into the promised land.

Just so Christ, God of gods, priest of priests, and king of 2 kings, performs the Father's legation into the world. He is received by angels and shepherds, who prefigure the pastors

filios Dei qui erant dispersi in unam fidem congregat, mundum variis signis subiugat. Oppressos a diabolo liberans, de inferno educit, in patriam paradisi inducit. Hoc totum repraesentat nobis processio episcopi, qui gerit figuram Christi.

4

De processione episcopi

Postquam campanae sonaverint, pontifex ornatus procedit. Quem septem acolythi cum luminibus praeeunt, post quos septem subdiaconi cum plenariis incedunt. Item post hos septem diaconi gradiuntur, quos duodecim seniores sequuntur. Post hos tres acolythi cum thuribulis vadunt, qui incensum gerunt. Post quos Evangelium ante episcopum fertur, quod ipse inter duos ambulans sequitur, eumque principes cum populo comitantur. Qui dum chorum ingreditur, a cantoribus cum versu *Gloria Patri* excipitur. Quibus ipse pacem porrigit, deinde ad altare vadit, finito cantu orationem dicit, et tunc sedere pergit. Quidam de ministris cum eo sedent, quidam ei assistunt. Hoc quasi praesentia Christi nobis exhibet.

of the Church. He who gathers the dispersed sons of God into one faith subdues the world through various miracles. Freeing them from the devil's oppression, he leads them out of hell and into the homeland of paradise. The bishop's procession reenacts all of this for us, as he bears the figure of Christ.

4

On the Bishop's Procession

After the bells have sounded, the vested bishop goes in procession. Seven acolytes precede him with candles, and behind them seven subdeacons advance with plenaries. Likewise after these come seven deacons followed by twelve seniors. After these come three acolytes with thuribles and bearing incense. After these the Gospel is carried before the bishop, who follows it, walking between two others, accompanied by princes along with the people. When he enters into the choir, he is received with the verse *Gloria Patri* sung by the cantors, to whom the bishop extends peace. Then he goes to the altar and, when the chant is finished, says the prayer and proceeds to sit. Some of the ministers sit with him and others stand near him. All of this indicates Christ's presence to us.

5

De campanis significatio

Campanae sunt prophetae. Campanae sonabant, quia prophetae Christi adventum praenuntiabant. Pontifex templum ingreditur, et Christus hunc mundum ad Ecclesiam ingreditur. Episcopus de sacrario ornatus procedit, et Christus de utero virginis decore indutus *tamquam sponsus de thalamo* processit. Diaconi et subdiaconi et acolythi, qui episcopum praecedunt, designant prophetas, et sapientes, et scribas, qui adventum Christi in carne mundo nuntiaverunt. Diaconi prophetas significant, qui Christum iam venisse et adhuc venturum populo praedicant, et ex Evangelio futuram vitam nuntiant. Subdiaconi cum plenariis sapientes praeferunt, qui *plenitudinem divinitatis in Christo corporaliter*
2 retulerunt. Acolythi cum luminibus typum scribarum gerunt, qui lumen scientiae scripturas exponendo fidelibus ministraverunt. Qui ideo singuli septem decernuntur, quia per septem dona Spiritus sancti sacramenta Missae perficiuntur. Priores cum capellanis qui eos sequuntur duodecim apostoli accipiuntur. Tres acolythi qui thuribula cum incenso ferunt, sunt tres Magi, qui nato Christo munera obtulerunt. Evangelium ante episcopum portatur, quia per
3 doctrinam Christi *nobis via ad vitam paratur.* Episcopus a duobus deducitur, et Christus a duobus Testamentis per

16

5

The Meaning of the Bells

The bells are the prophets. The bells rang out because the prophets foretold Christ's coming. The pontiff enters the temple, and Christ enters this world to the Church. The bishop comes out from the sacristy vested, and Christ came from the virgin's womb clothed in beauty *as a bridegroom coming from his bridal chamber.* The deacons, subdeacons, and acolytes who precede the bishop symbolize the prophets, wise men, and scribes who announced to the world Christ's coming in the flesh. The deacons signify the prophets because they preach Christ's past and future coming to the people, and proclaim the good news of the life to come. The subdeacons bearing the plenaries represent the wise, who announced *all the fullness of the Godhead in Christ corporeally.* The acolytes with candles act as a type of the scribes, who 2 furnished the light of wisdom to the faithful by expounding the scriptures. Each of these groups is seven in number because the sacraments of the Mass are accomplished through the seven gifts of the Holy Spirit. The officers with the chaplains who follow them are the twelve apostles. The three acolytes who carry thuribles with incense are the three Magi who brought gifts to the newborn Christ. The Gospel book is carried before the bishop because Christ's teaching *prepares the way for us* toward life. The bishop is escorted 3 by two people, and Christ was introduced to the world by

prophetas et apostolos mundo invehitur. Turba populi episcopum comitatur, quia Christum populus fidelium ad caelestia sequi conatur.

Dum praesens officium agitur, in ecclesia non sedetur, quia labori Christi deputantur, qui ad cultum Dei vocantur.

6

De curru Dei

Interim dum chorus canit, episcopus quasi in curru vectus ad sollemnitatem vadit, quia *currus Dei decem milibus multiplex* legitur, et comitatus episcopi decem ordinibus distinguitur. Scilicet primus ordo sunt ostiarii, secundus lectores, tertius exorcistae, quartus acolythi, quintus subdiaconi, sextus diaconi, septimus presbyteri, octavus cantores, nonus laici, decimus feminae. Ita Christus mundum intravit, dum chorus prophetarum cecinit, curru scripturae vectus, sanctorum ordinibus comitatus. Cantores venientem episcopum cum *Gloria Patri* excipiunt, et angeli Christum advenientem cum *Gloria in excelsis* susceperunt.

2   Duo chori laudes concinunt, quia duo populi scilicet

the two Testaments through the prophets and the apostles. A multitude of people accompany the bishop, because the faithful strive to follow Christ toward heavenly things.

While this office is being carried out, one does not sit in the church, since those who are called to worship God are assigned to Christ's work.

6

On God's Chariot

Meanwhile, as the choir sings, the bishop goes forth to the solemnity as if carried on a chariot because it is written that *the chariot of God is attended by ten thousands,* and the bishop's retinue is divided into ten orders. The first order are the porters, the second the lectors, the third the exorcists, the fourth acolytes, the fifth the subdeacons, the sixth the deacons, the seventh the presbyters, the eighth the cantors, the ninth the laymen, the tenth the women. In a similar manner Christ came into the world as the choir of prophets sang, carried on the chariot of scripture, accompanied by the orders of saints. The cantors welcome the bishop with the *Gloria Patri* when he enters, and the angels received Christ with the *Gloria in excelsis* at his advent.

Two choirs sing praises, because two peoples—namely 2

Iudaei et gentiles Christo advenienti cum laudibus occurre-
runt. Per cantum Introitus, accipitur laus Ecclesiae de Iudaeis, per *Kyrieleyson* laus Ecclesiae de gentibus, per *Gloria in
excelsis* autem, utriusque concors laudatio in fide Trinitatis,
3 pro adipiscenda aequalitate angelicae dignitatis. Per Introitum quoque ordo patriarcharum nobis repraesentatur, per
quos Christus venturus praefigurabatur. Per versum prophe-
ticum, ordo prophetarum insinuatur, per quos Christus nas-
citurus praenuntiabatur. Per *Gloria Patri,* ordo apostolicus
commemoratur, per quos Christus iam venisse praedicatur,
a quibus et Trinitas Ecclesiae insinuatur. Per Introitum secundo repetitum, ordo doctorum notatur, per quos Christus
adhuc venturus ad iudicium narratur. Porro per *Kyrieleyson*
diversarum linguarum populi declarantur, a quibus Christus
in *Gloria in excelsis* cum angelis collaudatur.

7

Ingressus episcopi quid significet

Episcopus ingrediens pacem clero porrigit, quia Christus mundum ingrediens pacem humano generi attulit, quam in primo parente amisit. Deinde sanctuarium intrat, inclinis coram altari orat, confessionem faciens, indulgentiam implorat, quia Christus Ierusalem passurus intravit, pro nobis

the Jews and the gentiles—ran to meet Christ at his advent with praises. The Introit chant stands for the praise of the Church of the Jews, the *Kyrie eleison* for the praise of the Church of the gentiles, and the *Gloria in excelsis* is the harmonious praise of both, in Trinitarian faith, to obtain a dignity equal to the angels'. The Introit also portrays for us the 3 order of patriarchs who prefigured Christ's coming. The prophetic verse signifies the order of prophets, who foretold Christ's birth. The *Gloria Patri* calls to mind the apostolic order, who preached that Christ has already come and made the Trinity known to the Church. The repetition of the Introit denotes the order of doctors, who tell that Christ will come again as a judge. Further, the *Kyrie eleison* proclaims the peoples of various tongues, who praise Christ together with the angels in the *Gloria in excelsis*.

7

What the Bishop's Entry Signifies

As he comes in, the bishop offers peace to the clergy, for when Christ came into the world, he brought peace to the human race, which had lost it through our first parent. Then he enters the sanctuary and prays bowing before the altar. Making his confession, he begs for forgiveness, for Christ entered Jerusalem in order to suffer and bowed himself in

levandis se in mortem inclinavit, in cena Patrem pro Ecclesia oravit, paenitenti et confitenti Petro vel latroni, deinde omni populo peccata donavit.

2   Post haec duos sacerdotes osculatur, quia *per Christum lapidem angularem* duo parietes in una fide copulantur. Deinde ceteris ministris a dextra laevaque pacem dabit, quia *Christus pacem his qui longe et his qui prope praedicavit,* et *ab oriente et occidente venientes in vinculo pacis* sociavit. Altare et Evangelium osculatur, quia per Passionem Christi homines angelis in pace sociantur. Per altare namque Iudaei, per Evangelium gentes denotantur. Post haec thuribulum accipiens altare thurificat, in figura angeli qui in Apocalypsi cum aureo thuribulo altari astiterat, de quo *fumus aromatum in conspectu Domini ascendebat,* quia Christus *magni consilii angelus* in ara Crucis *se pro nobis obtulit,* cuius corpus thuribulum Ecclesiae fuit, ex quo Deus Pater *suavitatem odoris* accepit, et propitius mundo extitit. *Fumus aromatum orationes sunt sanctorum,* quae *super auream aram* Christum per caritatis ardorem, vel illuminationis Spiritus sancti *carbones succensae* ad Deum ascendunt. Deinde altare osculatur, quia Christus pro nostra pace in ara Crucis immolabatur.

3   Deinde *Gloria in excelsis* incipit, et chorus concinit, quia Christus per mortem suam, gloriam angelorum hominibus restituit, in qua sanctorum populus laetabundus laudes perstrepit. Deinde ad populum se convertens *Pax vobis* dicit, quia Christus a mortuis resurgens, pacem Ecclesiae reddidit, suisque *Pax vobis* dixit. Deinde in dextra parte

death in order to raise us up. At the Last Supper, he prayed to the Father for the Church and then forgave the sins of Peter and the thief who repented and confessed, and then those of the entire people.

After this he kisses the two assisting priests, for *by Christ* 2 *the cornerstone* two walls are joined together in one faith. Then he will bestow peace upon the other ministers to his right and left, for *Christ preached peace to those far off and nigh,* and joined together *in the bond of peace those coming from east and west.* He kisses the altar and Gospel, for through the Passion of Christ men are joined in peace with the angels. The altar designates the Jews, the Gospel the gentiles. Then, taking the thurible, he censes the altar as a figure of the angel of the Apocalypse who stood by the altar with a golden thurible, from which *the smoke of spices rose in the sight of God,* because Christ, the *angel of great counsel, offered himself up for us* on the altar of the Cross, and his body was a thurible for the Church, from which God the Father accepted *a fragrant odor* and showed himself merciful to the world. The *smoke of spices* are *the prayers of the saints* that rise from *the golden altar* of Christ toward God, kindled *like burning coals* by the ardor of charity and the Holy Spirit's illumination. Then he kisses the altar, for Christ was sacrificed on the altar of the Cross for our peace.

Then he intones the *Gloria in excelsis* and the choir sings 3 along, for through his death Christ restored to mankind the glory of the angels, in which the crowds of saints joyfully resound his praises. Then, turning to the people, he says *Pax vobis,* for rising from the dead Christ restored peace to the Church and said *Pax vobis* to his own. Then he says the

orationem dicit, quia Christus iam *de morte ad vitam transiit,* nosque de exilio in patriam transtulit. Oratio autem illam benedictionem significat, qua caelos ascensurus suos benedicebat. His peractis episcopus sedere pergit, et Christus omnibus rite peractis caelos ascendit, et *in dextera Patris sedens* quiescit. Quidam cum episcopo sedent, quidam ei assistunt, quia quidam electi nunc cum Christo requiescunt, plurimi adhuc in labore ei hic serviunt.

8

Quid cereostata significent

Episcopo ascendente ad sedem cereostata mutantur de locis suis in ordine unius lineae, excepto primo, usque ad altare. Per cereostata varia dona Spiritus sancti exprimuntur, per lineam unam unitas Spiritus sancti in singulis donis denotatur. A primo incipit, quia Spiritus sanctus a Christo procedit, usque ad altare, id est ad corda electorum pervenit.

Collect on the right side, for Christ *has already crossed from death to life* and conveyed us from exile to our native land. The Collect signifies the blessing he gave to his own just before he ascended into heaven. After doing these things, the bishop proceeds to sit, and Christ, after everything was fitly accomplished, ascended into heaven and *sitting at the right hand of the Father* now rests. Some sit with the bishop and others attend him, for some of the elect now rest with Christ, while many others still in travail serve him here below.

8

What the Candlesticks Signify

As the bishop goes up to his seat, the candlesticks, except for the first, are moved from their places into a single line leading up to the altar. The candlesticks express the various gifts of the Holy Spirit, and the single line denotes the unity of the Holy Spirit in each of its gifts. The line begins from the first candle because the Holy Spirit proceeds from Christ. It is aligned toward the altar, that is, he comes into the hearts of the elect.

9

Quid ministri designant

Diacones qui episcopum praecedentes altare deosculan-tur, designant iustos qui ante Christi adventum pro veritate patiebantur. Deinde post episcopum erecti stabunt, quia plurimi *Christi vestigia sequentes* pro eo mortem subierunt. Quidam a dextris, quidam a sinistris stant, quia dextra con-templativam, sinistra activam vitam significat. In dextra stantes, sunt in contemplativa vita Christo ministrantes; in sinistra consistentes, sunt in activa vita Christo servientes. Duo diaconi vicissim vadunt altrinsecus osculari latera alta-ris, quia Christus *misit binos discipulos ante faciem suam in om-nem civitatem.* Osculum eorum signat ubi intrantes dicunt, *"Pax huic domui."* Altare, corda electorum. Postea revertun-tur ad episcopum, et discipuli reversi sunt ad Christum, nuntiantes opera signorum.

2   Septem diaconi ideo sunt, quia apostoli septem diaconos in ministerium elegerunt, et quia septem dona Spiritus sancti sacramenta Missae conficiunt. Ideo etiam septem diaconi ministrant, quia septem discipuli post Resurrecti-onem in piscando laborabant, quos Dominus ad prandium invitabat. Per septem autem subdiaconos, septem columnae domus sapientiae accipiuntur. Per septem acolythos, sep-tem lucernae tabernaculi vel septem candelabra in Apoca-

3 lypsi intelliguntur. Si quinque diaconi ministrant, tunc hos

9

What the Ministers Represent

The deacons who precede the bishop and kiss the altar represent the just men who suffered for the truth before Christ's advent. Thereafter they stand behind the bishop because many *followed in Christ's footsteps* and suffered death for him. Some stand to the right, others to the left, because the right signifies the contemplative life, the left the active life. Those who stand on the right are those who minister to Christ in the contemplative life; those stationed on the left are those who serve Christ in the active life. The deacons come in pairs to kiss opposite sides of the altar, for Christ *sent the disciples two and two before his face into every town.* Their kiss signifies what they say when they enter, "*Peace to this house.*" The altar signifies the hearts of the elect. Then they return to the bishop, and the disciples returned to Christ, announcing the miracles they had performed.

There are seven deacons, because the apostles chose 2 seven deacons for the ministry, and because the seven gifts of the Holy Spirit confect the mysteries of the Mass. Again there are seven ministers because our Lord invited to supper the seven disciples who toiled at fishing after the Resurrection. The seven subdeacons are interpreted as the seven columns in the house of wisdom. The seven acolytes are understood as the seven lamps of the tabernacle and the seven candelabra in Revelation. If five deacons minister, 3

quinque designant, qui Domino in resuscitatione puellae af-
fuerant. Quinque autem subdiaconi serviunt, quia haec sacramenta quinque partes scripturae docuerunt. Vetus enim
Testamentum in legem et prophetas dividitur, novum in Actus apostolorum, et Epistulas eorum, et prophetiam Apoca-
lypsis partitur. Quinque acolythi sunt, quia quinque libri
Moysi haec mysteria testificati sunt. Tres diaconi si ministrant, significant tres apostolos qui Domino in monte trans-
figurato aderant. Tres subdiaconi sunt, quia lex et psalmi et
prophetae haec sacramenta praedixerunt. Tres acolythi serviunt, quia fides spes et caritas haec mysteria perficiunt.
4 Unus diaconus si ministrat, illum adulescentem qui Domino
in Passione adhaesit, scilicet Iacobum signat, quando relicta
sindone nudus profugerat. Per unum quoque diaconum designatur Stephanus, qui solus sua morte Christum est se-
cutus.

10

Quid subdiaconus et acolythus designant

Unus subdiaconus servit, quia universitas scripturae haec
sacramenta docuit. Ab uno acolytho servitur, quia in unitate
tantum Ecclesiae hoc sacramentum conficitur.

they represent the five disciples with our Lord at the damsel's resuscitation. Five subdeacons also minister because the five parts of scripture taught these sacraments. For the Old Testament is divided into the Law and the prophets; the New into the Acts of the Apostles, their Epistles, and the prophecy of the Apocalypse. Five acolytes serve because the five books of Moses testified to these mysteries. If three deacons minister, they signify the three apostles present with the Lord as he was transfigured on the mount. There are three subdeacons because the Law, prophets, and psalms predicted these sacraments. Three acolytes serve because faith, hope, and charity perfect these mysteries. If one deacon serves, he represents the young man who cleaved to Jesus during his Passion, the one who cast aside his tunic and ran away naked, namely James. By one deacon we may also understand Stephen, who followed Christ in dying alone.

4

10

What the Subdeacon and Acolyte Represent

One subdeacon serves because the entirety of scripture teaches this sacrament. One acolyte serves because this sacrament can be confected only in the unity of the Church.

II

Quid acolythi designant

Acolythi usque ad *Kyrieleison* lumina tenent, quia doctores illuminatores Ecclesiae verbo et exemplo lumen fidelibus praebere debent, quoadusque ipsi Dominum moribus invocare incipiant, et *Christum veram lucem omnem animam illuminare* cognoscant. Septem cerei, sunt septem dona Spiritus sancti. Cereus in medio stans est Christus. Deinde lumina Christi ordinatim versus episcopum disponuntur, quia septem dona Spiritus sancti per Christum Ecclesiae tribuntur. Acolythus qui fert thuribulum, designat Ioseph qui undique circumtulit Christum. Significat etiam Paulum apostolum, qui praedicando Christi odorem portavit per totum mundum. Sex vel quattuor vel duobus ministrare non licet, quia par numerus dividi potest, et Ecclesia scindi non debet, et ideo *numero Deus impare gaudet.*

11

What the Acolytes Represent

The acolytes hold their candles until the *Kyrie eleison* because doctors, the enlighteners of the Church, should offer light to the faithful by word and example until the faithful themselves begin to invoke the Lord by their conduct and realize that *Christ, the true light, is the one who enlightens every soul.* The seven candles are the seven gifts of the Holy Spirit. The candle that stands in the middle is Christ. Then the candles are arranged in order toward the bishop, for the seven gifts of the Holy Spirit are bestowed upon the Church through Christ. The acolyte who carries the thurible represents Joseph, who carried Christ around everywhere. It also signifies the apostle Paul, who bore the sweet odor of Christ throughout the whole world by his preaching. It is not permitted that six, four, or two perform a ministry, for an even number can be divided, and the Church must not be split. Therefore, *an odd number is God's delight.*

12

De thuribulo

Thuribulum namque significat corpus Dominicum, incensum eius divinitatem, ignis Spiritum sanctum. Si est aureum, signat eius divinitatem, omnia praecellentem; si argenteum, demonstrat ipsius humanitatem, omni sanctitate nitentem; si cupreum, declarat eius carnem, pro nobis fragilem; si ferreum, insinuat eius carnem mortuam, in Resurrectione mortem superantem. Si quattuor lineas habet thuribulum, significat quattuor elementis constare corpus Dominicum, quod quattuor virtutibus prudentia, fortitudine, iustitia, temperantia fuit plenum. Quinta linea quae thuribulum ab invicem separat, designat animam Christi quae se in morte a corpore sequestraverat. Si autem tribus lineis continetur, significat quod humana caro et anima rationalis et Verbi divinitas una persona Christi efficitur. Quarta quae partes dividit, est potestas quae *animam pro ovibus in morte posuit*. Si vero una tantum linea sustentatur, designat quod ipse solus absque sorde a virgine generatur, et solus *inter mortuos liber* praedicatur. Circulus cui haec omnia innectuntur, est deitas a qua haec omnia continentur, cuius maiestas nullo termino concluditur.

12

On the Thurible

The thurible signifies our Lord's body, the incense his divinity, the fire the Holy Spirit. If the thurible is golden, it designates his divinity, surpassing all things; if it is silver, it shows his humanity, shining with all holiness; if it is copper, it makes manifest his flesh, made frail for our sake; if it is of iron, it signifies his dead flesh, overcoming death in his Resurrection. If the thurible has four chains, it signifies that four elements make up our Lord's body, which was also filled with the four virtues of prudence, fortitude, justice, and temperance. A fifth chain, which separates the thurible into two parts, designates Christ's soul, which removed itself from his body in death. If, however, the thurible has three chains, it signifies that human flesh, a rational soul, and the Word's divinity make up the one person of Christ. The fourth chain that separates the parts is the power that *laid down his soul in death for the sheep*. But if the thurible is held by only one chain, it designates that he alone was without impurity begotten of a virgin, and that he is proclaimed as the only *free one among the dead*. The ring to which all these chains are fastened is the divinity that contains all these things, while being itself endless in majesty.

2

13

De Ecclesia et secundo officio

In superiori officio de capite nostro Christo agebatur, in sequenti vero de corpore eius Ecclesia agitur. Quam Maria soror Moysi praefigurabat, quae populo liberato praecinebat, et turba canticum respondebat.

Sic episcopo residente, lector Epistulam in pulpito recitat, et chorus cantum resonat, quia Christo in caelis residente, doctorum ordo scripturam mundo intonuit, et omnis ubique populus laudem Christo sonuit. Altior locus ponitur episcopo, ut superintendat, et tamquam populum custodiat, ut vinitori altior locus fit, ut vineam custodiat. Sic Dominus in alto caelorum sedens custodit currum suum, id est civitatem suam, videlicet Ecclesiam. Subdiacono legente, solemus sedere. Lectio est praedicatio; sessio, obauditio; responsio, credentium confessio. Lectores et cantores, sunt Domini negotiatores.

13

On the Church and the Second Office

The previous office was concerned with Christ the head, but the next is about his body, the Church, which was prefigured by Miriam, Moses's sister, when she sang before the liberated people and the throng responded in song.

So now that the bishop is seated, the lector recites the Epistle from the pulpit and the choir responds in song. In the same way, Christ took his seat in heaven, the order of doctors thundered forth scripture in the world, and all peoples in all places resounded Christ's praise. The higher place is reserved for the bishop so that he may watch over and, so to speak, guard the people, just as the overseer of a vineyard is given a higher place so he may watch over the vineyard. In the same way our Lord sits in the heights of the heavens watching over his chariot, which is to say his city, namely the Church. While the subdeacon reads, we sit. The reading is preaching; the sitting, attentive listening; the response, the confession of believers. Lectors and cantors are our Lord's merchants.

14

De subdiacono

Subdiacono Epistulam legente, cerei verso ordine ab oriente in occidentem transponuntur, quia lumen doctrinae ab oriente in occidentem, id est per totum orbem per apostolos diffundebatur. Per Graduale conversio Ecclesiae de Iudaeis intelligitur, per versum conversio Ecclesiae de gentibus accipitur, per Alleluia, utriusque in fide laetitia exprimitur. Sequentia cantum victoriae designat, quo iustorum animae *in Deo vivo* pro sua liberatione *exultant,* sicut filii Israel pro sua ereptione canticum victoriae canebant. Unde quidam longam neumam cum organis iubilant, quae iubilus vocatur, quia plausum victorum laetantium imitantur.

15

De episcopo

Episcopus a dextris altaris sedens versa facie ad chorum laborantes intuetur, quia Christus a dextris Dei sedens versa

14

On the Subdeacon

While the subdeacon reads the Epistle, the arrangement of the candles is reversed and they are placed from east to west, for through the apostles the light of Christian doctrine was spread from east to west, that is, throughout the whole world. By the Gradual we understand the conversion of the Church of the Jews; by its verse, the conversion of the Church of the gentiles; the Alleluia expresses the joy both of them take in the faith. The Sequence is a victory song in which the souls of the just *exult in the living God* on account of their liberation, just as the sons of Israel sang a song of victory for their deliverance. This is why some joyfully sing a long melisma with organum, which they call a jubilus, for they are imitating the applause of exultant victors.

15

On the Bishop

Sitting to the right side of the altar facing the choir, the bishop shall gaze upon the laborers, because Christ, sitting

facie ad Ecclesiam singulorum corda intuetur, et pro se laborantes remunerari pollicetur. Unde dum Stephanus pro eo laboravit, ad adiuvandum ei surrexit.

16

De cantoribus

Cantores qui choros regunt, sunt apostoli qui Ecclesias laudes Dei instruxerunt. Hi qui Graduale canunt, significant eos qui in activa vita Christo serviunt. In gradibus cantantes stabunt, quia iusti *de virtute in virtutem* in scala caritatis *ibunt*. Qui Alleluia cantant, designant eos qui in contemplativa vita Christum laudant. Hi cantantes altius consistunt, quia tales in celsitudinem virtutum caelestia contemplando scandunt. Sequentiam chori alternatim iubilabunt, quia frequentiae angelorum et hominum in domo Dei Deum *in saeculum saeculi laudabunt*.

at the right hand of God facing toward the Church, gazes upon the hearts of every individual, and promises to reward those toiling on his behalf. Thus when Stephen toiled for him, he rose up to help him.

16

On the Cantors

Cantors who direct choirs are the apostles who taught the churches God's praises. Those who sing the Gradual signify those who serve Christ in the active life. The singers will stand on the steps because the just *will go from virtue to virtue* on the ladder of charity. Those who sing the Alleluia signify those who praise Christ in a contemplative life. These stand in a higher place to sing because such men scale the heights of virtue by contemplating heavenly things. The choirs will jubilate the Sequence in alternation because in God's house crowds of men and angels *will praise the Lord unto the ages of ages.*

17

De servo arante

Legitur in Evangelio de servo arante, quod peracto opere de agro domum redeat, et post servitium Domino suo impensum ad convivium recumbat. Ager Dei corda sunt fidelium; servus arans, est ordo praedicatorum. Per lectorem Epistulae doctores exprimuntur, qui agrum Dei praedicando coluerunt; per responsum fideles qui per bonam operationem respondentes *fructum iustitiae* protulerunt. Aratrum, est nostrum servitium. Boves hinc inde trahentes, sunt utrinque totis viribus Domino canentes. Praecentor qui cantantes manu et voce incitat, est servus qui stimulo boves minans dulci voce bubus iubilat.

2   Lector legem Domini dat auditoribus, qui nuper vocati sunt per officia cantorum in schola Dei ad nuptias. "Schola" dicitur vocatio. In qua si quis adhuc surdis auribus cordis torpescit, cantor cum *excelsa tuba* sonat in aurem eius dulcedinem melodiae ut excitetur. Cantores qui respondent primo canenti vox est auditorum quasi evigilantium et Deum laudantium. Versus, est servus arans. Per dulcedinem modulationis, scinduntur corda carnalium, et se aperiunt more fulci in confessionem vocis et lacrimarum. Arat, qui

17

On the Plowing Servant

In the Gospel we read about the plowing servant, who when his work in the field is finished goes back home, and after serving his master, sits down to eat. The field of God is the hearts of the faithful; the plowing servant is the order of preachers. The reader of the Epistle expresses the doctors, who have tilled God's field by preaching; the Gradual represents the faithful, who responded with good works and bore the *fruit of justice.* The plow is our service. The oxen that drag the plow back and forth are those who sing to God from both sides of the choir with all their strength. The precentor who conducts the singers with his hand and voice is the servant who drives the oxen with the goad and sings merrily to them with a sweet voice.

The lector gives the Law of the Lord to his hearers, who 2
have just been summoned to the wedding by the cantors' services in God's *schola. Schola* means a summoning, for if someone is still languorous and deaf in the ears of the heart, the cantor sounds a sweet melody in his ear with his *lofty trumpet,* so he may be roused. The cantors who respond to the first singer are the voice of the listeners who are watchful and praising God. The verse is the plowing servant. The hearts of carnal people are rent by the sweetness of his song, and open up like a furrow into a confession of faith through voice and tears. The plowman is he who rends hearts with

aratro compunctionis corda scindit. In lectione pascitur auditor, quasi quodammodo bos. Bos ad hoc pascitur, ut in eo opus agriculturae exerceatur. Bos est praedicator, cantor bubulcus qui iubilat bubus ut hilarius aratrum trahant, scilicet instigat canentes ut laetius canant. Terra scinditur, quando corda auditorum compunguntur. Tales operarii cum de agro huius mundi redeunt, aeternum convivium cum Domino suo ineunt.

18

De alia figura

Episcopus tribus horis Missae sedet, scilicet dum Epistula legitur, dum Graduale et Alleluia canitur, quia Christus tribus diebus inter doctores in templo sedisse legitur. Subdiaconus qui lectionem legit, significat Iohannem baptistam qui ante Christum praedicavit. Per Epistulam quippe Iohannis praedicatio accipitur, per Evangelium Christi praedicatio innuitur. Ideo Epistula Evangelium praecedit, quia praedicatio Iohannis praecessit, et sicut Iohannes praecursor Christi memoratur, ita Epistula ante Evangelium quod est Christus praeconatur. Evangelium in altiori loco quam Epistula legitur, quia Christi praedicatio dignior quam

the plow of compunction. The listener is fed by the reading, as it were like an ox. The ox is fed so that he may be used for the work of agriculture. The ox is the preacher, the singer is the plowman who sings merrily to the oxen so that they may drive the plow more cheerfully, which is to say he incites the singers to sing more gaily. The earth is furrowed when the hearts of the listeners are inspired with devotion. These workers, when they return from the field of this world, enter into the eternal banquet with their Lord.

18

On Another Figure

The bishop remains seated during three parts of the Mass, namely while the Epistle is read, and while the Gradual and Alleluia are sung, for we read that Christ sat for three days among the doctors in the Temple. The subdeacon who reads the lesson signifies John the Baptist who preached before Christ. The Epistle signifies John's preaching, the Gospel Christ's preaching. The Epistle precedes the Gospel because John's preaching preceded Christ's, and just as John is remembered as the forerunner of Christ, so the Epistle comes before the Gospel, which is Christ. The Gospel is proclaimed in a place higher than the Epistle because Christ's preaching is more worthy than John's. But the

Iohannis cognoscitur. Subdiaconus tamen in eodem pulpito quo et diaconus legit, quia omnis populus Iohannem Christum esse putavit. Graduale signat vocationem apostolorum, qua se ad Christum converterunt, Alleluia vero laetitiam eorum quam de praesentia Christi et miraculis eius habuerunt, Sequentia vero animae eorum iubilationem qua de promissa spe exultaverunt.

Hic episcopus ministros Ecclesiae ordinat, quia Moyses Aaron et Levitas in ministerium tabernaculi ordinabat, et Christus septuaginta duos ordinavit, quos in praedicationem destinavit.

19

De tertio officio

In tertio officio ad caput reditur, et praedicatio Christi nobis ad memoriam reducitur.

Hoc officium Moyses praefiguravit, quando in montem ad Deum ascendit, et ab eo tabulas Testamenti accepit, Dominusque cuncto populo audiente mandata proposuit, et Moyses iustitias legis eis exposuit, et populus se omnia servaturum respondit. Sic diaconus ad episcopum vadit, librum ab altari accipit, Evangelium in quo divina praecepta sunt

subdeacon reads from the same pulpit as the deacon because the whole people thought that John was the Christ.
The Gradual is the calling of the apostles, by which they began to follow Christ; the Alleluia signifies their happiness in
the presence of Christ and his miracles; the Sequence portrays the jubilation of their souls when they rejoiced in the
hope that was promised them.

At this point in the Mass the bishop ordains the Church's
ministers, because Moses ordained Aaron and the Levites to
serve in the tabernacle, and Christ ordained the seventy-
two he had chosen to preach.

19

On the Third Office

In the third office we return to the head and recall Christ's
preaching.

Moses prefigured this office when he ascended to the
Lord upon the mountain and received from him the tablets
of the covenant, and the Lord gave out his commandments
while the entire people listened, and Moses expounded the
justices of the Law, and the people responded that they
would keep them all. Just so the deacon goes to the bishop,
takes the book from the altar, and reads the Gospel containing the divine precepts before the people, and the bishop

coram omni populo legit, episcopus sermonem faciens populo ea exponit, et populus per *Kyrieleison,* clerus autem per *Credo in unum* se spondet cuncta servaturum.

Qualiter hoc per Christum et apostolos sit gestum, breviter est dicendum.

20

De diacono

Per episcopum repraesentatur nobis Christus, per diacones ordo apostolicus. Diaconus qui legit, est Petrus, qui pro omnibus respondit. Episcopus lecturum diaconum benedicit, quia Christus *convocatis apostolis* benedictione eos replevit, dum *eis potestatem super omnia daemonia dedit,* et *eos regnum Dei praedicare misit.* Diaconus Evangelium ab altare accipit, et legere pergit, quia *de Syon lex, et verbum Domini de Ierusalem exivit.* In hoc quippe loco altare Ierusalem designat, in qua apostoli verbum praedicationis a Domino acceperunt; et *exeuntes per totam terram praedicaverunt.* Diaconus in sinistro brachio librum portat, quia sinistra praesentem vitam significat, et in hac vita tantum praedicari Evangelium debet, quia in futura vita nullus doctrina eget, ubi omnis a minimo usque ad maximum Deum cognoscent. Ab australi parte in ambonem ascendit, quia Christus a

preaches a sermon expounding them to the people, and the people through the *Kyrie eleison* and the clergy through the *Credo in unum* promise they will keep them all.

Now, in what way this was done by Christ and the apostles, we must briefly say.

20

On the Deacon

The bishop represents Christ for us, the deacons the order of apostles. The deacon who reads is Peter, who responded on the other apostles' behalf. The bishop blesses the deacon who is about to read because Christ, *having called his disciples together,* filled them with blessing, *giving them power over demons and sending them to preach the kingdom of God.* The deacon takes the Gospel from the altar and proceeds to read because *the Law went out from Sion and the word of the Lord from Jerusalem.* For at this point the altar signifies Jerusalem, in which the apostles received the word of preaching from our Lord and *going forth preached it throughout the whole world.* The deacon carries the book in his left arm because the left signifies the present life, and the Gospel is preached only in this life because in the future life no one will lack doctrine, for all from the least to the greatest will know the Lord. He mounts the ambo on the south side

Bethlehem quae est ad austrum Ierusalem venit. Unde dicitur, *Deus ab austro veniet.*

21

Quid duae candelae designant

Duae candelae Evangelium praecedunt, quia lex et prophetae praecesserunt, quae Evangelium praedixerunt. Duo candelabra quae praeferuntur, sunt duo praecepta caritatis quae per Evangelium instruuntur. Duo acolythi qui ea portant, sunt Moyses et Helias, inter quos Dominus ut sol in monte fulgebat. Dum Evangelium legitur, cerei in pavimento deponuntur, quia umbrae legis, et enigmata prophetarum per Evangelii lumen ab humilibus intelliguntur. Perlecto Evangelio candelae extinguuntur, quia praedicante Evangelio lex et prophetia in littera extinguuntur, dum per lucem Evangelii spiritualiter prolatae intelliguntur. Thuribulum ante Evangelium portatur, quia Christus *odor suavitatis* in igne Passionis pro nobis sacrificatus praedicatur.

because Christ arrived in Jerusalem from Bethlehem, which is to the south, whence it is said that *the Lord will come from the south.*

21

What the Two Candles Represent

Two candles precede the Gospel because the Law and the prophets came first, announcing the Gospel. The two candlesticks that are carried before it are the two precepts of charity taught by the Gospel. The two acolytes who carry them are Moses and Elijah, between whom the Lord shone like the sun on the mountain. While the Gospel is read, the candles are placed on the floor because the shadows of the Law and the mysteries of the prophets are understood by the humble through the light of the Gospel. After the Gospel is read, the candles are extinguished because at the preaching of the Gospel the Law and prophecy are extinguished according to the literal sense, while by the light of the Gospel their spiritual sense is disclosed and understood. A thurible is carried before the Gospel because Christ is proclaimed to have been sacrificed for us as a *fragrant odor* in the fire of his Passion.

22

Quid designet quod Evangelium in ambone legitur

Evangelium in alto loco legitur, quia in monte Christus praedicasse perhibetur. Ideo etiam in sublimi legitur, quia sublimia sunt Evangelica praecepta, per quae altitudo caelorum scanditur. Inter Evangelium lumen ardet, eo quod Evangelica doctrina Ecclesiam illuminet, et quia verbum Dei *lumen* nobis *ad vitam* praebet. Diaconus secundum ordinem se vertit ad austrum, dum legit Evangelium, quia in hac parte viri stare solent, quibus spiritalia praedicari debent. Per viros quippe spiritales significantur, et per austrum Spiritus sanctus designatur. Nunc autem secundum inolitum morem se ad aquilonem vertit, ubi feminae stant, quae carnales significant, quia Evangelium carnales ad spiritalia vocat. Per aquilonem quoque diabolus designatur, qui per Evangelium impugnatur. Per aquilonem etiam infidelis populus denotatur, cui Evangelium praedicatur, ut ad Christum convertatur.

22

What Reading the Gospel from the Ambo Represents

The Gospel is read from a high place because we are told that Christ preached on a mount. Moreover, it is read in a lofty place on account of the loftiness of the evangelical precepts, by which one scales the heights of the heavens. A light burns during the Gospel because the Gospel's doctrine enlightens the Church, and because the word of God offers us the *light of life*. According to the Roman order, the deacon turns toward the south to read the Gospel because the men stand in this direction, to whom we must preach spiritual things. Men, of course, signify the spiritual, and the south represents the Holy Spirit. According to established custom, however, he now turns toward the north where the women stand, who represent the carnal people, for the Gospel calls the carnal toward spiritual things. The north also represents the devil, who is assailed by the Gospel. The north also denotes the heathen people, to whom the Gospel is preached that they may be converted to Christ.

23

De signis et salutatione diaconi

Diaconus cum ascendit in analogium, primum salutat populum per *Dominus vobiscum,* quia apostoli quandocumque domum praedicaturi intraverunt, primum per *Pax huic domui* auditores salutaverunt. Cum "Sequentiam secundum Evangelium" dicit, signum sanctae Crucis fronti suae in qua sedes est verecundiae imprimit. Per hoc se de verbis Domini non erubescere innuit. *Qui enim sermones Domini non erubuerit, hunc Filius coram Patre et angelis in iudicio non erubescit.* Crux enim et Evangelium apud incredulos magnae confusionis fuit opprobrium. Deinde os signat, quia verba Dei se ore confiteri pronuntiat, cum *ore confessio ad salutem* fiat. Exinde cor signat, ut spiritum elationis a se excludat, et ea quae ore confitetur, se corde credere ad iustitiam innotescat. Igitur per cordis signationem, fides verbi accipitur; per oris signationem, confessio Christi intelligitur; per frontis signationem, operatio Evangelii exprimitur. Deinde clerus et populus se signat, *Gloria tibi Domine* exclamat, quia Christum crucifixum se adorare, suis verbis obedire se pronuntiat. Ita dum apostoli verba Dei praedicaverunt, populi Deum laudaverunt.

23

On the Deacon's Signs and Greeting

When the deacon goes up to the pulpit, he first greets the people with *Dominus vobiscum,* because whenever the apostles entered a house to preach, they first greeted their listeners with *Pax huic domui.* When he says, "A continuation of this or that Gospel," he makes the sign of the holy Cross on his forehead, which is the seat of shame. In this way he shows that he is not ashamed of God's words, for *whoever is not ashamed of the words of God, him the Son will not be ashamed of in the judgment before the Father and the angels.* Now the Cross and the Gospel were scandals of great confusion for the unbeliever. Then he signs his lips, proclaiming that he confesses the words of God with his mouth, for *the mouth makes confession unto salvation.* Then he signs his heart to banish the spirit of pride, and to make known for the sake of justice that what he confesses with his lips he believes in his heart. Therefore, we take signing the heart to mean faith in the word; signing the lips to mean confessing Christ; and signing the forehead to mean living the Gospel. Then the clergy and people sign themselves and cry out *Gloria tibi Domine,* proclaiming by their words that they adore Christ crucified and obey his words. Likewise when the apostles preached God's words, the people praised God.

24

De baculis

Cum Evangelium legitur, baculi de manibus deponuntur, quia praedicante Evangelio legales observantiae a populo deponebantur. Ex legis quippe praecepto baculos manibus tenebant, qui paschale agnum edentes ad patriam tendebant. Secundum hunc morem cantores in officio Missae baculos tenere noscuntur, dum verus paschalis agnus benedicitur, significantes quod hi qui ad supernam patriam et ad festum angelorum cupiunt festinare, esu caelestis agni et baculis contra hostes, id est sententiis scripturarum contra daemones se debent defensare. Hos inter Evangelium deponunt, quia cum ad Christum quem Evangelium signat pervenerint, nullis scripturarum sustentaculis indigebunt. Per baculos etiam sacerdotes denotantur, per quorum doctrinam infirmi in fide sustentantur. Qui baculi in Evangelio deponuntur, quia omnium sacerdotum doctrinae Christi Evangelio postponuntur. Tunc etiam velamina capitis auferuntur, quia Christo evangelizante velamina legis tollebantur. Et nos capita denudamus, quia *revelata facie non in aenigmate Deum* in Evangelio videmus.

2   Perlecto Evangelio diaconus revertitur ad episcopum, librum ei offert ad osculandum, quem mox reponit in locum suum, quia apostoli peracta praedicatione ad Christum

24

On Staves

As the Gospel is read, anyone holding a staff puts it down because at the preaching of the Gospel the people put aside the observances of the Law. For the Law commanded them to hold a staff in their hands when, bound for their fatherland, they ate the paschal lamb. Following this custom, cantors bear staves during the Mass office when the true paschal Lamb is blessed, signifying that those who want to hasten toward the heavenly fatherland and the feast of the angels by eating the heavenly lamb must defend themselves from their enemies with staves, that is, from the demons with the verses of scripture. These they put down during the Gospel, for when they reach Christ whom the Gospel signifies, they will no longer need the aid of the scriptures. The staves also signify priests, upon whose teaching the weak in faith lean for support. These staves are put down during the Gospel because the teachings of all priests are put after the Gospel of Christ. Head coverings are removed also at this time because when Christ was preaching the Gospel the veils of the Law were removed. We bare our heads too because in the Gospel we see Christ *face to face, and no longer in a dark manner.*

Having read the Gospel, the deacon returns to the bishop 2 and offers him the book to kiss, then returns it to its place, because after their preaching the apostles returned to

reversi sunt, sibi *etiam daemonia in nomine eius subiecta* retulerunt. Quasi librum in locum suum reposuerunt, dum non sibi sed Domino cuncta adscripserunt.

25

De sermone

Deinde episcopus sermonem ad populum facit, quia postquam Christus populo per apostolos innotuit, ipse omnibus praedicare coepit. Episcopus populum de paenitentia et fide et confessione instruit, quia Christus paenitentiam et fidem in Deum et remissionem peccatorum per confessionem et baptisma docuit. Post haec populus *Kyrieleyson* et clerus *Credo in unum* cantant, quia quod diaconus legit, et quod episcopus praedicavit, se credere affirmant. Ita postquam Christus et apostoli populum docuerunt, fide recepta laudes Deo personuerunt. Interim Evangelium cum incensu per chorum defertur, et singulis ad osculandum porrigitur, quia apostoli Christum *odorem vitae* per mundum portaverunt, et cunctis gentibus per verbum eius pacem aeternam praebuerunt.

Christ, and brought back news that *the devils also were subject to them in his name.* They put the book in its place, as it were, when they ascribed everything not to themselves but to God.

25

On the Sermon

Then the bishop delivers a sermon to the people, for after Christ made himself known to the people through the apostles, he began to preach openly to all. The bishop instructs the people on penance, faith, and confession, for Christ taught penance, faith in God, and the remission of sins by confession and baptism. After this the people sing *Kyrie eleison* and the clergy *Credo in unum Deum,* affirming that they believe what the deacon has read and what the bishop has preached. Likewise after Christ and the apostles had taught the people and they had received the faith, they broke forth in praise of God. Meanwhile, the Gospel is carried through the choir with incense, and held out for each person to kiss, for the apostles carried Christ, *the odor of life,* through the whole world, and through his word brought everlasting peace to all the nations.

26

De quarto officio et de Ecclesia

In quarto officio ad corpus Christi id est ad Ecclesiam significatio recurrit, et eius actionem nobis exprimit.

Cuius figuram populus Israel olim praeferebat, quando Moysi de monte descendenti diversa dona ad faciendum tabernaculum offerebat, in quo altare fiebat, super quo sacerdos sacrificia populi immolabat. Sic episcopo de pulpito descendenti populi diversas oblationes offerunt, pro quibus sacerdos et ministri in altari cum cantu immolabunt. Ita Christo ad Ierusalem passuro de monte Oliveti descendenti turba occurrit, palmas floresque cum cantu laudis obtulit, pro quibus ipse se sacrificium in ara Crucis obtulit. Pontifex repraesentat Christum, ministri turbam discipulorum. Populi offerentes, sunt illi cum palmis occurrentes; cantores cantantes, sunt *Hosanna* resonantes.

26

On the Fourth Office and on the Church

In the fourth office the meaning returns to the body of Christ, that is the Church, and portrays for us her act of sacrifice.

Of old, the people of Israel prefigured this act when they offered Moses, as he descended from the mountain, various gifts for the construction of a tabernacle. An altar was built there, where the priests offered up the people's sacrifices. In the same manner the people offer various oblations to the bishop as he descends from the pulpit, and the priest and ministers will offer sacrifices for them with song. Likewise the crowds went out to receive Christ as he came down from the Mount of Olives into Jerusalem to suffer, offering him palms and flowers with songs of praise, and he offered himself as a sacrifice for them on the altar of the Cross. The bishop represents Christ, his ministers the crowds of disciples. The people bringing up the offering are those who met him with palms; the cantors singing are the ones who shouted *Hosanna*.

27

De sacrificio

Quidam de populo aurum, quidam argentum, quidam de substantia alia sacrificant; sacerdos et ministri panem et vinum cum aqua immolant. Qui aurum offerunt, significant Magos qui aurum Deo obtulerunt; qui argentum offerunt, designant eos qui pecuniam in gazophylacium miserunt. Qui de aliis rebus sacrificant, sunt hi qui Domino necessaria quae Iudas portabat mittebant; et hos significant, qui per Paulum et Barnaban apostolis oblationes Hierosolimam transmittebant. Qui panem offerunt, sunt hi qui spiritum suum *in sacrificium laudis Domino* impendunt; qui vinum offerunt, sunt hi qui *animas pro fratribus ponunt;* qui aquam offerunt, sunt hi qui corpus suum ad supplicia tradunt.

28

De tribus sacrificiis

Primo viri offerunt, qui *fortes in Christo* designant, quia in primitiva Ecclesia iusti sub persecutoribus dura perpessi

27

On the Sacrifice

Some of the people sacrifice gold, some silver, and some other substances; the priest and his ministers immolate bread and wine mixed with water. Those who offer gold signify the Magi who offered our Lord gold; those who offer silver signify those who put money into the Temple treasury. Those who sacrifice other substances are those who sent our Lord basic necessities, which Judas used to carry, and those who sent their oblations to Jerusalem through the apostles Paul and Barnabas. Those who offer bread are those who pour out their spirit *in a sacrifice of praise to the Lord;* those who offer wine are *those who lay down their lives for their brothers;* those who offer water are they who hand over their body to be tortured.

28

On the Three Sacrifices

The men bring their offerings first, signifying those who are *strong in Christ,* because in the early Church the just

victima Christi occubuerant. Deinde feminae sacrificant, quae fragiliores significant, quia tempore pacis fideles non se ipsos sed *hostiam laudis Domino* immolant. Ad ultimum sacerdotes et ministri offerunt, qui doctores et ductores populi sunt, quia sub Antichristo fideles per diversa tormenta *sacrificium vivum* se Christo offerunt.

<h1 style="text-align:center">29</h1>

De septem sacrificiis legalibus

Septem autem sacrificia ab antiquis secundum legem offerebantur, quae adhuc Christiani imitantur. Ritus namque Synagogae, transivit in religionem Ecclesiae; et sacrificia populi carnalis, mutata sunt in observantiam spiritalis. Sunt autem haec: legale sacrificium, voluntarium, pro peccato, pro gratiarum actione, dona, vota, holocausta. Sacrificium legale obtulit, qui decimas vel primitias, vel ea quae lex praecipit obtulit. Sacrificium voluntarium obtulit, qui aliquid de rebus suis Deo sponte obtulit. Sacrificium pro peccato obtulit, qui pro transgresso legis mandato hircum obtulit. Sacrificium pro gratiarum actione obtulit, qui pro victoria

suffered grievously under the persecutors and died as sacrificial victims of Christ. Then the women sacrifice, signifying the weaker, for in peacetime the faithful do not immolate themselves but the *sacrifice of praise to the Lord.* Lastly the priests and ministers, who are the teachers and leaders of the people, make their offering, because the faithful, through their various torments under Antichrist, offer themselves to Christ as a *living sacrifice.*

29

On the Seven Sacrifices of the Law

Now the ancients offered seven sacrifices in accordance with the Law, which Christians imitate to this day. For the rite of the Synagogue passed over into the religion of the Church, and the carnal people's sacrifices were changed into the spiritual people's divine worship. These are the sacrifices: the tithe, the voluntary, the sin offering, thanksgiving, gifts, vows, holocausts. He offered the tithe who offered one tenth of his income, or firstfruits, or whatever the Law prescribed. He offered a voluntary sacrifice who of his own will offered something from his possessions to God. He offered a sacrifice for sin who offered a goat for a transgression against a commandment of the Law. He offered a thanksgiving sacrifice who offered God a victory gift. He

munus Deo obtulit. Dona obtulit, qui aliquid in ornatum Templi contulit. Vota obtulit, qui in periculo belli constitutus aliquid Deo vovit, quod postea solvit. Holocausta obtulit, qui agnum offerens totum in altari incendit. "Holocaustum" namque totum incensum dicitur.

30

De sacrificio Christianorum

Ita Christiani legale sacrificium offerunt, dum decimas rerum suarum Deo dabunt. Voluntarium offerunt, dum de rebus suis Deo servientibus aliquid conferunt. Pro peccato offerunt, dum pro paenitentia iniuncta sacerdotibus vel religiosis vel indigentibus aliquid impendunt. Pro gratiarum actione offerunt, dum pro dignitate vel pro aliqua collata gratia Deo quicquam offerunt. Dona offerunt, dum in aedificia ecclesiarum, vel in ornatus earum aliquid conferunt. Vota offerunt, dum in bello vel naufragio vel aliquo periculo positi, aliquid vovent, quod liberati Deo et sanctis offerunt. Holocausta offerunt, qui saeculum relinquunt, et omnia sua vel indigentibus distribuunt, vel monasteriis conferunt.

offered gifts who contributed something for the decoration of the Temple. He offered vows who made a vow to God amid the danger of war and afterward fulfilled it. He offered holocausts who burned a whole lamb on the altar. For "holocaust" means burned completely.

30

On the Christian Sacrifice

In the same way Christians offer the legal sacrifice when they give a tenth part of their wealth to God. They offer the voluntary sacrifice when they bestow something of their wealth on the clergy. They offer the sacrifice for sin when, to fulfill a penance enjoined upon them, they pay something to priests, religious, or to the poor. They offer the thanksgiving sacrifice when they offer God anything in return for an official appointment or for any other favor they receive. They offer gifts when they contribute something to the fabric or decoration of churches. They offer vows when they vow something in war, or shipwreck, or any other danger, which they offer to God and the saints upon their deliverance. They offer holocausts when they leave the world and distribute all their possessions to the poor or endow monaster-

Haec sacrificia populi offerunt; sacerdotes autem et ministri Christo instituente panem et vinum offerunt.

31

De sacrificio panis

Hoc sacramentum ideo ex pane fit, quia Christus se *panem vivum* astruxit, quem scriptura *panem angelorum* praedixit. Qui panis fit absque fermento, quia Christus fuit sine peccato. Ideo autem panis ex frumento fit, quia Christus se granum frumenti asseruit. Granum autem per trituram de theca sua excutitur, arefactum duobus molae lapidibus molitur. Farina cribrata aqua conspersa conpastinatur, panis formatus in clibano coctus in candorem mutatur. Ita Christus nobile granum *cum gladiis et fustibus* de comitatu apostolorum per Iudaeos quasi de theca sua excutitur; contumeliis et opprobriis arefactus; a Iudaeis et gentibus quasi duobus lapidibus flagellis atteritur; cribratur, conspersus conpastinatur, dum a suis separatus, sanguine proprio perfusus, Cruci conpingebatur, in qua quasi panis in igne Passionis excoctus in immortalitatem mutabatur.

ies. These are the sacrifices people offer; the priests and his ministers offer bread and wine as Christ established.

31

On the Sacrifice of Bread

This sacrament is made of bread because Christ gave himself as the *bread of life,* and scripture spoke of him as *the bread of angels.* This bread is made without yeast because Christ was without sin. It is made with wheat because Christ called himself a grain of wheat. A grain is extracted from its husk by rubbing, and once dried it is crushed by two millstones. Once the flour is sifted and moistened to make dough, shaped into bread, and cooked in an oven, it becomes white. Just so, Christ the noble grain is extracted by the Jews from the company of the apostles *with swords and clubs,* as from a husk; is dried by reproaches and insults; is crushed by the Jews and gentiles with scourgings as if by two stones; and is sifted, moistened, and made into dough when, separated from his own, he poured out his blood and was fixed to the Cross where, baked like bread in the fire of his Passion, he became immortal.

32

De Ecclesia et significatione

Ideo etiam corpus Christi de pane fit, qui ex multis granis conficitur, quia Ecclesia corpus Christi per illud reficitur, quae ex multis electis colligitur. Quae grana scilicet electi flagello praedicationis de theca veteris vitae excutiuntur, paenitentia arefacti, quasi duobus lapidibus moluntur, dum duabus legibus in scrutinio minutatim imbuuntur. Cribrati, conspersi, conpastinantur, dum ab infidelibus segregati, aqua baptismatis renati, vinculo caritatis per Spiritum sanctum in fide copulantur. Ut panes in clibano excocti, in candorem mutantur, dum in camino tribulationis examinati ad imaginem Dei reformantur. Tali modo panis effecti de pane Christi reficiuntur, et hi *in aeternum non moriuntur.*

32

On the Church and Its Meaning

The body of Christ is made from bread, which is composed of many grains, because the Church, which is assembled out of the many elect, both is Christ's body and is restored through his body. The grains, that is, the elect, are removed from the husk of their old life by the whip of preaching, dried by penance, and milled as if by two stones, as they are carefully instructed by the two Laws, in the scrutiny. They are sifted, moistened, and worked into a dough when they are separated from the unfaithful, reborn in the water of baptism, and joined in faith by the bond of charity through the Holy Spirit—just like bread baked in the oven, they become white when, having been tried in the furnace of tribulation, they are remade unto the image of God. Once made into bread in this way, they are nourished by the bread of Christ, and *they will not die forever.*

33

De sacrificio vini

Ideo vero hoc sacramentum de vino fit, quia Christus se vitem dixit, et scriptura eum vinum iucunditatis asseruit. Uva autem in praelo duobus lignis expressa in vinum liquatur, et Christus, duobus lignis Crucis pressus, sanguis eius in potum fidelibus fundebatur. Ideo etiam sanguis Christi de vino conficitur, quod de multis acinis exprimitur, quia per illum corpus Christi Ecclesia recreatur, quae de multis iustis congregatur. Haec pressuris mundi quasi in torculari calcatur; et Christo per passiones incorporatur.

34

De aqua

Ideo autem hoc sacramentum de aqua fit, quia aqua de Christi latere exivit, et Iohanni angelus aquas populos esse retulit. Et ideo aqua vino admiscetur, quia populus sanguine

33

On the Sacrifice of Wine

The sacrament is made of wine because Christ said that he was the vine, and scripture proclaims him the wine of gladness. Now, the grape is squeezed in the winepress by two wooden beams and strained into wine, and Christ was pressed by the two wooden beams of the Cross, and his blood was poured out as a drink for the faithful. Again, the blood of Christ is confected from wine, which is pressed from many grapes, because this wine refreshes Christ's body, the Church, which is assembled from many just men. She is trodden by the pressures of the world as if in a winepress, and incorporated into Christ by martyrdoms.

34

On the Water

The sacrament is made of water, because water flowed out of Christ's side, and the angel told John that the waters were the people. The water is mixed with the wine because the people, redeemed by the blood of Christ and cleansed

Christi redemptus, per aquam baptismatis ablutus, per pastum huius cibi, et potum huius vini Christo counitur. Panis autem hic in carnem convertitur, quia Christus paschalis agnus pro nobis occiditur, et caro nostra a morte redimitur. Vinum in sanguinem transit, quia Christus sanguinem fundens, pro nobis animam posuit, et animam nostram quae in sanguine habitat a peccatis expiavit. Sine aqua autem hoc sacramentum non conficitur, quia solius populi causa hoc mysterium agitur, qui et eo cottidie reficitur.

35

De forma panis

Panis vero ideo in modum denarii formatur, quia panis vitae Christus pro denariorum numero tradebatur, qui verus denarius in vinea laborantibus in praemio dabitur. Ideo imago Domini cum litteris in hoc pane exprimitur, quia et in denario imago et nomen imperatoris scribitur, et per hunc panem imago Dei in nobis reparatur, et nomen nostrum in libro vitae notatur.

by the water of baptism, are united with Christ by eating this food and drinking this wine. Now, this bread becomes flesh because Christ the paschal lamb is slain for us and our flesh is ransomed from death. The wine turns into blood because Christ poured out his blood when he laid down his life for us and thus purified our soul, which dwells in the blood, of its sins. This sacrament cannot be confected without water because this mystery is done solely for the sake of the people, who are daily refreshed by it.

35

On the Shape of the Bread

Now the bread is made in the shape of a penny because Christ, the bread of life, was betrayed for a few pence and, as the true penny, will be given as a reward to those who labor in the vineyard. The image of our Lord and several letters are stamped in this bread because the image and name of the emperor are stamped on a penny, and because by this bread the image of God is restored in us and our name is recorded in the book of life.

36

Cur cottidie Missa canatur

Et cum Christus semel sua morte credentes redemerit, hoc tamen sacramentum cottidie ob tres causas Ecclesia necessario repetit. Una ex causa ut in vinea laborantes cottidie eo reficiantur; alia ut hi qui numero fidelium cottidie associantur per illud incorporentur; tertia ut memoria Passionis Christi cottidie mentibus fidelium ad imitationem inculcetur. Tali autem ordine offertur.

37

De subdiacono

Subdiaconus calicem in sinistra, patenam in dextra, desuper corporale portat, quia subdiaconus in loco hoc Christum, calix Passionem, sinistra praesentem vitam, patena Crucem, dextra aeternam vitam, corporale Ecclesiam significat. Et Christus calicem Passionis in praesenti vita bibit,

36

Why Mass Is Sung Daily

Though Christ redeemed the faithful once and for all by his death, yet the Church must repeat this sacrament each day for three reasons. One reason is so that those who labor in the vineyard might be refreshed by it daily; another is so that those who are daily added to the faithful's number may be incorporated by it; the third is to daily etch the commemoration of Christ's Passion into the faithful's minds for them to imitate. Now it is offered according to the following order.

37

On the Subdeacon

The subdeacon carries the chalice in his left hand, the paten in his right, and the corporal covering them both, because at this point the subdeacon signifies Christ, the chalice his Passion, the left hand the present life, the paten the Cross, the right hand eternal life, and the corporal the Church. And Christ drank the chalice of the Passion in the

quem prius a se transferri Patrem petiit. Per Crucem autem gloriam Patris intravit, cuius Passionem Ecclesia imitari non desinit. Corporale multo labore candidatur, et Ecclesia per multas tribulationes Christo conformatur. Subdiaconus noster Christus quasi patenam cum calice portavit, quando Crucem ad Passionem baiulavit.

38

De cantoribus

Unus cantor oblatam cum fanone et vinum cum ampulla offert, alter aquam vino admiscendam praebet. Qui vinum offert significat Ecclesiam de Iudaeis, quae legis ritus in Christi sacrificium commutavit; qui aquam offert Ecclesiam de gentibus, quae populum gentile Christo sacrificavit. Hi etiam duo typum Enoch et Heliae praeferunt, qui Iudaicum populum Christo in sacrificium oblaturi sunt. Oblata non nudis manibus sed fanonibus multo labore candidis offertur, quia Christi corpus ab his tantum qui *carnem suam cum vitiis et concupiscentiis crucifigunt* digne suscipitur. Ampulla in qua vinum offertur, significat nostram devotionem, quae in vasculis cordis portatur. Archidiaconus ad ultimum aquam in

present life, though he first asked the Father for it to be taken from him. Through the Cross he entered into the Father's glory, and the Church never ceases to imitate his Passion. The corporal is made white by strenuous effort, and the Church is conformed to Christ by many tribulations. Christ our subdeacon carried the paten and chalice, as it were, when he bore the Cross to his Passion.

38

On the Cantors

One cantor offers the communion bread on a linen cloth and wine in a cruet; a second provides water to be mixed in the wine. The one who offers wine signifies the Church of the Jews, which transformed the rites of the Law into the sacrifice of Christ; he who offers water signifies the Church of the gentiles, which made of the gentile people a sacrifice to Christ. These two also present a type of Enoch and Elijah, who will offer the Jewish people to Christ in sacrifice. The communion bread is brought forward not with bare hands, but with linen cloths made white by much labor, because the body of Christ can be received worthily only by those who *crucify their flesh with the vices and concupiscences.* The cruet in which the wine is offered signifies our devotion, which is carried in the heart's vessels. Finally, the

calicem fundens episcopo offert, quia Christus quem hic diaconus signat Ecclesiam sibi in Passione miscuit, Patri in Cruce obtulit, et in ultimo corpus capiti consociabit, cum regnum Deo et Patri tradiderit.

39

De oratione sacerdotis

Post acceptum sacrificium episcopus se inclinans coram altari orationem *Suscipe sancta Trinitas* dicit, quia Christus ad pedes discipulorum se inclinans, post traditum sacramentum in cena ante mensam stans, orationem ad Patrem fecit. Deinde dicit "Orate," quia Christus apostolos orare monuit. Dehinc orationem *super oblatam* secreto dicit, quia Christus in monte Oliveti secreto prolixius oravit, cum ei angelus confortans eum apparuit. Spatium silentii post Offertorium illud tempus signat, quo Christus ante Passionem in Ierusalem latebat, velut paschalis agnus quem Iudaei decima luna reclusum decima quarta luna immolabant.

archdeacon pours the water into the chalice and offers it to the bishop because Christ, whom the deacon signifies here, mingled the Church with himself in his Passion, offered it to the Father on the Cross, and in the end shall join the head to the body when he hands over the kingdom to his God and Father.

39

On the Priest's Prayer

After taking the sacrifice, the bishop bows low before the altar, and says the prayer *Suscipe sancta Trinitas,* because at the Last Supper, Christ, having bent down over the feet of the apostles, and after handing them the sacrament, made a prayer to the Father while standing before the table. Then he says "Orate," because Christ told the apostles to pray. Then he says the *Super oblatam* in silence, because on the Mount of Olives Christ prayed secretly at great length, and at that time an angel appeared to comfort him. The interval of silence after the Offertory signifies that time when Christ was lying low in Jerusalem before his Passion, just like the paschal lamb, which the Jews sacrificed on the fourteenth day of the month, after keeping it confined since the tenth.

40

De Secreta

Composito sacrificio sacerdos orationem sub silentio recitat, quia idem sacrificium in sacrificio patrum absconditum latebat. In agno quippe Abel delitescebat; in ariete Abrahae pro Isaac se occultaverat; in agno paschali, in vitula rufa, in hirco emissario se celaverat. Tunc pontifex offert pro populo sacrificium, quia Christus obtulit pro Ecclesia semetipsum. Tunc sacrificium thurificatur, quia Christus *odor suavitatis* pro nobis oblatus a Deo acceptatur.

41

De Praefatione

Sequitur in Praefatione sacrificium angelorum, qui huic sacrificio interesse creduntur. Summo enim imperatori ut milites assistunt, et laudes suo regi concinunt. Per ter autem tria distincti Trinitatem sacrificio laudis honorificant, et hostiam iubilationis iugiter unitati immolant. Ideo etiam

40

On the Secret

Once the sacrifice has been arranged, the priest recites a prayer in silence, for the same sacrifice lay concealed in the sacrifice of the fathers. For he lay hidden in Abel's lamb and concealed himself in Abraham's ram, taking Isaac's place; in the paschal lamb, in the red calf, in the scapegoat he was there in disguise. Then the bishop offers the sacrifice for the people because Christ offered himself for the Church. Then the sacrifice is incensed because, when offered up to God as *a fragrant odor,* Christ is always accepted.

41

On the Preface

Next, in the Preface, comes the sacrifice of the angels, who we believe are present for this sacrifice. For like soldiers they stand by assisting the supreme commander and singing praises to their king. Thrice three times divided, they honor God's Trinity in a sacrifice of praise, and to his unity they perpetually sacrifice a host of jubilation. The

hoc sacerdos alta voce cantat, quia sacrificium angelorum, quod est laus repraesentat.

42

De sacrificio angelorum

Angeli itaque, et archangeli maiestatem Dei laudant, dominationes adorant, principatus et potestates admirando tremunt, caeli—id est throni—et virtutes iubilant, cherubin et seraphim dulciter concelebrant. Hoc sacrificium concentus angelorum David et Salemon sunt imitati, qui instituerunt hymnos in sacrificio Domini organis et aliis musicis instrumentis concrepari, et a populo laudes conclamari. Unde solemus nos adhuc in officio sacrificii organis concrepare, clerus cantare, populus conclamare. Sacrificium itaque laudis angeli immolant, dum "Sanctus, sanctus, sanctus" consonant. Ter "sanctus" repetitur, quia Trinitas collaudatur; "Dominus Deus" semel dicitur, quia unitas veneratur. Sacrificio angelorum coniungitur sacrificium spirituum iustorum qui Christi humanitatem adorant, et pro humani generis redemptione cantant "Benedictus qui venit in nomine Domini." Hic hymnus partim ab angelis, partim ab hominibus

priest sings the Preface aloud because he represents the angels' sacrifice, which is praise.

42

On the Sacrifice of the Angels

Therefore the angels praise God's majesty together with the archangels and the dominions adore him, the powers and principalities tremble in awe, the heavens—that is the thrones—and the virtues sing joyfully, and the cherubim and seraphim join in sweet celebration. This sacrifice of the concert of angels was imitated by David and Solomon, who ordered that hymns sound forth to the accompaniment of organs and other musical instruments during the Lord's sacrifice, and that the people join in singing praises with lively voice. To this day, following their example we sound the organ during the office of sacrifice, the clergy sing, and the people join in with lively voices. The angels immolate a sacrifice of praise when they ring out, "*Sanctus, sanctus, sanctus.*" *Sanctus* is repeated three times to praise God's Trinity; *Dominus Deus* is said once to venerate his unity. The sacrifice of the angels is joined by the sacrifice of the spirits of the just, who adore Christ's humanity and sing for the human race's redemption, "Blessed is he who comes in the name of the Lord." This hymn is sung partly by angels, partly by men,   2

concinitur, quia per Christum immolatum humanum genus angelis coniungitur. Laus quippe angelorum est "Sanctus, sanctus, sanctus Dominus Deus Sabaoth, pleni sunt caeli et terra gloria tua, hosanna in excelsis." Laus vero hominum est, "Benedictus qui venit in nomine Domini, hosanna in excelsis." In hoc cantu se signant, quia signum Christi cui contradicitur se recipere designant.

43

De quattuor ordinibus

Notandum quod primo loco masculi offerunt, quia primo tempore patriarchae suo sacrificio hoc sacrificium pertulerunt. Secundo loco feminae offerunt, quia secundo tempore Iudaei legalibus sacrificiis hoc sacrificium praemonstraverunt. Tertio loco sacerdotes et ministri offerunt, quia tertio tempore apostoli ipsum sacrificium exceperunt, et hoc fideles docuerunt, qui cottidie septem suprascripta sacrificia offerunt. Quarto loco angeli sacrificium laudis offerunt, quia post hanc vitam angeli cum *beatis hominibus in saeculum saeculi Deum laudabunt.*

because through Christ's immolation the human race is joined to the angels. The angel's praise is "Holy, holy, holy Lord, God of Hosts, heaven and earth are full of your glory, hosanna in the highest," and man's praise is "Blessed is he who comes in the name of the Lord, hosanna in the highest." During this chant they sign themselves with a cross to show that they receive Christ's sign, a sign of contradiction.

43

On the Four Orders

Note how the men offer first, because in the first age the patriarchs heralded this sacrifice when they performed their own. The women make their offering second, because the Jews in the second age prefigured this sacrifice in the sacrifices of the Law. The priests and ministers offer in third place because the apostles in the third age received the sacrifice itself and taught it to the faithful, who offer the seven aforementioned sacrifices every day. In fourth place the angels offer their sacrifice of praise because after this life the angels together with *the blessed shall praise the Lord forever and ever.*

44

De quinto officio et de pugna Christi

Quintum officium alis cherubin velatur, in quo summi Pontificis hostia, et Regis gloriae pugna repraesentatur. Hoc Moyses praefigurabat, quando in monte extensis manibus orabat, dum Iosue qui et Iesus cum Amalech pugnabat, devicti regnum vastabat, ac populum cum victoriae laetitia reducebat. Sic Christus in monte Crucis *extensis manibus pro populo non credente et contradicente* oravit, et verus dux cum Amalech—id est cum diabolo—vexillo sanctae Crucis pugnavit devicti regnum devastavit, dum infernum superato maligno hoste spoliavit, populum de tenebris ereptum cum gloria victoriae ad caelestia revocavit.

44

On the Fifth Office and Christ's Battle

The fifth office, which represents the sacrifice of the supreme Pontiff and the battle of the King of glory, is veiled by the wings of the cherubim. Moses prefigured it when he prayed on the mountain with outstretched hands, while Joshua, who is also Jesus, fought with Amalek, defeated him, laid waste to his kingdom, and brought the people back in the joy of victory. Just so, Christ prayed upon the mount of the Cross *with hands outstretched for an unbelieving and gainsaying people,* and as a true leader fought with Amalek—that is with the devil—under the banner of the holy Cross, vanquished him, and laid waste to his kingdom when he overcame the wicked enemy and plundered hell, rescued the people from darkness, and called them back to heaven in the glory of victory.

45

Mysterium

Hoc totum episcopus imaginatur, et quasi tragicis gestibus exprimere conatur. Christum namque in Cruce fixum repraesentat, dum expansis manibus Canonem recitat. Quasi contra Amalech pugnat, dum contra diabolum Christi Passionem cum signis crucis simulat. Ministri autem quasi acies pugnantium utrimque ordinantur, dum diaconi retro episcopum, subdiaconi retro altare locantur. Exercitus cum triumpho regreditur, quia populus percepta communione *ad propria cum gaudio revertitur.*

46

De Passione Christi

In hoc officio agitur Christi Passio. Altare Crux intelligitur, in quod corporale in forma corporis Christi distenditur. Corporale de puro lino terrae conficitur, et cum multo labore in candorem vertitur, et Christi corpus de munda

45

A Mystery

The bishop creates an image of this whole event for us and endeavors to express it using the gestures of a tragic actor. He depicts Christ nailed to the Cross when he recites the Canon with hands outspread. He fights against Amalek when he reenacts Christ's Passion against the devil with signs of the cross. The ministers, for their part, are drawn up on each side like ranks of warriors when the deacons are arranged behind the bishop and the subdeacons behind the altar. The army returns in triumph, for once Communion is taken the people *return joyfully homeward.*

46

On Christ's Passion

This office enacts Christ's Passion. The altar is the Cross, on which the corporal is spread in the manner of Christ's body. The corporal is made of pure linen taken from the earth, and made white with much hard effort, and Christ's body is born from a pure Virgin, and through many suf-

virgine nascitur, et per multas passiones in candorem Resurrectionis redditur. Corporale cum plicatur nec initium nec
finis eius apparet, quia Christi divinitas initio caret, et finem
non habet. Super quod oblata ponitur, quia caro a divinitate
suscepta in Cruce affigitur. Calix cum vino et aqua in dextra
locatur, quia sanguis cum aqua de latere Christi manasse
praedicatur. Cum sacerdos "Hanc igitur oblationem" dicit,
se usque ad altare inclinat, quia ibi Passio Christi inchoat,
qui se usque ad aram Crucis obediens Patri pro nobis incli-
naverat.

2   Deinde oblata vel calix in manu sacerdotis exaltatur, quia
Christus pro salute nostra in Crucem levatur, et sanguis eius
in redemptionem nostri immolatur. Interim diaconi retro
episcopum stantes figuram apostolorum gerunt, qui in Passione Domini eo relicto omnes fugierunt; subdiaconi vero
retro altare stantes contra episcopum aspiciunt, mulieres et
notos Iesu praeferunt, qui a longe stantes eius Passionem
viderunt. Ante altare se sacerdos inclinat, cum "Supplices te
rogamus" dicit, quia ibi Passio Christi finit, et *Christus incli-
nato capite spiritum emisit.* Infra Canonem diaconus manus
lavat, quia Pilatus in Passione Domini manus lavabat, dum
se sic mundus a sanguine eius quam manus suas a sorde pro-
clamabat. Sacerdos vocem levat, dum "Nobis quoque peccatoribus" dicit, designans quod Ecclesia de Christi latere iam
formata in confessione redemptoris erupit, dum per vocem
centurionis sic clamavit, *"Vere Dei Filius est iste."*

ferings attains the whiteness of the Resurrection. When the corporal is folded, neither its beginning nor its end is visible, because Christ's divinity lacks any beginning and has no end. The bread is placed upon it because the flesh assumed by the divinity is fixed to the Cross. The chalice containing the water and wine is set on the right side because blood and water flowed from Christ's side. When the priest says "*Hanc igitur oblationem,*" he bends down over the altar, because Christ began his Passion there when, in obedience to the Father, he bent over the altar of the Cross for us.

Then the bread and chalice are raised in the priest's hand 2 because Christ is raised on the Cross for our salvation and his blood is sacrificed for our redemption. Meanwhile the deacons standing behind the bishop cut the figure of the apostles, who all fled during our Lord's Passion and abandoned him; the subdeacons standing behind the altar facing the bishop display the women and noblemen who saw his Passion while standing far away. The priest bows before the altar when he says "*Supplices te rogamus,*" because there Christ's Passion ends, and *bowing his head, Christ gave up his spirit.* During the Canon the deacon washes his hands because Pilate washed his hands during our Lord's Passion, thus proclaiming that his hands were as clean of his blood as his hands were from dirtiness. The priest raises his voice at *Nobis quoque peccatoribus,* showing that the Church sprang fully formed from Christ's side when she cried through the voice of the centurion, "*Indeed this was the Son of God.*"

47

De Ioseph

Dicente sacerdote "Per omnia saecula saeculorum" diaconus venit, calicem coram eo sustollit, cum fanone partem eius cooperit, in altari reponit, et cum corporale cooperit, praeferens Ioseph ab Arimathia, qui Christi corpus deposuit, faciem eius sudario cooperuit, in monumento deposuit, lapide cooperuit. Hic oblata et calix cum corporale cooperitur, quod sindonem mundam significat, in quam Ioseph corpus Christi involvebat. Calix hic sepulchrum, patena lapidem designat, qui sepulchrum clauserat. Tres articuli, scilicet *Oremus praeceptis,* et *Pater noster,* et *Libera nos Domine,* tres dies significant, quibus Christus in monumento quiescebat.

48

De acolytho qui patenam tenet, quod Nichodemum figuret

Acolythus infra Canonem patenam involutam tenet, quam hic subdiacono defert, subdiaconus archidiacono

47

On Joseph

When the priest says "*Per omnia saecula saeculorum*," the deacon comes, raises the chalice before him, covers part of it with a cloth, places it back on the altar, and covers it with the corporal. In all this he symbolizes Joseph of Arimathea as he laid Christ's body to rest, covered his face with the shroud, placed him in the tomb, and sealed it with a stone. At this point the host and the chalice are covered with the corporal, which signifies the white sindon Joseph used to wrap Christ's body. The chalice represents the tomb, the paten the stone that sealed the tomb. These three articles, namely *Oremus praeceptis,* and *Pater noster,* and *Libera nos Domine* signify the three days Christ lay in the tomb.

48

On the Acolyte Who Holds the Paten, a Figure of Nicodemus

During the Canon the acolyte holds the wrapped paten, which he now takes to the subdeacon, and the subdeacon

praebet, quam ipse osculatam uni de diaconibus ad tenendam, et corpus Domini in ea confringendam porrigit. Acolythus qui patenam tenuit, formam Nichodemi gerit, qui mirram et aloen ad sepulturam Domini attulit. Porro subdiaconus et archidiaconus cum alio diacono patenam tenenti tres Marias praeferunt, quae cum aromatibus ad monumentum venerunt.

2   Dum septem petitiones in Dominica oratione dicuntur diaconi inclinati stant, et communione confirmari expectant, quia apostoli septem hebdomadas post mortem Christi confirmari a Spiritu sancto expectabant. Subdiaconi autem interim quiescunt, quia mulieres in Sabbato, quae septem dies est siluerunt.

49

De Cruce

Hoc sacramentum tantum per Crucem fit, quia Christus sacrificium Patris in Cruce pependit, et in Cruce quadruplum mundum redemit. Sex autem ordines crucum fiunt quia sex diebus mundus perficitur, et senario numero corpus Christi conficitur. Per imparem vero numerum qui in duo paria non potest dividi benedicitur, quia corpus Christi unum permanens non finditur. Aut enim tres cruces facimus,

gives to the archdeacon, who kisses it and hands it to one of the deacons to hold, so that our Lord's body may be broken upon it. The acolyte who holds the paten is Nicodemus, who brought myrrh and aloe for our Lord's burial. The sub-deacon and archdeacon along with the other deacon holding the paten are figures of the three Marys, who came to the tomb with perfumes and spices.

As the seven petitions in the Lord's Prayer are said, the deacons stand bowed and wait to receive communion. For the seven apostles waited to receive the Holy Spirit for seven weeks after Christ's death. Now the subdeacons are at rest in the meantime, for the women kept silence on the Sabbath, which is the seventh day. 2

49

On the Cross

This sacrament is done through the Cross alone because Christ hung on the Cross as the Father's sacrifice, and on the Cross redeemed the world in a fourfold manner. There are six orders of crosses because the world was created in six days, and Christ's body is confected by the same number six. Blessing is given using an odd number, which cannot be divided into two equal parts, because the eternal body of Christ remains one and cannot be divided. We make either

et fidem sanctae Trinitatis exprimimus, aut per quinque signamus, et quinquepartitam Christi Passionem denotamus. Per sex crucum ordines cuncta mundi tempora comprehendimus, quae per Crucem Christo unita exprimimus.

50

De primo ordine et de tribus crucibus

In primo ordine tres cruces facimus, ubi *Haec dona* dicimus, et primum tempus ante legem innuimus, quod tribus interstitiis distinguimus, quia unum ab Adam usque ad Noe, aliud a Noe usque ad Abraham, tertium ab Abraham usque ad Moysen distendemus. In quibus iusti in fide Trinitatis Christum a longe suis sacrificiis salutaverunt, et multos cruciatus in hac fide pertulerunt. In prima quippe aetate Abel Christum in agno obtulit, et pro eo cruciatum mortis pertulit. In secunda Melchisedech Christi carnem et sanguinem in pane et vino obtulit, qui cruciatus bellorum a regibus gentium in fide Christi pertulit. In tertia, Abraham Christum in Isaac sacrificavit, in ariete mactavit, et varios cruciatus in hac fide toleravit.

three crosses, and thus express our Trinitarian faith, or five crosses, and denote the fivefold Passion of Christ. These six orders of crosses encompass all the ages of the world, which are united to Christ by the Cross.

50

On the First Order and the Three Crosses

In the first order we make three signs of the cross at *Haec dona,* an allusion to the first period before the Law, which we divide into three phases, one stretching from Adam to Noah, the next from Noah to Abraham, and the third from Abraham to Moses. The just men of these times had faith in the Trinity and greeted Christ from afar through their sacrifices, and also bore many terrible crosses for their faith. For in the first age, Abel offered Christ in the form of the lamb and for his sake suffered the cross of death. In the second age, Melchizedek offered Christ's body and blood in bread and wine and for his faith in Christ he suffered the crosses of war with the kings of the gentiles. In the third age, Abraham sacrificed Christ in the person of Isaac, slaughtered the ram, and bore various crosses for his faith.

51

De secundo ordine et de quinque crucibus

In secundo ordine quinque cruces facimus, ubi *Benedictam adscriptam* dicimus, et tempus legis exprimimus, quo iusti per quinque librorum legis sacrificia Christum expresserunt, et multos cruciatus pro eius fide pertulerunt. Quinque namque in duas partes scilicet ternarium et binarium solvitur, et illud tempus in duo interstitia dividitur. Unum a Moyse usque ad David fuit, alterum a David usque ad Christum extitit. Per ternarium iudices a Iosue usque ad David et reges a David usque ad captivitatem Babylonis et principes a Zorobabel usque ad Christum notantur, per binarium vero sacerdotes et prophetae significantur. Ex quibus Moyses Christum in paschali agno immolavit, qui a populo multa adversa pro fide Christi toleravit, quem lege praedicavit. Samuel Christum in David unxit, qui uterque Christum et sacrificiis expressit, et in figura Christi persecutionem a perfido rege Saul pertulit. Helias et alii prophetae Christum sacrificiis, scriptis, vocibus praemonstraverunt, et pro eius fide varia supplicia perpessi sunt.

51

On the Second Order and the Five Crosses

In the second order we make five signs of the cross at *Benedictam adscriptam,* portraying the time of the Law, in which the just men portrayed Christ through the sacrifices of the five books of the Law and suffered many crosses for their faith. Five is divided into two parts, three and two, just as this time is divided into two intervals. One was from Moses to David, another from David to Christ. The number three signifies the judges from Joshua to David, the kings from David to the Babylonian captivity, and the princes from Zerubbabel to Christ. The number two on the other hand signifies the priests and prophets, among them Moses, who immolated Christ in the paschal lamb, and suffered many hardships from the people for his faith in Christ, whom he preached in the Law. Samuel anointed Christ in the person of David and both of them expressed Christ in their sacrifices, and as figures of Christ bore persecution at the hands of the treacherous king Saul. Elijah and the other prophets gave figures and signs of Christ in their sacrifices, words, and writings, and were stricken with many punishments for their faith.

52

De tertio ordine

In tertio ordine panem in manus suscipimus, et benedicimus, et tempus gratiae innotescimus, quo Simeon Christum iam natum panem vivum in manus accepit, et gaudens benedixit. Deinde calicem levamus et benedicimus, et tempus Cenae exprimimus, quo Christus panem et calicem manibus elevavit, et benedixit, et inde corpus et sanguinem apostolis tradidit. Unde cum adhuc verba in hoc ordine recitantur, panis et vinum in corpus et sanguinem Domini commutantur.

53

De quarto ordine et
de quinque crucibus

In quarto ordine quinque cruces facimus, ubi *Hostiam puram* dicimus, et illud tempus ad memoriam reducimus, quo Christus in Cruce quinque vulnera accepit, et quinque saecula redemit.

52

On the Third Order

In the third order we take bread in our hands and bless it, signifying the time of grace in which Simeon received the newborn Christ into his hands as the living bread and blessed him with great joy. Next we raise the chalice and bless it, portraying the time of the Supper, in which Christ raised up bread and wine in his hands, blessed them, and gave them to the apostles as his body and blood. For this reason, to this very day whenever our Lord's words are recited in this order, bread and wine are changed into his body and blood.

53

On the Fourth Order and the Five Crosses

In the fourth order we make five crosses at *Hostiam puram,* recalling the time when Christ received five wounds on the Cross and redeemed all five ages.

54

De quinto ordine et tribus crucibus

In quinto ordine tres cruces facimus, ubi *Omnia bona creas sanctificas* dicimus, et corpus Christi scilicet primitivam Ecclesiam innuimus, quae fidem Trinitatis excepit, et multos cruciatus pro Christo sustinuit.

55

De sexto ordine et de quinque crucibus

In sexto ordine quinque cruces facimus, ubi *Per ipsum* dicimus, et item corpus Christi videlicet Ecclesiam de gentibus exprimimus, quae Christi quinquepartitam Passionem veneranter excepit, et eam imitando patienter diversa tormenta pertulit.

54

On the Fifth Order and
the Three Crosses

In the fifth order we make three signs of the cross at *Omnia bona creas sanctificas,* alluding to the body of Christ, that is, the early Church, which took up the Trinitarian faith and withstood many crosses for Christ.

55

On the Sixth Order and
the Five Crosses

In the sixth order we make five crosses at *Per ipsum,* likewise expressing the body of Christ, that is, the Church gathered from among the gentiles, which reverently welcomed Christ's fivefold Passion and in its desire to imitate it bore varied agonies with patience.

56

De quinque ordinibus crucum

Item per quinque ordines crucum quinque aetates mundi designantur, quae per crucem et Christi corpus salvantur. Unde et in Canone quinquies *Per Christum Dominum nostrum* dicitur, quia per quinque vulnera Christi mundus redimitur. In sexto ordine calix cum oblata tangitur, quia in sexta aetate Christus calicem Passionis in Cruce pro omnibus bibisse innuitur. Cum *Per ipsum* dicimus, quattuor cruces super calicem cum oblata facimus, quintam lateri calicis imprimimus, quia Christum quattuor vulnera in manibus et pedibus, et quintum in latere suscepisse innotescimus. Confecto igitur Christi corpore labia calicis tangimus, ac per hoc quod formato primi hominis corpore *Deus spiraculum vitae in faciem eius spiravit,* et mulierem ex eo vivificavit, significamus. Et hoc, Deus *per quem, cum quo, in quo omnia,* in faciem mortui humani generis Spiritum sanctum spiravit, Ecclesiam ex eo per corpus suum vivificavit. Per quattuor autem partes calix tangitur, quia humanum genus in quattuor mundi partes dispersum, per quattuor crucis partes vivificatum, in fine mundi per Christum ad vitam resuscitatur.

56

On the Five Orders of Crosses

Moreover, through the five orders of crosses we symbolize the five ages of this world, which are saved by the Cross and Christ's body. For that reason *Per Christum Dominum nostrum* is said five times in the Canon because the world is redeemed through Christ's five wounds. In the sixth order the host is touched to the chalice because in this way it is shown that Christ drank the chalice of his Passion on the Cross for the sake of all during the sixth age. When we say *Per ipsum,* we make four signs of the cross over the chalice with the host and a fifth on the side of the chalice because thereby we make known that Christ received four wounds in the hands and feet and a fifth in his side. Once the body of Christ has been confected, we touch it to the edge of the chalice, and in this way we signify that having formed the body of the first man, *God breathed the breath of life into his face* and brought the woman into being from him. In a similar way God, *through whom, with whom, and in whom* all things exist, breathed the Holy Spirit into the face of the perishing human race and out of it gave life to the Church through his body. The chalice is touched in four places because the human race, scattered to the four corners of the world and brought to life by the four parts of the Cross, will be raised to life through Christ at the end of the world.

57

De numero signorum

Notandum quod per totum Canonem viginti et tria signa fiunt, quia in veteri Testamento iusti sub decalogo legis, et in novo Testamento iusti per decalogum legis in fide Trinitatis huius sacramenti participes existunt. Tribus autem digitis signa facimus, quia Trinitatem exprimimus. Quod si viginti et tria triplicaveris, sexaginta et novem habebis. Porro cum *Pax Domini* dicimus, non cum digitis sed cum oblatae particula tria signa super calicem facimus. Quae si superioribus adieceris septuaginta duo signa habebit. Porro hoc significat quod septuaginta duae linguae per superbiam dispersae, per Christi humilitatem sunt in unum congregatae, per crucem et Passionem redemptae, per corpus et sanguinem eius ei counitae.

57

On the Number of Signs

In the whole Canon there are twenty-three signs of the Cross, because the just of the Old Testament were participants in this sacrament under the Decalogue of the Law, and the just of the New Testament are participants through the same Decalogue in Trinitarian faith. We make the sign of the Cross with three fingers to represent the Trinity. But if you multiply twenty-three by three, you get sixty-nine. When we say *Pax Domini,* we use the particle of the host rather than the fingers, making three signs over the chalice. If you add this number to the one above, you will have seventy-two. What this means is that seventy-two languages were dispersed because of pride, but gathered together by Christ's humility, redeemed through his Cross and Passion, and united to him through his body and blood.

58

De septem sacrificiis

In Canone septem sacrificiorum actio commemoratur, quibus corpus Ecclesia capiti Christo copulatur. In primis sacrificium Innocentum, secundo apostolorum et martyrum, tertio confessorum, quarto religiosorum et continentium, quinto coniugatorum, sexto in Christo defunctorum, septimo in anima mortuorum, scilicet paenitentium.

2   A *Te igitur* usque *Communicantes* sacrificium Innocentum notatur, qui se in Christi sacrificium obtulerunt, dum pro eo immolati sunt. A *Communicantes* usque *Hanc igitur oblationem,* sacrificium apostolorum et martyrum repraesentatur, ubi et nomina illorum recitantur, qui se hostiam vivam Deo obtulerunt, dum sanguinem suum pro eo fuderunt. Ab *Hanc igitur* usque *Quam oblationem* sacrificium confessorum commemoratur, qui ab haereticis multa pericula perpessi sunt, et sacrificium laudis Christo iugitur obtulerunt. A *Quam oblationem* usque *Supplices te rogamus,* sacrificium religiosorum demonstratur, qui *carnem suam vitiis et concupiscentiis crucifixerunt,* et sic hostia Christi effecti sunt. A *Supplices te rogamus* usque *Memento Domine,* sacrificium coniugatorum declaratur, qui fide et eleemosynis Christi corporis participes efficiuntur. A *Memento Domine* sacrificium defunctorum

58

On the Seven Sacrifices

The Canon recalls the seven sacrifices by which the body, the Church, is united to its head, Christ. First, the sacrifice of the Holy Innocents; second, of the apostles and martyrs; third, of confessors; fourth, of religious and those who practice continence; fifth, of the married; sixth, of those who have died in Christ; and seventh, in the souls of the dead doing penance.

From the *Te igitur* to the *Communicantes* we mark the sacrifice of the Holy Innocents, who offered themselves in union with the sacrifice of Christ when they were killed for his sake. From the *Communicantes* to the *Hanc igitur oblationem* we represent the sacrifice of the apostles and martyrs, where we recite the names of those who offered themselves to God as living victims and poured out their blood for him. From *Hanc igitur oblationem* to *Quam oblationem,* we recall the sacrifice of the confessors, who suffered many perils at the hands of heretics and offered Christ an unending sacrifice of praise. From *Quam oblationem* to *Supplices te rogamus,* we illustrate the sacrifice of the religious, who have *crucified their flesh to vice and concupiscence* and so are made victims of Christ. From *Supplices te rogamus* to *Memento Domine,* we manifest the sacrifice of the married, who are made participants in Christ's body through faith and almsgiving. From *Memento Domine,* we show the sacrifice of the faithful

ostenditur, qui in confessione Christi migraverunt, et fidelibus associati sunt.

3   Sacerdos Christi mortem repraesentat, cum se ad *Supplices te rogamus* inclinat, et post mortem eius apte comme-
moratio defunctorum agitur, qui pro eis mortuus creditur. A
Nobis quoque usque in finem Canonis sacrificium paenitentium exprimitur, qui se lacrimis et paenitentiae doloribus
Christo in sacrificium mactant, cum se animas suas peccatis
occidisse doleant, ut in eo vivificentur, qui pro impiis mortuus praedicatur. Unde et sacerdos ibi vocem exaltat, quia
paenitentes a vocis et cordis gemitu saepius rugire constat,
cum amaros singultus edant. Hos Dominus expressit, cum
Lazarum magna voce de monumento vocavit. In hoc etiam
capitulo nomina martyrum recitantur, quia paenitentes variis cruciatibus macerantur.

Per haec septem sacrificia corpus Christi Ecclesia efficitur, et capiti Christo coniungitur. Hoc per Dominicam orationem exprimitur, quae septem petitionibus haec sacrificia
sequitur, quia per orationem et hoc singulare sacrificium Ecclesia Christo counitur.

departed, who have passed away confessing Christ and are reckoned among the company of the blessed.

The priest represents Christ's death when he bows at the *Supplices te rogamus,* and it is fitting to do the commemoration of the dead after the death of the one who died for them. From the *Nobis quoque* to the end of the Canon we express the sacrifice of the penitents, who sacrifice themselves for Christ through the tears and the pains of their penance, for they grieve the fact that they have killed their souls by their sins, so that they may be brought back to life in him who, according to the Gospel, died for the impious. The priest raises his voice at this point because penitents often groan in heart and voice and heave bitter sighs. Our Lord represented them when he summoned Lazarus out from the tomb in a loud voice. Under this heading we also recite the names of martyrs because the penitents are tormented by various punishments.

Through these seven sacrifices the Church, the body of Christ, is confected and joined to her head, Christ. All this is expressed in the Lord's Prayer, which follows these sacrifices with its seven petitions, for the Church is made one with Christ through prayer and through this unique sacrifice.

59

De quinque orationibus

Oratio autem Canonis ideo in quinque distinguitur, quia oratio fidelium per quinquepartitam Christi Passionem tantum exauditur. In tribus locis pro praelatis et subiectis oramus, quia Ecclesiam in doctores, continentes, coniugatos discernimus, quarto loco pro defunctis offerimus, quinto pro paenitentibus petimus.

Primo loco pro praelatis offerimus, ubi dicimus "In primis quae tibi offerimus pro Ecclesia tua" et tunc papam, et episcopum et regem nominamus. Pro subiectis oramus, ubi "Memento Domine famulorum famularumque" recitamus, ubi et nominare possumus quos volumus. Secundo loco pro praelatis petimus, cum "Hanc igitur oblationem servitutis" dicimus. Pro subiectis subiungimus, cum "Et cunctae familiae tuae" dicimus. Tertio loco pro praelatis supplicamus, cum "Unde et memores, Domine, nos servi tui" recitamus. Pro subiectis poscimus, cum *"Sed et plebs tua sancta"* subiungimus. Pro defunctis sacrificamus, cum "Memento etiam, Domine" dicimus, ubi etiam nomina eorum recitare possumus. Pro paenitentibus offerimus, ubi "Nobis quoque peccatoribus" dicimus. Haec omnia ideo in Canone commemorantur, quia cuncta in morte Redemptoris reconciliantur.

59

On the Five Prayers

Now, the prayer of the Canon is divided into five parts because the prayer of the faithful is efficacious only through the five-part Passion of Christ. In three places we pray for superiors and their subjects because the Church is composed of the doctors, the continent, and the married. In the fourth place we offer sacrifice for the faithful departed. Fifthly, we intercede for the penitent.

In the first place we offer sacrifice for superiors, where we say, "In the first place, which we offer thee for thy Church," and then name the pope, bishop, and king. We pray for subjects at "Remember, O Lord, thy servants," where we can also add the names of whomever we wish. We pray for superiors a second time when we say, "This oblation of our service." We add another prayer for subjects when we say "And that of thy whole family." We pray for superiors a third time when we recite "Wherefore, O Lord, we thy servants." We intercede for subjects when we add "And likewise thy holy people." We sacrifice for the dead when we say "Remember also, O Lord," where we may even recite their names. We sacrifice for the penitent when we say "To us also, thy sinful servants." All of these things are mentioned in the Canon because all of them are reconciled through the death of our Redeemer.

60

De sexto officio et benedictione episcopi

Sextum officium in quo pontifex populum benedicit, Christi descensionem ad inferos exprimit.

Huius rei figuram Moyses gessit, quando moriturus filios Israel benedixit, educatosque de Aegypto in patriam introduci per Iesum qui et Iosue iussit. Hoc etiam Iacob moriens expressit, qui filios suos benedixit, et eis de futura hereditate multa praedixit. Has utrasque benedictiones Christus moriens complevit, cum ad inferna descendit, populum *sedentem in tenebris et umbra mortis* visitando benedixit, de carcere eductos caelesti patriae induxit. Quod episcopus ostendit dum populum benedicit, moxque eum spiritali cibo reficit.

2   Notandum autem quod semper ternis capitulis benedicit, et omnes quarto scilicet *Quod ipse praestare dignetur* confirmabit; quinto vero reliquas per *Benedictio Dei Patris* concludit, quia nimirum Deus tribus vicibus huic mundo benedicit, quarta reliquas firmavit, quinta *benedictionem hereditate possidere* dabit. Primo primis hominibus benedixit, cum eos crescere et multiplicare praecepit. Secundo hominibus benedixit, dum mundo diluvio deleto Noe et filios suos

60

On the Sixth Office and the Episcopal Blessing

The sixth office, when the bishop blesses the people, expresses Christ's descent into hell.

Moses acted as a figure of this when he blessed the sons of Israel just before he died and ordered them to be led from Egypt into their fatherland through Jesus, also called Joshua. Jacob also expressed this in his death, when he blessed his sons and predicted many things about their future inheritance. Christ brought both these blessings to fulfillment when, dying, he descended into hell to the people *sitting in the darkness and the shadow of death,* blessed them with his visitation, and led them out of prison to their heavenly fatherland. The bishop performs all of this when he blesses the people and then refreshes them with spiritual food.

Observe that the blessing he gives always includes three 2 elements, and, fourthly, he confirms the whole with *Quod ipse praestare dignetur;* fifthly, he concludes the rest with *Benedictionem Dei Patris*—with good reason, for God blessed this world three times, then fourthly confirms the rest, and with a fifth blessing he will *cause them to inherit a blessing.* First, God blessed the first human beings when he commanded them to *be fruitful and multiply.* He blessed mankind a second time after the world had been destroyed by the Flood, when he ordered Noah and his descendants to *be fruitful and*

posteros crescere et multiplicari iussit. Tertio per Abraham Deus mundo benedixit, cum ei in benedictionem Christum repromisit. Quarto mundum benedixit, dum Filium suum nobis benedicentem misit, qui caelos ascensurus suis benedixit, et per Spiritum sanctum reliquas firmavit. Quinto mundo benedicet, dum patriam intraturis ultimam benedictionem sic complet: *Venite benedicti,* et cetera.

61

De septimo officio et de Resurrectione Domini

Septimum officium Dominicam Resurrectionem insinuat, quando devicta morte, et spoliato inferno pacem omni mundo dabat, quia iam omnia in caelis et in terris pacificaverat, et cum suis discipulis comedit, eisque reliquias dedit.

Sic pontifex diabolo per spirituale bellum superato "Pax vobiscum" dicit, astantibus pacem porrigit, panem caelestem distribuit. Hoc Iesus qui et Iosue figuraliter praetulit, cum introducto populo ac superatis hostibus terram sorte distribuit. Pontifex partem oblatae in calicem mittit, designans quod anima Christi ad corpus rediit.

multiply. Thirdly, God blessed the world through Abraham, when he promised him Christ as a blessing. He blessed the world a fourth time when he sent his Son to bless us, who blessed his own before ascending to heaven and strengthened the other blessings through the Holy Spirit. At last he will bless the world a fifth time when he fills those who are about to enter into their fatherland with a final blessing: *Come, ye blessed of my Father, possess you the kingdom prepared for you.*

61

On the Seventh Office and on Our Lord's Resurrection

The seventh office shows us our Lord's Resurrection when, having conquered death and despoiled hell, he gave peace to the whole world. For when he had pacified all things in heaven and on earth, he ate with his disciples and gave them what was left over.

Thus the bishop, having conquered the devil in spiritual warfare, says, "Peace be with you," extending peace to those in attendance, and distributes the heavenly bread. Jesus, also known as Joshua, heralded this in a figurative manner when, after overcoming his enemies, he distributed the land to the people by lot. The bishop places a part of the oblation in the chalice, signifying that the soul of Christ returned to his body.

62

De pace Domini

Deinde "Pax Domini vobiscum" dicit, quia Christus suis apparens "*Pax vobis*" dixit. Pacem porrigit, quia Christus pacem amissam humano generi resurgens reddidit. Propter tres causas pacis osculum datur. Ob unam causam clerus et populus se invicem osculantur, quia homines Domini sui gratiam, angelorumque amicitiam, per Christum qui est pax nostra se promeruisse gratulantur. Alia est causa quod se per pacis osculum fratres in Christo, Dei Patris Ecclesiae matris filios per Christi reconciliationem demonstrant, atque uno pane Christi qui est Deus pacis, concordiae, et dilectionis refici desiderant. Tertia causa est, quia sicut in osculo caro carni, spiritus spiritui coniungitur, ita omnis homo in necessitate carnis per dilectionem proximi, in necessitate spiritus per dilectionem Dei diligi praecipitur. Qui non tali pacis osculo foederati corpus Christi comedunt, ut Iudas *iudicium sibi* per falsam pacem *sumunt*.

62

On Our Lord's Peace

Then he says, "The peace of the Lord be with you," because when Christ appeared to his own he said, "*Peace be to you.*" He offers peace because by his Resurrection Christ restored to the human race the peace it had lost. The kiss of peace is given for three reasons. For one, the clergy and people kiss one another because men congratulate one another for having gained our Lord's grace and the friendship of the angels through Christ, who is our peace. Another reason is that, through this kiss of peace, they demonstrate that by means of Christ's reconciliation they are all brothers in Christ and sons of God the Father and Mother Church, and that they desire to be refreshed by the one bread of Christ, who is the God of peace, concord, and love. The third reason is that, just as a physical kiss unites flesh to flesh and spirit to spirit, so we are commanded to love everyone with respect to his fleshly needs out of love of neighbor, and to love everyone with respect to his spiritual needs out of love of God. Those who eat the body of Christ without being bound together by this kiss of peace are like Judas, *eating and drinking condemnation on themselves* through their false peace.

63

De fractione oblatae

Oblata frangitur, quia panis angelorum nobis in Cruce frangitur, ut fractio peccatorum nostrorum per comestionem ipsius redintegretur.

2   Papa oblatam non frangit, sed partem ex ea mordet, reliquam in calicem mittit, quia Christus infernum *momordit,* et inde sumptos in paradisum misit. Diaconus calicem tenet dum papa sanguinem sumit, significans angelum qui Christo surgente lapidem de monumento tulit. Communicato sacerdote mox calix de altari tollitur, quia Christus resurgens ultra non moritur, et corpus eius in sepulchro non invenitur. Diaconus sanguinem distribuit, quia angelus Resurrectionem Domini innotuit. Subdiaconus corpus Domini accipit a diacono, et fert presbyteris frangendum populo, designans quod mulieres verba de Resurrectione Domini ab angelo perceperunt, et apostolis detulerunt, ipsique omni populo praedicando distribuerunt. Cum apostolicus ab altari descendit, populus communicat, quia cum Christus ab ara crucis descendens, a morte resurgit, populus aeterna gloria participat.

3   Episcopus oblatam frangit, quia Dominus panem in Emmaus discipulis fregit. In tres partes oblatam dividit, sibi

63

On the Fraction of the Host

The host is broken because the bread of angels is broken for us on the Cross, so that the brokenness of our sins may be repaired by eating him.

The pope does not break the host, but rather tears a mor- 2 sel off with his teeth and places the rest in the chalice, for Christ *took a bite out of* hell and placed those he took from there into paradise. The deacon holds the chalice while the pope receives the blood, signifying the angel who at Christ's Resurrection removed the stone from the tomb. As soon as the priest has communicated, the chalice is taken from the altar because Christ having risen will die no more and his body is not found in the tomb. The deacon distributes the blood because the angel made known our Lord's Resurrection. The subdeacon receives our Lord's body from the deacon and carries it to the priests to be broken for the people, thereby signifying that the women understood the angel's words about Christ's Resurrection and carried the news to the apostles, who distributed it to the whole people by their preaching. When the apostolic lord descends from the altar, the people communicate, because when Christ descends from the altar of the Cross and rises from the dead, the people participate with him in eternal glory.

The bishop breaks the host because our Lord broke bread 3 for his disciples at Emmaus. He divides the host into three

una retenta, duas diacono et subdiacono tribuit, quia Dominus fracto pane unam partem sibi, duas Cleopae et Lucae divisit.

64

De tribus partibus oblatae

Oblata non integra sumitur, sed in tria dividitur. Unum in calicem mittitur, aliud a sacerdote consumitur, tertium in pyxidem morituris ad viaticum reponitur, quia *corpus Domini est triforme:* illud quod de Maria sumptum a morte resurgens caelos penetravit, et illud quod adhuc in electis in terra laborat, et illud quod in sepulchris iam pausat. Pars in calicem missa, est corpus Christi iam sumptum in gloria. Pars a sacerdote vel a populo comesta, est corpus Domini id est Ecclesia adhuc laborans in terra. Pars in altari relicta, est corpus Domini in sepulchris quiescens id est Ecclesia in Christo mortua, per unionem corporis Christi resurrectura.

parts. He takes one for himself and gives two to the deacon and subdeacon because at Emmaus our Lord, having broken the bread, kept one part for himself and gave two to Cleophas and Luke.

64

On the Three Parts of the Host

The host is not consumed whole but divided into three parts. One is placed in the chalice, the second is consumed by the priest, the third is placed in a pyx as a viaticum for the dying. For *Christ's body is threefold:* the one taken from Mary that went into the heavens after rising from the dead, the one that still labors on earth in the elect, and the one that already rests in the grave. The part placed in the chalice is the body of our Lord already taken into glory. The part eaten by the priest and people is the body of Christ, that is, the Church still laboring on earth. The part left on the altar is the body of our Lord that rests in the grave, which is the Church dead in Christ, bound to rise through its union with Christ's body.

65

De tribus communicationibus

Primitus episcopus communicat, quia Christus coram apostolis partem piscis assi et favum mellis manducabat, reliquias eis dabat. Deinde ministri communicant, quia Dominus cum discipulis ad Mare Tiberiadis prandebat. Post hoc populus communicat, quia Dominus ascensurus cum multitudine discipulorum comedebat. Corporale plicatur, quia sudarium involutum invenitur. *Agnus Dei* et cantus in Communione, significat laetitiam fidelium de Christi Resurrectione. Oratio quam postea episcopus dicit, est benedictio qua Dominus ascensurus fideles benedixit. Diaconus se ad populum vertit, *Ite missa est* dicit, significans angelos qui apostolos alloquentes eos abire iusserunt, atque eis Christum ad iudicium rediturum praedixerunt. Clerus Deo gratias respondit, et populus abit, quia visa credentes ascensione Christi gratias egerunt, *in Ierusalem abierunt, in templo cottidie Deum benedixerunt.*

2 Benedictio quam papa vel sacerdos post Missam super populum facit, est spiritalis benedictio quam Spiritus sanctus in die Pentecostes fidelibus attulit, quando credentes *omni benedictione spiritali replevit,* et illam ultimam benedictionem exprimit, per quam Ecclesia thalamum sponsi sui intrabit. His peractis ad propria episcopus regreditur, quia

65

On the Three Communions

The bishop communicates first because Christ ate a piece of grilled fish and honeycomb before the apostles, then gave them what was left over. Next the ministers communicate, for our Lord ate with the disciples beside the Sea of Tiberias. After this the people communicate, since before his Ascension our Lord ate with a multitude of his disciples. The corporal is folded because the shroud was found rolled up. The *Agnus Dei* and the Communion chant signify the faithful's joy in Christ's Resurrection. The Postcommunion prayer the bishop pronounces next is the blessing by which our Lord blessed the faithful before his Ascension. The deacon turns to the people and says *Ite missa est,* signifying the angels who addressed the apostles, ordered them to leave, and foretold to them that Christ would return in judgment. The clergy responds *Deo gratias* and the people leave because the believers gave thanks when they saw Christ's Ascension, *went away to Jerusalem and blessed the Lord daily in the Temple.*

2   The blessing that the pope or priest gives after Mass is the spiritual blessing that the Holy Spirit conferred upon the faithful on the day of Pentecost when *he filled the faithful with every spiritual blessing.* It also expresses that final blessing that will grant the Church entry into the chamber of the Bridegroom. These things completed, the bishop returns to

et Christus legatione sua peracta in gloriam Patris revertitur. Sic Ecclesia omnibus adhuc agendis rite peractis, ab hoc
exilio per Christum eripitur, et in caelestem Ierusalem indu-
cetur. Corporale in altari remanet, quia munditia castitatis
in sacerdotibus permanere debet. Per altare quoque Christus, per corporale Ecclesia designatur, quae hic et in futuro
perenniter in Christo permanere affirmatur.

66

De Dominico pane

Fertur quod olim sacerdotes de singulis domibus vel fami-
liis farinam accipiebant, quod adhuc Graeci servant, et inde
Dominicum panem faciebant, quem pro populo offerebant,
et hunc consecratum eis distribuebant. Nam singuli farinam
offerentium Missae interfuerunt, et pro his in Canone dicebatur, "Omnium circumstantium qui tibi hoc sacrificium
laudis offerunt." Postquam autem Ecclesia numero quidem
augebatur, sed sanctitate minuebatur, propter carnales statutum est ut qui possent singulis Dominicis, vel tertia Dominica, vel summis festivitatibus, vel ter in anno com-
municarent, ne ante confessionem et paenitentiam pro

his own, because when Christ had finished his legation, he returned to the Father's glory. Likewise the Church, after all these things have been completed in proper order, is snatched up from this exile along with Christ and conducted into the heavenly Jerusalem. The corporal remains on the altar because priests must always maintain the cleanness of chastity. The altar signifies Christ, the corporal the Church, and so by this the truth is affirmed that the Church will remain in Christ now and forever.

66

On the Lord's Bread

It is said that in former times priests received flour from each household or family—as the Greeks do even today—and used it to make the Lord's bread that they offered for the people and, once consecrated, they gave it back to them. For whoever offered flour was present at the Mass, and the Canon refers to them when it says, "And all here present who offer to you this sacrifice of praise." But later, as the Church grew in number but diminished in sanctity, on account of carnal men it was decided that those who were able should receive communion each Sunday, or every third Sunday, or on the great feasts, or thrice in the year. This was in order to avert people bringing judgment upon themselves

aliquo crimine iudicium sibi sumerent. Et quia populo non communicante non erat necesse panem tam magnum fieri, statutum est eum in modum denarii formari, et ut populus pro oblatione farinae denarios offerret, pro quibus Dominum traditum recognosceret, qui tamen denarii in usum pauperum, qui membra sunt Christi cederent, vel in aliquid quod ad hoc sacrificium pertinet.

67

De Oratione super populum

Statutum est ut panis post Missam benediceretur, et populo pro benedictione communionis partiretur, hocque *eulogia* dicebatur. Sed quia hoc in Quadragesima fieri non licuit, Oratio super populum dici Ecclesia statuit, ut per hanc particeps communionis sit.

before confessing and doing penance for a criminal sin. Since the people did not receive communion usually and thus it was not necessary to make so much bread, it was decided to form the bread in the shape of a denarius, and that in place of the flour offering the people should offer real coins, recognizing that our Lord was betrayed by a similar offering of coins. But these coins were for the use of the poor, who are members of Christ, or for other things pertaining to the sacrifice.

67

On the Prayer over the People

It has been decided that bread should be blessed after the Mass and shared among the people as a communion blessing. This was called the *eulogia*. But because it was not permitted in Lent, the Church instituted the Prayer over the People, as a means of participating in the communion.

68

De processione

Nunc ut legentium vel audientium mentibus quiddam dulcedinis infundamus, aliquid de processione dicamus.

In Missa quidem agebatur Christi pro nobis in mundum legatio, in processione agitur nostra ad patriam reversio. Per processionis itaque sollemnitatem, imitatur Ecclesia populi Dei de Aegypto egredientis iucunditatem. Qui signis et prodigiis liberatus ad Montem Sinai pervenit, ibi accepta lege et facto tabernaculo quasi quadam processione ad terram repromissionis tetendit. Populus namque armatus incedebat, *per turmas* signa et vexilla anteferebant. Levitae tabernaculum gerebant, sacerdotes tubis clangebant. Arca foederis a sacerdotibus portabatur, et Aaron summus sacerdos decoratus et Moyses dux populi cum virga sequebatur. Quibus in via Amalech cum exercitu occurrit, iter armis obstruere voluit, cum quo Iesus pugnans victor extitit, populo iter ad patriam aperuit. Qui Iesus normam nobis processionis dedit, quando cum arca omnique populo Iericho circuivit, sacerdotalis ordo tubis cecinit, populus clamore personuit, Iericho corruit, et victor populus regnum obtinuit.

68

On the Procession

That we may pour some sweetness into the minds of our readers and hearers, we shall now say something about the procession.

If the Mass represented Christ's legation for us into the world, the procession represents our return to our fatherland. In her solemn procession, the Church imitates the joy of the people of God as they left Egypt and, liberated through many signs and wonders, finally arrived at Mount Sinai. There, having received the Law and built the tabernacle, they wended in a sort of procession toward the promised land. For the people went forth *by companies* under arms, carrying banners and emblems before them. The Levites bore the tent of meeting, the priests blared with their trumpets. The priests carried the ark of the covenant, and Aaron the high priest follows in his vestments, and Moses, the leader of the people, with his rod. On their way, Amalek met them with his army and tried to block their way. But Joshua came out victorious and opened the way for the people toward their fatherland. Joshua gave us the norm for our procession when he circled Jericho with the ark and the entire people, and the priestly order sounded their trumpets, and the people raised a very great shout. Jericho fell, and the victorious people gained possession of their kingdom.

69

Significatio processionum

Populus a Pharaone per Moysen ereptus, est Christianus populus a diabolo per Christum redemptus. Tabulae Testamenti a monte accipiuntur, et libri Evangelii ab altari ad portandum sumuntur. Populus abit armatus, et populus Christianus vadit fide et baptismate signatus. Prae turmis illorum signa ferebantur, et ante nos cruces et vexilla portantur. Eos columna ignis praecessit, et nos candelae lumen praecedit. Ille populus sanguine aspergebatur, iste aqua benedicta aspergitur. Levitae tabernaculum foederis portaverunt, et hic diaconi et subdiaconi plenaria et capsas gerunt. Arca Testamenti a sacerdotibus portabatur, et scrinium vel feretrum cum reliquiis a presbyteris portatur. Aaron summus sacerdos sequitur ornatus, et apud nos episcopus scilicet summus sacerdos sequitur infulatus. Rex si adest cum sceptro rector populi, significat Moysen cum virga ductorem populi. Si rex non aderit, tunc pontifex utrumque exprimit. Moysen baculum portando, Aaron mitra caput velando. Clangor tubarum, exprimitur per sonum campanarum.

69

The Meaning of Processions

Moses delivering his people from Pharaoh is Christ redeeming the Christian people from the devil. They received the tables of the Law on the mountain, and we take the Gospels from the altar; the people went out under arms, and the Christian people go forth emblazoned with faith and baptism. They carried their standards before their companies, and we carry crosses and banners. A column of fire went before them, and candlelight goes before us. That people were splashed with blood, this one is splashed with holy water. The Levites carried the tent of meeting, and here the deacons and subdeacons carry plenaries and reliquary capsules. The ark of the covenant was carried by priests, and the shrine and feretory of relics are carried by our presbyters. The high priest Aaron follows in stately array, and among us the bishop, the high priest, follows in his pontifical vestments. If the king is present with his scepter ruling his people, he signifies Moses leading his people with his staff. If the king is not present, then the bishop expresses both: Moses by carrying his rod, and Aaron by covering his head with a miter. The sound of trumpets is expressed by the sound of bells.

70

Quid designat processio ad aliam ecclesiam facta de patria

Cum ad aliam ecclesiam processionem facimus, quasi ad terram repromissionis tendimus. Cum ecclesiam cantando intramus, quasi gaudentes ad patriam pervenimus. Cum circa monasterium scrinium vel feretrum cum cantu et pulsatione ferimus, quasi cum arca Iericho cum sono tubarum et clamore populi circuimus. Iericho coram nobis corruit, cum mundi concupiscentia in cordibus nostris aruerit. Ideo quippe crucem praecedentem sequimur, quia Christum crucifixum in omnibus sequi praecipimur. Et nullus ad eum pervenire poterit, nisi qui se mundo *vitiis et concupiscentiis crucifixerit.*

71

De arca

David quoque et Salemon ad processionem nos informaverunt, qui arcam Dei hymnis et canticis produxerunt, et David in tabernaculum, Salemon in Templum, sub alas

70

The Meaning of the Procession from Our Homeland to Another Church

When we make a procession to another church, it is as if we are wending our way toward the promised land. When we enter the church singing, we arrive in our fatherland rejoicing. When we carry a relic chest and feretory around the minster, singing and ringing bells, it is as if we were walking around Jericho with the ark to the sound of trumpets and the shouts of the people. Jericho falls before us when the worldly concupiscence in our hearts dries up. We follow the cross before us, for we are commanded to follow Christ crucified in all things, and no one shall reach him unless he *crucifies himself to the world with its vices and concupiscences.*

71

On the Ark

David and also Solomon taught us how to conduct the procession when they carried forth the ark of God with hymns and canticles, and David set it down in the tabernacle, Solomon in the Temple under the wings of the

cherubin reposuerunt. Cum ecclesiam cum scrinio intramus; quasi arcam in Templum cum gaudio portamus, et cum Christo atque Ecclesia quod utrumque arca designat, caelestem aulam nos intraturos clamamus. Arca sub alas cherubin ponitur, et a populo laus concinitur, quia Christi humanitas inter summos ordines angelorum cherubin et seraphin locabitur, et a turba angelorum et hominum perenni iubilatione adorabitur.

72

De pugna Christianorum spirituali

Missa quoque imitatur cuiusdam pugnae conflictum, et victoriae triumphum, qua hostis noster Amalech prosternitur, et via nobis ad patriam per Iesum panditur. Iesus quippe imperator noster cum diabolo pugnavit, et caelestem rem publicam ab hostibus destructam hominibus reparavit. Qui cum posset producere duodecim legiones angelorum vel septuaginta duo milia militum, instruxit tantum agmen duodecim apostolorum et expugnavit septuaginta duo genera linguarum.

2   Pontificis namque et cleri populique processio, est quasi imperatoris et cuiusdam exercitus ad bellum progressio. Hi cum subtus albis desuper cappis, vel aliis sollemnibus

cherubim. When we enter the church with the relic chest, we are joyfully carrying the ark into the Temple, and with Christ and the Church—for the ark signifies both—we are proclaiming that we shall enter into the heavenly palace. The ark is placed under the wings of cherubim and the people sing praises because the humanity of Christ is set among the highest orders of the angels—the cherubim and seraphim—to be adored by the whole host of angels and mankind with unending jubilation.

72

On the Spiritual Warfare of Christians

In another way, the Mass portrays the harsh battle and triumphant victory in which our enemy Amalek was laid low and a way was opened for us toward our fatherland through Jesus. For Jesus, our commander, fought with the devil and recovered for man the heavenly commonwealth that had been destroyed by his enemies. Though *he might have called forth twelve legions of angels* or seventy-two thousand soldiers, he mustered the tiny band of the twelve apostles and with them subdued seventy-two kinds of tongues.

The procession of the bishop, clergy, and people is like 2 an emperor and his army marching off to battle. Their vesture—albs under copes, or other solemn vestments—make

vestibus induuntur, quasi milites pugnaturi subtus loricis desuper clipeis muniuntur. Cum de choro exeunt, quasi de regia curia cunei prodeunt. Quasi imperiale signum, et vexilla
a signiferis ante feruntur, cum ante nos crux et vexilla gerun-
tur. Quasi duo exercitus sequuntur, dum hinc inde ordinatim cantantes gradiuntur. Inter quos vadunt magistri et
praecentores, quasi cohortium ductores ac belli incitatores.
Sequuntur priores, quasi exercitus duces, atque agminum
ordinatores.

73

Quod episcopus spiritualiter agat vicem imperatoris

Procedit pontifex cum baculo, quasi imperator cum sceptro. Ante pontificem portantur sancta, sic ante regem im-
perialia. Ante archiepiscopum crux portatur, sic et ante imperatorem gestatur. Qui pallio decoratur, sic rex corona
perornatur. Comitatur turba plebis, quasi exercitus pedes-
tris. Cum de basilica procedunt, quasi de regia urbe turmae
proruunt. Cum ad aliam ecclesiam procedimus, quasi ad
castellum expugnandum pergimus. Quod cum cantu intra-
bimus, quasi in deditionem accipimus, et inde auxiliarios

them look like war-bound soldiers who go out to battle armored with cuirasses and shields. When they leave the choir, they are like columns filing forth from the royal court. The cross and banners we carry in procession are like the ensign and standards of the imperial army. They are followed by two more armies, since the cantors follow behind in good order. Among them walk the choir masters and precentors, like the captains and sergeants who stir up the cohorts for battle. Then the officers follow as the leaders of an army and officers who dress the ranks.

73

How the Bishop Spiritually
Plays the Role of an Emperor

The bishop proceeds with his staff, like the emperor with his scepter. The *sancta* are carried in front of him, as the imperial ensigns before the king. A cross is carried before the archbishop, as if before the emperor; he is decorated with the pallium, like a king is adorned by his crown. A crowd of people follow like an army of infantry. When they process from a basilica, it is as though the troops sally forth from the king's city. When we process to another church, we are marching to seize a fortified town; when we enter it with song, we accept that town's submission as it were and con-

nobis ascimus. Cum vero ad monasterium redimus, quasi ad locum certaminis tendimus. Scrinium cum reliquiis portamus contra daemones, sicut filii Israel portaverunt arcam Dei contra Philistiim hostes. Cum ecclesiam intramus, quasi ad stationem pervenimus. Cum campanae sonantur, quasi per classica milites ad proelium incitantur. Quasi vero acies ad pugnam ordinantur, dum utrimque in choro locantur. Qui crucem cum vexillo coram archiepiscopo tenet, est signifer qui vexillum coram imperatore in pugna fert.

74

Quod cantor sit signifer
et tubicina

Cantor qui cantum inchoat, est tubicina qui signum ad pugnam dat. Praecentores qui chorum utrimque regunt, sunt duces qui agmina ad pugnam instruunt. Cantores caput pilleolis tegunt, baculos vel tabulas manibus gerunt, quia proeliantes caput galeis tegunt, armis bellicis se protegunt.

script auxiliaries for our army. When we return to the minster, we are hastening to the field of battle. We carry the reliquary against the demons, as the sons of Israel carried the ark against their Philistine foes. When we enter the church, we arrive at our station. When the bells ring, the war trumpet stirs up the soldiers for battle. Now they are arranged in battle lines when they take their places on each side of the choir. The one who holds the cross with the banner before the archbishop is the standard-bearer who carries the flag before the emperor in battle.

74

How the Cantor Is the Standard-Bearer and Trumpeter

The cantor who begins the chant is the trumpeter who gives the signal to join battle. The precentors who direct the choir on each side are the leaders who dress the lines for battle. Cantors cover their heads with caps and carry rods or tablets in their hands, because in a fight soldiers protect their heads with helmets and guard themselves with weapons of war.

75

De bello spirituali

Bellum cum tubarum clangore et turbarum clamore committitur, et nostrum spiritale bellum cum campanarum compulsatione et cleri cantatione incipitur. Geritur namque bellum *non contra carnem et sanguinem, sed adversus principes et potestates, adversus rectores tenebrarum harum, contra spiritalia nequitiae in caelestibus*. Quasi ergo strenui milites pugnant, dum totis viribus utrimque cantant. Ignea tela concupiscentiarum nequissimi hostes immittunt, quae fortes viri fortiter scuto fidei repellunt, hostes vitiorum acriter insistentes gladio verbi Dei prosternunt.

76

Quod cantores vicem
ducum agant

Cantores manu et voce alios ad harmoniam incitant, quia et alios duces manibus pugnando, et voce hortando ad certamen instigant. Interim stat pontifex ad altare, et pro

75

On Spiritual Warfare

Battle is joined to the clash of trumpets and shouts of the throngs, and our spiritual combat begins with the clash of bells and the clergy's singing. For our battle is waged *not against enemies of blood and flesh, but against the rulers, against the authorities, against the cosmic powers of this present darkness, against the spiritual forces of evil in the heavenly places.* We fight like stout soldiers when we sing with all our might from each side of the choir. Our villainous enemies cast fiery darts of concupiscence into our ranks, which the strong repel with the shield of faith. The throngs of vices press in close, but we knock them down with the sword of God's word.

76

How the Cantors Play the Role of Captains

The cantors stir the rest into harmony with hand and voice, like captains leading others in hand-to-hand combat and spurring them to great deeds with their voices. Mean-

laborantibus orationem recitat, sic et Moyses in monte
stans pro pugnantibus orabat.

77

De cantore quod vicem
praeconis agat

Lector qui Epistulam recitat, est praeco qui edicta imperatoris per castra praedicat. Meliores voce ad Graduale vel
Alleluia cantandum eliguntur, et fortiores manu ad duellum
producuntur. Iam deficientibus in cantu alii succurrunt, ita
multum laborantibus in proelio, alii constantes corde subveniunt. Deinde Sequentiam cum voce et organis iubilant,
quia victoriam cum plausu et cantu celebrant. Diaconus qui
Evangelium in alto recitat, est praeco qui peracto bello agmina dispersa cum tuba convocat. Quod episcopus populum exhortando alloquitur, significat quod imperator victores laudando affatur. Quod tunc oblationes offeruntur,
significat quod spolia victoribus coram imperatore dividuntur. Cantus Offertorii est laus quam offerunt imperatori.

while the bishop stands at the altar and recites a prayer for his struggling men, just as Moses prayed for his warriors on the mountain.

77

How the Cantor Plays the Role of a Herald

The reader who recites the Epistle is the herald who cries the emperor's orders through the camp. The better voices are chosen to sing the Gradual and Alleluia, as the strongest fighters are picked for single combat. When some people falter in song, others come to their aid; so when some are sorely oppressed in battle, sturdy hearts hasten to help. Next, the cantors jubilate the Sequence with voice and organum, celebrating their victory with applause and song. The deacon who reads the Gospel from a high place is the herald after the battle who calls the dispersed army together with his trumpet. When the bishop addresses and exhorts the people, this signifies the emperor praising his victorious troops. Then when the oblations are brought up, it means that the spoils are being divided among the victorious army while the emperor looks on. The Offertory chant is the praise they offer their emperor.

78

De David cum Christo et Goliath cum diabolo comparatis

Multiplici itaque hoste ab Iesu qui et Iosue superato et victori populo ob pacis abundantiam negligentia resoluto, rursus Philistaei adversus Israel conveniunt, crudele bellum inducunt. Ex quibus Golias procedit, duellum petit. Cui David cum pastorali pera occurrit, funda et lapide eum deicit, proprio mucrone perfodit. Populus autem liberatus pro victoria Deo victimam immolat, pro gratiarum actione laudes iubilat. David Ierusalem venienti turba populorum obviam ruit, salvatorem populi hymnis excipit. Sic quoque vitiis a Christiano populo superatis denuo consurgunt, negligenti animae acrius bellum inferunt. Ex quibus gigas Goliath scilicet diabolus procedit, duellum petit, dum quemlibet Christianum ad singula vitia illicit. Cui fortis animus cum sacra scriptura ut David cum mulctro lactis occurrit, funda et lapide deicit, dum per humanitatem Christi qui sitienti populo erat petra et credentibus populis lapis angularis eum devincit. Proprio ense prostratum iugulat, dum hostem malignum fragili carne superat.

78

On David Compared with Christ and Goliath with the Devil

When Jesus, who is Joshua, had defeated many foes and the victorious people became lax in the long peace that followed, the Philistines once again rose up against Israel and waged a bloody war with it. Goliath steps out from their lines and asks for a duel. David comes against him with his shepherd's bag, knocks him down with his sling and stone, and kills him with his own sword. The liberated people sacrifice a victim to God for the victory and sing their praise and thanksgiving. Then this crowd of peoples meets David on his way to Jerusalem and receives him as their savior with hymns. In the same way, when once the Christian people have overcome their vices, they rise again and wage a more bitter war upon the negligent soul. The devil, our giant Goliath, comes forth and asks for a duel when he tempts Christians to each of the vices. The sturdy soul comes against him with sacred scripture like David with his milk pail, and slings a stone when it defeats him through the humanity of Christ, which was a stone to the thirsty people and the cornerstone to those who believe in him. Having laid the devil low, the soul beheads him with his own sword when it overcomes the malignant foe through fragile flesh.

79

Mysterium

Cum ergo a subdiacono et aliis sacrificium instruitur, quasi David a Saul et populo armis induitur. Cum oblationes super altare ponuntur, quasi arma a David deponuntur. Porro cum pontifex ad altare venit, quasi David adversum Philistaeum procedit. Per calicem mulctrale accipitur, per corporale funda, per oblatam petra intelligitur. Praefatio quae cantatur, fuit clamor quo pugil gygas ad duellum provocabatur. Per Canonis deprecationem, intelligimus populi orationem. Sacerdotis inclinatio, est fundae lapide imposito rotatio. Panis elevatio, est lapidis iactatio. Ubi denuo inclinatur, significat quod hostis prosternitur. Ubi autem diaconus ad sacerdotem venit, et calicem cum eo elevans deponit, designat quod David ad prostratum cucurrit, extracto gladio caput abstulit. Deinde data pace populus communicat, quia accepta per David pace populus Deo sacrificans participat. Cantus in Communione, est laus populi pro victoriae exultatione. Oratio et benedictio quae sequitur, est tropheum quo David a populo Ierusalem veniens excipiebatur. His peractis populus ad propria remeat, quia populus tunc post victoriam cum gaudio ad propria repedabat.

79

The Mysteries

Thus when the subdeacon and other ministers arrange the sacrifice, Saul and the people are, as it were, arming David. When the oblations are placed on the altar, David puts aside his weapons. Then when the pontiff comes to the altar, David goes forth against the Philistine. The chalice is his milk pail, the corporal his sling, the bread his stone. The sung Preface is the cheering of Goliath's comrades egging the giant on to fight. The Canon is the people's prayer. The priest's bow is the stone's swinging in the sling. The elevation of the bread is the casting of the stone. When he bows again, he signifies that the enemy has been knocked down. When the deacon comes to the priest, elevates and puts down the chalice with him, he indicates that David has run up to the prostrate giant, drawn his sword, and cut off his head. Finally, after giving the peace the people communicate because having received peace through David they participate in God through sacrifice. The Communion chant is the praise of the people flush with victory. The Postcommunion prayer and blessing that follows is the trophy the people of Jerusalem gave to David upon his return. At the end of all these things, the people go back to their homes because after their victory the people returned home with joy.

80

Item de Missa et et de iudicio

Missa et quoddam iudicium imitatur, unde et Canon "actio" vocatur. Actio autem est causa quae in publico conventu coram iudicibus agitur, quia in Missa causa populi cum Deo iudice agitur. Cum campana sonatur, quasi populus ad placitum per praeconem convocatur. Nempe oratorium, est quasi praetorium, in quo iudex Deus pro tribunali sedere creditur, cui populus reus sistitur. Diabolus est accusator, sacerdos defensor. Quia ergo accusatione diaboli, et reatu populi iudex offenditur, sacerdos qui causam populi suscepit, duellum subire compellitur, quatenus delatoris fallacia refutetur, populi innocentia comprobetur, iudicis ira placetur. Mox spiritalibus armis induitur, adversario congreditur, et populus anxius eripitur.

80

More on the Mass and on the Trial

The Mass also resembles a sort of trial, which is why the Canon is called the *actio*. For an *actio* is a trial held in public before judges, and in the Mass the people's case is heard with God as judge. When the bell rings, the herald summons the people to the court. For the place of prayer is like a praetorium, where God sits in judgment before the tribunal and the accused people stand trial. The devil is the plaintiff, the priest the defense attorney. Because the judge is dissatisfied with both the devil's accusation and the people's defense, the priest who has taken up the people's case is obliged to fight a judicial duel to refute the accuser's lies, prove the people's innocence, and soothe the judge's anger. He takes up spiritual weapons, engages the enemy, and saves the troubled people.

81

De pugna Philistaei

Hoc ut dictum est in figura praecesserat, quando David cum Golia congressus, populum a tyrannide eius eruerat, quia Christus eum diabolo duellum subierat, et populum oppressum ab eo eripiebat. Philistiim namque Israel impugnabat, et daemonum caterva humanum genus vexabat. Hostes contra populum Dei aciem direxerant, et daemones contra iustos tyrannos incitaverant. Hostes se vallo munierant, et daemones per philosophos et poetas errores firmaverant. Golias agminibus Dei exprobrabat, et diabolus cultoribus Dei per idolatriam insultabat. David a patre suo ad pugnam mittitur, et Christus a Patre in mundum ad certamen dirigitur. David oves pavit, et Christus innocentes ad pascua vitae congregavit. David ursum vel leonem superavit, et Christus diabolum se tentantem superavit. David ovibus relictis ad locum certaminis tendit, et Christus a discipulis derelictus, ad conciliabula hostium venit.

2 Veniente David clamor in castris oritur, et Christo inter Iudaeos veniente clamor *"Reus est mortis!"* exoritur. David a militibus armis Saul induitur, moxque eisdem exuitur, et Christus a militibus vestibus Pilati scilicet purpura et chlamyde coccinea induitur, moxque eisdem exuitur. David

81

On the Battle with the Philistine

Now, as we have said, this duel took place figuratively when David met Goliath and freed the people from his tyranny, for Christ also dueled the devil and saved the people who had been oppressed by him. For the Philistines were making war on Israel, and the host of demons was waylaying the human race. Their enemies had sent troops against the people of God, and the devils raised up tyrants against the just. Their enemies were protected by a rampart, and the demons made their errors strong through the philosophers and poets. Goliath taunted God's armies, and the devil mocked God's devout through idolatry. David is sent into battle by his father, and Christ is dispatched into the world to wage his contest by the Father. David tended sheep, and Christ gathered the innocent into the fields of life. David beat a bear and a lion, and Christ defeated the devil's temptation. David left his sheep and hastened to the place of battle, and Christ, deserted by his disciples, came into the enemy's assembly place.

At David's arrival there was great shouting in the camp, and when Christ came among the Jews the cry went up, *"He is guilty of death!"* The soldiers dress David in Saul's suit of arms, but he takes them off again, and Christ is dressed up by Pilate's soldiers in the royal purple and the scarlet mantle, then stripped of them immediately. David carried a

baculum contra Philistaeum portavit, et Christus Crucem contra diabolum baiulavit. David mulctrum, et Christus accepit vas aceto plenum. Hostis funda et lapide prosternitur, et diabolus Christi carne vincitur. Per fundam quippe Christi caro, per lapidem eius anima, per David deitas intelligitur. Petra itaque de funda excussa frontem superbi penetrat, quia anima Christi de carne tormentis excussa, regnum tyranni superans infernum spoliat. Proprio ense victum iugulat, quia per mortem auctorem mortis vicerat. Reverso David populus laetatur, et Christo ab inferis regresso populus fidelium congratulatur. David Ierusalem veniens a turbis cum cantu excipitur, et Christus ab Ierusalem caelos ascensurus ab angelis hymnologis laudibus suscipitur.

82

De armis sacerdotis

Sacerdos itaque pugil noster cum hoste pro populo congressurus, armis munitur spiritalibus, quia pugnaturus est *contra spiritalia nequitiae in caelestibus.* Denique sandaliis se pro ocreis induit, caput humerili pro galea tegit, totum corpus alba pro lorica vestit. Cum stolam collo circumdat, quasi

staff against the Philistine, and Christ carried the Cross against the devil. David took a milk pail, and Christ took a pot of vinegar. The enemy is toppled by a sling and stone, and the devil is beaten by Christ's flesh. For we should understand the sling to be Christ's flesh, the stone his soul, and David his divinity. The stone hurled by the sling pierces the proud man's forehead because Christ's soul, driven from his flesh by cruel torture, invaded and despoiled the tyrant's dominion of hell. He kills him with his own sword because by his death Christ conquered the author of death. The people rejoice at David's return, and the faithful people celebrate Christ's return from hell. David is received by singing crowds on his way back to Jerusalem, and at his ascension from Jerusalem into heaven, Christ is met by angels singing hymns of praise.

82

On the Priest's Weapons

Before facing the enemy on the people's behalf, our team's fighter, the priest, steels himself with spiritual arms because he is about to fight against *the spiritual forces of evil in the heavenly places.* Sandals are his greaves, the amice his helmet, and to cover his body he dons the alb for a cuirass. When he drapes the stole around his neck, he is shaking his spear in

hastam ad resistendum vibrat. Cingulo pro arcu se cingit, subcingulo pro pharetra sibi appendit. Casula pro clypeo protegitur, manipulo pro pugilis clava utitur. Porro libro in quo est verbum Dei pro gladio armatur, per confessionem diaboli dominio renuntiatur, sicque hostis ad singulare certamen provocatur. Quasi enim totis viribus pugnat, dum cantum et orationem et reliquas contra diabolum recitat. Dum ad Evangelium casula super humerum proicit, quasi gladium arripit. Dum legit Evangelium, quasi ense petit diabolum.

83

De tragoediis

Sciendum quod hii qui tragoedias in theatris recitabant, actus pugnantium gestibus populo repraesentabant. Sic tragicus noster pugnam Christi populo Christiano in theatro ecclesiae gestibus suis repraesentat, eique victoriam redemptionis suae inculcat.

2   Itaque cum presbyter "Orate" dicit, Christum pro nobis in agonia positus exprimit, cum apostolos orare monuit. Per Secreti silentium, significat Christum velut agnum sine voce ad victimam ductum. Per manuum expansionem, designat

defiance. He girds himself with a cincture instead of a bow, and ties on the subcingulum as a quiver. The chasuble protects him like a shield. He uses the maniple like a war club, and the book of the word of God is his sword. He renounces the devil in his confession and thus challenges the enemy to single combat. He fights with all his might when he recites the chant, the prayer, and the rest against the devil. When he throws his chasuble over his shoulder to read the Gospel, this is him drawing his sword. When he reads the Gospel, he thrusts at the devil with his sword.

83

On Tragic Theater

The actors who once recited tragedy in the theaters depicted fight scenes for the audience using dramatic gestures. Now our very own tragic actor uses gestures to represent Christ's duel to the Christian audience in the theater of the church, and in this way impresses upon them the victory of their redemption.

So when the priest says "*Orate,*" he imitates Christ in his 2 agony, when he admonished the apostles to pray. By his silence during the Secret, he signifies Christ as a lamb led dumbly to the slaughter without uttering a word. By extending his arms, he signifies Christ's arms stretched out on the

Christi in Cruce extensionem. Per cantum Praefationis, exprimit clamorem Christi in Cruce pendentis. Decem namque psalmos scilicet a *Deus Deus meus respice,* usque *In manus tuas commendo spiritum meum* cantavit, et sic expiravit. Per Canonis secretum, innuit Sabbati silentium. Per pacem et communicationem, designat pacem datam post Christi Resurrectionem, et gaudii communicationem. Confecto sacramento pax et communio populo a sacerdote datur, quia accusatore nostro ab agonotheta nostro per duellum prostrato, pax a iudice populo denuntiatur, ad convivium invitatur, deinde ad propria redire cum gaudio per *Ite missa est* imperatur. Qui gratias Deo iubilat, et gaudens domum remeat.

84

Item de Missa et de septem *Dominus vobiscum,* septemque donis sancti Spiritus et de mysterio Missae

Missa legatio dicitur. Totum tempus quo Christus mundum intravit, usque quo Ecclesia caelum intrabit, est tempus legationis; et tunc Christi legatio finietur, cum sponsa

Cross. By chanting the Preface, he voices the cry of Christ as he hung on the Cross. For Christ sang ten psalms, from *Deus Deus meus respice* to *In manus tuas commendo spiritum meum,* and when he finished them he died. By the silence of the Canon, he points to the silence of the Sabbath. By the peace and the communion, he symbolizes the peace Christ gave after his Resurrection and the joy he communicated to the apostles. After the sacrament has been confected the priest gives the people peace and communion, because once our accuser is laid low in the duel by our champion, the judge announces the peace to the people and invites them to a banquet. Then through *Ite missa est* the people are ordered to return home rejoicing, and so they cheerfully sing "*Deo gratias*" and go back home rejoicing.

84

More on the Mass, on the Sevenfold *Dominus vobiscum,* the Seven Gifts of the Holy Spirit and on the Mystery of the Mass

The Mass is called a legation. The period of this legation runs from the moment Christ entered the world to the time when the Church shall enter into heaven. Christ's legation

Christi ab ista Babylonia in supernam Ierusalem ducetur.
Quod tempus septem interstitiis distinguitur, significat
quod legatio Christi septem donis Spiritus sancti perficitur.
Unde et ad Missam septem vicibus *Dominus vobiscum* dicitur, quia mysterium Missae septem donis Spiritus sancti
peragitur.

Primo post Introitum *Dominus vobiscum* dicitur. Introitus
signat ingressum Christi in hunc mundum, quo sua incarna-
tione salutavit genus humanum. Cantus enim Introitus est
gaudium, et angelorum et hominum, quod in eius nativitate
habuerunt. Primum donum Spiritus sancti est sapientia,
quia Dei Sapientia venit incarnata. Oratio quae sequitur,
signat nostram reconciliationem per eum. Lectio autem
signat doctrinam vel exemplum quod praebuit in baptismate. Graduale, ieiunium vel tentationem eius, Alleluia ministerium angelorum quo ministrabant ei. Secundo dicitur
Dominus vobiscum ante Evangelium quo mundum salutavit
sua praedicatione. Evangelium enim signat tempus praedicationis Christi. Secundum donum est spiritus intellectus,
quia tunc docuit omnes intellegere spiritalia. Tertio dicitur
Dominus vobiscum ante Offertorium, est illud tempus quo
ivit Ierosolimam pati et salutavit turbam sibi cum palmis
obviam. Cantus Offertorii, significat laudem illius populi.
Unde et in eadem significatione solet adhuc populus ad offe-
rendam sacrificare. Tertium donum est spiritus consilii, quia
tunc consilium Dei aperuit, propter quod venit, scilicet homines redimere sua Passione. Silentium quod sequitur, est
illud tempus quo Christus in Ierusalem usque ad Passionem

will end on that day when his bride is led out of this Babylon into the heavenly Jerusalem. This time is divided into seven intervals, signifying that the legation is carried out through the seven gifts of the Holy Spirit. Wherefore *Dominus vobiscum* is said seven times at the Mass because the sacrament of the Mass is accomplished through the seven gifts of the Holy Spirit.

It is said first after the Introit. The Introit signifies Christ's entry into the world, because by his incarnation he saluted the human race. The Introit chant is the joy angels and men shared in his Nativity. The first gift of the Holy Spirit is wisdom, since God's Wisdom came to us incarnate. The prayer that follows signifies our reconciliation through him. The Lesson signifies the teaching and example he gave in his baptism. The Gradual signifies his fasting and temptation, the Alleluia the service of the angels who ministered to him. *Dominus vobiscum* is said a second time before the Gospel because he greeted the world through his preaching. For the Gospel signifies the time of Christ's preaching. The second gift of the Holy Spirit is the spirit of understanding because at that time he taught men to understand spiritual things. It is said a third time before the Offertory. This is the time when he went to Jerusalem to suffer and greeted the crowd that went out to meet him with palms. The Offertory chant signifies the praise of this people. Even now the people offer sacrifice at the Offertory with the same signification. The third gift of the Holy Spirit is the spirit of counsel, because at that time God revealed his plan to redeem men by his Passion. The silence that follows is that time when Christ, penned up like the paschal lamb, remained in Jerusalem until his Passion, which happened

2

quae sexta die statim contigit, quasi agnus paschalis inclusus
3 mansit. Quarto dicitur *Dominus vobiscum* in Praefatione expansis manibus, significat illud tempus quo Christus pependit in Cruce extensus. Quartum donum, est spiritus fortitu-
dinis, quia tunc expugnavit diabolum. Quod Praefatio alta
voce dicitur, significat decem psalmos quos ipse in Cruce
clamavit, scilicet a *Dominus Deus meus* usque *In manus tuas
commendo;* vel signat strepitum qui circa crucem fiebat turba-
tis caelestibus et terrestribus. Silentium Canonis quod sequitur, fuit illud tempus quod post mortem eius sui in timore et
tremore fuerunt absconditi. Quinto dicitur *Pax vobiscum* pro
Dominus vobiscum, est illud tempus quo Christus surrexit et
suos his verbis salutavit. Quintum donum est spiritus scientiae, quia tunc aperuit illis sensum ut intelligerent scripturas. Cantus qui sequitur, est gaudium quod habuerunt
4 usque ad eius ascensum. Sexto *Dominus vobiscum* post communionem dicitur, est illud tempus quo Christus et homines
derelinquens, et angelos sibi obviantes ascendens salutavit.
Sextum donum est spiritus pietatis, quia maxima pietas fuit,
qua humanam naturam super astra vexit. Oratio quae sequitur, est hoc quod interpellat Patrem nunc pro nobis. Septimo *Dominus vobiscum,* in fine Missae dicitur, significat illud
tempus quo Christus in fine mundi veniens sanctos sibi ad
iudicium obviantes salutabit. Septimum donum est spiritus
timoris, quia tunc angeli contremiscent.

Sequitur *Ite missa est,* hoc est ad sinistros, *"Ite maledicti in
ignem aeternum."* Benedictio vero quae sequitur, est ad dexte-
ros, *"Venite benedicti Patris mei, percipite regnum."*

immediately on the sixth day. The priest says *Dominus vobis-* 3
cum a fourth time, with arms extended, in the Preface dia-
logue, signifying the time when Christ hung stretched out
on the Cross. The fourth gift is the spirit of fortitude because at that time he subdued the devil. The fact that the
Preface is said in a loud voice signifies the ten psalms Christ
recited on the Cross, namely from *Dominus Deus meus* up to
In manus tuas commendo; or it signifies the noise heard around
Calvary when the heavens and earth were shaken. The silence of the canon that follows was that time when his own
were hidden in fear and trembling. In the fifth place, *Pax vo-*
bis is substituted for *Dominus vobiscum.* It is that time when
Christ rose and greeted his own with these words. The fifth
gift is the spirit of knowledge, because at that time he
opened their eyes to understand the scriptures. The *Agnus*
Dei chant that follows is the joy that they had up until his
Ascension. The sixth *Dominus vobiscum* said after the comm- 4
union is that time when Christ greeted the men as he left
them and the angels as they came to meet him. The sixth
gift is the spirit of piety because it was an act of the greatest
piety for him to carry human nature beyond the stars. The
Pater noster is his intercession for us with the Father. The
seventh *Dominus vobiscum* is said at the Mass's end, and
means that time when Christ will come at the end of the
world to greet the saints gathering for the judgment. The
seventh gift is the spirit of fear, because at that time the angels shall tremble.

The *Ite missa est* follows, when he shall say to those on the
left, "*Depart from me you cursed into the eternal fire.*" The blessing that follows is said to those on the right, "*Come, you that*
are blessed by my Father, receive the kingdom."

85

Amalarius de Missa

Quae celebrantur in officio Missae ante lectum Evangelium respicientia sunt ad primum adventum Domini usque
ad illud tempus, quando properabat in Ierusalem passurus.
Introitus vero ad chorum prophetarum respicit, quia ut Augustinus dicit, *Moyses minister fuit Veteris Testamenti, propheta
Novi. Kyrieleyson* ad eos prophetas respicit, qui circa adventum Domini erant. *Gloria in excelsis* ad coetum angelorum
qui gaudium nativitatis Christi pastoribus annuntiabant.
Prima Collecta ad hoc respicit, quod Dominus circa duode-
cimum annum egit, cum in medio doctorum audiens eos et
interrogans sedit. Epistula ad praedicationem Iohannis pertinet. Responsum ad benevolentiam apostolorum, quando
vocati a Domino secuti sunt. Alleluia, ad laetitiam mentis
eorum quam habuerunt de promissionibus eius vel de miraculis eius quae per eum fieri videbant. Evangelium ad suam
praedicationem usque ad praedictum tempus.

2   Deinceps vero quod agitur in officio Missae ad illud tempus respicit, quod est a Dominica quando pueri obviaverunt
ei, usque ad ascensionem eius sive Pentecosten. Orationem
vero quam presbyter dicit a Secreta usque *Nobis quoque,* hanc
orationem designat, quam Iesus exercebat in monte Oliveti.
Illud quod sequitur, signat tempus quando Dominus in
sepulchro iacuit. Et quando panis in vinum mittitur, animam Domini ad corpus redire demonstrat. Quod postea

85

Amalarius on the Mass

The things we celebrate in the Mass office before the reading of the Gospel pertain to the time from our Lord's first advent to the time when he hastened to Jerusalem to suffer. The Introit refers to the choir of prophets because as Augustine said, *Moses was a minister of the Old Law, a prophet of the New.* The *Kyrie eleison* pertains to those prophets who were near to the time of our Lord's advent. The *Gloria in excelsis* refers to the band of angels who announced the joy of Christ's Nativity to the shepherds. The first Collect refers to the time when our Lord was around twelve years old and sat in the midst of the doctors, listening and asking them questions. The Epistle pertains to John's preaching. The Responsory pertains to the apostles' good will, when after being called by our Lord, they followed him. The Alleluia refers to the happiness they felt when they heard his promises and saw the miracles worked through him.

What happens next in the office of the Mass pertains to that Sunday when the Hebrew children came to meet him up till the Ascension or Pentecost. The prayer said by the priest from the Secret to the *Nobis quoque* signifies the prayer Jesus made on the Mount of Olives. What follows signifies the time when our Lord lay in the tomb. When the bread is cast in the wine, it shows that our Lord's soul has returned to his body. What we celebrate next signifies the greetings

2

JEWEL OF THE SOUL

celebratur, signat illas salutationes quas Christus fecit discipulis suis. Fractio oblatarum, illam signat fractionem, quam
duobus fecit in Emmaus.

86

Item de Missa

Nunc dicendum unde Missa exordium sumpserit, et quis
eam auxerit.

Missam inprimis Dominus Iesus *sacerdos secundum ordinem
Melchisedech* instituit, quando ex pane et vino corpus et sanguinem suum fecit, et ob memoriam sui suis celebrare hoc
praecepit. Hanc apostoli auxerunt, dum super panem et vinum verba quae Dominus dixit, et Dominicam orationem
dixerunt. Deinde successores illorum Epistulas et Evangelia
legi statuerunt; alii cantum et alii alia adiecerunt, qui *decorem
domus Domini dilexerunt.*

Christ gave to his disciples. The fraction of the hosts, the fraction our Lord made for the two disciples in Emmaus.

86

On the Mass

Now we must speak about the origin of the Mass, and who has added to it.

The Mass was first instituted by our Lord Jesus, a priest according to the order of Melchizedek, when he made his body and blood from bread and wine and ordered his own to do this in memory of him. The apostles added to this ritual when they said our Lord's words over the bread and wine and said the Lord's Prayer. Subsequently their successors determined that the Epistles and Gospels should be read, others added chant, and others other things, for they *loved the beauty of the Lord's house.*

87

De Introitu

Caelestinus itaque papa psalmos ad Introitum Missae cantari instituit, de quibus Gregorius papa postea antiphonas ad Introitum Missae modulando composuit. Unde adhuc primus versus eiusdem psalmi ad Introitum cantatur, qui olim totus ad Introitum cantabatur. *Gloria Patri* Nicaena synodus composuit, sed Damasus papa ad Missam cantari censuit. *Kyrieleyson* Silvester papa de Graecis sumpsit, quod Gregorius papa ad Missam cantari instituit. *Gloria in excelsis Deo* angelicus chorus in primis cecinit, sed Hilarius episcopus Pictaviensis ab illo loco *Laudamus te* usque in finem composuit. Telesphorus autem papa ad Missam cantari constituit. Symmachus vero papa in festis tantum cantari statuit. *Dominus vobiscum* de Veteri Testamento scilicet de libro Ruth est sumptum, *Pax vobiscum* de Novo id est de Evangelio acceptum. *Et cum spiritu tuo* de Epistulis Pauli. "Amen" vero de Apocalypsi. Quae apostolicus ordo tradente Domino dici docuit, et Clemens papa vel Anacletus papa ad Missam dici constituit. Orationes Ambrosius episcopus composuit, sed Gelasius papa auxit, et ad Missam dici constituit.

87

On the Introit

Pope Celestine instituted the singing of psalms at the Introit. Afterward, Pope Gregory composed antiphons for singing at the entrance of the Mass. That is why to this day the first verse of the psalm is sung with the Introit, where once the whole psalm was sung at the entrance. Pope Sylvester took the *Kyrie eleison* from the Greeks and Pope Gregory ordered it to be sung at Mass. The *Gloria Patri* was composed by the Council of Nicaea, but Pope Damasus ordered it to be sung at Mass. The *Gloria in excelsis Deo* was first sung by the angelic chorus, but Bishop Hilary of Poitiers composed everything after *Laudamus te,* and Pope Telesphorus was the one who ordered it to be sung at Mass. Pope Symmachus decided it should be sung only on feast days. The *Dominus vobiscum* is from the Old Testament, namely from the book of Ruth. The *Pax vobis* is again received from the New Testament, from the Gospel. The *Et cum spiritu tuo* is from Paul's Epistles. "Amen" is from Revelation. What our Lord handed down and the apostolic order had taught us to say, Popes Clement and Anacletus ordered to be said at Mass. Bishop Ambrose composed the collects. Pope Gelasius increased their number and ordered them to be said at Mass.

88

De Epistula et Evangelio

Epistulam et Evangelium Alexander papa legi ad Missam constituit. Ieronimus autem presbyter lectionarium vel evangeliarium, ut hodie habet Ecclesia collegit, sed Damasus papa ut nunc moris est legi censuit. Graduale et Alleluia Ambrosius composuit, sed Gregorius papa ad Missam cantari instituit. Qui etiam in festivis diebus neumam quae iubilum dicitur iubilare statuit. Sed abbas Nokkerus de sancto Gallo Sequentias pro neumis composuit, quas Nicolaus papa ad Missam cantari concessit. Anastasius papa decrevit, ut dum Evangelium legitur, nullus sedeat. *Credo in unum* Constantinopolitanus synodus composuit, sed Damasus papa ad Missam cantari instituit. Offertorium Gregorius papa composuit, et ad Missam cantari statuit.

88

On the Epistle and Gospel

Pope Alexander determined that the Epistle and Gospel be read at Mass. The priest Jerome compiled the lectionary and Gospel book the Church has today, but it was Pope Damasus who ordered them to be read in the current fashion. Ambrose composed the Gradual and the Alleluia, but Gregory ordered them to be sung at Mass. He also ordered the melisma we call the jubilus to be sung on feast days. Abbot Notker of Saint Gall composed Sequences for these melismas, which Pope Nicholas allowed to be sung at Mass. Pope Anastasius decreed that no one should sit during the Gospel reading. The Council of Constantinople composed the Creed, but Pope Damasus ordered it to be sung at Mass. Pope Gregory composed the Offertory and ordered it to be sung at Mass.

89

De vestibus et calicibus

Apostoli et eorum successores in quotidianis vestibus et ligneis calicibus Missas celebraverunt, sed Clemens tradente Petro apostolo usum sacrarum vestium ex lege sumpsit, et Stephanus papa in sacratis vestibus Missas celebrari constituit. Zephyrinus autem papa vitreis, Urbanus vero papa aureis vel argenteis calicibus et patenis offerri instituit. Alexander papa panem et vinum tantum offerri ad Missas statuit, sicut et Dominus instituit, et aquam admisceri censuit, sicut et apostolica traditio docuit. Silvester papa lineo corporali offerri statuit, sicut et Ioseph Dominicum corpus in sindonem mundam volvit. *Orate pro me* Leo papa dici statuit. Hic et Praefationes composuit. *Sursum corda* de Ieremia. *Gratias agamus Domino Deo nostro* de Apostolo est sumptum. Praefationes Dionysius Areopagita putatur composuisse, sed Gelasius papa ad Missam cantari instituit. *Sanctus,* Sixtus papa dimidium de Isaia, dimidium de Evangelio composuit, et ad Missam cantari statuit.

89

On Vestments and Chalices

The apostles and their successors celebrated Mass in everyday clothing and with wooden chalices. But Clement, handing on the teaching of Peter, took the use of sacred vestments from the Law, and Pope Stephen decided that Mass must be celebrated in sacred vestments. Pope Zephyrinus ordered Mass to be offered with glass chalices, and the martyr Pope Urban with gold or silver chalices and patens. Pope Alexander decided that only bread and wine should be offered, as our Lord had instituted it, and also ordered the admixture of water, as apostolic tradition had already taught. Pope Sylvester instituted the linen corporal, as Joseph wrapped our Lord's body in a clean shroud. Pope Leo ordered the *Orate pro me* to be said. He also composed the Preface. The *Sursum corda* is from Jeremiah. *Gratias agamus Domino Deo nostro* is taken from the Apostle. Dionysius the Areopagite is thought to have composed the Prefaces, but Pope Gelasius instituted the custom of singing them at Mass. Pope Sixtus composed the *Sanctus,* taking half from Isaiah and half from the Gospel, and ordered it to be sung at Mass.

90

De Canone

Canonem Gelasius papa composuit, sed Gregorius papa capitulum *Diesque nostros* intermiscuit, Leo papa *Sanctum sacrificium, immaculatam hostiam* apposuit. *Pater noster* Dominus quidem docuit, sed Matthaeus composuit. Gregorius vero papa ad Missam cantari censuit, sicut apostolica doctrina tradidit. Hic etiam praecedens capitulum *Oremus praeceptis,* et sequens *Libera nos Domine* addidit. Benedictionem episcopalem Martialis episcopus apostolorum discipulus ex magisterio apostolorum tradidit, quas probabile studium Deo servientium auxit. Ambrosius dicere coepit, isque mos ex eo usquequaque convaluit. Apostolicus autem hanc tamen quae finita Missa dicitur dicit *Pax Domini sit semper vobiscum.* Innocentius papa dici constituit, et pacem dari censuit. *Agnus Dei* Sergius papa composuit, et ad Missam cantari instituit. Iulius papa intinctionem corporis Domini in sanguinem prohibuit, et Gelasius papa illum excommunicavit, qui corpus Domini acceperit, et sanguinem non sumpserit. Communiones papa Gregorius composuit, et ad Missam cantari instituit. *Ite missa est,* de Veteri Testamento sumptum est, scilicet ubi Pharao populum de Aegypto ire iussit, sive ubi Cyrus populum a Babylonia ire praecepit. Sciendum quod ab hoc *Ite missa est* Missa nomen accepit. *Benedicamus Domino* acceptum est de Psalterio, *Deo gratias* de Apostolo, sed haec dici constituit papa Leo.

90

On the Canon

Pope Gelasius composed the Canon. Pope Gregory added the phrase *Diesque nostros.* Pope Leo inserted *Sanctum sacrificium, immaculatam hostiam.* Our Lord taught us the *Pater noster,* of course, but Matthew wrote it. And Pope Gregory caused it to be sung at Mass, following the apostolic tradition. He also added the preceding prayer *Oremus praeceptis salutaribus moniti* and the embolism *Libera nos Domine.* The bishop Martial, a disciple of the apostles, handed down the episcopal blessing from the teaching of the apostles, who were zealous to embellish the divine service. Ambrose was the first to use it, and from him the use spread elsewhere. The pope says only *Pax Domini sit semper vobiscum* at the end   2 of the Mass. Innocent ordered it to be said and also established the custom of giving peace. Pope Sergius composed the *Agnus Dei* and caused it to be said at Mass. Pope Julius prohibited the intinction of our Lord's body in the blood, and Pope Gelasius excommunicated anyone who does not take our Lord's blood along with the body. Pope Gregory composed Communions and ordered them sung at Mass. The *Ite missa est* is taken from the Old Testament, when Pharaoh ordered the people to leave Egypt, or when Cyrus ordered the people to go out of Babylon. Note that the Mass takes its name from the *Ite missa est.* The *Benedicamus Domino* is taken from the Psalter, *Deo gratias* from the Apostle, though Pope Leo instituted them.

Ex his omnibus Gregorius papa Missam ordinasse traditur, ut hodie per Ecclesiam canitur.

91

De Missae officiorum nominibus

Hic subnectendum est unde singula dicantur. Officium quasi efficium dicitur. Missa quasi transmissio dicitur, quia in hoc officio catechumeni, excommunicati, paenitentes, foras ecclesiam mittuntur. Introitus ab introitu sacerdotis dicitur; eo quod sacerdote ad altare introeunte a choro canitur. Introitum ideo canimus, quia Christum in sacerdote nos suscipere significamus. *Gloria Patri* ideo canimus, quia Trinitatem nos adorare innotescimus.

It is said that out of all these parts Pope Gregory composed the order of the Mass as it is sung today throughout the Church.

91

The Names of the Offices of the Mass

We should add something here about the origin of these terms. The word "office" comes from *efficium,* doing. *Missa* means dispatching, because during this office the catechumens, excommunicates, and penitents are sent out of the church. Introit refers to the priest's entrance, because while the priest enters and approaches the altar, this chant is sung by the choir. We sing the Introit to signify that we welcome Christ in the person of the priest. We sing the *Gloria Patri* to show that we adore the Trinity.

92

De *Kyrieleyson*

Kyrieleyson dicitur "Domine miserere"; *Christeleyson* dicitur "Christe miserere"; *ymas,* "nobis." Hoc ideo Graece canitur, quia Missa tribus linguis, Hebraica, Graeca et Latina cantari praecipitur, sicut et titulus in Passione Domini scriptus fuisse legitur. Hebraicum est quippe *alleluia, hosanna,* et *amen;* Graecum vero *Kyrieleyson,* et *Christeleyson;* Latinum reliquum officium. *Kyrieleyson* ter ideo dicitur, quia Trinitas adoratur, quae a patribus ante diliuvium, a patriarchis ante legem, a prophetis sub lege veneratur. *Christeleyson* ideo ter canitur, quia Christus in Patre et Spiritu sancto adoratur, qui Patris voluntate Spiritu sancto cooperante salutem nostram operatur. Item *Kyrieleyson* ter repetitur, quia Pater, Filius, et Spiritus sanctus ab angelis, a spiritibus iustorum, ab hominibus colitur. Ideo etiam *Kyrieleyson* cantatur, ut subsequens oratio sacerdotis exaudiatur.

92

On the *Kyrie eleison*

Kyrie eleison means "Lord, have mercy"; *Christe eleison*, "Christ, have mercy"; *imas,* "on us." This part is sung in Greek because we must sing the Mass in three languages, Hebrew, Greek, and Latin, those in which the inscription on Christ's Cross was written. In Hebrew we say *alleluia, hosanna,* and *amen;* in Greek, *Kyrie eleison* and *Christe eleison;* in Latin, the rest of the office. The *Kyrie eleison* is said three times on account of the Trinity adored by our ancestors before the Flood, by the patriarchs before the Law, and by the prophets under the Law. *Christe eleison* is sung three times because Christ is adored in the Father and the Holy Spirit, having accomplished our salvation according to the Father's will with the cooperation of the Holy Spirit. *Kyrie eleison* is repeated again because the Father, Son, and Holy Spirit are worshiped by the angels, the spirits of the just, and mankind. The *Kyrie eleison* is also sung so that God may accept the prayer of the priest that follows next.

93

De *Gloria in excelsis*

Gloria in excelsis solus sacerdos incipit, et chorus simul concinit, quia et solus angelus haec incepit, et *militia caelestis exercitus* simul concinit. Quod dum incipit, ad orientem se convertit, quia angelicus chorus hoc ad orientem Bethlehem apud turrim Adier cecinit. Per *Pax vobiscum* vel *Dominus vobiscum* populum salutat, sic Dominus ingressu suo mundum salutabat. Presbyter cum salutatione Veteris Testamenti et episcopus cum salutatione novi Testamenti salutat populum, quia dignius est novum quam vetus Testamentum. Populus autem Dominum cum spiritu eius esse orat, ut cum spiritu et mente orare admoneat. Ore orat, qui tantum verba pronuntiat. Ore et spiritu orat, qui verba per interpretationem discernit, quae ore pronuntiat. Spiritu et mente orat, qui per verba quae dicit, Deum et caelestia intendit. Non "Orem," sed "Oremus" dicit, quia vocem totius Ecclesiae exprimit.

93

On the *Gloria in excelsis*

First the priest intones the *Gloria in excelsis,* and then the choir joins in because the angel began this hymn alone and then *the hosts of the heavenly army* sang along. When he begins the hymn he faces east, because the angelic choir sang these words to Bethlehem in the east, near the tower of Eder. He greets the people with *Pax vobiscum* or *Dominus vobiscum,* as our Lord greeted the world upon entering it. The priest uses a salutation taken from the Old Testament, the bishop one from the New, because the New Testament is more honorable than the Old. The people pray that our Lord may be with his spirit, admonishing him to pray with his spirit and his mind. He prays with his mouth who only pronounces the words. To pray with mouth and spirit is to understand and interpret the words one pronounces with the mouth. To pray in spirit and mind is to attend to God and heavenly things through the words one says. He says "Let us pray" and not "Let me pray," because he represents the voice of the whole Church.

94

De oratione

Oratio ab orando vocatur, quia in ea populo et corporis et animae praesentia et futura bona orantur. Collecta ideo dicitur, quia sub ea populus in unum colligitur, vel quia in ea oratio totius populi in unum colligitur. Haec est autem differentia inter orationem et Collectam, quod hoc oratio vocatur, quod ad Missam dicitur, hoc autem Collecta quod ad processionem in statione super populum dicitur. Haec et *Missa* dicitur, quia in ea oratio populi per sacerdotem ad Deum mittitur. Hanc in dextra parte altari ideo dicimus, quia cum dextris in iudicio statui oramus. Omnes orationes ad Deum Patrem dirigimus, et per Dominum nostrum Iesum Christum in Spiritu sancto concludimus, quia cuncta iuste petita a Patre per Filium in unitate Spiritus sancti dari credimus. "Per eum qui venturus est" non nisi in exorcismis dicimus, in quibus diabolus per venturum iudicium adiuramus.

94

On the Collect

The name "oration" comes from praying because in it we pray for the people that they may enjoy present and future health of mind and body. It is called the Collect because the people are gathered together under it. But there is a difference between an oration and a Collect. An oration is said at Mass, while a Collect is said over the people gathered at a station church for a procession. The Mass is so named because in it the people's prayer is sent to our Lord through the priest. We say it on the right side of the altar because we pray to stand *with those on the right side* on the day of judgment. We direct all our prayers to God the Father and conclude them through our Lord Jesus Christ in the Holy Spirit, because we believe that everything we ask for justly from the Father through the Son in the unity of the Holy Spirit will be given to us. We say "through him who is to come" only in exorcisms, in which we adjure the devil through the future judgment.

95

De situ orationis

Propter tres causas ad orientem nos vertimus, cum oramus. Una est quia in oriente est patria nostra scilicet paradisus, unde expulsos nos dolemus. Orantes ergo contra paradisum nos vertimus, quia reditum illuc petimus. Alia est quia in oriente surgit corpus caeli, et lux diei. Ad orientem nos vertimus, quia Christum qui est oriens et lux vera nos adorare significamus. Cuius debemus esse caeli, ut eius lux in nobis velit oriri. Tertia est quia in oriente sol oritur, per quem Christus sol iustitiae exprimitur. Ab hoc promissum habemus, quod in resurrectione *ut sol fulgeamus*. In oratione ergo contra ortum solis nos vertimus, ut solem angelorum nos adorare intelligamus, et ut ad memoriam gloriam nostrae resurrectionis revocemus, cum solem quem in occidente quasi mori conspeximus, tanta gloria resurgere in oriente videmus.

95

The Direction of Prayer

We pray facing the east for three reasons. One reason is because our fatherland, that is, paradise, is in the east, and we grieve from our expulsion thence. We turn toward paradise when we pray, since we seek to return thither. The second reason is that the body of heaven and the light of day rise in the east. We turn ourselves east in order to signify that we adore Christ, the dawn and true light. We must be his skies, so that his light may deign to rise in us. A third reason is that the sun rises in the east, representing Christ the sun of justice. He has given us a sure promise that in the resurrection *we will shine like the sun.* Thus we turn toward the rising sun in prayer, so that we may understand that the one we adore is the sun of the angels, and may call to mind the glory of our resurrection when we see the sun, which had seemed to die in the west, rise again in the east with such glory.

96

De Epistula

"Lectio" dicitur a legendo. "Epistula" dicitur supermissa. *Epi,* "super," *stola* dicitur "missa"; quia sicut prophetiae super legem, ita Epistulae missae sunt super Evangelium. Hanc ideo legimus, quia viam nobis per eam ad Christum facimus. "Gradale" a gradibus dicitur, quia in gradibus canitur. Hoc etiam "Responsum" vocatur, quia choro cantante, ab uno versus respondetur, et illo versum cantante a choro respondetur. "Versus" ideo dicitur, quia ad inceptionem revertitur. "Alleluia" dicitur "Laudate Dominum": *Allelu,* "Laudate," *Ia,* in decem Dei nominibus unum ponitur, quod "Dominus" dicitur. Huius cantus "versus" ideo dicitur, quia iterum ad Alleluia revertitur. Sequentia ideo canitur, quia neumam iubili sequitur. "Tractus a trahendo" dicitur, quia trahendo, id est tractim canitur. Graduale ideo cantamus, quia *de virtute in virtutem* gradatim ire debemus. Alleluia ideo canimus, quia ad gaudium angelorum tendimus. Sequentiam ideo iubilamus, quia *faciem Domini* in iubilo *videbimus.* Tractum ideo canimus, quia per laborem illuc perveniemus.

96

On the Epistle

The word "lesson" comes from the word for reading. "Epistle" means sent in addition. *Epi,* "in addition," *stola,* "sent"; because just as the prophecies were sent in addition to the Law, so the Epistles were sent in addition to the Gospel. We read the Epistle because through it we make our way to Christ. "Gradual" comes from the word for steps because it is sung on the steps. It is also called the "Responsory" because first the choir sings, then one singer responds with the verse, and then the choir responds when he sings the verse. "Verse" refers to a reversion to the beginning. "Alleluia" means "Praise the Lord": *Allelu,* "give praise," *Ia,* one of God's ten names, meaning "Lord." The "verse" of the Alleluia chant is so called because from it we revert to the Alleluia. The name of the Sequence comes from the fact that it follows the melismatic jubilus of the Alleluia. "Tract" comes from the word for drawing out because it is a slow, drawn-out chant. We sing the Gradual because we must go gradually *from virtue to virtue.* We sing the Alleluia because our goal is to join the angels in joy. We jubilate the sequence because *we will see the Lord's face* in jubilation. We sing the Tract because we shall get there through travail.

97

De Evangelio

Evangelium ideo legimus, quia per eius doctrinam gaudia percepturi sumus. "Evangelium" dicitur bonum nuntium: *Eu,* "bonum," *angelium,* dicitur "nuntium." Nuntiat enim vitam post mortem, requiem post laborem, regnum post servitium. "Sequentia" ideo dicitur, quia praecedentia initii sequitur. Ideo etiam "initium Evangelii" dicitur, quia ibi liber Evangelii incipitur. Ubi post Evangelium "Oremus" dicitur, apud Graecos oratio sequitur.

"Offertorium" dicitur, quasi offerentium canticum. Hoc ideo cantamus, quia nos ipsos in sacrificium Deo offerre debemus. Sacerdos lavat manus, id est opera, per lacrimas compunctionis. Hic liber in sinistra parte ponitur, ut expeditior ad suscipiendum sacrificium reddatur, et quia per sinistram tristitiam designatur, quae tunc in Passione Christi repraesentatur.

97

On the Gospel

We read the Gospel because through its teaching we shall receive joy. *Evangelium* means good news. *Eu* means "good," and *angelium* means "news." The news is that there is life after our death, rest after our labor, and a kingdom after our servitude. We say "a continuation of the Gospel" when the text to be proclaimed is not the beginning of a Gospel, and "the beginning of the Gospel" when it is. After the Gospel, where we say "Let us pray," the Greeks have a prayer.

"Offertory" means the song of the offerers. We sing it because we must offer our very selves in sacrifice to God. The priest washes his hands, that is, his works, through the tears of compunction. At this point, the book is placed on the left side of the altar to leave the right open for receiving the sacrifice, and because the left side signifies the sadness of Christ's Passion, which is being represented.

98

De sacrificio

"Sacrificium" dicitur quasi sacrum factum. "Immolatio" dicitur, quia in mola altaris terebatur. "Hostia" dicitur quia ante ostium pugnae offerebatur. "Victima" dicitur quia pro victoria offerebatur. "Holocaustum" totum incensum dicitur, totum enim in altari incendebatur. "Sacramentum" dicitur, quasi sacrum iuramentum. "Secretum" dicitur, quia secreto dicitur. Cum sacrificium super crucem in altari cum christmate a pontifice factam ponitur, quasi corpus Christi Cruci affigitur.

99

De sacrificio panis et vini

"Panis" omne dicitur. Ideo hoc offertur, quia omnis salus animae et corporis in eo percipitur. "Vinum" quasi a "vite natum" dicitur. Hoc ideo offertur, ut sicut palmites viti ita Christo inseramur. "Aqua" ab aequalitate dicitur. Haec ideo

98

On the Sacrifice

"Sacrifice" means made holy. It is also known as an "immolation," because it is ground fine on the millstone of the altar. A "host" is so called because it used to be offered before the commencement of a battle. A "victim" was sacrificed in gratitude for a victory. "Holocaust" means entirely burned, for the whole animal used to be burned on the altar. A "sacrament" is a sacred oath. The "Secret" is so called because it is said inaudibly. When the sacrifice is placed on the altar over the cross made by the bishop with the chrism oil, then Christ's body is nailed to the Cross.

99

On the Sacrifice of Bread and Wine

"Bread" means all. Bread is offered because in it we receive all salvation of mind and body. "Wine" derives from "born of the vine." Wine is offered because we are grafted into Christ as young branches to a vine. "Water" comes from the word equality, and is mixed into the sacrifice so that

sacrificio admiscetur, ut ex aqua renati fonte vitae satiemur, et angelis coaequemur. "Per omnia saecula saeculorum" dicitur, quia se sequuntur. Aliis enim decedentibus, alia succedunt. *Amen* dicitur verum. Per hoc totum sacramentum confirmatur, quia per hoc et saeculum creatur. Dicitur enim "fiat," quo verbo usus est Deus in creatione mundi quando dixit: "*Fiat lux,*" et cetera. Ipse quoque Filius Dei *Amen* cognominatur, ut in Apocalypsi dicitur: *Haec dicit Amen testis fidelis.* "Dominus vobiscum" ideo hic dicimus, quia Regem caelorum praesentem populo innotescimus. "Sursum corda" ideo dicimus, quia angelorum exercitum adventare non dubitamus. Huic enim sacrificio aderunt, et nostra vota suscipientes ad Deum perferunt. "Gratias agamus Domino Deo nostro ideo" dicimus, quia ei pro omnibus beneficiis grates reddimus.

Nihil autem sine causa rationabilis significationis fit in isto sacramento.

100

De Ꝏ

Ideo et forma huius litterae Ꝏ non fit absque magno sacramento. Significat quippe duas substantias in Christo. *U* enim quod ex una parte aperitur, ex altera sequenti *D* innectitur, est Christi humanitas quae a parte matris inchoatur, et

reborn in water we may drink from the fount of life and be made equal to the angels. We say "for all ages of ages," because the ages follow one after another, one more beginning as each one ends. *Amen* means true. We say "amen" to confirm the whole sacrament, because through this word the world is created. For *amen* means "let it be," the word God used to create the world when he said, "*Let there be light*" and the rest. The Son of God himself is called *Amen* in the book of the Revelation: *These things saith the Amen, the faithful and true witness.* We say "The Lord be with you," to indicate that the King of heaven is present with his people. We say "Lift up your hearts," because we are certain that the angelic host are present, for they are present at this sacrifice and they *bear* our prayers to the Lord. We say "Let us give thanks to the Lord our God" to show that we are thankful to him for all of his benefits.

Nothing that is done in this sacrament is done without the purpose of some rational signification.

100

On Ʊ

The form of this letter Ʊ contains a great mystery. It signifies that there are two substances in Christ. For the *U,* being open on one side and linked with the *D* on the other, is Christ's humanity, which had a beginning with his mother

divinitati copulatur. Per *D* quod circuloso orbe undique clauditur, est Christi divinitas, quae nec initio aperitur, nec fine terminatur. Apex quo litterae in modum crucis + coniunguntur, est sancta Crux, per quam humana divinis sociantur.

101

De Praefatione

"Praefatio" dicitur praelocutio, scilicet sequentis Canonis. Haec et praeparatio dicitur, quia mentes nostras ad mysterium Christi praeparat. In hoc ideo ordines angelorum commemoravimus, quia frequentiam supernorum civium adesse demonstramus. "Maiestas" dicitur quasi maior potestas. "Caelum" dicitur quasi casa *elios,* id est solis. *Seraphin* per *n* sunt plures angeli; *seraphim* per *m* unus.

and is joined to divinity. The *D*, which is a closed circle, signifies Christ's divinity, which has neither beginning nor end. The stroke by which the letters are joined in the shape of a cross + is the holy Cross, through which humanity and divinity are brought together.

101

On the Preface

"Preface" means foreword, that is, to the Canon that follows. It also means preparation, because it prepares our minds for Christ's mysteries. In it we commemorate the orders of angels, demonstrating that the crowds of heavenly citizens are present. "Majesty" means mightier power. *Caelum* (heaven) means, as it were, house of *helios*, that is, of the sun. *Seraphin*, ending in *n*, are many angels; *seraphim*, ending in *m*, is one angel.

102

Quare dicatur *Sanctus*

*S*anctus ideo cum angelis cantamus, quia terrena caelestibus coniungi per hoc sacrificium clamamus. "Sanctus" dicitur sanguine tactus, vel sane auctus; "Dominus" dans minas; "Deus" delens scelus; *Sabaoth* exercituum, scilicet Rex exercitus angelorum. *Hosanna* dicitur salvifica id est "Salva nos habitans in excelsis."

103

De Canone

"*C*anon" dicitur regula, quia per eum regulariter fit sacramentorum confectio. Hic et "actio" dicitur, quia causa populi in ea cum Deo agitur.

Hic ob tres causas sub silentio dicitur. Una est quia cum Deo loquitur, cui non ore sed corde clamare praecipimur. Ideo autem verba dicimus, ut sciamus quid intendere vel petere debeamus. Secunda est, ne populus tam prolixa

102

Why We Say the *Sanctus*

We sing the *Sanctus* with the angels to proclaim that through this sacrifice heaven and earth become one. *Sanctus* means touched by blood or exceedingly magnified. *Dominus* (Lord) means issuing threats; *Deus* (God) means obliterating crime; *Sabaoth* means of armies, for he is king of the angelic hosts. *Hosanna* means saving, as if to say, "Save us, thou who livest in the highest heavens."

103

On the Canon

"Canon" means rule, because by means of it the sacraments are validly confected. It is also called an "action," because in it the people's suit is heard before God.

The Canon is said silently for three reasons. First, because we are speaking with God, and we must speak to God with the heart not the mouth. We use words so that we may know what our intention should be and what we should ask for. Second, so that the people do not leave out of boredom

declamatione attaediatus abscedat, vel sacerdos tam longo clamore voce deficiat. Tertia est, ne tam sancta verba tanti mysterii vilescant, dum ea vulgus per quotidianum usum sciens in inconvenientibus locis dicat.

2   Unde fertur, dum Canon primitus publice cottidie recitaretur, ab omnibus per usum sciretur, et cum eum pastores in agro super panem et vinum dicerent, repente carnem et sanguinem ante se invenirent, atque inde divinitus percussi interirent! Unde synodali decreto sub anathemate est praeceptum, ut nullus canonem dicat nisi in libro, et in sacris vestibus, et nisi super altare et super sacrificium, et ut nullus hoc sacrificium nisi in aureis vel argenteis vasis offerat, cum haec omnes habere nequeant, et ideo incongruum non faciant.

3   Hic in libris crucifixus ideo depingitur, quia per illud Passio Christi oculis cordis ingeritur, Christus quippe est via et veritas, ipse Deus et Dominus. "Te igitur" ideo dicitur, quia Deum quasi praesentem aspicit. Ideo autem per litteram *T* incipit, quia haec forma Crucis exprimit. "Clemens" dicitur, quasi clara mens. Dum homo timet, turbescit; dum Deum propitium sentit, mens ei clarescit. "Haec dona," quantum ad panem, in quo aqua et farina. "Haec munera," quantum ad vinum, in quo aqua et vinum. "Haec sancta sacrificia," ad utrumque. "Illibata," id est sine labe, agnus enim paschalis debuit esse immaculatus, et absque macula peccati fuit

at such a long declamation, and so that the priest does not lose his voice from shouting so long. Third, so that the holy words of this great sacrament be not cheapened when the common folk, knowing them through daily habit, repeat them in unsuitable places.

For it is said that in olden days, when the Canon was still 2 recited out loud every day, all the people came to know it, and shepherds would say it in the field over bread and wine, and suddenly they would find meat and blood before their eyes and were immediately struck dead! Henceforth it was commanded through synodal decree, under pain of anathema, that no one should say the canon except he read it from a book, in sacred vestments, and on an altar, and over the sacrifice, and that no one should offer this sacrifice except in gold and silver vessels, since few are able to acquire all these things, and therefore would not do anything incongruous.

At this point in our books a crucifix is painted, because 3 through it Christ's Passion is brought before the eyes of our heart. For Christ is the way and the truth, our very God and Lord. The priest says "You, therefore," because he sees our Lord as if present before him. This prayer begins with the letter *T* because this letter is the form of the Cross. God is called "clement," as in clear minded, because when a person is afraid he becomes muddled and confused, but when he sees that the Lord is well-disposed toward him, his mind becomes clear. "These gifts" refers to the bread, made of water and wheat flour. "These presents" refers to the wine, mixed with water. "These holy sacrifices" refers to both. "Unblemished" means without defect, because the paschal lamb had to be spotless and Christ was without any stain of sin.

Christus. "Ecclesia" dicitur convocatio, quia non timore sed amore Spiritus sancti in unam fidem convocatur. "Catholica" dicitur universalis, quia haec religio per totum mundum servatur. "Papa" dicitur pater patrum. "Orthodoxus" dicitur recte glorians, scilicet in recta fide existens. "Memento Domine famulorum": Hic possumus nominare quos volumus. Pro fidelibus tantum offertur, sicut dicitur, "quorum tibi fides cognita est."

104

De duodecim apostolis et de sancta Maria

Communicantes: ideo sancta Dei genetrix virgo Maria hic nominatur, quia hoc sacrificium de ea mundo generatur. Ideo autem duodecim apostoli nominantur, quia illorum doctrina et sanguine haec sacramenta affirmantur. Pro testimonio namque huius sacrificii, Petrus et Andreas et Philippus sunt crucifixi, Paulus et Iacobus, Matthaeus et Bartholomaeus decollati, Iacobus et Simon et Thaddaeus enecati. Iohannes veneno et exilio excruciatus, Thomas transfossus.

"Church" means convocation because it is called together in one faith, not out of fear but by the love of the Holy Spirit. "Catholic" means universal because this religion is kept throughout the whole world. "Pope" means the father of all. "Orthodox" means rightly worshiping, that is having the true faith. At "Remember, Lord, thy servants," we may mention whomever we wish, though this prayer is offered only for the faithful, as it says, "whose faith is known to you."

104

On the Twelve Apostles and Our Lady

Communicantes: The holy mother of God, the Virgin Mary, is named in this place, because through her this sacrifice is conceived for the sake of the world. The twelve apostles are named because their doctrine and blood guarantee these sacraments. Peter, Andrew, and Philip were crucified for their testimony regarding this sacrifice; Paul, James, Matthew, and Bartholomew were beheaded; James, Simon, and Thaddaeus were killed. John was tortured by poison and exile, and Thomas was stabbed to death.

105

De duodecim nominibus martyrum

Deinde duodecim martyrum nomina recitantur, quorum cruciatu hoc sacrificium commendatur. Ex quibus quidam summi pontifices, quidam episcopi, quidam diaconi, quidam laici extiterunt, quia omnes gradus, omnesque ordines huic sacramento testimonium praebuerunt. Linus quippe et Cletus, Clemens, Sixtus et Cornelius Romani pontifices; Cyprianus Carthaginensis archiepiscopus; Laurentius archidiaconus; Chrysogonus, Iohannes, et Paulus milites; Cosmas et Damianus medici fuerunt, qui omnes pro Christo, nostro sacrificio sanguinem fuderunt. "Quam oblationem . . . benedictam," id est materiam hanc terrenam, ad corpus Filii tui sicut Adam de terra formatam, Spiritu sancto benedicendo repleas. "Adscriptam," id est ad formam Filii tui signatam, divinitati adscribas. "Ratam," id est veritate firmam facias. In fide nostra rationabilem, pro devotione nostra facias acceptabilem. "Pridie," id est priori die. "Hoc est corpus meum": Sicut ex verbis Domini ex nihilo factus est mundus, ita per verba Domini haec species rerum mutatur vere in Domini corpus.

105

On the Twelve Names of the Martyrs

Next the names of twelve martyrs are recited because their torments give credit to this sacrifice. Some of them are supreme pontiffs, some bishops, some deacons, and some laymen, because every grade and all the orders gave testimony to this sacrament. Linus, Cletus, Clement, Sixtus, and Cornelius were Roman pontiffs; Cyprian of Carthage an archbishop; Laurentius an archdeacon; Chrysogonus, John, and Paul were soldiers; Cosmas and Damian were doctors, and all shed their blood for Christ, our sacrifice. "Which oblation do thou, O God, vouchsafe in all respects, to make blessed": In other words, by your blessing, may you fill up this earthly material with the Holy Spirit, for it has been made to become the body of your Son, just as Adam was formed from the earth. "Approved": In other words, consent to reckon it divine, given that it is stamped with the image of your Son. "Ratified": In other words, make it legitimate in the truth. By our faith make it spiritual, and acceptable in virtue of our devotion. "The day before": That is, on the previous day. "This is my body": Just as through the Lord's words the world was made out of nothing, so through our Lord's words these appearances are truly changed into our Lord's body.

106

De calice

"Hunc praeclarum calicem": Idem calix est in ministerio quam Christus in manibus tenuit, quamvis in materia
metalli alius sit. "Aeterni testamenti": Testamentum illa
scriptura vocatur, per quam mortui hereditas vivis confirmatur. "Novum et aeternum testamentum" est nobis Christi
sanguine scriptum, per cuius mortem caeleste regnum in
hereditate confirmatum. "Mysterium" vocatur, ubi aliud videtur, aliud intelligitur. Species panis et vini cernitur, corpus
Christi et sanguis creditur. "Hostiam puram," quantum ad
corpus. "Hostiam sanctam," quantum ad sanguinem. "Hostiam immaculatam," ad utrumque. Aliter: "Hostiam puram,"
scilicet ab aliis hostiis separatam. "Hostiam sanctam," id est
nos sanctificantem. "Hostiam immaculatam," id est a macu-
2 lis emundantem. "Panem vitae aeternae," scilicet quo pasti
aeterni efficiamur; "et calicem salutis perpetuae," videlicet
cuius gustu aeternam salutem consequamur. "Iusti Abel":
Ideo mentio Abel hic fit, quia ipse hoc sacrificium suo agno
protulit, et ipse innocens ut Christus occubuit, triginta
namque annorum occiditur, sicut Christus triginta annorum
crucifigitur. "Sacrificium patriarchae nostri Abrahae": Patriarcha dicitur summus pater. Hic figuram Dei habuit, qui
Filium suum pro nobis ut ille Isaac obtulit. Aries immolatur,
et Isaac evadit; et caro Christi pro nobis sacrificatur,

106

On the Chalice

"This excellent chalice": The chalice used in our service is the same as the one Christ held in his hands, only it is made of metal. "Of the eternal testament": A testament is a document in which the estate of a deceased person is legally assigned to the living. The "new and eternal testament" is written in the blood of Christ, whose death assigns the kingdom of heaven as our inheritance. A "mystery" is when we see one thing but understand another: we perceive the appearance of bread and wine, we believe they are the body and blood of Christ. "A pure Host" refers to the body, "a holy Host" to the blood, "an unspotted Host" to both. Another explanation: "A pure Host," because it is set apart from other offerings; "a holy Host," that is, sanctifying us; "an unspotted Host," that is, cleansing from stain. "Holy bread of eternal life," that is, bread that makes those who eat it eternal, "and the chalice of everlasting salvation," that is, by drinking which we attain eternal salvation. "Of Abel the just": Abel is mentioned here because he prefigured our sacrifice with his lamb, and died innocent like Christ. He was slain at thirty years old, the same age Christ was crucified. "The sacrifice of our patriarch Abraham": Patriarch means great father. Abraham was an image of God, who offered his Son for us as Abraham offered Isaac. A ram is sacrificed and Isaac escapes; Christ's flesh is sacrificed for us, but his

divinitas vero illaesa existit. "Summus sacerdos Melchisedech," quod sonat rex iustitiae. Hic sine patre sine matre assimilatur Filio Dei, qui in caelis matrem non habuit, et in terris patrem caruit. Hic rex iustitiae existit, quia iustos remunerabit, iniustos iuste damnabit. Melchisedech sacrificium Christi pane et vino expressit, quae Christus in sacramentum corporis et sanguinis sui transtulit.

3   Ideo in hoc loco horum sacrificia recitantur, quia protinus per inclinationem sacerdotis mors Christi commemoratur, quae per haec praefigurabatur. "Iube haec perferri per manus sancti angeli tui in sublime altare": Angelus dicitur nuntius. Christus *magni consilii angelus* extitit, dum consilio Patris per Filium hunc mundum redimi nuntiavit. "Sublime altare in conspectu Dei," est Christus in dextera Dei. Super quod altare Ecclesia hostias spiritales immolat, super quod Deus vota fidelium et *sacrificium iustitiae acceptat.* Hic angelus haec sacramenta "in sublime altare" fert, dum interpellans pro nobis vultui Dei apparet. Qui ex hoc altari scilicet Christo participantur omni benedictione caelesti et gratia replebuntur.

divinity remains unharmed. "Thy high priest Melchizedek," whose name means king of justice: Having no father or mother, he is like the Son of God, who had no mother in heaven and no father on earth. Christ was a king of justice because he will reward the just and justly punish the unjust. Melchizedek expressed the sacrifice of Christ in bread and wine, which Christ took up in the sacrament of his body and blood.

The sacrifices of these men are recalled at this point be- 3 cause the bow made by the priest signifies Christ's death, which was prefigured through these sacrifices. "Command these offerings to be borne by the hands of thy holy angel to thine altar on high": An angel is a messenger. Christ was the *angel of great counsel,* announcing the Father's plan to redeem this world through his Son. The "altar on high in the sight of God's majesty" is Christ at the right hand of God, over which the Church burns spiritual sacrifices and God *is pleased to accept* the faithful's votive offerings and *the sacrifice of justice.* This angel bears these sacraments "to the altar on high" when he appears before God's face to intercede for us. Those who receive from this altar, meaning Christ, will be filled with every grace and heavenly blessing.

107

De nominibus

"Memento Domine famulorum," hic poteris quos vis nominare, sed non in Dominica die. Nomina vivorum in libro scribebantur, quae ad altare infra Canonem recitabantur, et hic liber viventium vocabatur. Similiter hic nomina defunctorum de libro recitabantur, sed hoc Dominicis diebus intermittebatur, quia a quibusdam animae ob Resurrectionem Dominicam requiem habere credebantur. "Cum apostolis et martyribus, cum Iohanne": Quidam Iohannem baptistam volunt intelligi, quidam Marcum, qui etiam Iohannes dictus legitur, qui magis hic intelligitur. Octo martyres et septem virgines hic ponuntur, quorum sanguine hoc sacramentum approbatur, quia per hoc sacrificium in septem donis Spiritus sancti ad octo beatitudines pervenitur.

107

On the Names

"Remember, O Lord, thy servants": In this place you may mention the names of whomever you wish, save on Sundays. In former times, the names of the living were written down in a book and read out at the altar during the Canon. It was called the book of the living. In the same way, the names of the dead were read out from a book, but this was forbidden on Sundays because some people believed that souls attained their rest on account of the Sunday Resurrection. "With thine apostles and martyrs, with John": Some people understand this to refer to John the Baptist and some to Mark who was also called John, and this latter is probably correct. Eight martyrs and seven virgins are placed here, whose blood endorses this sacrament. For through this sacrifice one attains the eight beatitudes in the seven gifts of the Holy Spirit.

108

De ordinibus

Diversi ordines et sexus hic introducuntur, quia per omnes ordines et sexus hoc sacramentum confirmatur. Ex evangelistis quippe Iohannes qui et Marcus ponitur, qui Alexandriae praesul et martyr fuit; ex diaconibus Stephanus, qui primus martyr post Christum extitit; ex apostolis Mathias, qui pro Christo occubuit; ex septuaginta duobus discipulis Barnabas, qui se pro Christo obtulit; ex patriarchis Ignatius, Antiochensis episcopus; ex papis Alexander Romanus pontifex; ex presbyteris Marcellinus; ex exorcistis Petrus; ex coniugatis Felicitas et Perpetua; ex virginibus Agatha; et reliquae omnes quae hoc sacrificium suo sanguine firmaverunt, et in corpore Christi conumerari meruerunt.

2   "Per quem omnia bona": "Creas" nos novam creaturam in Christo; "sanctificas" per baptismum in ipso; "vivificas" per Spiritum sanctum in anima; "benedicis" spiritali benedictione, sive in ultima benedictione, "Venite benedicti"; "et praestas nobis," scilicet vitam aeternam post mortem. "Per ipsum" nos creas, "cum ipso" nos recreas, "in ipso" nos ad vitam resuscitas.

3   Sciendum quod in Canone nulli aliquid dicere vel adicere licebit, nisi quod ab apostolicis viris positum fuerit. Quod si quis praesumpserit, non devotioni sed praesumptioni adscribitur. Ideo *Pater noster* alta voce cantatur, ut communicaturi

108

On the Orders

Several orders and sexes are mentioned here, because all the orders and both sexes endorse this sacred oath. Of the evangelists: John, who is called Mark, bishop of Alexandria and martyr. Of the deacons: Stephen, the first martyr after Christ. Of the apostles: Matthias who died for Christ. Of the seventy-two disciples: Barnabas, who offered himself for Christ. Of the patriarchs: Ignatius, bishop of Antioch. Of the popes: Alexander, pope of Rome. Of priests: Marcellinus. Of exorcists: Peter. Of the married: Felicity and Perpetua. Of virgins: Agatha and the rest. All of these signed this sacrifice with their blood and so merited to be incorporated into the body of Christ.

"Through whom thou dost create all these good things": 2 "Dost create" as a new creation in Christ; "sanctify" through baptism in him; "give life" through the presence of the Holy Spirit in the soul; "bless," with a spiritual blessing, or in the final blessing, "Come, ye blessed"; "and bestow upon us" eternal life after death. You create us "through him," you recreate us "with him," and "in him" you raise us to life.

Note that no one may add to the Canon anything that 3 was not placed there by apostolic men. If anyone presumes to do so, it should be counted as presumption, not devotion. The *Pater noster* is sung in a loud voice, so that those about to

ante alterutrum offensas dimittendo per pacem reconcilientur.

109

In Orationem Dominicam

"Pater noster": Deus voluit esse dominus Iudaeorum, quasi servorum, pater vero Christianorum, quasi filiorum. Ideo illos quasi inutiles servos de domo eiecit, istis quasi filiis hereditatem tribuit, quos et nunc pane angelorum et carne saginati vituli pascit. "Qui es in caelis," id est in sanctis. "Sanctificetur nomen tuum": Nomen Dei sanctificatur, cum nos Filio eius uniti in regno Patris coheredes assumimur. Tunc "regnum eius advenit," cum Ecclesia regnum eius ad caelestia pervenit. "Voluntas" eius "sicut in caelo ita in terra" fiet, cum terrena caro caeleste corpus induet, et homines nihil mali concupiscunt, sed aequales angelis erunt. "Panem quotidianum hodie dat," quando in hoc exilio suo corpore nos recreat. "Debita nostra dimittit," si nos aliis dimittere posse praestiterit. "In tentationem nos non inducit," si nos a tentatione liberaverit. "A malo liberabit," si nos a peccato et ab inferno eruerit.

2   Nomen sanctae Mariae ideo hic commemoratur, ut per

communicate may be reconciled with one another in peace by forgiving one another's offenses.

109

On the Lord's Prayer

"Our Father": God wished to be a lord to the Jews, who were as his servants, but a father to Christians, who are as his sons. Thus he cast the former out from his house as useless servants and gave the latter the inheritance of sons, whom he also feeds with the bread of angels and the flesh of the fatted calf. "Who art in heaven": That is, among your saints. "Hallowed be thy name": The name of God is sanctified when we are united to his Son and adopted as coheirs into the Father's kingdom. His "kingdom comes" when the Church, his kingdom, comes into heaven. His "will shall be done on earth as it is in heaven" when earthly flesh puts on a heavenly body and men desire nothing evil but are made equal to the angels. He "gives us today our daily bread" when he refreshes us with his body during our exile on earth. He "forgives us our trespasses" if he enables us to forgive those of others. He "does not lead us into temptation" if he frees us from temptation. He "will deliver us from evil" if he saves us from sin and hell.

We mention the name of Mary here so that, through her   2

eam *a praeteritis et praesentibus ac futuris malis* liberemur, per cuius partum filii Dei efficimur. Ideo autem tres apostoli Petrus, Paulus et Andreas nominantur, quia *in ore duorum vel trium testium omne verbum stare* affirmatur, et huic sacramento tres ordines scilicet doctores, continentes, coniugati testificantur. Hic poteris de sanctis nominare quos vis, quia quaeque membra Ecclesiae participant Christi sacramentis.

110

De pace

Cum osculata patena sacerdos se signat, quia per Crucem et hoc sacrificium omnia in caelis et in terris pacificata denuntiat. "Pax" dicitur a "pacto," quia Deus pactum cum hominibus fecit, quod eis per Filium suum propitius sit.

by whose childbirth we become sons of God, we may be freed *from all evils past, present, and to come.* The three apostles Peter, Paul, and Andrew are named because *every word is confirmed by the evidence of two or three witnesses* and in this sacrament three orders—doctors, the continent, and the married—act as witnesses. In this place you can name whatever saints you wish because all the Church's members participate in Christ's sacraments.

110

On the Peace

The priest signs himself with the paten he has kissed, announcing that through the Cross and this sacrifice all things in heaven and on earth have been restored to peace and harmony. "Peace" comes from "pact," because God has made a pact with mankind, promising to look with favor upon them on account of his Son.

III

De *Agnus Dei*

Christus ideo agnus dicitur, quia ipse est qui secundum legem in Pascha immolabatur, per quem populus a servitute liberabatur. Hunc Iohannes vocavit *agnum Dei qui tolleret peccata mundi.* Ideo in fractione *Agnus Dei* cantamus, ut digne carnes huius agni sumamus. Qui agnus licet ab omni populo totus, et a singulis totus sumatur, tamen totus et integer in caelo permanere non dubitatur. Sacramentum namque quod ore percipitur, in alimentum corporis redigitur, virtus autem sacramenti qua interior homo satiatur, per hanc vita aeterna adipiscitur. Populus communicaturus tres dies debet ante ab uxoribus abstinere, et tribus postea ab eis vacare. Tot enim diebus populus Dei abstinuit, quando legem accepit. Ter *Agnus Dei* canitur, quia corpus Christi triforme intelligitur, illud quod in caelo residet, et quod in terra ambulat, et quod in sepulchris requiescit. "Eucharistia" dicitur bona gratia; "eulogia" bona benedictio; "communio" participatio.

2   Hanc ideo cantamus, ut cum iustis gratiae Dei communicemus. Complendum ideo cantamus, quia per illud Missa completur. *Ite missa est,* est licentia abeundi, *Deo gratias* interiectio gratulandi. His quippe peractis populus Deo

III

On the *Agnus Dei*

Christ is called a lamb because he is the very lamb that was sacrificed on Passover in accordance with the Law, and through whom the people were liberated from slavery. John called him *the Lamb of God who takes away the sins of the world.* We sing the *Agnus Dei* during the Fraction so that we may receive the flesh of this Lamb in a worthy manner. Although the whole Lamb is eaten by all the people and by each individually, yet it remains whole and entire in heaven. For the sacrament we receive with our mouths is turned into nourishment for our bodies, while the power of this sacrament feeds the interior man, and through it he attains eternal life. Those of the people who wish to communicate must abstain from their wives for three days before and also stay away from them for three days after. For the people of God abstained for this period before receiving the Law. The *Agnus Dei* is sung three times to signify the threefold body: the one that resides in heaven, the one that walks on earth, and the one that rests in the grave. "Eucharist" means good thanks; "eulogia," good blessing; "communion," participation.

We sing the Communion antiphon to share in the grace 2 of God with the just. The *Oratio ad complendum* is so called because it ends the Mass. *Ite missa est* is a permission to leave, *Deo gratias,* an exclamation of gratitude. For when all these things are finished, the people give thanks to God and

grates reddit, et ad propria redit. Sicut populus Israel pro-
missu Pharaonis de Aegypto abiit, et grates Deo retulit, sive
quando Cyro praecipiente de Babylonia ad Ierusalem rediit,
et gratias Deo egit; ita nos accepta ultima benedictione ad
patriam caelestem ibimus, et in gratiarum actione semper
manebimus. Ideo hymnum trium puerorum scilicet *Benedicite* post Missam cantamus, quia Deum pro omnibus beneficiis suis benedicimus, quem post in saeculum saeculi laudamus. Hunc Toletanum Concilium cantari instituit, et hunc
negligentes anathemate subdidit.

112

De quattuor speciebus Missae

Missa dividitur in quattuor species, scilicet *obsecrationes,
orationes, postulationes, gratiarum actiones.* Ab initio Missae usque ad offertorium, sunt obsecrationes. A Secreta usque ad
Pater noster, sunt orationes. Deinde usque ad communionem,
postulationes. Exinde usque in finem gratiarum actiones.

return home, just as when the people of Israel left Egypt with Pharaoh's permission, and when they returned from Babylon to Jerusalem by Cyrus's command, they gave thanks to God; in the same way, once we have received the final blessing we shall return to the heavenly fatherland and remain forever in the state of thanksgiving. That is why after Mass we sing the hymn of the three young men, called the *Benedicite,* because we bless the Lord for all of his blessings, as we will praise him later unto the ages of ages. The Council of Toledo ordered this hymn to be sung and anyone who neglects it is subject to anathema.

112

On the Four Species of Prayer in the Mass

There are four species of prayer in the Mass, namely *supplications, prayers, intercessions, and thanksgivings.* From the beginning of Mass to the offertory are supplications. From the Secret to the *Pater noster* are prayers. Thence to the communion are intercessions. And finally the rest are thanksgivings.

113

De tribus horis Missae

Tribus horis licet Missam cantare, scilicet tertia, sexta, nona. In festis tertia, in privatis diebus sexta, in Septuagesima vel in diebus ieiunii nona hora. Hora tertia ideo Missa cantatur, quia hora tertia Christus ad Passionem iudicabatur, quando Iudaei *"Crucifige, crucifige"* clamaverunt, et milites eum flagellaverunt. Hora sexta ideo Missa celebratur, quia hora sexta Christus pro nobis in Cruce immolabatur. Hora nona ideo Missa celebratur, quia hora nona Christus mortem subiisse traditur.

114

Quod una Missa debeat celebrari

Semel in die debet Missa ab uno sacerdote celebrari, sicut et Christus semel voluit immolari. Si autem necessitas cogit, id est si duae festivitates simul occurrerint, duae vel tres celebrari poterunt, quia et Romani hoc in die Natalis Domini

113

On the Three Hours at Which Mass May Be Said

It is permitted to sing Mass at three different hours, namely the third, sixth, and ninth. On feast days at the third; on ferial weekdays at the sixth, and in Lent or on fasting days at the ninth hour. Mass is sung at the third hour because at that hour Christ was condemned to death, when the Jews shouted, *"Crucify him, crucify him!"* and the soldiers scourged him. Mass is celebrated at the sixth hour because at the sixth hour Christ was sacrificed for us on the Cross. Mass is sung at the ninth hour because we are told that Christ died at the ninth hour.

114

On Celebrating Only One Mass per Day

A priest should celebrate Mass only once per day, just as Christ willed to be sacrificed once. In case of necessity, however, for example if two feast days fall on the same day, two or three Masses may be celebrated because the Romans do

faciunt. Et Christi Passio est tripartita. Passus est enim linguis insultantium, manibus verberantium, clavis crucifigentium. Ipse etenim in figura a patriarchis est immolatus, ipse a prophetis sacrificatus, ipse idem a Patre et seipso pro nobis oblatus. Legitur de Leone papa, quod saepius in una die septem Missas, aliquando novem celebraverit. Nullus absque sacerdotalibus vestibus—et his singulis consecratis—et altari consecrato Missam celebrare debet, et nulli nisi ordinato Epistulam vel Evangelium legere licet, sicut nulli non ordinato Missam cantare licet. Post acceptam lavationem nulli Missam celebrare vel communicare licebit, quod si fecerit gravi paenitentia obnoxius erit.

Interrogatio

2 Licet laico plus in die quam semel communicare? Responsio: Si presbytero licet duas vel tres Missas cantare, communicare licet et laico. Licet presbytero plusquam unam Missam celebrare? Responsio: Legitur de Leone papa quod aliquando in die septem vel plures Missas celebraverit. Si ei licuit, et aliis sacerdotibus licet.

this on the day of Christ's Nativity, and because Christ's Passion is threefold. For he suffered from the tongues of those who insulted him, the hands of those who struck him, and the nails of those who crucified him, and further indeed he was immolated by the patriarchs, sacrificed by the prophets, and offered for use by the Father and by himself. On the other hand, we read that Pope Leo sometimes celebrated seven or even nine Masses in one day. No one may celebrate Mass without priestly vestments—all of them consecrated—and on a consecrated altar, and only an ordained man may read the Epistle and Gospel or sing the Mass. After purifying the chalice, no priest may celebrate Mass or communicate a second time, but, if he does so, shall incur a grave penance.

Question

May a layman communicate more than once per day? Response: If a priest may sing two or three Masses, then a laymen may communicate. May a priest celebrate more than one Mass? Response: We read that Pope Leo sometimes celebrated seven or more Masses each day. If he was allowed to, other priests are too. 2

115

De *Gloria in excelsis Deo*

Gloria in excelsis, numquam nisi ad horam tertiam canitur, qua Spiritus sanctus super credentes descendisse, et eos gloria et exultatione replevisse legitur. In duobus etiam Sabbatis Paschae et Pentecosten ad nonam cantatur, quia baptizatis gloria amissa redditur.

116

De una Oratione in Missa vel pluribus

Una Oratio regulariter dicitur, sicut et una Epistula vel unum Evangelium legitur. Si autem festivitas in die Dominico occurrit, duas dici licebit, quia et hoc Romana auctoritas in die Natalis Domini ad secundam Missam facit. Interdum tres ideo dicimus, quia Deum ter ante Passionem orasse legimus. Aliquando quinque dicimus, quia quinquepartitam Passionem Domini in hoc officio agimus. Nonnumquam septem usurpamus, propter septem petitiones in Dominica oratione quas tantum apostolos super hoc sacramentum dixisse cognovimus. Qui hunc numerum supergressus fuerit, ut caecus errabit.

115

On the *Gloria in excelsis Deo*

The *Gloria in excelsis* is only ever sung at the third hour, when the Holy Spirit descended upon the believers and filled them with glory and exultation. But on the Saturdays before Easter and Pentecost it is sung at the ninth hour because then the baptized regain their former glory.

116

On One or Many Collects at Mass

The usual rule is that there is one Collect at Mass, just as there is one Epistle and one Gospel. But if a feast occurs on a Sunday it is allowed to say two, following the Roman authority which does this at the second Mass on the day of our Lord's Nativity. From time to time we say three, because we read that our Lord prayed three times before his Passion. Sometimes we say five, acting the five-part Passion of our Lord in this office. Occasionally we use seven, on account of the seven petitions in the Lord's Prayer, which is the only thing that the apostles said over this sacrament. If anyone should exceed this number, he will be as lost as a blind man.

117

De genuflexione in Quadragesima

In Quadragesima ideo ad Missam *Flectamus genua* dicimus, quia corpus et animam in paenitentia nos humiliare innuimus. Ob tres autem causas ad terram cadimus. Una est quod Christum adoramus in carne, quem ad terras descendisse, et carnem de terra induisse, ad levandos nos venerando memoramus. Alia est quod ad memoriam reducimus, quia qui in paradiso cum angelis stetimus, nunc inter bruta animalia in terra iacemus, et animam nostram corporali mole ad terram deprimi ingemiscimus. Tertia causa est haec. Qui stat aliis hominibus coaequatur; qui in terra iacet, bestiis assimilatur. Et nos dum in iustitia stetimus, rationalibus similes fuimus; postquam vero in carnis desideriam cecidimus, cum bestiis quasi irrationabiles in luto repimus.

2 Quia ergo aliis hominibus nos dissimiles in factis cernimus, eis etiam ipso corporis statu aequari erubescimus. Et lapsus animae nostrae in vitia paenitendo clamamus, dum corpore ad terram cadimus. Et *ventrem nostrum terrae* et *animam pavimento* facimus *adhaerere,* ut per Christum propter nos terram factum a terrenis desideriis valeamus resurgere. Hic autem ritus ab Abraham exordium sumpsit, qui in terram prostratus Dominum adoravit. Quem prophetae imitati sunt, qui in terram cadentes Deum adoraverunt.

117

On Genuflecting during Lent

In Lent we genuflect at Mass to signify the humiliation of our body and soul through penance. Now, we fall to the ground for three reasons. One is that thereby we adore Christ in the flesh, recalling with veneration how he descended to earth and took on flesh from that earth in order to wash us clean. Another reason is to recall that formerly we stood with the angels in paradise, and now lie down among the brute beasts, and thus we bemoan how our soul is weighed down to the earth by our corporal nature. The third reason is this: one who stands is at the same level with other humans, but the one who lies on the ground is like the beasts. Just so, when we still stood in the state of original justice we were like rational beings; but later we fell to the desires of the flesh, and now we wallow in the mud with the irrational beasts.

Therefore, since we recognize that we are not like human beings in our deeds, we are ashamed even to stand equal to them in our bodily posture. Instead, we fall to the ground, with our bodies proclaiming our soul's fall into vice. We make *our bellies cleave to the earth* and *our soul to the pavement,* so that through Christ who became earth for our sake, we may rise from our earthly desires. This rite has its origin in Abraham, when he fell on his face and adored the Lord. The prophets imitated him when they fell to the ground to adore

Genuum autem flectio a gentilibus est sumpta. Quem honorem ipsi regibus exhibuerunt, quos proni vel flexo genu adoraverunt. Nos autem cum apostolo dicimus Deo, "*Flecto genua mea ad Deum.*"

118

De lumine ad Missam

Lumen Spiritum sanctum signat, ideo cum lumine Missa celebratur, quia hoc sacramentum per Spiritum sanctum consecratur, et digne haec percipientes a Spiritu sancto illustrantur. Lumen etiam laetitiam designat, quia sacramentum Missae aeternam laetitiam donat. In *Credo in unum,* cum "et homo factus est" dicimus genua flectimus, quia Christum hominem factum et crucifixum pro nobis adoramus.

the Lord. Genuflection comes from the gentiles, who used this reverence to honor their kings, adoring them from either a prostrate or kneeling position. But we say to God along with the apostles, "*I bow my knees before the Lord.*"

118

On the Use of Light at Mass

Light signifies the Holy Spirit. Light is used during the celebration of the Mass, because the sacrament is consecrated through the Holy Spirit, and those who receive it are filled with light by the same Holy Spirit. Light also symbolizes happiness, because the sacrament of the Mass gives eternal happiness. During the *Credo in unum,* when we say "and was made man," we genuflect to adore Christ made man and crucified for us.

119

De *Credo in unum Deum,* quando sit cantandum

*C*redo *in unum* in Dominicis omnibus et festis Domini, et sanctae Crucis canitur, et in festis sanctae Mariae, et in natalitiis apostolorum et in festivitate omnium sanctorum et in dedicatione templi canitur, quia aliquid de his in illo sonare videtur. Liber Evangelii infra *Credo in unum* osculatur, quia per Christum pax reddita declaratur.

120

De Praefationibus

*P*elagius papa novem praefationes cantari statuit, scilicet *Quia per incarnati verbi* de Nativitate Domini; *Quia cum unigenitus* de Epiphania; *Qui corporali ieiunio* Dominicis in Quadragesima; *Qui salutem humani* de Passione, vel de Cruce; *Te quidem Domine* de Pascha; *Qui post Resurrectionem* de Ascensione; *Qui ascendens super omnes* de Pentecosten; *Qui cum unigenito* de sancta Trinitate; *Te Domine supplices exoramus* de

119

When *Credo in unum Deum* Should Be Sung

Credo in unum should be sung on all Sundays, feasts of our Lord and of the holy Cross, on feasts of Mary and the birthdays of the apostles, on the feast of All Saints, and at the dedication of a church, because the Creed makes mention of each of these in some way. The Gospel book is kissed during *Credo in unum* to manifest that peace has been restored through Christ.

120

On the Prefaces

Pope Pelagius instituted nine prefaces to be sung: *Quia per incarnati* for the Nativity; *Quia cum unigenitus* for Epiphany; *Qui corporali ieiunio* for Sundays in Lent; *Qui salutem humani generis* for our Lord's Passion or the holy Cross; *Te quidem Domine omni tempore* for Easter; *Qui post Resurrectionem* for Ascension; *Qui ascendens super omnes caelos* for Pentecost; *Qui cum unigento filio,* for the most holy Trinity; *Te Domine*

sancto Petro et Paulo, quae et de pluribus apostolis dicitur. Gregorius vero papa decimam *Qui Ecclesiam tuam* de sancto Andrea adiecit, quae de uno quolibet apostolo usquequaque dici consuevit. Noviter autem Urbanus papa undecimus de sancta Maria addidisse non ignoratur, quae a pluribus ubique frequentatur.

Soter papa constituit, ut nullus Missam celebret, nisi saltem tertius sit. Zacharias papa constituit, ne sacerdos cum baculo ad altare intret, et ne velato capite ad altare stet.

121

Quare pro defunctis *Gloria Patri* et *Alleluia* non cantetur

Ad Missam pro defunctis *Gloria Patri,* et *Alleluia* quod laetitiam designat non cantatur, quia luctum imitatur, et nos per hoc in hunc mundum ad tristitiam venisse, et per luctum hinc exire admonemur. Corpora vero mortuorum non debent interesse Missae vivorum, quia nobiscum non respondent, et cum vivis non communicant. Hoc autem significat, quod hii qui in peccatis mortui sunt, et Christi sacramenta in percipiunt, in terra viventium communicatoribus Christi interesse non poterunt.

supplicter exorare, for Peter and Paul, though it is also said for feasts of several apostles. Pope Gregory added a tenth, *Qui Ecclesiam tuam,* for Saint Andrew, which it is customary to use for each of the apostles. Recently Pope Urban II added one for Mary, which is used in many places.

Pope Soter decided that none should celebrate Mass without a third person present. Pope Zachary decreed that no priest should approach the altar with a staff or stand at the altar with his head covered.

121

Why the *Gloria Patri* and Alleluia Are Not Sung in Masses for the Dead

At a Mass for the dead, *Gloria Patri* and Alleluia—which indicate happiness—are not sung, as a gesture of mourning by which we are admonished that we have come into this world for sadness and will leave it in mourning. The bodies of the dead should not be present in a Mass for the living, because they do not make the responses with us and do not communicate with the living. By not allowing the bodies to be present, we signify that those who are dead in their sins and do not receive Christ's sacraments will not be among Christ's faithful in the land of the living.

De ecclesia

Haec breviter de Missa diximus. Nunc pauca de ecclesia in qua agitur videamus.

122

De altari

Noe primus altare Domino construxisse, deinde Abraham, Isaac, et Iacob altaria aedificasse leguntur, quae non aliud quam lapides erecti intelliguntur. Super quos sacrificia mactabant, quae subposito igne cremabant. Aliquando vero ignis de caelo descendit, et oblatum sacrificium consumpsit. Unde Cain fratrem suum occidit, quia ignis caelestis Abel sacrificium consumpsit, suum intactum remansit. Haec autem differentia est inter altare et aram, quod "altare" quasi alta res vel alta ara dicitur, quia sacerdotes incensum adolebant; "ara" vero quasi "area," id est plana, vel ab "ardore" dicitur, eo quod in ea sacrificia ardebant. "Ara" etiam Graece, dicitur Latine "precatio."

On the Church Building

We have said this much briefly about the Mass. Now let us look at a few things concerning the church in which it is celebrated.

122

On the Altar

Noah was the first to construct an altar for our Lord. Subsequently we read that Abraham, Isaac, and Jacob built altars which were nothing more than a raised pile of stones over which they offered sacrifices and burned them with fire. Sometimes fire descended from heaven and consumed the oblation. Wherefore Cain killed his brother, because heavenly fire consumed Abel's sacrifice but left his own untouched. Now there is this difference between *altare* and *ara:* an *altare* is elevated, as in a high *ara,* in which the priests burned incense. Further, *ara* is similar to the word "area," which means a flat surface, or it comes from "ardor," since sacrifices were burned there. *Ara* is Greek; the Latin is *precatio.*

123

De tabernaculo Moysi

Quando vero Dominus populum suum de Aegypto eduxit, spiritale tabernaculum Moysi in monte Sinai ostendit, ad cuius exemplar materiale fieri praecepit. Vasa quoque pretiosa, et sacras vestes fieri iussit; altare ad sacrificia, sacerdotes et Levitas in ministeria constituit; et tubas argenteas vel aereas ad convocandum populum fieri statuit. Quae cuncta Moyses secundum ostensum exemplar miro opere consummavit, et tabernaculum cum gaudio populi dedicavit.

2   Quod postquam est vetustate consumptum, iussit Dominus sibi fieri templum, atque chartam David regi per prophetam misit, in qua erat descriptio, qualiter templum construi debuerit. Salemon vero mirificum templum toto orbe famosum aedificavit, sicut Dominus in carta imperavit. Altare quoque aureum, et vasa pretiosissima, et vestes sacras fecit, sacerdotes, cantores, Levitas in ministeria templi distribuit, prout Dominus in brevi praecepit. Omnibus rite peractis, Templum maximo cultu dedicavit, et arcam in eo locavit.

Quod quia utrumque Ecclesiam praefiguravit, secundum formam utriusque populus Christianus ecclesias formavit.

123

On Moses's Tabernacle

But when our Lord led his people out from Egypt, he showed Moses a spiritual tabernacle on Mount Sinai and ordered him to build a material one on this model. He also commanded precious vessels and sacred vestments to be made. He established an altar for sacrifices, priests and Levites for the ministries, and commissioned silver and bronze trumpets for calling the people together. Moses brought all this work wondrously to completion according to the divine exemplar and dedicated the tabernacle while the people rejoiced.

When this tabernacle had become worn with age, our   2 Lord ordered a temple to be built for himself, and through the prophet he sent King David a brief, on which there was a description of how the temple ought to be built. But it was Solomon who built a marvelous temple that became famous the world over, following our Lord's commands as written on the brief. He also made a golden altar and very precious vessels and sacred vestments; priests, cantors, and Levites he assigned to minister in the temple as our Lord had prescribed on the piece of paper. When all had been fittingly completed, he dedicated the temple with a sumptuous ceremony and placed the arc inside.

Since both of these structures prefigured the Church, the Christian people have modeled their churches on them both.

124

De tabernaculo populi

Tabernaculum quod populus in itinere habuit, formam mundi tenuit, et typum Ecclesiae gessit, quae in itinere huius mundi *non manentem civitatem habet, sed futuram inquirit.* Tabernaculum secundum mundum erat formatum, et elementa atque omne quod est in mundo in eo fuerat praefiguratum, quia totus hic mundus iam factus est Dei templum, sanguine Christi dedicatum, in quo universalis Ecclesia tabernaculum Dei existens, *Deum vivum et verum* laudibus iugiter concelebrat, et ex tabernaculo templum fieri desiderat. Cuius tabernaculi una pars dicebatur sancta, in qua populus sacrificabat, et est activa vita, in qua populus in dilectione proximi laborabat. Altera pars dicebatur sancta sanctorum, in qua sacerdotes et Levitae ministrabant, et est contemplativa vita, in qua religiosorum sinceritas in dilectione Dei caelestibus inhiat.

2   Porro secundum formam tabernaculi, faciunt ecclesias Christiani. Secundum sancta fit anterior domus ubi populus stat, sanctuarium vero secundum sancta sanctorum ubi clerus stat. Ministerium Levitarum et sacerdotum mutuavit Ecclesia in ordinem Christi ministrorum. Vasa et vestes et

124

On the People's Tabernacle

The tabernacle that the people carried with them on their journey was made as a likeness of the cosmos and acted as a type of the Church, which *has no abiding city* on its journey through this world, *but seeks one to come.* The tabernacle had been fashioned after the shape of the universe and all the elements and everything in the world had been prefigured in it, because this whole world has become God's temple, dedicated by the blood of Christ, in which the universal Church, as God's tabernacle, celebrates *the living and true God* with endless praise and strives to be changed from a tabernacle into a true temple. The part of this tabernacle where the people sacrificed was called the holy place and stands for the active life, in which the people labored each in the love of his neighbor. The other part was called the holy of holies, in which the priests and Levites ministered, and stands for the contemplative life, in which the fervor of the religious eagerly thirsts after heavenly things in the love of God.

Christians too build their churches according to the design of this tabernacle. The inner part of the house, where the people stand, is made like the holy place. The sanctuary is made like the holy of holies, where the clergy stands. In the Church the order of Christian ministers is modeled on the ministry of the Levites and priests. She converted the

ritus sacrificiorum, convertit in morem ecclesiasticorum. Clangorem tubarum, transtulit in sonum campanarum.

125

De Templo

Templum autem quod populus in patria cum pace possidebat, praefert templum gloriae de vivis lapidibus in caelesti Ierusalem constructum, in quo Ecclesia perenni pace exultat. Hoc etiam in duo dividitur, quia templum supernae curiae in angelorum et hominum differentiam discernitur. In quo altare aureum, est Christus gloria sanctorum. In hoc templo omnes electi sacerdotes et cantores erunt, ipsi et vasa pretiosa in camino tribulationis examinata *ut sol fulgebunt, veste salutis et indumento iustitiae* splendescunt. A templo itaque quod Salemon fecit, ecclesia nostra formam accepit. Per hanc quippe domum Ecclesia significatur, ideo et ecclesia vocatur.

vessels, vestments, and the sacrificial rituals into the customs of the Church. The blare of trumpets she transposed into the sound of bells.

125

On the Temple

Now when the people had established a lasting peace in their fatherland, they built a temple. This prefigured the temple of glory built out of living stones in the heavenly Jerusalem, in which the Church rejoices in an eternal peace. But this temple is divided into two parts, for the temple of the heavenly curia is divided into men and angels. There is also a golden altar, which is Christ, the glory of the saints. In this temple all the elect will be priests and cantors, and as precious vessels tested in the furnace of tribulation, they *will shine like the sun, with the garment of salvation and with the robe of justice.* And so our church takes its form from the temple that Solomon made. This house signifies the Church, and so it is called a church.

126

De ecclesia habente
septem vocabula

Ecclesia autem septem vocabulis insignitur, quia Ecclesia Christi septem donis Spiritus sancti velut septem columnis domus sapientiae fulcitur.

127

De basilica caeterisque
templi nominibus

"Ecclesia" vero convocatio dicitur, quia in ea populus fidelium ad audienda iudicia Dei, et ad convivium Christi convocatur. "Synagoga" congregatio dicebatur, quia virga legis velut grex irrationalium pecorum congregabatur. Ecclesia autem merito convocatio vocatur, quia amore Spiritus sancti in unam fidem convocatur. Haec domus et basilica, id est regalis nuncupatur, quia in ea Regi regum ministratur. *Basileus* namque rex quasi *basis loas,* id est columna *loas,* id est

126

On the Seven Names for the Church Building

Now a church has seven names because the Church of Christ is sustained by the seven gifts of the Holy Spirit, akin to the seven columns of the house of wisdom.

127

On the Basilica and Other Names for Temples

"Church" means a convocation or calling together, because in it the faithful people are called together to hear God's judgments and attend Christ's banquet. "Synagogue" meant a flocking together, because it was gathered together like a herd of irrational beasts by the rod of the Law. The Church is rightly called a convocation, because it is called together into one faith by the love of the Holy Spirit. This house is called a basilica, meaning regal, because in it we serve the king of kings. For *basileus* means king, from *basis*

columna populi dicitur, quia eius regimine fulcitur. Haec domus et *kyricha,* id est dominicalis appellatur, quia in ea Domino dominorum servitur. *Kyrus* quippe dicitur Dominus. Haec quoque domus Dei vocatur, quia in ea Deus adoratur. Haec domus orationis appellatur, quia in ea populus fidelium ad orationem congregatur. Haec etiam aula Dei nuncupatur, quia in ea convivium aeterni regis celebratur. Haec quoque dicitur oratorium, quia locus est orationis fidelium. Haec templum quasi "amplum tectum" vocatur, quia conventus populi in ea quasi sub unum tectum coadunatur. Monasterium dicitur habitatio monachorum. *Monas* quippe solus, *sterion* dicitur habitatio. Maiores autem ecclesiae templa appellantur; minores vero capellae a caprarum pellibus vocantur.

128

De capellis

Antiqui enim nobiles ecclesiolas in itinere de pellibus caprarum factas habebant, quas inde capellas vocabant, et earum custodes capellanos nominabant. Sunt etiam capellani a cappa sancti Martini appellati, quam reges Francorum in proeliis semper habebant, et eam deferentes capellanos dicebant. "Capenum" dicitur domus ad quam pauperes ad postulandam eleemosynam confluunt. Inde diminutivum

laos, which means the people's column, because the people are made secure by his government. This house is also called *kyriaka,* which means of the Lord, because in it we serve the Lord of lords. For *Kyrios* means Lord. It is also called the house of God because in it we adore our Lord; or again a house of prayer because in it the faithful people are gathered to pray; or again God's hall because in it we celebrate the banquet of the eternal king; or again it is called an oratory because it is a place for the faithful to pray; or again a temple, from "ample house," because the assembly of the people is united in it as if under one roof. A habitation of monks is called a monastery, for *monos* means alone and *sterion* means habitation. Now major churches are called temples, but minor churches are called chapels, from goat's skin.

128

On Chapels

For while on a journey, noblemen of ancient times carried with them little churches made out of goat skins, which therefore they called chapels. Those who kept them were called chaplains. Chaplains are also named after the cape of Saint Martin that the Frankish kings always had with them in battle, and they called those who carried them chaplains. A *capenum* is a house where paupers go to beg for alms. From

"capella" dicitur in qua Christiani pauperes spiritu ad postulandam animae eleemosynam conveniunt.

129

De situ ecclesiae

Ideo autem ecclesiae ad orientem vertuntur, ubi sol oritur, quia in eis Sol iustitiae adoratur, et in orientem paradisus nostra patria esse praedicatur. Per ecclesiam ergo Ecclesia figuratur, quae in ea ad servitium Dei congregatur. Domus haec super petram locatur, et Ecclesia super Christum firmam petram fundatur. Quattuor parietibus surgit in altum, et Ecclesia crescit quattuor Evangeliis in altum virtutum. Domus haec ex duris lapidibus construitur, et Ecclesia ex fortibus in fide et operatione colligitur. Lapides caemento conglutinantur, et fideles vinculo dilectionis compaginantur. Sanctuarium est primitiva Ecclesia de Iudaeis collecta, anterior domus Ecclesia de gentibus ad fidem convecta. Sanctuarium etiam sunt in contemplativa vita degentes, anterior domus in activa vita Deo servientes.

there we have the diminutive form *capella,* because Christians who are poor in spirit come there to ask for spiritual alms.

129

On a Church's Position

Churches are turned toward the east where the sun rises, because in them the Sun of justice is adored, and in the east is paradise, our fatherland. Thus the church building is a figure of the Church that is gathered in it for the divine service. This house is set on rock, and the Church is founded on the firm rock of Christ. It rises upward with four walls, and the Church grows to the lofty heights of virtue through the four Gospels. This house is constructed out of hard stones, and the Church is gathered from among those strong in faith and works. The stones are held together by cement, and the faithful are jointed together by the bond of love. The sanctuary is the early Church, gathered from among the Jews; the anterior part of the house is the Church of the gentiles drawn to the faith. The sanctuary also represents those who live a contemplative life, and the anterior part of the house those serving God in the active life.

130

De fenestris ecclesiae

Perspicuae fenestrae quae tempestatem excludunt, et lumen introducunt, sunt doctores qui turbini haeresium obsistunt, et lucem doctrinae Ecclesiae infundunt. Vitrum in fenestris per quod radius lucis iaculatur, est mens doctorum, quae caelestia quasi *per speculum in aenigmate* contemplatur.

131

De columnis ecclesiae

Columnae quae domum fulciunt, sunt episcopi qui machinam Ecclesiae vitae rectitudine in alta suspendunt. Trabes quae domum coniungunt, sunt saeculi principes qui Ecclesiam continendo muniunt. Tegulae tecti quae imbrem a domo repellunt, sunt milites qui Ecclesiam a paganis et hostibus protegunt.

130

On the Church's Windows

The clear windows that shut out storms and let in the light are the doctors who stand against the tempests of the heresies and shed the light of the Church's doctrine upon us. Light shines through the glass in the windows, and this glass is the mind of the doctors, which contemplates heavenly things as if *through a glass in a dark manner.*

131

On the Church's Columns

The columns that hold up the house are the bishops, who by their righteousness raise the structure of ecclesial life to lofty heights. The beams that join the house together are the princes of the world, who provide protection and support to the Church. The shingles of the roof, which repel rain from the house, are the soldiers who protect the Church from pagans and enemies.

132

De pictura

Laquear picturae, sunt exempla iustorum, quae Ecclesiae repraesentant ornatum morum. Ob tres autem causas fit pictura: primo quia est laicorum litteratura, secundo ut domus tali decore ornetur, tertio ut piorum vita in memoriam revocetur.

133

De corona

Lumina quae circa capita sanctorum in ecclesia in modum circuli depinguntur, designant quod lumine aeterni splendoris coronati fruuntur. Idcirco vero secundum formam rotundi scuti pinguntur, quia divina protectione *ut scuto* nunc muniuntur. Unde ipsi canunt gratulabundi, "*Domine ut scuto bonae voluntatis tuae coronasti nos.*" Usus autem formas sculpendi a lege coepit, ubi Moyses Domino duos cherubim ex auro fecit. Usus vero ecclesias pingendi, a Salemone exordium sumpsit, qui *varias caelaturas* in Templo Domini fieri instituit. Usus etiam candelabri et thuribuli a

132

On Painting

Painted panels are the examples of the just, who show the Church the loveliness of good conduct. Painting is done for three reasons: first, because it is the literature of the laity; second, to give the house fitting decoration; third, to recall the lives of the saints.

133

On the Halo

The circles of light that are painted around the heads of the saints signify that they are now crowned by the light of eternal splendor. The crown is depicted in the form of a round shield because they are defended by a divine protection *as if by a shield*. Thus they gratefully sing, "*O Lord, thou hast crowned us, as with a shield of thy good will.*" The practice of sculpting images is taken from the Law, where Moses, by God's command, made two cherubim out of gold. But the practice of painting churches began with Solomon, who placed *divers engravings* in the Temple of God. The use of the

lege coepit. Pavimentum quod pedibus calcatur, est vulgus cuius labore Ecclesia sustentatur. Cryptae sub terra constructae, sunt cultores secretioris vitae.

134

De altari

Altare super quod sacrificatur, est Christus super quem sacrificium Ecclesiae acceptatur. Ideo corpus Christi super altare conficitur, quia populus in eum credens qui ex eo reficitur, unum cum Christo quasi multi lapides unum altare efficitur. In altari reliquiae reconduntur, quia in Christo *omnes thesauri sapientiae et scientiae absconduntur.* Super altare capsae ponuntur; sunt apostoli et martyres qui pro Christo passi leguntur. Pallae et vestes quibus altare ornatur, sunt confessores et virgines quorum opibus Christus decoratur.

candelabrum and thurible began in the Law. The pavement that is trod underfoot is the mass of men whose labor sustains the Church. Crypts built underground are those who lead a more withdrawn life.

134

On the Altar

The altar on which we sacrifice is Christ, upon whom the Church's sacrifice is acceptable to God. The body of Christ is confected upon the altar because the people who believe in Christ and eat of him become one with him, just as many stones are made into one altar. Relics are enclosed in the altar because in Christ *are hid all the treasures of wisdom and knowledge.* Capsules containing saints' relics are put on the altar; they are the apostles and martyrs who suffered for Christ. The linens and other cloths that decorate the altar are the confessors and virgins, by whose works Christ is adorned.

135

De cruce

Crux ob tres causas super altare erigitur. Primo quod signum Regis nostri in domo Dei quasi in regia urbe figitur, ut a militibus adoretur; secundo ut Passio Christi semper Ecclesiae praesentetur; tertio, ut populus Christianus *carnem suam crucifigendo vitiis et concupiscentiis* Christum imitetur. Vexilla ideo eriguntur, ut trophaeum Christi Ecclesia iugiter memoretur.

136

De propitiatorio et de lavacro

Propitiatorium quod super altare locatur, est divinitas Christi quae humano generi propitiatur. Gradus per quos ad altare ascenditur, sunt virtutes per quos ad Christum pertingitur. Lavacrum quo iuxta altare manus abluuntur, est misericordia fluens de Christo qua homines in baptismo vel in paenitentia a sordibus diluuntur.

135

On the Cross

A crucifix is set up above the altar for three reasons. Firstly, because our King's banner hangs in God's house, as in a royal city, so that his soldiers may give it homage. Secondly, so that Christ's Passion may always be made present to the Church. Thirdly, so that the Christian people may imitate Christ by *crucifying their flesh, with the vices and concupiscences.* The banners are set up for this reason, that the Church may always remember Christ's trophy.

136

On the Propitiatory and on the Lavabo

The propitiatory that is fixed on the altar is Christ's divinity, which intercedes for the human race. The stairs by which one ascends the altar are the virtues by which one strives toward Christ. The lavabo beside the altar where the washing of hands takes place is the mercy flowing from Christ, by which men are cleansed from their filth in baptism or in penance.

137

De paliis

Pallia quae in ecclesia suspenduntur, sunt miracula Christi quae in Ecclesia leguntur. Pulpitum quod in altum sustollitur, et in quo Evangelium legitur, est perfectorum vita ad quam per Evangelicam doctrinam pervenitur, dum *relictis omnibus* quis Christum sequitur. Ecclesia iugi lumine lucernae illuminatur, et Ecclesia Christi lumine Spiritus sancti semper illustratur. Baptismus in ecclesia celebratur, quia Catholica Ecclesia est mater de qua nova progenies Christo generatur.

138

De ostio

"Ostium" ab obstando vel ostendendo dicitur. Ostium quod inimicis obstat, et amicis aditus introeundi ostendit, est Christus qui per iustitiam obstans, infideles a domo sua arcet, et fideles aditum ostendendo per fidem introducit.

137

On the Tapestries

The tapestries hung up in the church are the miracles of Christ we read about in the Church. The raised pulpit from which the Gospel is read is the life of the perfect, which one attains through the Gospel's doctrine when *one leaves behind everything* and follows Christ. The church is always lit by lamplight and Christ's Church is always brightened by the light of the Holy Spirit. Baptism is celebrated in the church because the Catholic Church is our mother and from her new offspring are begotten for Christ.

138

On the Door

"Door" comes from obstruction or showing. The door that keeps out enemies and shows friends the way in is Christ, who resists the unfaithful through justice and bars them from his house, while showing the faithful the way in through faith.

139

De chorea

Chorus psallentium a chorea canentium exordium sumpsit, quam antiquitas idolis instituit, ut videlicet decepti deos
suos et voce laudarent, et toto corpore eis servirent. Per
choreae autem circuitionem, voluerunt intelligi firmamenti
revolutionem; per manuum complexionem, elementorum
connexionem; per sonum cantantium, harmoniam planeta-
rum resonantium; per corporis gesticulationem, signorum
motionem; per plausum manuum, vel pedum strepitum, to-
nitruorum crepitum.

2   Quod fideles imitati sunt, et in servitium veri Dei converterunt. Nam populus de Mari Rubro egressus choream
duxisse, et Maria eis cum tympano praecinuisse, et David
ante arcam totis viribus saltasse, et cum cithara psalmos ce-
cinisse legitur, et Salemon cantores circum altare instituisse
dicitur, qui voce, tubis, organis, cymbalis, citharis cantica
personuisse leguntur. Unde et adhuc in choreis musicis instrumentis uti nituntur, quia globi caelestes dulci melodia
circumferri dicuntur.

139

On the Ring Dance

Our choir of psalmists originates in the ring dance of singers that the ancients established for their idols, in order to praise their false gods in voice and serve them with their whole body. In the circular motion of their dance they wanted to express the revolution of the firmament; in the clasping of their hands, the binding of the elements; in the sound of the singers, the harmonious music of the spheres; in the gestures of their bodies, the motion of the zodiac signs; and in the clapping of their hands or the stamp of their feet, the crack of thunder.

Christians imitated this practice and converted it to the service of the true God. For we read that once the people of God had come through the Red Sea, they broke into a ring dance and Miriam sang before them with a timbrel, just as David danced mightily before the ark and sang psalms to the tune of his harp. Solomon also is said to have set up singers around the altar who made music with voice, trumpets, organs, cymbals, and harps. Thus, even to this day they use musical instruments in ring dances, because the heavenly spheres are said to revolve to a sweet melody. 2

140

De concordia chori

"Chorus" dicitur a concordia canentium, sive a corona circumstantium. Olim namque in modum coronae circa aras cantantes stabant, sed Flavianus et Diodorus episcopi choros alternatim psallere instituebant. Duo chori psallentium, designant angelos et spiritus iustorum, quasi reciproca voce Deum laudantium. Cancelli in quibus stant, mansiones multas in domo Patris designant. Quod aliquando de choro cum processione ad aliquod altare vadunt, et ibi in statione canunt, signat quod animae de hac vita exeuntes ad Christum perveniunt, et ibi in consortio angelorum Deo concinunt.

141

De corona

Corona ob tres causas in templo suspenditur. Una quod ecclesia per hanc decoratur, cum eius luminibus illuminatur. Alia quod eius visione admonemur, quia hi *coronam vitae* et

140

On the Harmony of the Choir

The word "choir" refers to the musical harmony of the singers, or to a ring of people standing around something. For in former times they sang standing around the altar in the form of a crown, until the bishops Flavian and Diodorus established the custom of antiphonal psalmody. The two choirs of singers signify the angels and the spirits of the just, who praise our Lord as it were in turns. The stalls in which they stand signify the many rooms in the Father's house. When they leave the choir in procession to an altar and sing a station there, it means that the souls who leave this life come to Christ and praise God together in company with the angels.

141

On the Crown Chandelier

A crown chandelier is hung in our temple for three reasons. One reason is to beautify the church, which is illuminated by its candles. Another reason is that when we see it,

lumen gaudii percipiunt, qui hic Deo devotae serviunt. Tertia ut caelestis Ierusalem nobis ad memoriam revocetur, ad cuius figuram facta videtur. Constat enim ex auro, argento, aere, et ferro. Aurum, sunt sapientia fulgentes; argentum, eloquentia nitentes; aes, in doctrina caelesti dulciter sonantes; ferrum, vitia domantes. Turres coronae sunt scriptis ecclesiam munientes, lucernae eius bonis actibus lucentes. Aurum etiam sunt martyres, argentum virgines, aes continentes, ferrum coniugio servientes. Gemmae in corona coruscantes, sunt quique in virtutibus rutilantes. Metalla in igne excocta ad ornatum coronae sumuntur, et electi in camino tribulationis probati, ad caelestis Ierusalem decorem eliguntur. Catena qua corona in altum continetur, est spes qua Ecclesia a terrenis ad caelestia suspenditur. Supremus circulus cui innectitur, est Deus a quo omnia continentur.

we are reminded that those who serve God with devotion in this life will one day see *the crown of life* and the light of joy. The third reason is to remind us of the heavenly Jerusalem, in whose image the chandelier is made. For it is made of gold, silver, bronze, and iron. The gold stands for those who are resplendent in wisdom; silver for those of brilliant eloquence; bronze for those of sweet-sounding doctrine; the iron for those who have conquered their vices. The towers of the chandelier are those who protect the Church with their writings; the torches are those who shine through their good works. The gold stands for the martyrs; the silver, the virgins; the bronze, the continent; the iron, those who serve their spouses. The gems in the chandelier sparkle like the coruscations of the virtues. Metals forged in flame are used to decorate the chandelier, just as the elect who are proven in the furnace of tribulation are chosen to decorate the heavenly Jerusalem. The chain that holds the chandelier aloft is hope, that virtue by which the Church on earth strains devotedly toward heavenly places. The higher circle to which it is attached is God, who upholds all things.

142

De campanis

Signa quae nunc per campanas dantur, olim per tubas dabantur. Haec vasa primum in Nola Campaniae sunt reperta, unde etiam sic sunt dicta. Maiora quippe vasa dicuntur "campanae" a Campania regione, minora "nolae" a civitate Nola. Campanae itaque praedicatores designant, qui populum ad ecclesiam convocant. Earum sonatio, est illorum praedicatio, quorum *sonus in omnem terram exivit, et in fines orbis terrae verba eorum*. Ex aere sunt fusae quod est durum et sonorum, quia praedicatio illorum contra vitia est dura, et de virtutibus sonora. Ideo autem in modum vasorum formantur, quia praedicatores vasa Spiritus sancti appellantur.

143

De turribus

Turres in quibus suspensae sonant, sunt duae leges quibus praedicatores a terrenis ad caelestia suspensi regnum Dei

142

On the Bells

The signals that were once given by trumpets are now given by bells. These contrivances were invented first in Nola in Campania, and thence they get their names. The larger ones are called *campanae* after the region of Campania, and the smaller are called *nolae,* after the city of Nola in Campania. Bells designate preachers, who call the people to the church. Their sounding is their preaching, and *their sound hath gone forth into all the earth, and their words unto the ends of the world.* They are forged from bronze, which is strong and sonorous, because their preaching against vices is strong, and they are sonorous in their virtues. They are formed in the shape of vessels because preachers are called vessels of the Holy Spirit.

143

On the Towers

The towers where the bells hang are the two Laws from which preachers, braced by the ground beneath and dan-

praedicant. Plectrum fit ex ferro, quod omnia dura domat, est illorum lingua quae omnia adversa superat. Vinculum quo ligatur, est moderatio qua illorum lingua temperatur. Funis quo campanae moventur ad sonandum, est Sacra Scriptura ex multis sententiis contexta, qua praedicatores moventur ad praedicandum. Funis a ligno descendit, et sacra scriptura a ligno Crucis et Dominicae Passionis descendit. Lignum a superioribus continetur, quia Crux et Passio Christi a prophetis ante praedicatur, et Evangelium legi conectitur, et apostolica doctrina prophetiae contexitur. Sacerdos funem apprehendit, dum scriptura docente bona opera peragit. Funis eum sursum trahit, dum scriptura eum in contemplatione suspendit. Funem ipse deorsum trahit, dum a contemplatione ad activam vitam descendit. Ex tractu funis campana sonat, quia ex bona operatione praedicatio intonat.

144

De campanario

Campanarium quod in alto locatur, est alta praedicatio quae de caelestibus loquitur. Non autem sine causa gallus super campanarium ponitur. Gallus enim dormientes

gling upward in their devotion to the divine, preach the kingdom of God. The clapper made of iron, the hardest of materials, is the preachers' tongue, which overcomes every adversity. The chain it hangs on is moderation, which governs their tongue. The rope that moves the bells is sacred scripture, woven of many verses, by which preachers are moved to preach. The rope descends from a wooden beam, and sacred scripture descends from the wood of the Cross and our Lord's Passion. The beam is held in place by pieces above it because the Cross and Passion of Christ is preached beforehand by the prophets, the Gospel follows from the Law in close connection, and the teaching of the apostles is interwoven with prophecy. The priest grabs the rope when he does the good works scripture teaches. The rope drags him upward, as scripture suspends him aloft in contemplation. He draws the rope down as he descends from contemplation to the active life. The bell rings when the rope is pulled, as the preacher rings out through his good works.

144

On the Belfry

The belfry that sits at such a height is an exalted style of preaching, which speaks of heavenly things. Not without good reason is a cock placed on the belfry. For the cock

excitat, et per hoc admonetur presbyter, gallus Dei, ut per campanam dormientes ad Matutinos excitet.

145

De statione

In ecclesia masculi in australi parte stant, signantes quod fortiores in fide ardore Spiritus sancti fervidi, praelati fieri debeant, qui aestum tentationum mundi ferre valeant. Feminae vero in boreali parte stant, demonstrantes quod fragiliores sub esse debeant, qui aestum tentationum ferre nequeant, atque nuptiali medicamine aestum carnis temperare.

146

De mulieribus

Mulieres quoque post partum ecclesiam non intrant, quia immundos a caelesti templo excludi designant.

rouses those who are sleeping, and this teaches the priest, God's cockerel, to rouse the sleeping for Lauds by the bell.

145

On Where the People Stand

The men stand on the south side of the church, signifying that those of strong faith who burn with the ardor of the Holy Spirit must be placed over the rest because they are able to weather the storm of the world's temptations. The women stand on the north side, demonstrating that the weaker must be subject, because they cannot bear the heat of temptation and so must apply the medicine of marriage to moderate the flesh's heat.

146

On the Women

Women do not enter the church after giving birth, because they signify the unclean who are excluded from the

Alioquin si prae infirmitate valerent, eadem die qua parerent intrare eis ecclesias liceret, ut Deo gratias agerent. Propter hanc significationem in multis locis menstruatae viris commixtae foris ecclesiam stare solent, et ob hoc paenitentes intrare ecclesiam non debent.

2   Linus papa ex praecepto beati Petri constituit, ut mulieres in ecclesia velatae sint, et hoc propter tres causas fit. Una est cum sint decipula diaboli, ne laxis earum crinibus iuvenum animi illaqueentur. Alia est ne quaedam illarum ob formositatem capillorum superbia eleventur, quaedam vero ne ob deformitatem illorum deturpentur. Tertia autem est, ut reatus originalis peccati qui per mulierem evenit, ad memoriam nobis revocetur. Iudex quippe malorum est Christus, sacerdos eius vicarius. Ante sacerdotem ergo debet se mulier velare velut rea, et tanti mali sibi conscia coram iudice se celare. Unde dicit Apostolus, ut mulier velata sit *propter angelos,* id est sacerdotes. In ecclesiis etiam non permittitur eis loqui, id est populum alloqui. Et nobis quoque non licet in ecclesia loqui, nisi *in hymnis et psalmis, et canticis spiritalibus,* et orare ut coniungamus caelestibus.

heavenly temple. If their health permits, however, they may enter the church to give thanks to God on the day they give birth. On account of this same signification, it is customary in many places for women who have had intercourse with men during their period to stand outside the church, and in penance for doing this they ought not to enter the church.

Pope Linus decreed that women be veiled in church, following the teaching of blessed Peter. This was done for three reasons. First, since they are a trap of the devil, lest the hearts of young men be ensnared by their free tresses. Secondly, lest some women be puffed up with pride on account of the beauty of their hair, and others, on the other hand, appear repulsive because of their ugliness. Thirdly, so that women may recall how the guilt of original sin came through a woman. Christ is the judge of the wicked and the priest is his vicar. Therefore a woman has to veil herself before the priest, and as a guilty woman conscious of so great a sin, to hide her shame before the judge. Thus when the Apostle says a woman ought to be veiled *on account of the angels,* he means priests. Additionally, they are not permitted to speak in church, which means to address the people. Neither are we allowed to speak in church except in *hymns, psalms, and spiritual canticles,* and prayers, so that we may be married to heavenly things. 2

147

De coemeterio

Coemeterium quod dicitur mortuorum dormitorium, est Ecclesiae gremium. Quia sicut saeculo mortuos de utero baptismatis Christo genuit, ita post modum carne mortuos gremio suo confovens aeternae vitae reddit. Ecclesiae quae in modum crucis fiunt, populum Ecclesiae *mundo crucifigi* debere ostendunt. Quae autem rotundae in modum circuli fiunt, Ecclesiam per circulum orbis in circulum coronae aeternitatis per dilectionem construi ostendunt.

148

De claustro

Claustralis constructio iuxta monasterium, est sumpta a porticu Salemonis constructa iuxta Templum, in qua apostoli omnes unanimiter commanebant, et in Templo ad orationem conveniebant, et *multitudinis credentium cor unum et anima una erat, et omnia communia habebant.* Secundum hanc

147

On the Cemetery

The cemetery, which means the dormitory of the dead, is the bosom of the Church. For just as she bore them dead to the world for Christ through the womb of baptism, likewise when they are dead in the flesh, she cradles them in her bosom and restores them to an eternal life. The cruciform shape of our churches shows us that the people of the Church must be *crucified to the world.* But the round ones made in the form of a circle show us that the Church throughout the whole circle of the world is being built up into the circle of an eternal crown through love.

148

On the Cloister

We build a cloister beside the minster on the model of Solomon's portico built next to the Temple, where the apostles all remained together and met in the Temple to pray, and *the multitude of believers had but one heart and one soul, and all things were common unto them.* Following this form, religious

JEWEL OF THE SOUL

formam religiosi in claustro unanimiter degunt, nocte ac die in monasterium ad servitium Dei conveniunt. Et fideles adhuc saecularia relinquunt, communem vitam in claustro ducunt.

149

Quod claustrum sit paradisus

Porro claustrum praefert paradisum, monasterium vero Eden scilicet sacratiorem paradisi locum. Fons in hoc loco voluptatis, est in monasterio fons baptismatis. Lignum vitae in paradiso, est corpus Domini in monasterio. Diversae arbores fructiferae, sunt libri diversi sacrae scripturae. Secretum etiam claustri, gerit figuram caeli, in qua iusti ita a peccatoribus segregantur, sicut religiosae vitae professores a saecularibus in claustro sequestrantur. Porro monasterium, praefert caelestem paradisum. Fons et lignum vitae signat Christum, qui est *fons vitae,* et cibus beatorum aeternaliter viventium. In monasterio duo chori laudes Deo concinunt, et in caelesti paradiso angeli atque sancti in saeculum saeculi dulci concentu Deum laudabunt. *Multitudo* in claustro conversantium *unum cor et unam animam* in religione habent, et *omnia communiter possident,* et in superna patria omnes electi *cor unum et animam unam* in dilectione habebunt, et *omnes*

live together in the cloister and meet night and day in the minster for the divine service. To this very day, some of the faithful abandon the things of this world and lead a common life in the cloister.

149

How the Cloister is Paradise

The cloister also signifies paradise, and the minster Eden, the more sacred part of paradise. The spring of pleasure in this part is the baptismal font in the monastery. The tree of life in paradise is the body of our Lord in the monastery. The sundry fruit trees are the various books of sacred scripture. The cloister's enclosure is a figure of heaven, where the just are separated from sinners just as professed religious are segregated from worldly men. Moreover, the minster presents us an image of the heavenly paradise. The fountain and the tree of life signifies Christ, who is *the fountain of life* and the food of the blessed in their state of eternal life. In the minster two choirs sing God's praises, and in the heavenly paradise the angels and saints will praise the Lord in sweet concert unto the ages of ages. *The multitude* of persons living in the cloister *have one heart and one mind* in religion and *possess all things in common,* and in the heavenly fatherland all the elect will *have one heart and one mind* in love, and

omnia communiter possidebunt, quia unusquisque quod in se minus habet, in aliis habebit, et *Deus omnia in omnibus erit.* In claustro singuli singula loca secundum ordinem tenent, et in paradiso singuli singulas mansiones secundum merita recipient.

150

De dedicatione ecclesiae

Ecclesiae dedicatio est Ecclesiae et Christi nuptialis copulatio. Episcopus qui eam consecrat, est Christus qui Ecclesiam desponsaverat. Episcopus fontem in atrio benedicit, et in circuitu aspergit, quia Christus fontem baptismatis in Iudaea consecravit, et in circuitu mundi omnes gentes eo ablui imperavit.

all will *possess all things in common* because whatever each one lacks he will find in others and *God will be all in all.* In the cloister each monk has his own place assigned to him, and in paradise each will receive his own rooms according to his merits.

150

On the Dedication of a Church

The dedication of a church is the nuptial union of Christ and the Church. The bishop who consecrates her is Christ, who had made the Church his betrothed. The bishop blesses the font in the atrium and then goes all around the Church sprinkling it with water, because Christ consecrated a baptismal font in Judaea and ordered all the nations all around the world to be washed in it.

151

De domo non consecrata

Domus non consecrata, et vectibus obserata, est gentilitas Dei ignara, et perfidiae repagulis inclusa. In domo duodecim candelae in circuitu accensae eam illuminant, et duodecim apostoli in circuitu orbis gentilitatem lumine doctrinae illustrabant. Candela *lucet et ardet,* et apostoli verbo lucebant, et caritate ardebant. Pontifex super liminare ostii cum baculo ter percutit, "*Tollite portas principes vestras et elevamini portae aeternales*" dicit. Per pontificem Christus, per baculum sceptrum potestatis intelligitur. Trina autem percussio, terna potestas in caelo, in terra, et in inferno accipitur. Quasi ergo ter Dominus ianuam capuita percussit, dum Ecclesiae potestatem ligandi atque solvendi in caelo et in terra concessit, et *portas inferi adversus eam non praevalere* tribuit. Iubet etiam ut *principes* tenebrarum *portas* mortis ab Ecclesia *tollant, portae* vero *aeternales,* id est caelestes, *eleventur* et *iusti* ad vitam *ingrediantur.*

151

On an Unconsecrated House

While the house stands unconsecrated and bolted shut, it is like the heathen world, ignorant of God and trapped behind the bars of unbelief. The twelve lit candles set around the church illuminate it, as the twelve apostles illuminated heathendom all around the world by the light of their doctrine. A candle *shines and burns,* and the apostles shone in the word and burned with charity. The bishop strikes the lintel of the door three times with his staff saying, *"Lift up your gates, O ye princes, and be ye lifted up, O eternal gates."* In the bishop we are to understand Christ, and in his staff the scepter of power. The threefold striking is his threefold power in heaven, on earth, and in hell. Thus our Lord struck the door three times with the crosier, as it were, when he gave the Church its power to bind and loose in heaven and on earth, and promised that *the gates of hell shall not prevail against it.* He also commands *the princes* of darkness to *remove the gates* of death from the Church and the *eternal*—that is, heavenly—*gates to be raised,* so that *the just may enter* into life.

152

De portis

Portae quippe mortis sunt vitia et peccata. Portae vitae sunt fides, baptisma, operatio. Per eum qui intus respondet, diabolus intelligitur, qui de domo Ecclesiae expellitur. Ipse quippe quasi *fortis armatus atrium suum custodivit,* dum hunc mundum quasi iure possedit. Sed *fortior superveniens* eum expulit, *spolia eius distribuit,* dum Christus *eum* Passione *vicit,* et Ecclesiam ab eius iure eripuit.

Mox ostium aperitur, et episcopus ingreditur, quia Ecclesia ostium fidei Christo aperuit, et eum intra se devote recepit. Episcopus ingrediens "Pax huic domui" dicit, quia Christus in mundum ingrediens pacem hominibus contulit, quam resurgens a mortuis suis praebuit, *"Pax,"* inquit, *"vobis."* Ter "Pax huic domui" clamat, quia reconciliationem Ecclesiae per Trinitatem factam insinuat, vel quia *unus est Deus, una fides, unum baptisma.*

2   Deinde pontifex prosternitur, pro consecratione domus Deum precatur, et Christus se ante Passionem in monte prostravit, et pro Ecclesiae sanctificatione Patrem oravit. Clerus litanias pro consecratione domus cantat, et apostoli atque doctores pro Ecclesiae sanctificatione patrocinia sanctorum invocabant.

152

On the Doors

The gates of death are, of course, the vices and sins. The gates of life are faith, baptism, and good works. The one who responds from within represents the devil, who is expelled from the house of the Church. For like *a strong-armed man he has guarded his court,* the world, which he *possesses* by right. But *one stronger than he arrived,* expelled him, and *distributed his spoils,* when Christ *conquered him* in his Passion and redeemed the Church from his right of possession.

Then the door is opened and the bishop enters, because the Church opened the door of faith to Christ and devoutly received him in her midst. Upon entering, the bishop says, "Peace be upon this house," because when he entered the world, Christ brought peace to mankind, and rising again from the dead, he offered it to his own saying, *"Peace be with you."* He shouts "Peace be upon this house" three times, showing that the Church has been reconciled through the Trinity, or because there is *one God, one faith, one baptism.*

Then the bishop prostrates himself and prays that the Lord's house may be consecrated, just as Christ prostrated himself on the mountain before his Passion, and prayed the Father for the Church's sanctification. The clergy sings the litany beseeching God to consecrate the house, and the apostles and doctors invoked the saints' patronage for the Church's sanctification.

Surgens pontifex populum per "Dominus vobiscum" non salutat, sed per "Flectamus genua" ad orationem invitat, quia infideles et impii non sunt salutandi, sed ad conversionem et paenitentiam provocandi.

153

De alphabeto

Post haec alphabetum in pavimento cum capuita scribit, incipiens a sinistro angulo orientali, in dextrum occidentalem desinit. Deinde aliud alphabetum a dextro angulo orientis inchoat, et sic scribendo in sinistro angulo occidentis consummat. Quae duo alphabeta in medio ecclesiae in formam crucis conveniunt, et quid mysticent nobis aperte innuunt.

Upon rising, the bishop does not greet the people with "The Lord be with you," but invites them to pray through "Let us kneel," because the unfaithful and impious should not be greeted but encouraged to conversion and penance.

153

On the Alphabet

Next he writes the alphabet on the pavement with his staff, starting from the left corner on the eastern side and ending on the right corner on the western side. Then he begins another alphabet from the right corner of the eastern side and finishes in the left corner of the western side. These two alphabets meet in the middle of the church in the form of a cross and it is clear what mystical sense we are to gather from them.

154

De quattuor angulis ecclesiae

Quattuor ecclesiae anguli, sunt quattuor plagae mundi. Scripturae quae terrae inscribitur, est simplex doctrina quae cordibus terrenorum primitur. A sinistro angulo episcopus scribere incipit, quia Christus a Iudaea incepit. Ipsa quippe sinistro angulo comparatur, quia ob perfidiam cum sinistris reputatur. Ideo angulus orientis dicitur, quia Christus qui est oriens in ea secundum carnem oritur. Scripturam in dextrum angulum episcopus deducit, quia doctrina Christi ad Ecclesiam usque pervenit. Ipsa quidem dextro angulo assimilatur, quia cum dextris computatur. Ideo autem angulus occidentis existit, quia in ea perfidia corruit, et Christus Sol iustitiae pro ea in morte occidit.

154

On the Four Corners of the Church

The four corners of the church are the four regions of the world. The writing inscribed in the pavement is basic doctrine, inscribed on the hearts of earthly people. The bishop begins to write from the left corner because Christ began to teach in Judaea. It is likened to the left corner because it is reckoned with those standing on the left. The eastern corner is so called because Christ who is the East originates from that part of the world according to the flesh. The bishop writes toward the right corner because Christ's doctrine comes to the Church. She is likened to the right corner because she is reckoned with those standing on the right. The western corner exists because unbelievers have fallen into that region, where also Christ, the sun of justice, went down in death for them.

155

De dextro angulo

Iterum episcopus scripturam a dextro angulo orientis inchoat, et in sinistro occidentis eam consummat, quia Christus doctrinam suam in primitiva Ecclesia inchoavit, et eam in fine mundi in Israelitico populo consummabit. Primitiva Ecclesia ideo dexter angulus dicitur, quia ipsa est regina quae a dextris Dei stare scribitur. Ideo angulus orientis dicitur, quia *lumen rectis* in ea *exoritur.* Populus autem Israel ideo sinister angulus vocatur, quia adhuc in infidelitate perdurare non verecundatur. Ideo vero angulus occidentis dicitur, quia occidente iam mundo post *plenitudinem gentium* Israel ad Christum convertitur. Duo alphabeta quae ex diversis angulis in forma crucis conveniunt, sunt duo populi qui ex diverso ritu in unam fidem Crucis per Christum convenerunt.

2 Duo etiam Testamenta sunt quae insimul coniuncta Crucem Passionis Christi ediderunt. Unum autem Graece, alterum Latine scribitur, quia Graeca lingua propter sapientiam, Latina autem ob imperialem potestatem aliis potentior cognoscitur, quae utraque ad fidem Crucis convertitur. Utraque vero per baculum scribuntur, quia haec omnia per praedicatores peraguntur.

Hucusque totum quod praecessit, quasi proemium consecrationis fuit. Abhinc dedicatio incipit, et ideo per hoc quod

155

On the Right Corner

Again, the bishop begins writing from the right corner on the eastern side and ends on the left on the western side, because Christ began his teaching in the early Church and will bring it to completion at the end of the world in the people of Israel. The right corner signifies the early Church because she is the queen who stands at God's right hand. She is called the eastern corner because *a light is risen up* in her *to the righteous.* The people of Israel are called the left corner because they still remain in their shameful infidelity. The western corner is so called because, as the world passes away and *the full number of the gentiles* has come in, Israel too will be converted to Christ. The two alphabets that run from the various corners in the form of a cross are the two peoples, who come from two different systems of worship into the one faith of the Cross through Christ. Further- 2 more, there are two Testaments that when coupled together erect the Cross of Christ's Passion. One alphabet is written in Greek, the other in Latin, because the Greek language is prestigious on account of wisdom, but Latin on account of the imperial power, and both are converted to the faith of the Cross. Both are written with a staff because all of these things are carried out by preachers.

Everything that has been done up to this point has been a preface to the consecration. Now the dedication of the

sequitur, Christi Passio et Spiritus sancti effusio innuitur, per quae Ecclesia Catholica consecratur.

156

De illo *Deus in adiutorium*

Post haec pontifex ante altare stans, divinum auxilium per versum *Deus in adiutorium meum intende* invocat, ut domum eius nomini digne consecrare valeat. *Gloria Patri* absque alleluia subiungitur, quia gloriam Trinitatis in illa domo cantari innotescit. Alleluia non addit, eo quod adhuc ad *vocem exultationis* consecrata non sit. Post consecrationem autem alleluia cantabitur, quia exclusa iam omni daemonum phantasia Deus in ea laudabitur. Ita Christus verus pontifex ad aram Crucis accedens, Patris auxilium invocavit, quo Ecclesiam sanctificare velit. Quasi *Gloria Patri* cecinit, dum ad gloriam Trinitatis mortem pro Ecclesia subiit. Quasi alleluia non addit, dum totus mundus in eius Passione turbatus fuit. Post Resurrectionem autem, quasi post consecrationem, alleluia cantabatur, quia caelum et terra de eius Resurrectione laetabatur.

church begins, and so what follows signifies Christ's Passion and the outpouring of the Holy Spirit, through which the Church Catholic is consecrated.

156

On the *Deus in adiutorium*

After these things, the bishop stands before the altar and invokes God's help in the verse *O God, come to my assistance* that he may be able to consecrate the house worthily to God's name. He adds *Gloria Patri* without an alleluia, showing that in this house glory is sung to the Trinity. He does not add an alleluia because the house has not been consecrated yet to *the voice of exultation*. After the consecration, however, the alleluia will be sung because once every influence of demons has been cast out God will be praised in it. Likewise Christ, our true bishop, went up to the altar of the Cross and invoked his Father's aid, that he might deign to sanctify the Church thereby. He sang a sort of *Gloria Patri* when he suffered death for the Church to the glory of the Holy Trinity. He did not add an alleluia, as it were, when the whole world was thrown into confusion by his Passion. But after his Resurrection, as after a consecration, the alleluia was sung because heaven and earth rejoiced in his Resurrection.

157

De sale et cinere

Deinde aqua benedicitur, vinum admiscetur, sal quoque et cinis commiscentur. Per sal quo omnes cibi sapidi fiunt, Christus Dei sapientia designatur qua omnes sapere et intelligere acceperunt. Unde Eliseus sal in aquam misit, et sanatae sunt, quia Deus sapientiam id est Filium suum in homines misit et sanati sunt. In lege autem vitula rufa missa est igne cremari, et populi eius cinere expiari. Vitula rufa in expiationem populi in cinerem cremata, est Christi caro sanguine rubricata, igne Passionis in cinerem redacta, quo plebs fidelium est expiata. Hic cinis sali admiscetur, dum humanitas a divinitate in resurrectione resumitur. Cinis quoque sali commiscetur, dum nos Christiani qui cinis sumus et Ecclesia nominamur, divinitati Christi associamur.

157

On the Salt and Ashes

Then water is blessed, wine is added, and salt and ashes are mixed in. Salt, which makes all foods flavorful, signifies Christ as God's Wisdom, through whom all are given wisdom and understanding. Elisha cast salt in water and the waters were made clean because God cast Wisdom, his Son, into mankind and they were healed. In the Law a red calf was burned in fire, and the people expiated their sins with its ashes. The red calf burned to ashes to expiate the people's sins is Christ's flesh, reddened with blood and reduced to ashes by the fire of his Passion, by which the faithful people are redeemed. This ash is mixed with salt when humanity is taken up into divinity at the resurrection. Ash is also mixed with salt when we Christians, who are ash and are called the Church, are brought to share in Christ's divinity.

158

De vino et aqua

Item per vinum divinitas, per aquam intelligitur humanitas. Haec duo commiscentur, dum nostra humanitas per Christi sanguinem divinitati adiungitur. Ter crux cum sale et cinere super aquam fit, quia per Crucem Christus hominibus fidem Trinitatis impressit. Porro per haec singula sacrificium Ecclesiae exprimitur, quod in hac domo dedicata offertur; per sal et cinerem Christi corpus in divinitate praefiguratur, per vinum et aquam Christi sanguis qui cum aqua conficitur praenotatur.

159

De templo

Notandum quod hoc totum ad hominem refertur, qui *templum Dei* appellatur.

Primum pontifex ostium aperit, deinde preces fundit, post haec alphabetum scribit, deinde aquam cum sale et cinere benedicit, vinum admiscet, deinde ungit. Ita cuilibet ad

158

On the Wine and Water

Similarly, wine stands for divinity, and water for humanity. When the two are mixed, our humanity is joined to divinity through Christ's blood. Three times the sign of the Cross is made with the salt and ashes over the water because through his Cross Christ taught the Trinitarian faith to mankind. Further, through each of these things we indicate the Church's sacrifice, offered in this consecrated house: through salt and ashes, the body of Christ is prefigured in its divinity; through the wine and water we symbolize Christ's blood, which is confected with an admixture of water.

159

On the Temple

One must understand that this whole rite refers also to the individual man, who is *God's temple*.

First the bishop opens the door, then offers prayers, writes the alphabet, blesses water with salt and ashes, adds wine, then anoints the altar. In a similar way, the door of

Deum converso ostium fidei aperitur, deinde pro eo oratur, deinde scriptura menti eius inscribitur, dum catechumenus exorcismis imbuitur, exin per fidem Christi divinitatem et humanitatem docetur, deinde fonte baptismatis purificatur, ad extremum chrismate unguitur, et sic templum Dei efficitur.

160

De altari et cruce

Post haec sacerdos digitum tinguit, et crucem per quattuor cornua altari facit. Altare hic primitivam Ecclesiam in Ierusalem exprimit. Quasi crucem Christus pontifex super altare fecit, dum Crucem in Ierusalem pro Ecclesia subiit. Quattuor cornua altaris signavit, dum quattuor partes mundi Cruce salvavit. Deinde septies contra altare spargit, quia Christus post Resurrectionem in septem donis Spiritus sancti Ecclesiam baptizari iussit. Aqua cum hyssopo aspergitur, quae amara herba duritiam lapidum penetrare fertur, et signat Christi carnem in Passione amaricatam, per quam baptismus datur, et duritia gentilium ad fidem emollitur. Deinde altare spargendo circuit, quia Dominus *angelum*

faith is opened to everyone who turns to seek God, prayers are offered for him, scripture is etched in his heart, as a catechumen he is taught through the exorcisms, and through the Creed he is shown Christ's divine and human natures; then he is purified in the baptismal font, and finally he is anointed with the chrism, and in this way he becomes a temple of God.

160

On the Altar and Cross

After these things, the priest dips his finger into the oil and makes a sign of the Cross over the four corners of the altar. Now the altar represents the early Church in Jerusalem. Christ the bishop made a cross over the altar when he took up the Cross for the Church in Jerusalem. He signed the four corners of the altar when he saved the four parts of the world by his Cross. Then the bishop sprinkles the altar seven times because after his Resurrection Christ ordered the Church to be baptized in the seven gifts of the Holy Spirit. Water is sprinkled using hyssop, a bitter herb that is said to be able to penetrate hard stone, and it signifies the flesh of Christ made bitter in the Passion, whence baptism is given to us, and the stony hearts of the gentiles are softened to receive the faith. Next he circles the altar while

suum in circuitu timentium se mittit. Altare ter respergitur, quia Ecclesia a tribus peccatis mortis, scilicet operis, locutionis, cogitationis emundatur. Deinde per totam ecclesiam vadit, parietes ex utraque parte spargit, quia Christus per totam Iudaeam populum baptizari praecepit. Interim canitur psalmus *Exurgat Deus,* quia dum Christus resurrexit, daemones et Iudaei *inimici eius dissipati sunt.* Et cum Christi Resurrectio et Baptismus per mundum praedicabatur, inimici Dei ab Ecclesia dissipabantur.

161

De ministris

Pontifex mittit ministros qui ecclesiam cantando circueant, et Christus apostolos misit, qui baptismum per totum mundum praedicabant. Episcopus per mediam ecclesiam incedens cantat antiphonam "*Domus mea,*" et Christus Ecclesiam per doctores visitans, fecit eam domum suam. Incipiens autem antiphonam *Introibo* et psalmum *Iudica me Deus* vadit canendo ad altare et quod remansit de aqua ad basim altaris fundit, quia Christus fluenta doctrinae in Ierusalem effudit, et inde fons baptismatis erupit. Post haec altare

sprinkling it, because our Lord *sends his angel round about them that fear him*. The altar is sprinkled three times because the Church is cleansed of three deadly sins, namely sins of thought, word, and deed. Next he goes through the whole church sprinkling the walls on both sides, because Christ commanded the people to be baptized throughout all Judaea. Meanwhile the Psalm *Exurgat Deus* is sung because when Christ *rose* the demons and his Jewish *enemies were scattered,* and because when Christ's Resurrection and Baptism were preached throughout the world the enemies of God were scattered by the Church.

161

On the Ministers

The bishop sends the ministers to compass the church while singing, because Christ sent the apostles to preach his baptism to the whole world. Proceeding to the middle of the church, the bishop sings the antiphon "*My house,*" and Christ made the Church his home by visiting it in the person of the doctors. Having begun the antiphon *Introibo* and psalm *Iudica me Deus,* he goes to the altar singing and pours what is left of the water at the altar's base, because Christ poured the rivers of his doctrine into Jerusalem, and thence the spring of baptism gushed forth. Next the altar is wiped

cum linteo extergitur, per quod Dominica Passio intelligitur. Linum quippe de terra oritur et cum labore ad candorem convertitur, et Christus de virgine nascitur, et cum magno Passionis labore ad candorem Resurrectionis redditur. Hoc linteo altare extergitur, dum tribulatio Ecclesiae exemplo Passionis Christi delinitur. Deinde offertur incensum, hoc sunt orationes iustorum, qui se in odorem Deo offerunt, dum corpus suum pro eo affligunt.

162

De altari et oleo

Postea pontifex fundit oleum super altare faciens crucem in medio eius super quattuor cornua eius, quia Christus Spiritum sanctum super primitivam Ecclesiam in Ierusalem effudit, in qua et crucem subiit, deinde per quattuor mundi partes haec dona fidelibus tribuit. Tunc cantetur antiphona *Erexit Iacob lapidem in titulum.* "*Lapis*" unctus, fuit Christus Spiritu sancto a Patre scilicet *oleo laetitiae* unctus. *Hic in caput anguli est factus,* dum uterque populus in eo est coniunctus. Ter altare unguitur, bis oleo, tertio chrismate, quia Ecclesia insignitur fide, spe, caritate. Fuso autem oleo cantatur

dry with a linen cloth, which signifies our Lord's Passion. For linen comes from the earth and is made white through much labor, and just so Christ is born of a virgin and through the great suffering of his Passion attains the whiteness of the Resurrection. The altar is wiped off with this linen when the example of Christ's Passion gives an outline of the Church's tribulation. Then incense is offered, and this is the prayers of the just, who offer themselves to God as a fragrance when they afflict their bodies for his sake.

162

On the Altar and the Oil

Next the bishop pours oil over the altar, making a cross through the center and over its four corners, because Christ poured out the Holy Spirit over the early Church in Jerusalem, where he took up the Cross, then distributed these gifts to the faithful throughout the four parts of the world. Then the antiphon *Erexit lapidem Iacob in titulum* is sung. The "*stone*" he anointed was Christ, whom the Father anointed with the Holy Spirit, who is the *oil of gladness. He became the cornerstone* when both peoples were joined in him. The altar is anointed three times, twice with oil and a third time with the chrism, because the Church is marked with faith, hope, and charity. Once the oil has been poured the

responsorium *Ecce odor filii mei sicut odor agri pleni.* "*Ager*" latitudo mundi intelligitur, per quem Ecclesia ubique diffunditur. Hic ager vernat floribus, dum Ecclesia resplendet virtutibus. "*Odor*" florum, est fragrantia bonorum operum. Rosae sunt martyres, lilia virgines, violae saeculi contemptores; virides herbae sapientes, floridae proficientes, fructibus plenae animae profectae.

163

De chrismate

Deinde per parietes ecclesiae crucem de chrismate facit cum pollice, incipiens a dextro latere usque in sinistrum, quia unctio chrismatis a primitiva Ecclesia incipiens, pervenit in Ecclesiam gentium. Interim cantatur antiphona *Sanctificavit Dominus tabernaculum.* Ecclesia nunc est Dei tabernaculum in huius mundi itinere, quae postea erit templum in perventione. Deinde antiphona *Lapides pretiosi.* "*Lapides pretiosi*" sunt qui sacras scripturas ediderunt. "*Muri et turres*" Ierusalem, sunt munitiones scripturarum, quibus arcentur Iudaei, haeretici, atque pagani. "*Gemmae*" sunt sacrae sententiae.

responsory *Ecce odor filii mei sicut odor agri pleni* is sung. The "*field*" is the whole compass of the world where the Church is everywhere diffused. This field is verdant with flowers, and the Church is resplendent in the virtues. The flowers' "*perfume*" is the fragrance of good works. The roses are the martyrs, the lilies the virgins, the violets those who give up the world; the green plants are the wise, the flowery ones the proficient, and those that are heavy with fruits are the souls of the perfect.

163

On the Chrism

Next he uses his thumb to make crosses with the chrism on the church walls, moving from the right side to the left, because the unction of chrism began in the early Church and reached the Church of the gentiles. Meanwhile the antiphon *Sanctificavit Dominus tabernaculum* is sung. Now the Church is God's tabernacle in this earthly journey, but will become a temple when it reaches the place of rest. Next the antiphon *Lapides pretiosi.* The "*precious stones*" are those who wrote the holy scriptures. "*The walls and towers* of Jerusalem" are the ramparts of scripture, which hold off the Jews, heretics, and pagans. Its "*gems*" are the sacred commentaries.

164

De incenso

Tunc pontifex crucem incensi super altare facit, et se ad orationem submittit. Christus quoque pontifex pontificum incensum crucis super aram ponit, quia apud Patrem pro nobis intervenit. Crucem namque incensi facere, est Passionem suam pro Ecclesia Patri ostendere, et pro nobis interpellare. Unde pontifex incipit antiphona *Confirma hoc Deus* cum *Gloria Patri,* quia Christus Patrem pro Ecclesia exorat, ut redemptionem *quam ipse operatus est in ea confirmet,* et omnem terram ei subiiciat. Unde haec gratia processerit, subdit: *a templo sancto tuo, quod est in Ierusalem.* In Ierusalem quippe salvatio humani generis coepit, et inde in totum mundum manavit. Ierusalem est et Ecclesia in qua templum est Christo, in quo *habitavit plenitudo divinitatis corporaliter,* quae inde per Spiritum sanctum effusa humano generi profluxit largiter. *Gloria Patri* additur, quia hanc salvationem Trinitas operatur, et Trinitati laus et gloria proinde canitur.

164

On Incense

Then the bishop makes a cross of incense grains over the altar and gives himself over to prayer. Christ also, bishop of bishops, makes a cross of incense over the altar because he intercedes for us with his Father. For him to make a cross with incense is for him to show his Passion to the Father on the Church's behalf and to intercede for us. Thus the bishop begins the antiphon *Confirma hoc Deus* along with the *Gloria Patri* because Christ implores the Father on behalf of his Church that he may *confirm in her his work* of redemption and submit the whole world to her dominion. The antiphon continues, specifying where this grace comes from: *from your holy temple, which is in Jerusalem.* In Jerusalem the work of mankind's salvation was begun, and from there spread out to the whole earth. For Jerusalem is also the Church, in which is Christ's temple, in whom *all the fullness of the Godhead dwelt corporeally,* whence it flooded out to the whole human race through the outpouring of the Holy Spirit. He adds *Gloria Patri* because the Trinity worked this salvation, and that is why we sing glory and honor to the Trinity.

165

De vasis et ornamentis

Post haec subdiaconus vel acolythi vasa, linteamina, et omnia ornamenta offerunt pontifici benedicenda. Sunt hi qui ornatui Ecclesiae eliguntur, et ad servitium Ecclesiae ab episcopo consecrantur, et vasa Dei dicuntur. His peractis vadit episcopus in eum locum in quo reliquiae praeterita nocte cum vigiliis fuerunt, et elevat eas portans ad locum praeparatum. Ita Christus verus pontifex post quam nobis praeparavit locum, iustos qui in praesenti nocte se vigili mente a malo custodiunt assumit de locis suis, et perducit eos in domum sui Patris. Unde cantatur antiphona *"Ambulate sancti Dei, ingredimini civitatem Dei,"* id est caelestem Ierusalem. Quod autem sequitur, *"vobis aedificata est nova ecclesia,"* haec est Ierusalem nova *quae aedificatur ut civitas.* Diversae antiphonae quae cantantur, tripudium et exultationem angelicarum Virtutum imitantur, qui exeuntes de corpore animas comitantur usquequo pro meritis sibi debitis mansionibus recipiantur. Veniens pontifex ante altare ubi reliquiae sunt reconditae, extendit velum inter se et populum, quia loca animarum secreta sunt a visione mortalium.

165

On Vessels and Ornaments

After all these things, the subdeacons or acolytes offer the vessels, linens, and all the vestments to the bishop to be blessed. They represent the clergy who have been chosen to adorn the Church and are consecrated to her service by the bishop, and they are called God's vessels. Then the bishop goes to the place where the relics were kept during the vigil of the previous night, and raising them aloft he carries them to the place prepared for them. Just so Christ, the true bishop, after preparing a place for us, takes the just, those who guard themselves from evil with a vigilant mind during the night of this present life, from their places and leads them into the house of his Father. Thus we sing the antiphon *"Walk, O saints of God, enter the city of God,"* which is the heavenly Jerusalem. The following phrase, *"a new church is built for you,"* refers to the new Jerusalem, *built as a city.* We sing several antiphons, imitating the joy and exultation of the angelic Virtues, who accompany souls as they leave their bodies, conducting them unto the heavenly habitations they have merited. Coming before the altar where the relics are to be placed, the bishop draws a veil between himself and the people because the places where souls dwell are hidden from mortal sight.

166

De reliquiis sanctorum

Reliquiae in altari sigillantur, quia animae in caelestibus collocantur. Cantatur *"Exultabunt sancti in gloria,"* quia animae ovant in angelica curia.

167

De veste animarum

Post haec altare vestitur, quia animae in resurrectione corporibus vestiuntur. Nudum erat altare, dum animae sine corporibus in caelis fuerant collocatae. Altare vestitur, dum anima immortali et incorruptibili corpore induetur.

166

On Saints' Relics

Relics are sealed in the altar because the holy souls are settled in heaven. The antiphon "*The saints shall rejoice in glory*" is sung because the souls celebrate their triumph in the angelic court.

167

On the Soul's Vestments

Next the altar is dressed because in the resurrection souls are dressed once more in their bodies. The altar was bare while the souls were placed in heaven without bodies. The altar is dressed when the soul is clothed in the immortal and incorruptible body.

168

De die iudicii

Post haec pontifex altare benedicit, et Christus Ecclesiam his verbis benedicit: *"Venite, benedicti Patris mei, percipite regnum."* Pontifex revertitur in sacrarium cum ordinibus suis, et induit se vestimentis aliis, et Christus revertitur in mundum ad iudicium cum ordinibus angelicis. Aliis induitur vestimentis, quia *servile formam* praesentabit impiis, cum *videbunt in quem transfixerunt,* et iusti *regem* gloriae *in decore suo videbunt.* Deinde ornatur ecclesia, et accenduntur luminaria, quia tunc opera iustorum splendescunt, pro quibus ornati perenniter *ut sol fulgebit.* Tunc incipit cantor *Terribilis est locus iste.* Quid enim terribilius illa die, quando angeli timebunt, et impii in aeternum supplicium ibunt? Tunc procedit pontifex sollemniter, et fit officium cum omni laetitia, quia peracto iudicio *videbitur* Deus *facie ad faciem* in gloria sua, et *erit Deus omnia in omnibus,* et ut lux oculis, sic gaudium animabus.

168

On the Day of Judgment

Next the bishop blesses the altar, and Christ blesses his Church with these words, "*Come, ye blessed of my Father, receive the kingdom.*" The bishop returns to the sacristy with the sacred ministers and puts on other vestments, and Christ returns with the orders of angels to judge the world. He puts on other vestments because he will appear *in the form of a slave* to the impious when *they look on the one they have pierced,* while the just *shall see the king* of glory *in his beauty.* Next the church is decorated and the lamps are lit because the good works wreathing the just will *blaze forth* forever *like the sun.* Then the cantor begins *Terribilis est locus iste.* For what is more terrible than that day when the angels will tremble and the impious go to their eternal punishment? Then the bishop goes forth in solemn procession and the service is performed with great joy because at the end of the judgment God *will be seen face to face* in his glory, and *God will be all in all,* and joy will suffuse the blessed souls as light fills the eye.

169

De certo loco et sacrificio

Igitur sicut in Ecclesia dedicata rite Missa celebratur, sic in Catholica Ecclesia legitime sacrificatur, et extra hanc nullum sacrificium a Deo acceptatur. Et quamvis Deus ubique sive in agro, seu in eremo, vel in mari, vel *in omni loco dominationis eius* iuste possit ac debeat, benedici et invocari, utputa in templo totius mundi, tamen iure opportuno tempore ad ecclesiam a fidelibus curritur, ut ibi Deus invocetur atque adoretur, in qua omnem rem quam duo ex consensu petierint, se daturum pollicetur, et ubi ipse duobus vel tribus in nomine eius congregatis interesse perhibetur. Iustum quippe est ut Christianus populus in oratorium, quasi ad praetorium conveniat, iudicia ac mandata aeterni Regis audiat, atque de convivio vituli saginati percipiat. Cum ergo populus in ecclesiam congregatur, quasi templum Deo ad inhabitandum aedificatur. Ecclesia autem in ecclesia, est plebs Christiana in aula dedicata. Templum quoque est in templo, baptizatus quilibet in domo consecrata.

169

On the Place of Sacrifice

Likewise, just as the Mass is properly celebrated in a dedicated church, so all legitimate sacrifice is offered in the Catholic Church, and no sacrifice made outside it is accepted by God. Though God can and justly must be blessed and invoked everywhere, in the fields, in the desert, on the sea, and *in every place of his dominion,* to wit in the temple of the whole world, nevertheless it is right that the faithful have recourse to the church at certain times, where they may invoke and adore God who has promised to give them anything that two together may ask of him, and where he promises to be present with *two or three gathered in his name.* Just, indeed, it is for the Christian people to convene in an oratory, as if in a praetorium, to hear the judgments and mandates of the eternal King and to join in the banquet of the fatted calf. Accordingly, when the people do congregate at the church, it is as if they build a temple for God to dwell in. The Christian people in the dedicated hall are a Church within a church, just as every baptized person in a consecrated house is a temple within a temple.

170

De violata ecclesia

Si ecclesia homicidio vel adulterio violatur, iterum dedicatur, ita si homo Spiritus sancti templum in baptismate dedicatum criminali peccato violatur, necesse est ut denuo fonte lacrimarum renovetur. Si sigillum altaris amovetur, est praeceptum ut iterum consecretur; ita si sigillum fidei ab altari cordis aliqua haeresi amovetur, oportet ut denuo per paenitentiam reconcilietur. Si principale altare movetur, est decretum ut ecclesia denuo consecretur. Ita si episcopus princeps Ecclesiae a fide ad haeresim mutatur, tota plebs ei subiecta commaculatur, et ideo convenit, ut cum eo paenitentia et satisfactione ad Catholicam fidem recipiatur. Quae autem violata non denuo consecrata fuerit, immunda et canibus pervia erit; ita si homo templum Dei scilicet seipsum mortali crimine violaverit, atque per paenitentiam denuo non remundaverit, daemonibus habitatio erit. Interfecti ideo in ecclesiam non portantur, ne sanguine pavimentum maculetur. Ob hanc etiam causam putant quidam mulieres in partu defunctas, in ecclesiam non esse deferendas, quod tamen fieri licet.

170

On a Desecrated Church

If a church is desecrated by an act of murder or adultery it is dedicated anew, just as when a man, a temple of the Holy Spirit dedicated through baptism, is desecrated by a criminal sin, he must be renewed once more in the font of tears. If the altar's seal is removed, it must be reconsecrated; and likewise, when the seal of faith is removed from the heart's altar by heresy, it must be reconciled through penance. If the principal altar is moved, it is decreed that the church must be reconsecrated. Likewise, when the bishop, the prince of the Church, is moved from faith to heresy, the whole people subject to him are stained with his fault, and so it is fitting that they be received back into the Catholic faith along with him after a process of penance and satisfaction. But should a desecrated church not be reconsecrated, it should be held as a place unclean and a haunt for dogs; likewise when a man, a temple of God, desecrates himself by a criminal sin and does not make himself clean through penance, he will become a demons' dwelling place. Bodies of people recently killed are not brought into church, so that the pavement is not stained with their blood. For the same reason some think that women who die in childbirth should not be brought into the church, but in fact it is permitted.

171

De constructione ecclesiae

Itaque bonum est ecclesias aedificare, constructas vasis, vestibus, aliisque ornamentis decorare, sed multo melius est eosdem sumptus in usus indigentium expendere, et censum suum *per manus pauperum in caelestes thesauros* praemittere, ibique *domum non manufactam, sed aeternam in caelis* praeparare, in qua possit cum angelis aeternaliter habitare.

Sciendum autem quod loca sancta non salvant, quos prava opera ab Ecclesia separant, nec item horrida loca his obsunt, qui pie vivunt. Nadab quippe et Abiu sacerdotes in tabernaculo Dei igne consummuntur, Chore, Dathan, et Abiron ante tabernaculum a terra deglutiuntur. Heli pontifex in loco sancto fracta cervice periit, Oza iuxta arcam percussus interiit. Ioab iuxta aram occiditur, Ozias rex in Templo lepra perfunditur. Postremum Templum violatum subruitur, populus legis praevaricator ab eo captivus ducitur. Econtra Ioseph in cisterna et in carcere non periit. Moyses in fluvio necem non subiit. Iob in sterquilinio, et Ieremias non interiit in caeno. Daniel in lacu leonum, tres pueri non laeduntur in camino ignium. Petrus in carcere, Paulus non periit in mari. Immo diabolus de caelo, homo cecidit de

171

On the Construction of a Church

It is very good to build churches and to contribute vessels, vestments, and other ornaments for their decoration, but it is much better to expend the same means for the relief of the poor, and to dispatch one's wealth *through the hands of the poor* for deposit *in the heavenly treasury,* and there to make ready *a house not made with hands, eternal in heaven,* where he will live forever with the angels.

Mark you, however, that holy places do not save those whose wicked works cut them off from the Church, while not even the most dreadful places hinder those who live a pious life. For the priests Nadab and Abihu were consumed by fire in God's tabernacle, while Korah, Dathan, and Abiram were swallowed up by the earth in front of the tabernacle. The high priest Eli's neck was broken in the holy place, and Uzzah was struck down by the ark. Joab was killed next to the altar, and King Uzziah was covered with leprosy in the Temple. Finally, the Temple itself was desecrated and destroyed, and the people were led away into captivity as violators of the Law. On the other hand, Joseph did not perish in the cistern or in prison. Moses was not drowned in the river. Job did not die on his dung heap nor Jeremiah in his muddy cistern. No harm came to Daniel in the lions' den nor to the three young men in the furnace. Peter survived prison, and Paul did not perish on the sea. Indeed, the devil fell even

paradiso. Iusti autem in terra a Deo visitantur, de inferno ad caelestia sublevantur.

172

De ministris ecclesiae

De ecclesia quod Deus dedit, iam diximus, superest ut de ministris ecclesiae dicamus.

Ecclesia itaque usum sacerdotum et ministrorum de Synagoga accepit, quos primum Moyses ex praecepto Domini in ministerio tabernaculi constituit. Deinde David et Salemon nihilominus ex iussu Domini cantores et Levitas in Templo dedicaverunt, quos apostoli secuti ministros Ecclesiae in Christiana religione disposuerunt.

from heaven, and man from paradise. But God visits the just of the earth and, raising them out of hell, places them in heaven.

172

On the Ministers of the Church

Concerning the church, we have now said what God gave us: it remains for us to speak about the church's ministers.

Now the Church took the use of priests and ministers from the Synagogue, where Moses had established them to minister in the tabernacle in obedience to God's command. Thereafter David and Solomon, equally by the Lord's command, arranged for cantors and Levites in the Temple, and the apostles imitated them when they established ministers in the Christian religion.

173

De Christianis

Christiani autem a Christo dicuntur, et hi in tria scilicet in laicos, in monachos, in clericos dividuntur. *Loas* dicitur populus, inde "laici," id est populares. *Monas* dicitur singularitas, inde monachi, id est singulariter degentes.

174

De clericis

Cleros dicitur sors vel hereditas, inde "clerici," id est sortiti, scilicet ad hereditatem Domini. Ipsi enim decimam et sacrificia accipiunt, quae ideo pars vel hereditas Dei dicuntur, quia ex praecepto Dei in servitium Dei offeruntur. Idcirco vero a sorte clerici appellantur, quia sacerdotes in lege sorte eligebantur. Et apud gentiles qui plures liberos habuit, unum ad clericatum sorte elegit. Omnes autem Ecclesiae ministri dicuntur clerici, sed sunt in septem gradus dispositi, quia a septiformi Spiritu sunt consecrati. Sunt autem hi: ostiarii, lectores, exorcistae, acolythi, subdiaconi, diaconi, presbyteri.

173

On Christians

Christians take their name from Christ, and are divided into laity, monks, and clerics. *Laos* means people, whence we have "laity," meaning the people. *Monas* means solitude. Hence monks are those who live the solitary life.

174

On Clerics

Cleros means choice and inheritance. Hence we have the word "clerics," which means chosen by lot, namely for the Lord's inheritance. For they collect the tithes and offerings, which are called God's portion and inheritance because they are contributed at God's command for the maintenance of the divine services. The clergy take their name from the word for lot, moreover, because the priests of the law were chosen by lot. Among the gentiles, families with several children chose one for the priesthood, also by lot. All Church ministers are called clerics, but they are arranged in seven orders, since they are consecrated by the sevenfold Spirit. They are the following: porters, lectors, exorcists, acolytes, subdeacons, deacons, presbyters.

175

De ostiariis

Qui in Synagoga ianitores vel aeditui dicebantur, in Ecclesia ostiarii nuncupantur. Illorum autem officium in lege erat, quod Templum ut Samuel aperiebant vel claudebant, et de Iudaeis pollutos, de gentibus autem immundos, id est incircumcisos de domo Dei excludebant. In Ecclesia autem hoc officium habent, ut catechumenos baptizandos in ecclesiam introducant, et paenitentes per episcopum reconciliatos in ostio accipiant, et in domum Dei reducant. Dum hi ordinantur, claves ecclesiae eis ab episcopo traduntur, ut videlicet credentibus ianuas ecclesiae aperiant, incredulis claudant, et templum Dei quod ipsi sunt virtutibus aperiant, vitiis claudant.

176

De lectoribus

Qui in Templo erant cantores, apud nos sunt lectores. Illorum officium erat hymnos a David compositos vel cantica

175

On Porters

The men who were called janitors or doormen in the Synagogue are called porters in the Church. In the Law their duty was to open and close the Temple like Samuel, and to bar Jews who were ritually defiled and gentiles, who were uncircumcised and hence unclean, from entering God's house. In the Church their duty is to lead the catechumens into the church for baptism and to receive at the door the penitents who have been reconciled by the bishop, leading them back into God's house. When they are ordained, the bishop hands them the keys of the church, so that they may open the church's doors to believers and close them to unbelievers, and unlock the temple of their bodies to the virtues and close them to vices.

176

On Lectors

The men who were called cantors in the Temple are called lectors among us. Their duty in the Temple was, as with

a Salemone edita in Templo ut Asaph et Idithun resonare, et organis vel cymbalis Deo iubilare. In Ecclesia autem illorum est officium divinam scripturam recitare, et responsoria vel Gradalia vel Alleluia singulariter coram populo ad laudem Dei cantare. Dum hi ordinantur, liber eis ab episcopo traditur, ut videlicet operibus impleant, quae populo de libris pronuntiant. Est autem praecentor qui praecinit, succentor qui cantum subsequitur, centor vel cantor qui consonat, psalmista qui psalmos pronuntiat, symmista, id est secretarius vel secreti conscius, qui mysteria Christi explicat.

177

De exorcistis

"Exorcista" dicitur adiurator. Hi Salemone docente daemones adiurabant, et eos de obsessis hominibus expellebant, ut septem filii Scevae sacerdotis faciebant. In Ecclesia autem habent officium infantes catechizandos exorcizare, et per verbum Dei templa Dei, id est baptizandorum corpora daemonibus interdicere, ac de energuminis, id est de obsessis corporibus per exorcismos daemonia arcere. Et his codex ab episcopo traditur dum ordinantur, ut videlicet monita librorum impleant, quo daemones ab aliis expellere valeant.

Asaph and Jeduthun, to sing the hymns David composed
and the songs Solomon authored, and to sing joyfully to God
with organs and cymbals. In the Church their duty is to recite the divine scripture and sing the responsories, Gradu-
als, and Alleluias solo before the people to the praise of
God. When they are ordained the bishop hands them a
book, since they must fulfill by their works what they proclaim to the people from the books. Now, a precentor is the
one who sings first, a succentor one who follows him, a *centor* or cantor one who sings along, a psalmist one who recites
the psalms, and a *symmysta,* that is, a secretary or one who
knows secrets, is one who explains Christ's mysteries.

177

On Exorcists

"Exorcist" means one who adjures. Solomon instructed
these men to adjure demons and expel them from possessed
people, as the priest Sceva's seven sons did. But in the
Church their duty is to exorcize the children who are under-
going catechesis, and to forbid the demons access to the
bodies of the baptized, which are temples of God, using
God's word, and to ward off demons from possessed and obsessed bodies by performing exorcisms. The bishop gives
them a codex at their ordination, teaching them to keep the
teachings contained in books, so that they may be able to
expel demons from others.

178

De acolythis

Qui in lege luminum concinnatores dicebantur, apud nos acolythi, id est ceroferarii nuncupantur. Hi lumina in Templo accendebant vel extinguebant, oleo reficientes lucernas nutriebant, ex quibus Nadab et Abiu erant. In Ecclesia autem habent officium ut lumen vel thuribulum coram sacerdote ad Missam vel Evangelium deferant, ad ornandum altare vestibus vel pallia inserviant. His ordinandis candelabrum et urceus vel ampulla ab episcopo traditur, ut per hoc admoneantur, quatenus lucernae bonorum operum in manibus eorum luceant, et oleum bonae conscientiae in vasis cordis habeant.

179

De subdiaconibus

Qui apud Hebraeos Nathinaei, id est humilitate servientes scribuntur, apud nos subdiaconi, id est subministri dicuntur. Horum officium in lege erat, oblata sacrificia a populo suscipere, et aquam vel quaelibet necessaria in

178

On Acolytes

The men who were called tenders of the lights in the Law are now called acolytes, or rather candle bearers. They used to light and extinguish the lights of the Temple, restock them with oil, and feed the lanterns. Nadab and Abihu were of this number. In the Church their duty is to carry the candle or thurible before the priest at Mass and during the Gospel, and to help dress the altar in its paraments and linens. The bishop gives them a candelabrum and a jug or cruet. By this they are admonished to keep alive the lantern of good works and to keep the vessel of their heart fully stocked with the oil of a good conscience.

179

On Subdeacons

The men the Hebrews call Nathineans, that is, those who humbly serve, we call subdeacons, which means subministers. In the Law their duty was to take the sacrifices offered by the people and to fetch the water and all other things

ministeria templi deferre, ex quibus Nathanahel dicitur fuisse. In Ecclesia autem hoc officium habent ut Epistulam legant, calicem et patenam cum corporali diacono ad altare offerant. Unde et yppodiacones, id est sub diacono ministrantes dicuntur. Cum hi ordinantur, vasa sancta, id est calix et patena eis ab episcopo dantur, quatenus se vasa Dei sciant, et se huic ministerio mundos exhibeant.

180

De diaconibus

A Levi filio Iacob Levitae, id est assumpti denominantur, per quos cuncta sacrificia sub sacerdotibus administrabantur, ex quibus Eleazar et Ithamar praedicantur. Hos Ecclesia diacones, id est ministros nuncupat, quia sacerdotibus ministrant. Horum officium est in Ecclesia Evangelium legere, sacrificium in altari componere, sanguinem Domini distribuere, populo licentiam abeundi dare, et si necessse est praedicare et baptizare. His ordinandis episcopus stolam dat, ut se lege Dei constrictos cognoscant, ac se castitati in servitio Dei omnimodis subdant. Archidiaconus dicitur summus diaconus, ut fuit Stephanus vel Laurentius.

necessary for the Temple service. Nathaniel is said to have been one. In the Church their duty is to read the Epistle and to carry the chalice, paten, and corporal to the deacon at the altar. Thus they are called hypodeacons, or those who serve under the deacon. When they are ordained the bishop gives them the sacred vessels, namely the chalice and paten, that they may know they are God's vessels, and keep themselves clean for this ministry.

180

On Deacons

Levites, meaning those who are lifted up, are named after Jacob's son Levi. They used to administer all the sacrifices under the priests' direction. Eleazar and Ithamar were of their number. The Church calls them deacons, which means ministers, because they serve the priests. Their duty in the Church is to read the Gospel, arrange the sacrifice on the altar, distribute our Lord's blood, give the people permission to leave, and in cases of necessity to preach and baptize. When the bishop ordains them, he gives them a stole, so that they recognize that they are bound by God's law and must observe perfect chastity in God's service. An archdeacon is the highest rank of deacon, as were Stephen and Laurence.

181

De presbyteris

"Presbyter" dicitur senior non aetate sed sensu, *cani enim sunt sensus hominis.* Hi in lege principes populi, ut Chore, Dathan, et Abiron, vel magistratus templi ut Nichodemus et Gamaliel dicebantur, et per eos sacrificia populi offerebantur. "Presbyter" etiam dicitur praebens iter, scilicet populo de exilio huius mundi, ad patriam caelestis regni. Horum officium est Missas celebrare, pro populo sacrificare, corpus Domini dispensare, praedicare, baptizare, paenitentes absolvere, infirmos unguere, mortuos sepelire, populum ad Missam vel nuptias vel arma, vel peras cum baculis, vel iudicia ferri et aquae, et candelas, vel palmas, vel cineres, vel quaslibet res ad cibum pertinentes benedicere. His episcopus manus in ordinatione imponit, potestatem ligandi atque solveni tradit, quatenus ipsi ita vivant, ut alios ligare ac solvere valeant. Iugum Domini suave eis imponit, dum collum eorum stola cingit, quatenus sic legi Dei obediant, ut alios regere queant. Manus eorum chrismate unguit, ut cuncta quae benedicunt, benedicta sint, quatenus se ab omni immundo opere contineant, ut digne corpus Christi conficere valeant.

181

On Priests

"Presbyter" means elder, not in age but in understanding, for *wisdom is gray hair unto man.* In the Law they were princes of the people, such as Korah, Dathan, and Abiran; or teachers in the Temple like Nicodemus and Gamaliel, and the people offered sacrifices through them. "Presbyter" comes from *praebens iter,* that is, one who shows people the way out of the exile of this world into the fatherland of the kingdom of heaven. Their duty is to celebrate Masses, offer sacrifice on the people's behalf, dispense our Lord's body, preach, baptize, absolve penitents, anoint the sick, bury the dead, bless the people at Mass, bless marriages, arms, pilgrims' purses and staves, ordeals of water and fire, candles, palms, ashes, and all sorts of foods. The bishop lays his hands upon them at their ordination and gives them the power to bind and loose, that they may so live that they are able to bind and loose others. He places our Lord's sweet yoke upon them, hanging the stole on their neck so that they may be so obedient to God's law, that they may be able to rule over others. He anoints their hands with chrism so that everything they bless may be blessed, and so that they may keep themselves from every unclean deed so be worthy to confect the body of Christ.

182

De sacerdotibus iterum

"Sacerdos" dicitur quasi sacrum dans. Dat enim corpus Domini vel alia sacramenta populo. Sacerdos enim dicitur sacer dux, quia verbo et exemplo ducatum praebet populo ad vitam. Tam episcopus quam presbyter "sacerdos" vocatur, quia per utrumque sacramentum datur. Archipresbyter dicitur summus presbyter. Decanus qui decem presbyteris est praelatus. Praepositus, qui aliis est praelatus. Chorepiscopus qui de choro sacerdotum vicarius episcopi est praelatus. Vicedominus, qui episcopi vices agit. Hos septuaginta viri expresserunt, qui spiritum Moysi accipiente populo sunt praelati.

183

De episcopis

Episcoporum ordo in tria dividitur: in episcopos, in archiepiscopos, in patriarchas.

Epi, super, *scopon* dicitur intendens. Inde "episcopus"

182

More on Priests

Sacerdos comes from *sacrum dans,* one who makes a holy
thing. For he makes our Lord's body and the other sacraments for the people. *Sacerdos* also means *sacer dux,* holy
leader, because by word and example he gives the people a
model of life. Both the bishop and the presbyter are called
sacerdos because both make the sacrament. An archpriest is a
high-ranking priest. A dean is placed over ten priests. A provost is a priest who presides over others. A chorbishop is a
priest of the choir who presides as the bishop's vicar. A vidame performs the role of a bishop. The seventy men who
received the spirit of Moses and were placed over the people
prefigured them.

183

On Bishops

The order of bishops is divided into three: bishops, archbishops, and patriarchs.

The word *episcopus* comes from *epi,* over, and *scopon,*

dicitur superintendens, quasi de alto prospiciens mores et vitam subditorum. Sicut enim custos vineae in alto residens undique prospicit, sic episcopus Christi vineae, scilicet Ecclesiae custos, quasi in alto residens populum sub se positum prospiciens instruit. Unde et speculator dicitur, quia sicut speculator in alta turri ponitur, ut hostes adventantes speculetur, et cives ad resistendum adhortetur, sic episcopus quasi in specula collocatur, ut populum contra hostes daemones et haereses armare nitatur. Hic quoque "praesul" nominatur, quia praesidere ad consultum putatur. Hic etiam "antistes" quasi anti stans dicitur, quia populo praeminere videtur. *Anti* enim dicitur contra, inde "antistes," quasi contra stans dicitur, qui haereticis ut lupis pastor contra stare, et oves protegere cernitur. Est etiam "pontifex" dictus, quasi pons factus. Vita quippe episcopi debet esse pons populo super mare saeculi ad patriam parasdisi. Vel "pontifex" dicitur pontem faciens, quia quasi pontem populo facit, dum eum sana doctrina super paludes haeresium ad atria vitae ducit.

watching. Therefore, *episcopus* means an overseer, as in one who surveys the life and morals of his subjects from on high. For just as the keeper of a vineyard sits in a high place and peers carefully all about, so the overseer of Christ's vineyard, and the keeper of Christ's Church, instructs the people placed under his care while observing them from his high seat. Wherefore he is also called a lookout, for just as a lookout is put in a high tower to spy out approaching enemies and call upon the citizenry to resist them, so the bishop is placed in a sort of tower, whence he strives to arm the people against the hosts of demons and heretics. He is also called a *praesul* or presider because he presides at a council. He is also called an *antistes* or one who stands in front of, from *anti stans,* because he is ranked above the people. *Anti* means against, and thus *antistes* means standing against, because we see him standing against heretics as the shepherd stands against the wolves and protects his sheep. He is also called *pontifex,* as in one who has become a bridge, for the life of the bishop should be a bridge for the people over the sea of this world into the fatherland of paradise. Or *pontifex* could mean one who makes a bridge, because in a way he makes a bridge for the people when he leads them by his sound doctrine over the swamps of heresy into the courts of eternal life.

184

De summo sacerdote

Hic Aaron in veteri lege summus sacerdos appellabatur, quia ceteris sacerdotibus et Levitis principabatur. Hic nomen Dei Tetragrammaton portabat, et semel in anno pro populo offerebat. In lege Aaron primus est in summum sacerdotem oleo unctus, in Evangelio autem Iacobus apostolus est primus ab apostolis Ierosolimis episcopus ordinatus. Unde dum ordinatur, a duodecim episcopis consecrari imperatur. Etsi necessitas cogit, saltem a tribus, ut Paulus a Petro Iacobo et Iohanne est ordinatus. Quod oleo ungitur, hoc a lege accipitur, in qua rex et sacerdos vel propheta oleo ungebatur.

185

De manus impositione

Quod autem benedictio per manus impositionem datur, inde exortum creditur, quod Isaac Iacob manus imposuit, dum eum benedixit. Et Moyses Iosue manus imposuit, dum

184

On the High Priest

Under the Old Law, Aaron was called the high priest because he was chief among the other priests and Levites. He wore the name of God, the Tetragrammaton, and sacrificed for the people once a year. In the Law Aaron is the first man anointed to the high priesthood with oil. But in the Gospel the apostle James is the first bishop ordained in Jerusalem by the apostles. Accordingly, when a bishop is ordained, custom demands that he be consecrated by twelve bishops, or if necessary by at least three, as Paul was ordained by Peter, James, and John. The custom of anointing him with oil is taken from the Law, in which a king and priest or prophet was anointed with oil.

185

On the Imposition of Hands

It is believed that giving blessings through the laying on of hands began when Isaac laid his hands on Jacob as he blessed him. Moses also laid hands on Joshua when he appointed

eum ducem populo praefecit. Et Dominus in Evangelio apostolis manus imposuit, dum *eos principes* et sacerdotes Ecclesiae *constituit.* Sed et ipsi apostoli manus imposuerunt, cum Spiritum sanctum dederunt. Huius officium est presbyteros et reliquos Ecclesiae ministros ordinare, virgines velare, baptizatos confirmare, chrisma et oleum consecrare, ecclesias dedicare, vasa et vestes Ecclesiae benedictione sanctificare, rebelles excommunicare, paenitentes reconciliare, in synodo clericorum vel in conventu populorum ecclesiastica iura roborare. Huic dum regnum Ecclesiae committitur, baculus quasi pastori, et anulus velut apocrisiario, id est secretorum sigillatori traditur, quatenus gregem Christi ad pascua vitae baculo doctrinae minet, atque sponsae Christi secreta scripturarum anulo fidei consignet.

186

De archiepiscopis

"Archiepiscopus" dicitur summus episcopus, vel princeps episcoporum. *Archos* quippe summus, vel princeps dicitur. Idem etiam metropolitanus dicitur. *Metropolis* autem mater civitatum vocatur, et ideo principalium civitatum episcopi metropolitani nominatur. Horum officium est episcopos consecrare, concilia congregare, iura dilapsa

him the leader of the people. The Lord too laid hands on the apostles in the Gospel when *he appointed them rulers* and priests of the Church. The apostles also did this when they conferred the Holy Spirit. His duty is to ordain priests and other ministers of the Church, veil virgins, confirm the baptized, consecrate the chrism and holy oil, dedicate churches, consecrate ecclesiastical vessels and vestments with his blessing, excommunicate rebels, reconcile penitents, and to promote the Church's estate in Church synods and popular assemblies. When the government of the Church is committed to him, he is given a staff, for he is a shepherd, and a ring, for he is an apocrisiarius, which means a sealer of secrets, so that he may shepherd Christ's flock with the staff of doctrine toward the pasture of life and impress the secrets of scripture into Christ's bride with the ring of faith.

186

On Archbishops

"Archbishop" means highest bishop, or ruler of bishops. *Archos* means highest or prince. He is also called a metropolitan. For *metropolis* means mother of cities, and so the bishops of principal cities are called metropolitans. Their duty is to consecrate bishops, convene councils, and restore

reparare. Hoc officium Moyses habuit, qui Aaron pontificem oleo consecravit. Ante hos crux portatur, et pallio in modum torquis decorantur, quia si Christum crucifixum imitantur, torque victorae remunerantur.

187

De patriarchis

"Patriarcha" dicitur summus patrum, vel princeps patrum. "Patriarcha" etiam pater arcae dicitur, scilicet Ecclesiae.

Hi tantum tres scibuntur, quorum figuram Abraham, Isaac et Iacob gessisse leguntur. Horum unus principatum in Asia tenuit, qui praesulatu in Antiochia praefuit. Alius in Africa primatum habuit, qui in Alexandria pontificatum tenuit. Tertius in Europa principabatur, qui Romani apicis infula decorabatur. Has tres sedes ideo Ecclesia principales constituit, quia eas princeps apostolorum sua sessione consecravit. Duabus quippe praesedit, tertiam Marcus Evangelista nomini eius adscripsit. Postquam vero Nicaena synodus Romano pontifici hoc contulit privilegium, ut sicut augustus prae regibus, ita ipse prae omnibus episcopis haberetur, et papa vocaretur, ius patriarchatus ad Constantinopolitanam urbem, scilicet secundam Romam est translatus.

laws that have fallen into abeyance. Moses held this office, and he ordained Aaron with oil. In a procession the crucifix is carried before them and they wear the pallium around their neck, because by imitating Christ crucified they are rewarded with a wreath of victory.

187

On Patriarchs

"Patriarch" means highest of fathers, or ruler of fathers. The word "patriarch" also comes from father of the ark, which is the Church.

There are only three patriarchs, who were prefigured by Abraham, Isaac, and Jacob. One of them was primate in Asia as bishop of Antioch. Another had the primacy in Africa, holding the bishopric of Alexandria. The third was primate of Europe, adorned by the sacred fillet of the Roman episcopacy. The Church declared these three to be the principal sees because their occupation by the prince of the apostles made them sacred. For he presided over two of them directly, and the third is reckoned his by way of Mark the Evangelist. But after the Council of Nicaea awarded the Roman pontiff this privilege, that as the emperor was first among all kings so he should be held first among all bishops and be called pope, his patriarchal dignity was transferred to the city of Constantinople, that is to say to the second Rome.

2   Quod autem aliae sedes sunt mutatae, haec causa creditur esse. Cum Christiani relicta lege Dei paganos spurcis
operibus imitarentur, iudicio Dei traditi sunt in manibus
eorum qui deletis Christianis possederunt loca illorum.
Unde Antiochenus patriarchatus, est ad Ierosolimam translatus. Porro Alexandrinus, ad Aquileiam esse positus. Quia
huic civitati primum Marcus Evangelista praesedit, qui
postea Alexandriae praefuit; quamquam quidam conten-
dant, quod Carthaginensis episcopus hac translatione pol-
leat. Horum officium est archiepiscopos consecrare, concilia episcoporum congregare, decreta canonum instaurare.

188

De papa

"Papa" dicitur, quasi pater patrum, vel custos patrum.
Hic etiam universalis nuncupatur, quia universae Ecclesiae
principatur. Hic quoque apostolicus nominatur, quia principis apostolorum vice fungitur. Hic etiam summus pontifex
appellatur, quia caput omnium episcoporum esse videtur.
Huius nomen in ordinatione mutatur, quia Petri nomen in
praelatione Ecclesiae a Christo mutabatur. Huic etiam

The reason why the other sees were altered is thought to be the following. When Christians began to neglect God's law and imitate the pagans by their impure deeds, God gave them into the hands of their enemies who slaughtered them and occupied their lands. Wherefore the Antiochene patriarchate was transferred to Jerusalem. Then that of Alexandria was given to Aquileia, since Mark the Evangelist was also the first bishop of that city after he had been primate of Alexandria. Nevertheless, there are some who claim that it was the bishop of Carthage who became powerful from this transfer. A patriarch's duty is to consecrate archbishops, convoke regional synods of bishops, and ensure observance of the decrees of canon law.

188

On the Pope

"Pope" means father of fathers, or guardian of fathers. He is called universal because he rules the universal Church. He is also called apostolic lord because he acts in place of the prince of the apostles. He is also called the supreme pontiff because he is the head of all bishops. His name is changed at ordination because Peter's name was changed by Christ when he was appointed as a prelate over the Church. He is given the keys, as the keys of the kingdom of heaven

claves traduntur, sicut Petro a Domino claves regni caelorum tradebantur, ut se ianitorem caeli esse cognoscat, in quod Ecclesiam introducere debeat. Hunc Melchisedech in officio praetulit, cuius sacerdotium aliis incomparabile fuit. Papae autem officium est Missas et Divina Officia ordinare, canones pro tempore ad utilitatem Ecclesiae immutare, augustum consecrare, pallia archiepiscopis, privilegia episcopis, vel aliis religiosis dare, totam Ecclesiam ut Christus gubernare. Itaque papa in vice Christi Ecclesiam regit, episcopi in loco apostolorum ei praesunt, presbyteri septuaginta duos discipulos exprimunt, reliqui ministri diaconos ab apostolis constitutos praeferunt.

189

De consecratione papae

Papa vicarius Christi, omnesque episcopi, apostolorum vicarii, in Dominica die debent ordinari hora tertia, qua apostoli a Spiritu sancto sunt oleo invisibili consecrati. Oleum lucernis lumen ministrat, et vulnera curat, ita Spiritus sanctus apostolis lumen scientiae ministravit, et vulnera peccatorum curavit. Ideo episcopus oleo unguuntur, ut se Spiritum sanctum apostolis datum accepisse doceantur, et ut vita

were given to Peter by our Lord to remind him that he is the guardian of heaven's door, into which he must usher the whole Church. Melchizedek prefigured him in this office, he whose priesthood was incomparable to any other. The pope's duty is to establish the order of Masses and Divine Offices, to modify the canons for the good of the Church when circumstances require it, to consecrate the emperor, to give the pallia to archbishops and privileges to bishops and other religious, and to govern the whole Church as Christ. Thus the pope rules the Church in Christ's place, while bishops assist him in the place of the apostles. The presbyters signify the seventy-two disciples, and the other ministers are the deacons appointed by the apostles.

189

On the Pope's Consecration

The pope, as vicar of Christ, as well as all bishops, as vicars of the apostles, must be ordained on a Sunday at the third hour, when the apostles were consecrated by the invisible oil of the Holy Spirit. Oil furnishes light to lamps and cleanses wounds. Just so the Holy Spirit furnished the apostles with the light of knowledge and salved the wounds of sin. Bishops are anointed with oil to signify that they have received the Holy Spirit that was given to the apostles, and

et doctrina *coram hominibus luceant,* et eos a vitiis curare satagant. Ideo autem in Dominico die consecrantur, quia et ea
die apostoli a Spiritu sancto ordinabantur, ut se cum Christo
resurrexisse, et *in novitate vitae ambulare* admoneantur.

190

De ordine ministrorum

Ministri autem Ecclesiae vel altaris ideo in Sabbato ordinantur, quod requies dicitur, quia ipsis ab omni opere ser-
vili requiescere, et in Dei servitio vacare praecipitur.

191

De presbyteris

Presbyteri vero ad vesperam quae magis ad Dominicam
pertinet consecrantur, quia Christo cuius corpus conficiunt

so that their life and doctrine *may shine before men,* and so that they may do their utmost to cure men of the vices. They are consecrated on Sunday because on that day also the apostles were ordained by the Holy Spirit, and to remind them that they have risen with Christ to *walk in newness of life.*

190

On the Ordination of Ministers

Ministers of the church and altar are ordained on Saturday, which is the day of rest, because they are commanded to rest from all servile labor and to be free for the divine service.

191

On Priests

Priests are consecrated on Saturday evening, which belongs to the Sunday, because their ordination incorporates

JEWEL OF THE SOUL

incorporantur. Ideo autem in Quattuor Temporum ordines dantur, quia quattuor gradus Deum benedicentium—quod acolythi, subdiaconi, diaconi, presbyteri intelliguntur—sub custodia quattuor Evangeliorum ad ministeria Ecclesiae in quattuor partibus mundi diffusae eliguntur.

192

De virginibus

Virgines vero ideo in natalitiis apostolorum velantur, quia per apostolicos viros quasi per paranymphos sponsae Christo consecrantur. Et quia morem virginitatis primum apostoli Ecclesiae servandum tradiderunt, quem a perpetua virgine Maria acceperunt.

them into Christ whose body they confect. Orders are given during Ember Days because the four grades of those who bless the Lord—namely acolytes, subdeacons, deacons, and presbyters—under the protection of the four Gospels are chosen for ministries in a Church spread throughout the four quarters of the earth.

192

On Virgins

Virgins take the veil on the birthdays of apostles because they are consecrated to Christ by the successors of the apostles, as it were Christ's groomsmen, and because it was the apostles who first gave the Church the celibate life, which they had received from the ever-virgin Mary.

192b

Potestates saecularium

Potestates saecularium, versae sunt in honorem spiritalium. Papa Romanus, augustis et caesaribus comparatur. Patriarchae quorum tres sunt, unus in Asia apud Antiochiam, alius in Africa apud Alexandriam, tertius in Europa, apud Constantinopolim, aequantur patriciis. Archiepiscopi, regibus. Metropolitani, ducibus. Episcopi, comitibus. Chorepiscopi, praefectis. Tribunis militum, abbates vel praepositi. Cancellarii, praetoribus. Archipresbyteri, centurionibus. Decani, decurionibus. Presbyteri, advocatis. Diaconi et subdiaconi, quaternionibus, vel trium viris. Exorcistae, quaestionariis. Aulae ianitores, in Ecclesia ostiarii. Carminum relatores, vel comici, vel tragoedi, sunt acolythi, lectores, cantores, psalmistae.

193

De tonsura clericorum

Tonsura clericorum initium sumpsit ab usu Nazaraeorum. Hii ex iussu legis crines suos radebant, et in sacrificium

192b

On Secular Powers

Secular powers have been transposed into Church offices. The Roman pope may be compared to the augusti and caesars. The three patriarchs (one in Asia at Antioch, another in Africa at Alexandria, a third in Europe at Constantinople) are equivalent to patricians. Archbishops are equal to kings, metropolitans to dukes, bishops to counts, chorbishops to prefects, abbots and provosts to military tribunes, chancellors to praetors, archpriests to centurions, deans to decurions, priests to counselors, deacons and subdeacons to quaternions or triumvirs, exorcists to executioners, church porters to royal doorkeepers, and acolytes, cantors, and psalmists to minstrels, comedians, and tragedians.

193

On the Clerical Tonsure

The clerical tonsure takes its origin from the practice of the Nazarenes. These men followed the Law's command to

Domino incendebant. "Nazaraei" autem dicuntur sancti. Unde apostoli ad exemplum eorum ministros Ecclesiae docuerunt se ob signum tondere, quo recordarentur se *Domino in sanctitate servire* debere. Christus rex et sacerdos, *fecit nos sibi reges et sacerdotes.* Pars capitis rasa, est signum sacerdotale; pars crinibus comata, signum regale. Sacerdotes quippe legis tiaram, id est pilleolum ex bysso in modum mediae sphaerae rotundum in capite portabant; reges autem aureas coronas gestabant. Ergo rasa pars capitis tiaram, circulus crinium praefert coronam.

194

De Christo rege et sacerdote

Sacerdos quoque in lege caput et barbam rasit, dum sacrificium pro populo obtulit. Rex coronam gestabant, dum ad salutandum populum procedebat. Ita Christus rex noster spineam coronam portavit, dum humilis et praepotens ad duellum pro militibus pugnaturus processit, et regem superbiae devicit. Idem ipse summus sacerdos in Calvaria crines deposuit, dum se ipsum acceptum sacrificium in ara Crucis obtulit. Per circulum igitur crinium spineam coronam praeferimus, per nuditatem rasurae calvitium Christi

cut their hair and burned it in sacrifice to the Lord. "Naza-rene" means holy. The apostles followed their example and taught the ministers of the Church to tonsure themselves as a sign to remind them that they must *serve the Lord in holiness*. Christ the king and priest *has made us priests and kings for him*. The shaved part of the head is a sign of priesthood; the part covered by hair is a sign of royalty. For priests of the Law wore a tiara, a little round cap of cotton shaped like a half sphere, while kings wore golden crowns. Therefore the shaved part of the head recalls the tiara, and the circle of hair recalls the crown.

194

On Christ the King and Priest

In the Law, a priest shaved his head and beard when he was to offer sacrifice for the people. The king wore a crown when he went forth to greet or deliver his people. Likewise Christ our king wore a crown of thorns as, both humble and mighty, he processed before the Roman soldiers to the judicial duel and utterly defeated the king of pride. He too put aside his hair when he acted as high priest on Calvary, when he offered himself as a pleasing sacrifice on the altar of the Cross. By the circle of hair, therefore, we display the crown of thorns, and by the baldness of the shaved part we express

exprimimus. Mos quippe apud antiquos erat quod captivos decalvabant, quos crucifigere volebant. Unde scriptum est, *de capitivitate nudati inimicorum capitis.* Ideo locus in quo decalvabantur, Calvaria dicebatur, in quo et Dominus decalvatus putatur.

195

Quod Petrus apostolus tonsuram invenit clericorum primus

Petrus quoque a gentibus captus, et ad ludibrium Christianorum traditur, barba rasus, et capite est decalvatus. Quod ipse deinceps in mysterio fieri iussit, quod incredulos quamvis inscios, tamen Deo permittente in figura operatos intellexit, sicut et crux olim fuit subsannatio, nunc est Ecclesiae gloriatio.

Per caput principale animae scilicet mens denotatur, quae sicut caput capillis, ita mens cogitationibus perornatur. Quae novacula timoris Dei debet a superfluis cogitationibus radi, ut nuda facie cordis valeat caelestia contemplari. Rotunditas autem quae remanet crinium, est ornatus virtutum. Capilli vero omnes in circulum coaequantur, quia omnes virtutes in concordia caritatis consummantur. Quod autem barbam radimus, inberbes pueros similamus. Quos si

Christ's baldness. For it was customary in ancient times to shave captives' heads before crucifying them. Thus it is written, *of the captivity, of the bare head of the enemies.* Hence the place where they were shorn was called Calvary, and our Lord is thought to have been shorn there too.

195

How the Apostle Peter Was the First to Invent the Clerical Tonsure

The pagans once seized Peter too, and shaved his beard and head as a sign of mockery against Christians. Afterward he ordered this to be made into a symbol, because he understood that the unbelievers had, albeit unwittingly, done this thing by God's permission as a figure: for the Cross was once a mockery, and has become the Church's glory.

The head denotes the principal part of the soul, that is, the mind, which is adorned with thoughts, just as the head is with hair. The mind must be shorn of superfluous thoughts by the razor of the fear of God so that it may contemplate heavenly things in naked purity of heart. The round shape of the remaining hair is the crown of virtues. The hair is cut evenly in a circle all around because all the virtues reach their consummation in the concord of charity. When we cut our beards, we become like beardless children. If we imitate

humilitate imitabimur, angelis qui semper iuvenili aetate florent aequabimur.

196

De tonsura magorum

Sciendum vero quod Simon Magus et sui sequaces sibi caput radebant, et ab aure usque ad aurem per medium caput quasi plateam, unde adhuc vulgo platta dicitur faciebant. Et per caput caelum, per viam tonsurae zodaicum intelligi volebant, quia se caelestes asserebant.

197

De clericali corona

Nostra autem tonsura in lege exprimitur, dum coronula quattuor digitorum super mensam coram altare, et desuper

the humility of children, we will be made equal to the angels who enjoy everlasting youth.

196

On the Magicians' Tonsure

It is worth knowing that Simon Magus and his followers shaved their heads in the following way: cutting a sort of highway from ear to ear over the front part of the head, whence in the vernacular the tonsure is still known as a *platta*. They believed that the head shaved in this manner signified heaven and the path of the tonsure the zodiac, for they claimed they were celestial beings.

197

On the Clerical Crown

But our tonsure is portrayed in the Law, when God commands a small crown or rim of a hand's breadth to be fashioned for the table that stood before the altar, and above it a

minor coronula aurea fieri praecipitur. Per mensam quo pro-
positio panum ponebatur, nostrum altare accipitur, cui cottidie panis Christi imponitur. Corona quattuor digitorum
per circulum crinium nostrorum exprimitur, superior autem
coronula per plattam figuratur.

198

De sacris vestibus

Haec strictim de ministris Ecclesiae sint relata, nunc de
sacris vestibus pauca sunt subicienda.

Vestes namque sacrae a veteri lege sunt assumptae. Ideo
autem ministri Christi vel Ecclesiae in albis vestibus ministrant, quia angeli aeterni Regis ministri in albis apparebant.
Per albas itaque vestes admonemur, ut angelos Dei ministros per castitatis munditiam in servitio Christi imitemur.
Vestes vero quibus corpus exterius decoratur, sunt virtutes
quibus interior homo perornatur. Septem autem vestes sacerdotibus adscribuntur, quia et septem ordinibus insigniti
noscuntur, quatenus per septiformem Spiritum septem virtutibus resplendeant, quibus cum angelis in ministerium
Christi ornati procedant.

smaller molding of gold. The table placed there to receive the bread of the presence stands for our altar, on which the bread of Christ is placed daily. The crown or rim of four digits is signified by the circle of our hair. The *platta* represents the higher crown.

198

On the Sacred Vestments

Let these brief observations about the Church's ministers suffice. Now we should conclude with a few words about the sacred vestments.

Sacred vestments are taken over from the Old Law. The ministers of Christ and his Church serve in white albs because the angels, who are ministers of the eternal King, appeared in white. White albs teach ministers to imitate the purity and chastity of the angels, who are God's ministers, when they carry out Christ's sacred service. The vestments that decorate one externally stand for the virtues that adorn the interior man. Now, there are seven vestments assigned to priests, for they are sealed with the seven orders so that through the sevenfold Spirit they may shine with the seven virtues and, so adorned, may go forth to perform Christ's sacred service in the company of the angels.

199

De praeparatione sacerdotis

Sacerdos igitur Missam celebraturus, id est spiritale bellum pro Ecclesia pugnaturus, necesse est ut spiritalibus armis induatur, quibus contra hostes incentores vitiorum undique muniatur. Primo namque quotidianas vestes exivit, mundas vestes induit, quia corpus Christi tractatus vel sumpturus, veterem hominem cum actibus suis, quod sunt vitia et peccata debet exuere, et *novum hominem qui secundum Deum creatus est,* id est virtutes et bona opera debet *induere.* Deinde pexit crines capitis, quia sacerdos debet componere mores mentis. Aqua abluit manus, quia lacrimis debet abluere carnales actus. Deinde a sorde eas extergit, quia transacta carnis opera per paenitentiam eum extergere convenit.

199

On the Priest's Preparation

The priest who is to celebrate Mass, that is, who is about to wage spiritual warfare on behalf of the Church, must equip himself with spiritual weapons so that he may be defended on all sides against the enemies who stir us to vice. First he takes off his ordinary garments and puts on clean ones because one who is about to handle or receive the body of Christ must take off the old man and his works, which are vices and sin, and *put on the new man,* that is, the virtues and good works, *created according to the likeness of God.* Then he combs his hair because the priest must set his mind in order. He rinses his hands with water because he must wash away carnal deeds with his tears. Finally, he wipes off any filthiness from them because through penance he must wipe away all the works of flesh he has committed.

200

De lavandis manibus

Sacerdotes quoque legis sacrificaturi in labro de speculis mulierum facto se lavabant, quae ad ostium tabernaculi excubabant. Labrum ex speculis mulierum factum, sacra scriptura intelligitur, quae de perspicua sanctarum animarum vita conscribitur. Hae ad ostium tabernaculi excubabant, quia iugiter aeternum Dei tabernaculum intendebant. In hoc labro sacerdotes sacrificaturi debent se lavare, scilicet vitam suam diligenter in sacra scriptura considerare, exemplis sanctorum a maculis purgare, et sic ad sacrificium Domini intrare.

201

De humerali

Hinc humerale quod in lege *ephot,* apud nos "amictus" dicitur, sibi imponit, et illo caput et collum atque humeros unde et "humerale" dicitur cooperitur, et in pectore copulatum duabus vitiis ad mamillas cingit. Per humerale quod

200

On the Washing of Hands

Before they sacrificed, the priests of the Law washed themselves in a basin made from the mirrors of the women who served at the entrance of the tabernacle. The basin made from the mirrors of women is sacred scripture, which is written about the transparent lives of holy souls. The women kept watch at the entrance of the tabernacle because they yearned without ceasing for God's eternal tabernacle. Priests on their way to a sacrifice must wash in this basin, meaning examine their life in sacred scripture, purge it of faults by following the example of the saints, and only then enter into the Lord's sacrifice.

201

On the Amice

Next the priest puts on what the Law called the *ephod* and what we call the amice. It covers the head, neck, and shoulders—hence its name, "humeral"—and is fastened with two ribbons at the breast. We wear it on our head to

capiti impontiur, spes caelestium intelligitur. Caput amictu cooperimus, cum pro spe caelestium Deo servimus. Collum per quod vox depromitur, eo circumdamus, si pro spe vitae *custodiam ori nostro ponamus,* ut nihil nisi quod ad laudem Dei sonet de ore nostro proferamus. Humeros quibus onera portantur, eo velamus, si leve onus Dei patienter feramus. Hoc facimus si pro spe futurorum laborem activae vitae subimus, et proximis in necessitate subvenimus. Per oras humeralis fides et operatio intelliguntur, quae utrinque spei annectuntur. Hae ante pectus in invicem copulantur, et una apparet, altera occultatur, quia fides et operatio inunum copulantur, et fides quidem in corde occultatur, operatio autem ad aedificationem proximorum foris manifestatur. Una etiam ora latet, alia apparet, quia actio nostra proximis lucet, intentio vero coram Deo intus latet. Ad pectus humerale cingitur, quia spe supernae patriae prava cogitatio a pectore sacerdotis restringitur. Duae vittae quae amictum ad mamillas precingunt, sunt timor poenae, et desiderium vitae, quae spem caelestium pectori nostro imprimunt. Haec vestis est candida, quia haec omnia coram Deo sunt splendida.

signify hope for heavenly things and we cover our head with the amice when we serve God in hope of obtaining heavenly things. We also use it to cover our neck, through which the voice is expressed, and we do this in hope of life, *putting,* so to speak, *a watch before our mouth* as a warning not to let any word escape our mouths unless it be to the praise of God. We cover our shoulders, which carry burdens, if we bear patiently our Lord's light yoke. We do this if we undertake the works of the active life in hope of future things and come to our neighbor's aid in times of need. The fringes of the amice signify faith and works, which are both tied to hope. The edges are folded over one another in front of the breast, the upper one concealing the lower. This is because faith and works are joined in one, but faith is hidden in the heart, while works are manifest for the edification of our neighbor. One edge is hidden, the other exposed, because our acts shine before our neighbors, but our intention is hidden inside, visible only to God. The amice is fastened at the breast because wicked thoughts are excluded from the priest's heart because of his hope for the heavenly fatherland. The two ties that fasten the amice at the breast are fear of punishment and the desire for eternal life, which the hope for heavenly things engraves on our hearts. It is a white vestment because all of these things are splendid in the eyes of the Lord.

202

De alba

Dehinc alba induitur, quae in lege tunica linea vel talaris, apud Graecos *poderis* dicitur. Per hanc castitas designatur, qua tota vita sacerdotis decoratur. Haec descendit usque ad talos, quia *usque in finem* vitae debet in castimonia *perseverare* sacerdos. Caputium quo alba induitur, est professio, qua castitas servanda promittitur. Lingua quae in caputio nunc innectitur, nunc resolvitur, est potestas linguae sacerdotalis, quae nunc ligat peccantes, nunc solvit paenitentes. Haec vestis in medio coangustatur, in extremo dilatatur, multis etiam commissuris multiplicatur, quia castitas pressuris quidem mundi coartatur, sed in caritate dilatatur, multis virtutibus multiplicatur. Haec vestis albedine candet, quia sanctitas coram Deo inter angelos splendet.

202

On the Alb

Next he puts on the alb, which the Law called the linen tunic or the *talaris* and the Greeks call the *poderes*. It denotes chastity, which adorns the whole life of the priest. It descends to the ankles because the priest must *persevere* in chastity *unto the end* of his life. The opening through which the head passes is his profession, in which he promised to observe chastity. The string that tightens and loosens the opening is the power of the priestly tongue, which binds sinners and looses penitents. This garment is trimmed in the middle, wider at the base, and forms numerous folds, because the virtue of chastity is hemmed in on every side by the pressures of the world, but is nourished and expanded by charity and multiplies into many virtues. The whiteness of this vestment is brilliant because holiness shines forth before the face of God and his angels.

203

De cingulo

Exhinc cingulo cingitur, quod in lege baltheus, apud
Graecos zona dicitur. Per cingulum quod circa lumbos prae-
cingitur, et alba ne defluat et gressum impediat astringitur,
mentis custodia vel continentia accipitur, qua luxuria restringitur, et castitas cohibetur, ne ad carnalia dilabatur, et
gressus bonorum operum impediatur, et ipsa concupiscentia devicta ad ruinam impellatur.

204

De stola

Dehinc circumdat collum suum stola, quae "oratorium"
dicitur, per quam obedientia Evangelii intelligitur. Evangelium quippe est suave Domini iugum, obedientia vero lorum. Quasi ergo sacerdos ad iugum Christi loris ligatur, dum
collum eius stola circumdatur. Haec primitus sinistro humero imponitur, et trans cor in dextrum latus reflectitur,
quia obedientia Evangelii primum in activa vita suscipitur,

203

On the Cincture

Next the priest girds himself with the cincture, called a belt in the Law and a zone by the Greeks. The cincture is girded above the loins and tightened to prevent the alb from billowing out and hindering his step. It signifies custody of the mind and continence, which restrains wantonness and holds up chastity lest fall toward carnal deeds, and lest the stride of his good works be impeded and fall into ruin while chastity is vanquished.

204

On the Stole

The priest next places the stole or *orarium* on his neck, through which we are to understand obedience to the Gospel. For the Gospel is our Lord's sweet yoke, and obedience is the rein; so it is as if the priest is tied to the yoke of Christ with reins when he puts the stole around his neck. At first, it is placed on the left shoulder and drawn across the heart to the right side because obedience to the Gospel is first

ac inde per dilectionem in dextrum contemplativae porrigitur. Deinde per collum in dextrum humerum gyratur, et a
sinistro non levatur, quia postmodum obedientia per dilectionem Dei in contemplationem attolitur, et tamen a proximis in activa vita per dilectionem proximi non avellitur.

205

De innocentia

Per stolam quoque innocentia exprimitur, quae in primo
homine amissa, per vitulum saginatum occisum recipitur.
Beati qui hanc stolam a criminum labe custodiunt, vel macu-
latam lacrimis lavabunt, quia *illorum potestas est in ligno vitae*
scilicet in Christo amissam gloriam possidebunt. Hac etiam
patriarchae ante legem utebantur, et primogenita dicebatur.
Erat autem vestis sacerdotalis qua maiores natu cum benedictione patris ut Iacob ab Isaac induebantur, et victimas
Deo ut pontifices offerebant. Unde dicitur, "*Vende mihi primogenita tua*," et iterum, "*Stola Esau induit eum.*"

observed in the active life, then drawn through love to the right side of the contemplative life. Later it is rotated around the neck onto the right shoulder, without removing it from the left, because through his love of God his obedience is elevated into contemplation, and yet, on account of his love for his neighbor, he is not torn from his neighbors in the active life.

205

On Innocence

The stole also represents innocence, which was lost in the first man and regained when the fattened calf was slain. Blessed are they who keep this stole pure from the stain of sin, or if stained wash it with their tears, because *they have a right to the tree of life,* that is, in Christ they will possess the glory they had lost. The patriarchs used this vestment before the Law, and they called it a birthright. It was a priestly garment that elder sons, such as Jacob and Isaac, put on with their father's blessing and wore as they offered sacrifices to God as priests. Thus it is written, *"Sell me your birthright,"* and *"She put on him Esau's stole."*

206

De subcingulo

Exin subcingulum quod perizoma vel cinctorium dicitur contra pudenda duplex suspenditur. Per hoc eleemosynarum studium accipitur, qua confusio peccatorum contegitur. Hoc duplicatur, quia primum animae suae misereri peccata devitando, deinde proximo necessaria impendendo cuilibet imperatur.

207

De casula

Deinde casula omnibus indumentis superponitur, per quam caritas intelligitur, quae omnibus virtutibus eminentior creditur. Casula autem quasi parva casa dicitur, quia sicut a casa totus homo tegitur, ita caritas totum corpus virtutibus complectitur. Haec vestis et planeta quod error sonat vocatur, eo quod errabundus limbus eius utrimque in bracchia sublevetur.

2 Haec in duobus locis scilicet in pectore et inter humeros duplicatur, in duobus locis videlicet in utroque brachio

206

On the Subcingulum

Next the subcingulum, which is also called the *perizoma* or *subcinctorium,* is hung around the loins on both sides. It signifies the love of almsgiving, which restrains the disorder of sin. It has two parts because it is a precept binding on everyone to save his own soul first by avoiding sin and then by giving his neighbor whatever is due him.

207

On the Chasuble

The chasuble is worn over all the other vestments, and it represents charity, which stands over all the virtues. Chasuble means a small house, for just as a house covers a whole man, so charity enfolds the whole body with the virtues. This vestment is also called a *planeta,* which means wandering, because its free-flowing borders are draped over each forearm.

When it hangs, this garment forms two folds in two places, at the breast and between the shoulders; on each arm

triplicatur. In pectore duplicatur, quia per caritatem sancta cogitatio et bona voluntas generatur. Inter humeros duplicatur, quia per illam adversa a proximis et ab adversariis supportantur. Vestis ad bracchia elevatur, dum caritas bona operatur. In dextro bracchio triplicatur, dum in dilectione Dei monachis, clericis, laicis Christianis ministratur. In sinistro triplicatur, dum per dilectionem proximi malis Catholicis seu Iudaeis, sive paganis necessaria corporis praebentur. Casula super dextrum brachium levatur, ut in Deo amici amentur; super sinistrum plicatur, ut inimici propter Deum diligantur.

Huic in supremo humerale forinsecus annectitur, quia spes caritatem semper amplectitur.

208

De mappula

Ad extremum sacerdos fanonem in sinistrum brachium ponit, qui et mappula et sudarium vocatur, per quod olim sudor et narium sordes extergebantur. Per hoc paenitentia intelligitur, qua quotidiani excessus labes extergitur. Hoc in sinistro brachio gestatur, quia in presenti tempore tantum vita nostra paenitentia emundatur.

it forms three. It forms two folds at the breast because charity begets holy thoughts and good will. It forms two between the shoulders because through the same charity we are able to bear the hardships laid upon us by our neighbors and our enemies. The vestment is drawn up onto the arms when charity does good works. On the right arm it forms three folds when we render service to Christian monks, clergy, and laity out of love for God. It forms three folds on the left when we offer material necessities to bad Catholics, Jews, or pagans out of love for our neighbor. The chasuble is drawn up onto the right arm so that we may love our friends in God; it is folded over the left, so that we may love our enemies for God's sake.

The amice is tied to the outside of this garment because hope always entails charity.

208

On the Maniple

In the last place, the priest puts the *fano* on his left arm, which is also called the maniple or sudary because, formerly, it was used to wipe away sweat or clean the nose. It signifies penitence, by which we wipe off the regular discharge of our sin. It is worn on the left arm because our life can be washed clean by penitence only in the present time.

His vestibus sacerdos ornatus procedit, confessionem facit, quia licet his virtutibus fulgeat, dignum est ut inutilem servum se dicat, de transactis se accusans, ut reum diiudicet, et coram Deo gratiam inveniat.

209

De septem vestibus episcopi

Episcopus eisdem septem vestibus induitur, insuper et aliis septem redimitur, scilicet sandaliis, dalmatica, rationali, mitra, chirotecis, anulo, baculo.

"Sandalia" a sandice herba, vel a sandaraco colore dicuntur, quo depingi feruntur. Haec ab ipso Domino vel ab apostolis accepta creduntur, in quibus praedicasse traduntur. Est autem genus calciamenti incisi, quo partim pes tegitur partim nudus cernitur. Evangelica vero praedicatio intelligitur, quae partim auditoribus aperitur, partim clauditur.

Having put on all these vestments, the priest processes in and makes his confession, because even if his life shines with these virtues, he deserves to call himself an unworthy servant and accuse himself of his past sins, so that he may judge the guilty and find grace before the face of God.

209

On the Seven Vestments of the Bishop

The bishop wears the same seven vestments, and in addition he is girt with seven more, namely, sandals, the dalmatic, rational, miter, gloves, ring, and staff.

The word "sandal" comes from the sandyx plant or from the sandarac color with which the sandals are painted. Their use is received from our Lord himself and from the apostles, who wore them while preaching. It is a kind of open shoe in which the foot is partly covered and partly bare. Hence it signifies preaching of the Gospel, which is partly revealed to hearers and partly concealed.

210

De sandaliis

Fiunt autem sandalia ex pellibus mortuorum animalium, quia apostoli et doctores praedicationem suam munierunt scriptis prophetarum, videlicet Dei animalium. Pes subtus ad terram solea huius calciamenti est tectus, desuper nudus, quia Evangelii praedicatio debet carnalibus per litteram tegi, spiritalibus autem per allegoriam denudari. Lingua sub calcaneo surgit de albo corio, quia praedicator debet se separare a terreno negotio, et esse innocens et sine dolo. Lingua inde surgens separata a corio, est illorum lingua qui bonum testimonium ferunt episcopo. Lingua superior est spiritalium lingua, qui eum eligunt in praedicationis opera. Albo corio intrinsecus sunt circumdata sandalia, quia praedicatoris conscientia coram Deo debet esse puritate candida. Extrinsecus vero nigrum apparet, quia vita ipsius coram hominibus humilitate deiecta esse debet. Superior pars per quam pes intrat, multis filis est consuta, quia multis sententiis debet praedicatio mentibus infundere superna. Lingua super pedem, est lingua praedicatoris in plebem. Linea quae a lingua usque in finem descendit, est Evangelica perfectio quae in Deum tendit. Lineae quae ex utraque parte

210

On the Sandals

Sandals are made from the skins of dead animals because the apostles and doctors use the writings of the prophets, who are God's animals, to corroborate their preaching. The bottom of the foot is hidden by the sole of this shoe while the upper part is bare, because when the Gospel is preached, the truth should be hidden from carnal people by recourse to the literal sense, but laid bare for spiritual people by way of allegory. A tongue of white leather runs up from under the heel because the preacher must withdraw from all earthly business and be innocent and without guile. The tongue that rises up from it and is divided from the hide is the tongue of those who carry a good testimony of their preaching to the bishop. The upper tongue is the tongue of spiritual men, who choose him for the work of preaching. On the inside the sandals are lined with white hide because the preacher's conscience should shine with purity before God. On the outside, however, they seem black because his life should be cast down in humility before men. The upper part where the foot enters is stitched with many threads because he must pour heavenly preaching into men's hearts through many discourses. The thong that lies over the foot is the preacher's tongue speaking to the people. The line that runs down from the thong to the other side of the sole is evangelical perfection that stretches toward God. The lines that

2

procedunt, sunt lex et prophetia quae Evangelio testimonium ferunt. Ligatura, est mysterium Christi Incarnationis, quae solvitur manu praedicationis. Tapetia pedibus eius substrata calcat, ut *terrena despicere, et caelestia amare discat.* Legis sacerdotes habebant femoralia quibus turpitudinem tegebant, Ecclesiae sacerdotes sandalia portant, quia etiam aliis munditiam praedicant.

211

De dalmatica

Dalmatica a Dalmatia provincia est dicta, in qua primum est inventa. Haec a Domini inconsutili tunica et apostolorum colobio est mutuata. Colobium autem erat cucullata vestis sine manicis, sicut adhuc videmus in monachorum cucullis, vel nautarum tunicis. Quod colobium a sancto Silvestro in dalmaticam est versum, et additis manicis infra sacrificium portari institutum. Quae ideo ad Missam a pontifice portatur, ubi Passio Christi celebratur, quia in modum crucis formatur. Haec vestis est candida, quia caro Christi de casta virgine est genita, et pontificis vita debet castitate esse nitida. Haec habet formam crucis, quia Christus pro nobis subiit supplicium Crucis, et pontifex debet se

proceed from both sides are the law and prophecy, which bear testimony to the Gospel. The strap is the mystery of Christ's Incarnation, which is loosed by the hand of the preacher. He treads upon the rugs under his feet so that he may *learn to despise the things of this world and love those of heaven*. The priests of the Law wore breeches that covered their nakedness; the priests of the Church wear sandals because they preach cleanliness also to others.

211

On the Dalmatic

The dalmatic is named after the province of Dalmatia, where it was first invented. It stands for our Lord's seamless tunic and the apostles' colobium. The colobium was a hooded garment without sleeves, as can still be seen in monastic cowls or the tunics of sailors. Saint Sylvester substituted the colobium with the dalmatic, adding sleeves and ordering it to be worn during the sacrifice. It is worn by the bishop at Mass, when Christ's Passion is celebrated, because it is shaped like a cross. The vestment is white because Christ's flesh was begotten from a chaste maiden and because a bishop's life must be a shining example of chastity. It has the form of a cross because Christ underwent the punishment of the Cross for our sake and a bishop must

2 *crucifigere vitiis et concupiscentiis.* Huius vestis manicae, sunt nostrae gallinae alae. Dei quippe sapientia primos homines in paradiso velut gallina ova in nido fovebat, pullos Ecclesiae *sub alas* gratiae et misericordiae congregabat. Ita debet pontifex fideles *sub alas* veteris et novae legis praedicando congregare, et exemplis se super eos expandere, et oratione a caeli volucribus, id est a daemonibus protegere. Haec debet esse inconsutilis ut Domini tunica, quia fidei integritas esse indiscussa.

212

De dalmatica et quid designet

Per dalmaticam quoque *religio sancta et immaculata* designatur, qua *pupillorum et viduarum visitatio,* et *vitae immaculatae custodia* mandatur. Dalmatica duas coccineas lineas ante et retro habet, quia vetus et nova lex dilectione Dei et proximi refulget, qua pontifex redimitus esse debet. Idem tramites purpurei, designant sanguinem Christi, pro duobus populis effusi. Immaculatio pertinet ad dilectionem Dei, visitatio fratrum ad dilectionem proximi. Per colorem coccineum opus misericordiae accipitur, quod ob geminam dilectionem viduis et pupillis impenditur.

crucify himself to vice and concupiscence. The sleeves of this gar- 2
ment are like the wings of our mother hen, for God's wisdom nurtured the first humans in paradise like eggs in a
nest. He gathered up the Church, his chicks, *under his wings*
of grace and mercy. In the same way a bishop must gather up
the faithful *under the wings* of the Old and New Law by his
preaching, spread himself over them by his good conduct,
and by his prayer protect them from the fowls of the air,
who are the demons. The dalmatic must be seamless as our
Lord's tunic because he must keep the integrity of the faith
whole and entire.

212

On the Dalmatic and What It Signifies

The dalmatic also signifies *religion clean and undefiled,* for
we are commanded *to visit orphans and widows* and *to keep our
life spotless.* The dalmatic has two scarlet stripes in front and
back because the Old and New Law radiate love of God and
neighbor, with which the bishop must be girt. The two purple stripes also signify the blood of Christ, poured out for
both peoples. Spotlessness represents the love of God, visitation of brethren the love of neighbor. The scarlet color
signifies works of mercy, which are performed on account of
the twin love of widows and orphans.

2   Fimbriae quae de dalmatica procedunt, sunt verba et exempla praedicatoris, quae de religione sancta prodeunt. Fimbriae ante et retro pendent, quia mandata dilectionis in lege et Evangelio manent. In utrisque lineis sunt quindecim fimbriae altrinsecus ante et retro dispositae, quia in veteri Testamento quindecim psalmi quasi quindecim gradus de via caritatis exeunt, et in novo similiter quindecim rami de arbore dilectionis excrescunt. Sunt autem hi rami: *Caritas patiens est, benigna est. Caritas non aemulatur, non agit perperam, non inflatur, non est ambitiosa, non quaerit quae sua sunt, non irritatur, non cogitat malum, non gaudet super iniquitate, congaudet autem veritati, omnia suffert, omnia credit, omnia sperat, omnia sustinet. Caritas numquam excidit.* Sinistrum latus habet fimbrias, quod significat laboris aerumnas, quia activa vita *est sollicita, et turbatur erga plurima.* Dextrum latus non habet, quia in contemplativa vita quieta manet, et *regina a dextris stans* nihil in se sinistrum habet. Manicarum largitas, est *datoris hilaritas.*

The tassels that hang from the dalmatic are the preach-   2
er's words and example, which flow from the virtue of religion. The tassels hang in front and back because the twin
commandment of love is found in both the Law and the
Gospel. In both sets of stripes there are fifteen tassels on
each side, before and behind, because in the Old Law fifteen
psalms extend out like the fifteen steps from the way of
charity, and likewise in the New there are fifteen boughs
growing out from the tree of life. Now the branches are
these: *Charity is patient, is kind: charity envieth not, dealeth not
perversely; is not puffed up; is not ambitious, seeketh not her own, is
not provoked to anger, thinketh no evil; rejoiceth not in iniquity
but rejoiceth with the truth; beareth all things, believeth all things,
hopeth all things, endureth all things. Charity never falleth away.*
The left side has tassels that signify the toils of human labor
because the active life is *careful and troubled about many things.*
The right side does not have tassels because the contemplative life remains calm, and *the queen standing at the right hand*
has nothing sinister in her. The great size of the sleeves is *the
good cheer of the giver.*

213

De rationali

Rationale est a lege sumptum, quod ex auro, hyacintho, purpura unius palmi mensura erat factum. Huic Doctrina et Veritas ac duodecim pretiosi lapides intexti nominaque filiorum Israel insculpta erant, et hoc pontifex in pectore ob recordationem populi portabat. Hoc in nostris vestibus praefertur, per ornatum qui auro et gemmis summis casulis in pectore affigitur. Monet autem pontificem ratione vigere, auro sapientiae, hyacintho spiritalis intelligentiae, purpura patientiae, in Christum *qui caelum palmo mensurat,* tendere debet, doctrina et veritate radiare, gemmis virtutum coruscare, duodecim apostolos sancitate imitari, totius populi in sacrificio recordari.

213

On the Rationale

The rationale is taken from the Law, where it was made of gold, violet, and purple and measured one span. Doctrine and Truth were attached to it, and twelve precious stones in which the names of the sons of Israel were inscribed. The pontiff wore it on his breast as a remembrance of the people. Its equivalent among our vestments is a garment attached to the breast over the chasuble, covered in gold and gems. It warns the bishop to be vigorous in reason and by the gold of wisdom, the violet of spiritual intelligence, and the purple of patience to tend always toward Christ—*who measures the heavens with his palm*—to radiate doctrine and truth, to shine with the gems of virtue, to imitate the holiness of the twelve apostles, and to remember the whole people in the sacrifice.

214

De mitra pontificale

Mitra quoque pontificalis, est assumpta ex usu legis. Haec ex bysso conficitur, et thiara et cidaris, infula, pileum dicitur. Mitra quae caput velat in quo sensus sunt locati, est custodia sensuum ab illecebris mundi in mandatis Domini pro *corona vitae, quam repromisit Deus diligentibus se.* Mitra etiam est Ecclesia, caput vero Christus, cuius figuram gerit episcopus. Mitra ergo ex bysso facta, multo labore ad candorem perducta, caput pontificis circumdat, dum Ecclesia baptismate mundata, labore bonorum operum candidata, caput suum scilicet Christum in gloria videre anhelat, dum variis passionibus eum imitari pro gloriae corona non dubitat. Caput quoque pontificis mitra decoratur, dum Ecclesia, eius doctrina illustrata, dignitati eius congratulatur, dum eum turba cleri et populi comitatur.

214

On the Pontifical Miter

The pontifical miter is also taken from the practice of the Law. It is made from cotton and is called a tiara, *cidaris, infula,* or *pileum*. The miter veils the head, in which the senses are located, and indicates the bishop must guard his senses against the temptations of the world by following our Lord's commandments in order to obtain *the crown of life, which God hath promised to them that love him*. The miter represents the Church, and its head is Christ, of whom the bishop is a figure. The miter surrounds the bishop's head and is made of cotton, a material that is made white through much effort, while the Church is made clean by baptism, whitened by the labor of good works, and deeply yearns to see Christ her head in glory, never ceasing to imitate him through various sufferings in order to obtain the crown of life. Moreover, the bishop's head is adorned with the miter when the Church, enlightened by his doctrine, gives honor to his dignity, and the whole clergy and people gather around him.

215

De chirotecis

Chirotecarum usus, ab apostolis est traditus. Per manus operationes, per chirotecas designantur earum occultationes. Sic enim aliquando manus chirotecis velantur, aliquando extractis chirotecis denudantur, sic opera bona interdum propter arrogantiam declinanda celantur, interdum propter aedificationem proximis manifestantur. Chirotecae induuntur, cum hoc impletur, quod dicitur: *Cavete ne iustitiam vestram coram hominibus faciatis, ut videamini ab eis.* Rursus extrahuntur, cum hoc impletur: *Luceat lux vestra coram hominibus, ut videant opera vestra bona, et glorificent Patrem qui in caelis est.* Chirotecae sunt inconsutiles, quia actiones pontificis debent rectae fidei esse concordes.

216

De anulo

Anuli usus ex Evangelio acceptus creditur, ubi vituli saginati conviva *prima stola* vestitur, anulo insignitur. Olim

215

On the Gloves

The use of gloves was handed down by the apostles. Hands signify good works, and gloves signify their hiddenness. Sometimes the gloves cover the hands, and sometimes they are taken off to leave the hands bare. In the same way good works are sometimes concealed in order to avoid all show of arrogance, but at other times they are made manifest for the edification of our neighbors. Gloves are put on when the following passage is fulfilled: *Take heed that you do not your justice before men, to be seen by them.* They are taken off again when this one is fulfilled: *So let your light shine before men, that they may see your good works, and glorify your Father who is in heaven.* The gloves are seamless because the bishop's actions must be in accord with sound faith.

216

On the Ring

The use of the ring comes from the Gospel, when in preparation for the feast of the fattened calf, the prodigal son is vested with the *first robe* and honored with a ring. Formerly

solebant reges litteras cum anulo signare, cum hoc soliti erant et nobiles quique sponsas subarrare.

Fertur quod Prometheus quidam sapiens primus anulum ferreum ob insigne amoris fecerit, et in eo adamantem lapidem posuerit, quia videlicet sicut ferrum domat omnia, ita *amor vincit omnia,* et sicut adamans est infragibilis, ita amor est insuperabilis. Quem etiam in illo digito portari constituit, in quo venam cordis deprehendit, unde et anularis nomen accepit. Postmodum vero aurei sunt pro ferreis instituti, et gemmis pro adamente insigniti, quia sicut aurum cuncta metalla praecellit, ita dilectio universa bona excellit, et sicut aurum gemma decoratur, ita amor dilectione perornatur.

Pontifex vero anulum portat, ut se sponsum Ecclesiae cognoscat, ac pro illa animam si necesse fuerit sicut Christus ponat. Mysterium scripturae a perfidis sigillet, secreta Ecclesiae resignet.

217

De baculo episcopali

Baculus ex auctoritate legis et Evangelii assumitur, qui et virga pastoralis et capuita, et ferula, et pedum dicitur. Moyses quippe dum oves pavit, virgam manu gestavit. Hanc ex praecepto Domini in Aegypto pergens secum portabat,

kings used to sign their letters with a ring, and all noblemen were accustomed to betroth their wives with a ring.

It is said that a wise man named Prometheus first made an iron ring as a sign of love and placed a stone of adamant in it. For just as iron vanquishes all, so *love conquers all,* and as adamant cannot be broken, so love cannot be overcome. He decided to wear it on the finger through which the heart's vein runs, and that is why it is called the ring finger. But later, gold rings were substituted for iron ones and set with gems instead of adamant. For just as gold is the most excellent metal, so love is the most excellent of good things, and just as gold is embellished with a gem, so love is adorned by affection.

The bishop wears a ring to show that he is the Church's bridegroom and, like Christ, will lay down his life for her in time of need. Let him seal the mysteries of scripture from unbelievers, but unseal all secrets for the Church.

217

On the Episcopal Staff

The staff is used on the authority of the Law and the Gospel, and is called the shepherd's staff, baton, rod, or crook. Moses held a staff in hand when he pastured his sheep. At the Lord's command, he carried it into Egypt with him and

hostes signis per eam factis terruit, qui velut lupi oves Domini strangulabant. Gregem Domini de Aegypto per Mare Rubrum hac virga eduxit, pastum de caelo, potum de petra hac produxit, ad terram lac et mel fluentem, velut ad pascua hac virga induxit. Nihil autem aliud haec virga fuit, quam virga pastoralis, cum quo gregem utputa pastor minavit. Hic baculus apud auctores pedum vocatur, eo quod pedes animalium illo retineantur. Est enim lignum recurvum, quo pastores retrahunt pecudes gregum.

218

Item de virga et baculo episcopi

In Evangelio quoque, Dominus apostolis praecepit, ut in praedicatione nihil praeter virgam tollerent. Et quia episcopi pastores gregis Dominici sunt, ut Moyses vel apostoli fuerunt, ideo baculum in custodia fidelium praeferunt. Per baculum quo infirmi sustentantur, auctoritas doctrinae designatur. Per virgam qua improbi emendantur, potestas regiminis figuratur. Baculum ergo pontifices portant, ut infirmos in fide per doctrinam erigant. Virgam baiulant, ut per potestatem inquietos corrigant. Quae virga vel baculus est

used it to work wonders that terrified his enemies, who were
as wolves tormenting the Lord's flock. Like a shepherd leading his sheep to pasture, he led the Lord's flock out of Egypt
through the Red Sea with this staff, used it to draw bread
from heaven and water from the rock, and led them with it
into the land flowing with milk and honey. This staff was
none other than the shepherd's staff, and he used it to guide
his flock like a shepherd. Some authors call this staff a crook
because shepherds used it to restrain the animals' feet. It is a
curved piece of wood with which shepherds draw back the
sheep of their flocks.

218

More on the Episcopal Rod and Staff

Likewise in the Gospel our Lord commanded the apostles to carry nothing with them besides a staff when they
went forth to preach. And since bishops are the shepherds
of our Lord's flock, as Moses and the apostles were, so they
carry a staff to guard the faithful. The staff signifies the authority of Christian doctrine, which supports the weak. The
rod is a figure of the power of governing, by which the ways
of the unjust are corrected. Bishops carry a staff to raise up
the weak in faith through sound teaching. They bear a rod
to correct the unruly through their power. The rod or staff is

recurvus, ut aberrantes a grege docendo ad paenitentiam re-
trahat. In extremo est acutus, ut rebelles excommunicando
retrudat, haereticos velut lupos ab ovili Christi potestative
exterreat.

219

De genere baculi

Hic baculus ex osse et ligno efficitur, crystallina vel deau-
rata sphaerula coniungitur, in supremo capite insignitur, in
extremo ferro acuitur. Per baculum ut dictum est auctoritas
doctrinae accipitur, qua grex Dominicus a pastore reficitur,
et ad pascua vitae compellitur. Per durum os duritia legis,
per lignum mansuetudo Evangelii insinuatur, per gemmam
sphaerulae divinitas Christi. Per supremum caput regnum
caelorum, per extremum ferrum ultimum iudicium denotatur. Ex osse ergo baculus inciditur, dum ex dura lege duritia
peccantium reprimitur. Ex ligno tornatur, dum ex ligno vitae
Christo doctrina formatur, et populus in virtutibus robora-
tur. Os ligno per gemmam conectitur, quia vetus lex novae
per Christi divinitatem contexitur.

curved so that it can draw wayward sheep back toward penance through teaching. It is sharp at the tip so that he may cast out rebels by excommunication and frighten heretics like wolves away from Christ's sheepfold by their power.

219

On the Kinds of Staff

This staff is made from bone and wood joined together by a crystalline or gilded knop, bears an inscription on the top, and comes to an iron point at the tip. As we have already said, the staff represents the authority of Christian doctrine, which the shepherd uses to feed the Lord's flock and herd them toward the pastures of life. The hardness of the bone points to the severity of the Law, the wood to the humility of the Gospel, and the bejeweled knop to Christ's divinity. The top denotes the kingdom of heaven, the iron at the tip the Last Judgment. The staff is carved out of bone when the stubbornness of sinners is curbed by the firmness of the law. The staff is lathed from wood when doctrine is fashioned from Christ, the tree of life, and the people are strengthened in the virtues. The bone is joined to the wood with a jewel because the Old Law is connected to the New by Christ's divinity.

220

De sphaerula

Per sphaerulam etiam dilectio intelligitur, qua severitas vel lenitas pontificis complectitur. Oportet enim ut doctrina episcopi ex utraque lege sic dilectione copuletur, ut Ecclesiam Christo coniungere per caritatem conetur. Haec autem cuncta sunt rasili arte polita, quia ista sunt omni sanctitate redimita. Os recurvatur, ut populus errans per doctrinam ad Deum retrahatur. Caput in supremo ponitur, dum conversis vita aeterna proponitur. In extremo baculus ferro induratur, dum omnis praedicatio per ultimum iudicium terminatur. In curvatura est scriptum, *"Cum iratus fueris, misericordiae recordaberis,"* ne ob culpam gregis, superet ira mentem pastoris, sed verbo et exemplo revocet peccantes ad misericordiam Redemptoris. In sphaerula est scriptum, "Homo," quatenus se hominem memoretur, et de potestate collata non elevetur. Iuxta ferrum est scriptum, "Parce," ut subiectis in disciplina parcat, quatenus ipse a summo Pastore gratiam inveniat. Unde et ferrum debet esse retusum, quia iudicium sacerdotis per clementiam debet esse delibutum.

220

On the Knop

By the spherical knop we understand the loving affection that must imbue the bishop's severity and leniency. For the bishop's teaching of the two Laws must be bonded together by love to such an extent that he may dare to orchestrate the Church's marriage to Christ through charity. All these elements are very finely polished because they are enshrouded with all sanctity. The bone is curved in order to snatch the wayward people back for the Lord through Christian doctrine. The head is placed on the top when eternal life is offered to converts. The tip of the staff is reinforced with iron when all preaching ends in the final Judgment. On the curve of the top is written, "*When thou art angry, thou wilt remember mercy,*" so that the sins of the flock might not overwhelm the pastor's heart, and he might call sinners by word and example back to the Redeemer's mercy. On the knop is written, "Man," to remind the bishop that he is a man and that he must not be puffed up by the power he bears. On the iron is written, "Spare," so that in his teaching he might have mercy on those subject to him, and so obtain grace from the supreme Shepherd. The iron must be blunted because a priest's judgment should be tempered by clemency.

221

De ornatu archiepiscopi

His insignibus etiam archiepiscopus fulget, insuper et pallio pollet, ut se Christi Passionem populo praeferre demonstret. In duabus quippe lineis pallii ante et retro est purpureum sanctae Crucis signaculum, quia pontifex ex utraque lege debet proferre Christi Passioni testimonium. Duae etenim lineae propendentes, duae sunt leges Christi Passionem proferentes.

222

De pallio archiepiscopi

Spinulae quibus pallium affigitur, sunt clavi quibus corpus Christi crucifigitur. Circulus quo pontifex circa collum circumdatur, est torques aureus qui *legitime certantibus* in praemio datur. Itaque pallium monet pontificem ferre vitiorum mortificationem, cruces pallii in mente et corpore Christi imitari Passionem, duae lineae ut sit duabus legibus per

221

On the Archbishop's Vestments

The archbishop gleams in these splendid vestments, and in addition puts on the pallium, in order to show that his life is a representation of Christ's Passion for the people. For upon the two linen cloths of the pallium, on the front and back, there is a purple image of the holy Cross, since a bishop must furnish evidence for Christ's Passion from both Laws. Accordingly, the two linen cloths hanging down represent the two Laws that testify Christ's Passion.

222

On the Archbishop's Pallium

The pins that hold the pallium are the nails with which Christ's body was crucified. The round hole around the bishop's neck is the golden wreath given as a prize to those who *strive lawfully*. And so the bishop is taught by the pallium to bear the mortification of his vices, by the crosses on the pallium to imitate Christ's Passion in mind and body, by the two lines to be guided in all things by the two Laws, by

omnia instructus, spinulae ut per timorem Dei sit mundo crucifixus, circulus ut si sic praeesse studeat, torquem coronae vitae percipiat. Et quia in pallio tanta latent mysteria, ideo portatur inter Christi sacrificia. Unde etiam crux ante archiepiscopum portatur, quatenus Christum crucifixum sequi admoneatur, ut coronam gloriae adipiscatur.

2   Pallium vero pro aurea lamina est institutum, in qua summus pontifex in lege nomen Dei Tetragrammaton, id est quattuor litteris in fronte sua praeferebat inscriptum. Quattuor quippe litterae illius nominis quattuor cornua Crucis praemonstrabant, sicut nunc pallium Crucis modum repraesentat. Et quia haec lamina aurea cum forma crucis in fronte pontificis portabatur, ideo adhuc pretiosa Crux frontibus Christianorum chrismate impressa portatur.

3   Pallium autem a solo apostolico datur, quia haec dignitas a Romano pontifice iure accipitur. Quos enim apostoli provinciis praefecerunt archiepiscopi, quos illi pagis praetulerunt episcopi dicebantur. Et apostolorum successores patriarchae, Petri vero successor apostolicus nominabatur. Huic collata est potestas ab Ecclesia archiepiscopos per provincias constituere, quod per pallii largitionem accipitur.

the pins to be crucified to the world through the fear of God, by the round hole that, if he strives to excel in these things, he shall receive the crown of life. Since there are such great mysteries hidden in the pallium, accordingly it is worn during Christ's sacrifices. A cross is carried before an archbishop that he may be reminded to follow Christ crucified so that he may obtain the crown of glory.

The pallium was instituted in place of the gold plate the high priest wore on his forehead, inscribed with the four letters of God's name, the Tetragrammaton. The four letters of this name prefigured the four corners of the Cross, just as now the pallium displays the shape of the Cross. And because the high priest wore this gold plate with the shape of a cross on his forehead, Christians to this very day have the adorable Cross traced on their forehead with the chrism oil. 2

The pallium is granted only by the pope because the Roman pontiff has obtained this privilege by law. For the men the apostles appointed over provinces were called archbishops, while those they set over country districts were called bishops. The apostles' successors were called patriarchs, but Peter's successor was named the apostolic lord. He was granted the authority to appoint archbishops for the provinces, which he does through the gift of the pallium. 3

223

De vestibus patriarchae
et apostolici

Patriarchae quoque et apostolicus pallio utuntur, qui eodem officio praediti noscuntur. Porro apostolico in Pascha procedente, pharus ex stuppa super eum suspenditur, quae igne succensa super eum cadere permittitur, sed a ministris vel a terra excipitur, et per hoc ipse in cinerem redigi, et gloria ornatus eius in favillam converti admonetur.

224

De corona imperatoris
et augusti

Corona imperatoris, est circulus orbis. Portat ergo augustus coronam, quia declarat se regere mundi monarchiam. Corona quoque dicitur victoria, unde et victores coronabantur, et augusti victores orbis dicebantur. Arcus super

223

On the Vestments of the Patriarch and Pope

The patriarchs and the pope use the pallium because they are considered to be endowed with the same office. When the pope is going in procession at Easter, a lamp made of tow is hung over him. The tow is set on fire and allowed to fall over him, although it is caught by the ministers or falls to the ground. This ceremony reminds the pope that he is but ash, and that all his glorious splendor will one day be reduced to cinders.

224

On the Crown of the Emperor and the Augustus

The emperor's crown is the circle of the globe. Therefore the augustus wears a crown to show that he rules the kingdom of the world. "Crown" also means victory, and thus victors used to be crowned; likewise the augusti were called the conquerors of the world. The arch above the crown is curved

coronam curvatur, eo quod oceanus mundum dividere narratur. Virga sceptri, est potestas regni. Vestes imperiales,
sunt sibi subditae potestates. Monent autem imperatorem
purpureae vestes, ut habeat principales virtutes; sceptrum,
ut iudicium et iustitiam diligat, quatenus solium gloriae cum
principibus caeli possideat; corona ut sic vivat, quatenus a
Rege regum coronam vitae accipiat.

Dicitur quod augusto ab apostolico coronato, et regalibus
indumentis decorato, desuper pera imponatur, ut per hoc
admoneatur, quia sicut ad fastigium regni ascendit, ita ad
mendicitatem descendere possit, sicut Diocletianus qui
prius augustus fuit, postmodum hortulanus extitit.

Crux ante augustum portatur, ut in omnibus regem
Christum sequatur.

225

De diademate

Diadema autem regum, designat regni ambitum, et omnes qui in agone contendebant, diadema accipiebant. Innuit
ergo regibus diadema, quod si iustitia certabunt, cum Rege
omnium coronati regnabunt. Haec vero regalia insignia, a
Nino primum traduntur inventa.

because the ocean is said to divide the world. The rod of the scepter represents the power of rule. The imperial garments represent the powers subject to him. His purple garments admonish him to cultivate princely virtues; the scepter, to love wisdom and justice so that he may possess a throne of glory with the princes of heaven; the crown, that he should so live, that he may receive the crown of life from the King of kings.

It is said that, after the augustus has been crowned by the pope and clothed in his royal garments, a small beggar's purse is placed over him, and by this he is reminded that just as he has ascended to the heights of power, so he may also descend to the depths of poverty, just as Diocletian was once the augustus and ended up a gardener.

A cross is carried in front of the augustus, so that in all things he may follow Christ the king.

225

On the Diadem of Kings

A king's diadem signifies the compass of his kingdom, and contestants in public games used to receive the diadem. Hence it reminds kings that if they compete with one another in justice they will rule as kings with the King of all. Ninus is said to have been the first to invent this royal insignia.

226

De vestibus ministrorum
inferioris gradus

Ministris inferioris ordinis—scilicet ostiariis, lectoribus, exorcistis, acolythis—tres sacrae vestes conceduntur—superhumerale, tunica talaris, baltheum—quia videlicet angelis splendidis ministris associabuntur, qui hic ministerio Trinitatis fide, spe, et caritate vestiuntur. Portant namque superhumerale quo humeri teguntur, quibus onera feruntur, ut discant *alterutrorum onera portare,* et Christo in membris suis necessaria ministrare. Tunicam talarem, id est albam portant, ut humilitatem induant, et in hac *usque in finem* Christo serviant. Baltheo, id est zona iubentur renes praecingere, ut sciant carnales concupiscentias per continentiam restringere.

226

On the Vestments of the Lower Ministers

Ministers of the lower orders—porters, lectors, exorcists, and acolytes—are granted three sacred vestments—the amice, alb, and cincture—because those who are robed in faith, hope, and charity in their Trinitarian ministry here below shall one day take their place beside those brilliant ministers, the angels. They wear an amice that covers their shoulders, whereupon they carry their burdens, so that they may learn *to bear one another's burdens* and give all due service to Christ in his members. They wear an ankle-length tunic, namely the alb, so that they may put on humility, and humbly serve Christ until the end. They are ordered to tie a cincture or zone around their loins so they may know to tether carnal desires through continence.

227

De cappa

Cappa propria vestis est cantorum, quae pro tunica hyacinthina legis mutuata videtur. Unde sicut illa tintinnabulis, ita ista insignitur fimbriis. Per hanc vestem sancta conversatio praemonstratur, ideo a singulis ordinibus portatur. Haec in supremo habet caputium, quod designat supernum gaudium. Si enim Christi ministri *conversatio in caelis nunc stabit,* peracto ministerio *gaudium Domini intrabit.* Haec usque ad pedes pertingit, quia *in sancta conversatione in finem usque perseverare* convenit. Per fimbrias labor denotatur, per quem servitium Dei consummatur. Haec vestis in ante aperta manet, quia Christi ministris sancte conversantibus aeterna vita patet. Porro in tunica sonus tintinnabulorum, est vox Deo canentium cantorum. Quae septuaginta duo fuisse describuntur, quia de septuaginta duobus libris laudes Deo canuntur. Quibus totidem mala punica interserta referuntur, quia de eisdem libris opera iustorum nobis in exemplum proferuntur.

227

On the Cope

The cope is the proper vestment of cantors, and seems to have been substituted in place of the hyacinth tunic of the Law. And so, like the latter was decorated with bells, so the former is adorned with fringes. This vestment denotes a holy life, and thus is worn by all the orders. It has a hood at the top that signifies heavenly joy. For if *the conversation* of Christ's minister is *already in heaven,* when he has fulfilled his ministry he will *enter into the joy of the Lord.* It reaches down to his feet because he must *persevere to the end in holy living.* The fringes denote suffering, by which the service of our Lord is brought to perfection. The cope is open at the front because eternal life lies open to those of Christ's ministers who live a holy life. The sound of bells on the hyacinth tunic is the voice of cantors singing to God. They are described as having seventy-two bells because God's praises are sung from seventy-two books. As many pomegranates were set between them because these same books give us the works of the just as examples.

228

De pileis

Cantores etiam pilleis caput ornant, quia se *in atria Domini concupiscere* clamant, ut Deum qui est caput omnium *in saeculum saeculi laudare* valeant. Baculos manibus portant, ut quo ipse properant, alios secum invitare satagant.

229

De subdiaconorum veste

Subdiaconibus tres supradictae vestes conceduntur, insuper duae aliae, id est subtile et sudarium adduntur. Subtile quod constricta tunica dicitur portat, ut se *iustitia quasi lorica* induat, et *in sanctitate et iustitia* Deo *serviat*. Sudarium quo sordes a vasis deterguntur portat, ut transacta mala sordium a se per paenitentiam tergat. Notandum vero quod subdiaconi sudarium maius aliis formatur, quia ubi nunc fano, ibi olim mappula portabatur.

228

On Caps

The cantors adorn their heads with caps because they cry out with *longing for the courts of the Lord,* where they may *praise God,* who is the head of all, *unto the ages of ages.* They carry staves in their hands, so that they may invite others to go with them to the place where they are hastening.

229

On the Subdeacons' Vestments

The subdeacon is assigned the three vestments noted above. To these two more are added: the tunicle and the maniple. When he puts on the tunicle, which is also called the tight tunic, he *puts on justice like a breastplate* and *serves God in holiness and justice.* He carries a maniple to wipe the vessels, and to blot out the foulness of his sins through penance. Note, however, that the subdeacon's maniple is cut larger than others' because he formerly carried a *mappula* where he now carries a *fano.*

230

De veste diaconorum

Diacono dalmaticae usus conceditur, quae in modum crucis formatur, quia per illum sacrificium super altare tamquam corpus Christi in Cruce collocatur. Per hoc admonetur ut *Crucis mortificationem iugiter in suo corpore* sicut Lucas *circumferat,* et *in sancta religione viduas et pupillos visitando* ut Stephanus serviat, et in gradibus supradictis caritatis ut idem ferveat. Capitium dalmaticae angustatur, quia imitatio sanctae Crucis ab omnibus negotiis coartatur. Huic stola in sinistro humero ponitur, et trans scapulas ad dextrum latus reflectitur, quatenus se iugo Domini in activa vita subdat, et per pii laboris exercitium ad contemplativam proficiat.

231

De diaconi casula

Cum diaconus casulam portat, tunc praedicatores significat, qui toto desiderio contemplativae vitae inhiant, et in dilectione ferventes aliis caelestia praedicant. Qui interdum

230

On the Deacons' Vestments

The deacon is given the use of the dalmatic. This vestment is made in the form of a cross because his hands place the sacrifice on the altar as the body of Christ on the Cross. His duty is *always to carry the mortification of the Cross in his body,* as Luke did; to serve in *holy religion,* like Stephen, by *visiting widows and orphans,* and like him to burn eagerly in the aforementioned steps of charity. The dalmatic has a narrow opening for the head because his many duties make imitation of the holy Cross difficult. The stole is placed on his left shoulder and folded across to his right side, so that he may put on our Lord's yoke in the active life and advance to the contemplative life by performing pious works.

231

On the Deacon's Chasuble

When the deacon wears his chasuble, he signifies preachers, whose whole desire is for the contemplative life and who, on fire with love, preach celestial things to others.

casulam exuunt, et se illa praecingunt, quia illa quae ore praedicant, exemplis bonorum operum demonstrant. Unde diaconus de choro exiit, casulam exuit, duplicatam humero imponit, in dextro latere cingit eam, quia oportet praedicatores interdum opus praedicationis vel orationis vel lectionis intermittere, et proximis in necessitate succurrere. Quasi duplicatam casulam humeris imponit, dum ob geminam dilectionem laborem pro fratribus subit. In dextro cingit, si per hoc tantum aeterna requirit. Latus etiam denudatum, designat Christum pro nobis vulneratum. Diaconus in chorum redit, Evangelium legit, quia postquam praedicator Christo in membris suis ministraverit, ad opus praedicationis redire debet quod deseruit. Peracto ministerio diaconus induitur casula, quia praedicator qui prius ministravit cum Martha, debet postmodum audire verbum Dei cum Maria. Subdiaconus etiam casulam portat, quia imitatur diaconem cui ministrat.

232

De indumentis clericorum

Clericorum induviae ab antiquis sunt acceptae. His nempe cantores in Templo usi sunt, sicut David et Salemon

Sometimes they take off their chasuble and fold it because what they preach with their lips they show by the example of their good works. Thus the deacon leaves the choir, takes off his chasuble, folds it and puts it on his shoulder, and ties it on the right side because sometimes preachers must leave aside the work of preaching, praying, or reading, and run to the aid of their neighbor in need. The chasuble is folded when he willingly takes on suffering for his brothers on account of the twofold love of God and neighbor. He ties it on the right side if through this ministry he seeks only the things of heaven. The side that is bared represents Christ wounded for us. The deacon returns to the choir and reads the Gospel because once the preacher has ministered to Christ in his members, he must return to the work of preaching he left behind. His ministry complete, the deacon dons his chasuble again because the preacher, having first ministered with Martha, must now listen to the word of the Lord with Mary. The subdeacon also wears a chasuble in imitation of the deacon, whom he serves.

232

On the Garb of the Clergy

The use of distinctive clothing by the clergy comes from the ancients. The cantors in the Temple, indeed, used such

instituerunt. Huiuscemodi etiam vestibus senatores usi sunt, ex quibus in ecclesiasicum usum transierunt. Hae autem albae vestes munditiam vitae indicant, quia iustum est ut clerici *in sanctitate et iustitia* Deo serviant. Haec vestis est laxa, quia clericalis vita debet esse in eleemosynis et bonis operibus larga. Est etiam talaris, quia docet *usque in finem perseverare* in bonis. Lingua huius vestis, est lingua clericalis, quae Deum debet laudare, et populum ad laudes Dei instigare.

233

De tunicis clericorum

Diebus Quadragesimae vel alio congruo tempore laneis tunicis utuntur, quia ministri Ecclesiae regi Christo in humilitate servire praecipiuntur. Si enim Christi mansuetudinem et humilitatem sequuntur, ad Christum in consortium angelorum perducuntur. In veste clericali lingua formatur, quia tunica Domini inconsutilis sic formata traditur.

clothing, as Solomon and David prescribed. Roman senators also used proper dress, which passed on from them into ecclesiastical use. The clerical tunic is white, signifying purity of life, because it is fitting that clerics serve God *in holiness and justice*. This tunic is loose, since a cleric's life should be generous in almsgiving and good works. It reaches down to the ankles, teaching *perseverance unto the end* in good works. The lace of this tunic is a cleric's tongue, which must both praise God and excite the people to his praise.

233

More on the Clerical Tunic

On Lenten days and at other appropriate times they use woolen tunics because the ministers of the Church are ordered to serve Christ the king with humility. For if they imitate Christ's meekness and humility, they will be admitted to the presence of Christ and the company of the angels. The clerical tunic has one lace because our Lord's seamless tunic is thought to have been made this way.

234

De camisiis clericorum

Camisia autem sacerdotum duabus linguis formatur, quia eis bina potestas traditur. Una quippe lingua ligant peccantes, alia solvunt paenitentes.

Cappa videtur a casula tracta. Per hanc admonentur clerici *in caritate ambulare,* hanc aliis verbo et exemplo demonstrare, quae solet omnes virtutes decorare.

235

Clerici non debent arma deferre

Clerici ideo non debent arma portare, quia non contra homines, sed contra daemones debent virtutibus pugnare. Sic Moyses arma non portavit, sed Iesu cum Amalech pugnante ipse precibus pugnavit. Sic apostoli et eorum successores non armis sed precibus pugnaverunt, et nos non resistere, sed magis iniuriam pati docuerunt.

234

On the Priestly Frock

A priestly frock, however, has two laces, because a two-fold power is granted to them. One lace binds sinners, the other looses penitents.

The cope seems to be derived from the chasuble. It teaches clerics *to walk in charity* and exercise it toward others in word and deed, for charity adorns all the other virtues.

235

Clergy Forbidden to Bear Arms

Clerics should not bear arms because it is their duty to struggle against demons, not men, just as Moses did not bear arms but strove against Amalek with his prayers, while Joshua led the battle. In the same way the apostles and their followers fought with prayers, not weapons, and taught us rather to suffer injuries than to resist them.

236

Laici possunt portare arma

Laici autem arma debent portare, ut Ecclesiam a paganis protegant, et clerum ad servitium Dei expediant. Unde et illorum vestes sunt constrictae, quatenus expediti reddantur pugnae. Sicut autem laicis non licet clericale officium usurpare, ita non debent clericalem vestem portare. Et sicut clericis non licet nec contra paganos arma portare, ita non debent laicas vestes portare.

237

Cuculla quid significet

Cuculla monachorum, sumpta est a colobio apostolorum. Illorum vero tunica formatur, ut dalmatica. Hae duae vestes formam crucis praeferunt, quia monachi se *vitiis et concupiscentiis crucifixerunt*. Per has etiam septem alae seraphim exprimuntur, qui proximi Deo scribuntur. Duae quippe partes capitii, sunt duae alae quibus caput velabant, duae vero partes cucullae, in ante et retro, duae alae sunt

236

Laymen May Bear Arms

But laymen must bear arms to protect the Church from pagans and so that the clergy may be free for the divine service. Thus their clothes are more close-fitting so that they are ready for battle. A layman may not usurp the clerical function, nor wear a clerical vestment. Similarly, clerics may not bear arms even against the pagans, and must not wear lay clothes.

237

What the Cowl Signifies

The monastic cowl is taken from the colobium, a garment worn by the apostles. The monastic tunic, however, is shaped like the dalmatic. These two garments form a sign of the Cross because monks *crucify themselves to vices and concupiscences.* They also symbolize the six wings of the seraphim, who are the angels closest to God. The two parts that cover the head are the two wings that cover the seraph's head, signifying faith and hope. The two sleeves are the seraph's two

quibus corpus tegebant, quae autem manicae, sunt duae alae quibus volabant. Alae seraphim in capite, fides est et spes, in brachiis gemina dilectio, in corpore paenitentia et operatio. Hos si Deum laudando imitantur, in gaudio angelis associabuntur. Nigredo huius indumenti, est contemptus mundi, longitudo vestis, est perseverantia in bonis.

238

Virga abbati conceditur

Abbati conceditur pastoralis virga, quia ei traditur Dominici gregis custodia, quem debet baculo doctrinae sustentare, et virga magisterii ad pascua vitae minare. Per baculum quippe doctrina, per virgam accipitur disciplina. Unde dicitur, *"Virga tua et baculus tuus ipsi me confortati sunt."* Huius baculi flexura, non ex albo, sed ex nigro osse debet esse, quia in commissa cura non debet mundi gloriam quaerere. Summitas curvaturae debet esse sphaerica, quia cuncta eius disciplina, debet esse deifica.

wings for flying, and stand for the twofold love of God and neighbor. The two parts of the cowl in front and back are the two wings that cover the seraph's body, and they are symbols of penance and good works. If the monk imitates the seraphim by praising God, he will join the angels in eternal joy. The black color of this garment signifies contempt for the world, its length perseverance in good works.

238

The Staff Granted to the Abbot

The abbot is given the crosier because he is charged with guarding the Lord's flock, which he must uphold with the rod of Christian doctrine and lead to the pastures of life with the staff of teaching. For the rod means doctrine, and the staff discipline. Thus it is said, *"Thy rod and thy staff they have comforted me."* The crook of this staff must not be white but black, because in the office committed to him he must not seek worldly glory. The tip of the curved crook must be spherical because all his discipline must be deifying.

239

Conversationis monialium initium

Vestis et conversatio monialium, a sancta Maria sumpsit exordium. Nigredo vestis, est contemptus amplexus virilis. Velum est signum pudoris, et futuri honoris. In nuptiis quippe puellae caput et faciem velant, ne pudorem ab inspicientibus habeant. Ita istae sponsae Christi se velant, ut omnibus viris illicitae appareant, et pro hoc sibi coronam vitae repositam sciant.

240

De vestitu monialium

Quod quaedam virgines candidis vestibus utuntur a sancta Cecilia sumptum videtur, quae foris veste splendebat, intus castitate fulgebat, et tamen mundi concupiscentia in corde eius sordebat. Candida etiam vestis, praefert votum virginitatis.

239

The Origin of the Way of Life of Nuns

The nuns' garments and way of life take their origin from the blessed Virgin Mary. The blackness of their habit is contempt for man's embraces. The veil is a sign of modesty and future honor. At weddings maidens veil their head and face to keep from being embarrassed by onlookers; similarly these brides of Christ veil themselves to show that they are unlawful to all men, and so that they may know that in exchange for their consecration a crown of life lies in store for them.

240

On the Habit of Nuns

Some virgins wear white vestments, perhaps in imitation of Saint Cecilia, whose exterior habit shone as white as her interior chastity, and whose heart refused to house worldly passions. The white habit manifests the vow of virginity.

241

De viduis

Viduarum prima Dina filia Iacob ante legem extitit, a qua usus viduarum coepit. Hanc sub lege Iudith et aliae multae imitatae sunt, sub gratia vero Anna et aliae plurimae secutae sunt, quae secundas nuptias contempserunt. Harum quoque habitus est mundi despectus.

242

De conversis

Conversae autem quae eundem habitum gerunt, Maria Magdalena formam sumpserunt.

241

On Widows

The first widow was Dinah the daughter of Jacob, who lived before the Law, and the widows' way of life began with her. Under the Law Judith and many other women imitated her example. In the time of grace Anna and many others followed, scorning second marriages. Their habit too is a sign of contempt for the world.

242

On Lay Sisters

The lay sisters, who wear the same habit, took their form of life from Mary Magdalene.

243

Baptizati albas portant vestes

Baptizati vero albas vestes portant, quia amissam innocentiam se recepisse insinuant.

243

The Baptized Wear White Clothes

The baptized wear white clothes to show that they have recovered their lost innocence.

BOOK 2

In superiori libello de Missa et de ecclesia eiusque ministris, quae Dominus largiri dignatus est digessimus. Nunc de reliquis horis quae Dominus rursus inspiraverit dicamus ut promisimus, et a Dominica nocte incipiamus, in qua redempti a servitute ad libertatem, de morte ad vitam translati sumus.

I

De nocturnorum officio

Nocturnale officium, repraesentat nobis excubias supernorum civium. Caelestis namque Ierusalem *quae aedificatur ut civitas,* conservatur per angelicas vigilias. Qui vices suas quasi in tres vigilias distribuunt, ac singulis tribus horis distinguuntur, et unamquamque tribus ordinibus custodiunt, dum Trinitati ter trinis agminibus laudes dulcisono concentu iugiter concinunt. Et quia praesens Ecclesia in hanc civitatem et in horum civium contubernium ventura praedicatur, ideo et ipsa Ierusalem nuncupatur, et idcirco illius civitatis vigiles in suis vigiliis imitatur. Quia vero umbram illius gerit, ideo hoc officium in nocte agit. Ideo autem in nocte Dominica, quia in hac meruit angelorum consortia.

BOOK 2

In the previous book we treated the Mass, the church, and its ministers, saying what the Lord deemed fit to grant us. Now we shall speak whatever the Lord again inspires us to say about the remaining hours, as we have promised, beginning from Sunday night, the night we were redeemed out of slavery into freedom and borne from death into life.

I

On the Office of Matins

The night office reenacts for us the watches of heaven's citizens. For the heavenly Jerusalem, *which is built as a city,* is kept secure by the angelic night watches. They share out their rounds in three vigils, dividing each into three hours, and each hour into three orders, as in thrice-three lines they sing praises to the Trinity in sweet harmony without end. It is foretold that the present Church will one day enter that city and become messmates with its citizens, and for this reason she too is called Jerusalem, and therefore she imitates the sentinels of that city in her vigils. Because this Jerusalem is only a shadow of that one, she performs this office at night, and on Sunday night, because that is when she merited to join the company of the angels.

2   Haec itaque urbs per basilicam praefiguratur, in quam clerus et populus quasi exercitus in militia congregatur. Signa militibus dantur per tubas, et Christianis dantur signa per campanas. Qui quasi milites convenientes imperatorem salutant, dum per versum *Domine labia mea aperies* laudes Christi inchoant. Dum enim in nocte dormitum eunt, signaculo crucis quasi sigillo se muniunt. Quod nunc aperiunt, dum ora in nocte clausa ad laudem Dei solvunt. Sed quia *frustra vigilant nisi Dominus custodiat civitatem* per versum *Deus in adiutorium meum* divinum auxilium invocant. Cantor qui invitatorium inchoat, est praeco qui tuba vigiles ad excubias convocat. Post *Venite,* hymnum omnes cantant, velut milites quando in castra conveniunt, regem laudibus 3 efferunt. Deinde vigilias inter se distribuunt, dum tres nocturnos psallunt. Singulae vigiliae tribus horis distinguuntur, et singulis nocturnis tres psalmi decernuntur. Angelicae excubiae tribus ordinibus servantur, et in nostris vigiliis tres ordines, scilicet psalmorum, lectionum, responsoriorum denotantur. Ideo autem novem lectiones cum responsoriis suis recitantur, quia caelestes excubiae per novem ordines angelorum celebrantur. Tres itaque nocturni totius Ecclesiae militiam nobis commemorant, qua in castris Domini sub tribus temporibus, videlicet ante legem, sub lege, sub gratia militant.

Now this city is prefigured in the basilica, where the 2
clergy and people gather like an army for their military service. Trumpets give signals to soldiers and bells to Christians
who, like mustered soldiers, salute their emperor when they
begin Christ's royal praises through the versicle *Domine labia
mea aperies*. When they go to sleep at night, they safeguard
themselves with the sign of the cross as with a seal, which
they open now when they loose for God's praise the mouths
that were closed during the night. But since *they keep watch
in vain unless God guards the city,* they invoke the divine help
through the verse *Deus in adiutorium meum*. The cantor who
begins the Invitatory is the herald who summons the sentinels to their posts. After the *Venite* all sing a hymn, as when
soldiers muster in the camp and give honor to the king.
Then they distribute the watches among themselves when 3
they sing the three nocturns. Each watch is divided into
three hours and there are three psalms in each nocturn. The
angelic night guard is kept in three turns, and in our vigils
three orders are marked out, namely, of psalms, readings,
and responsories. There are nine readings with their responsories because the heavenly watches are celebrated by the
nine orders of angels. In a similar way, the three nocturns
call to mind the whole Church militant, who have cam-
paigned in the Lord's service during three times: before the
Law, under the Law, and under grace.

2

De prima vigilia

Prima vigilia tempus ante legem intelligitur, quod quasi tribus horis adscribitur, dum tribus interstitiis distinguitur.

Prima hora huius vigiliae, ab Adam usque ad Noe erat, in qua excubias huius civitatis Abel, Enos, Enoch, Lamech, sicut primi psalmi indicant servabant. *Beatus vir* Abel exprimit, qui *tamquam lignum in tempore suo fructum* iustitiae protulit, dum ab hostibus urbis huius occubuit. *Quare fremuerunt* Enos denuntiat, qui *Domino in timore* serviebat, quem scriptura primus *nomen Domini invocasse* commemorat. *Domine quid multiplicati sunt* Enoch innuit, quem *Dominus suscepit,* dum eum de terrenis transtulit. *Domine ne in furore* Lamech depromit, cuius *deprecationem Dominus exaudivit,* cum ei talem filium dedit, qui humanum genus a furore Domini in arca servavit. Hi psalmi ideo sub una *Gloria Patri* canuntur, quia iusti illius temporis Trinitatem coluisse creduntur. Ideo autem quattuor psalluntur, quia quattuor virtutibus prudentia, fortitudine, iustitia, et temperantia fulsisse noscuntur. Antiphona per quam modulantur, laudatio eorum in Deum denotatur.

2

On the First Watch

The first vigil stands for the time before the Law. It is assigned three hours of watch time, as it were, because it is divided into three parts.

The first hour of this vigil lasted from Adam to Noah, during which time the night watch of this city was served by Abel, Enos, Enoch, and Lamech, as the first psalms indicate. The psalm *Beatus vir* portrays Abel, who *brought forth the fruit* of justice *in due season* when he was struck down by the enemies of this city. *Quare fremuerunt* proclaims Enos, who *served the Lord in fear* and whom scripture mentions as the first *to call upon the name of the Lord*. *Domine quid multiplicati sunt* signifies Enoch, whom *the Lord protected* when he took him up to heaven. *Domine ne in furore* introduces Lamech. *The Lord heard his supplication* when he gave him a son who saved the human race in the ark from the wrath of God. These psalms are sung under one *Gloria Patri* because we believe that the just men of that time worshiped the Trinity. The reason four are chanted is that these men were radiant with the four virtues of prudence, fortitude, justice, and temperance. The antiphon under which the psalms are sung signifies their praise of God.

2

3

De secunda hora

Secunda hora huius vigiliae a Noe usque ad Abraham erat, in qua Noe, Sem, Heber, et Thare vigilabant, ut sequentes psalmi insinuant. *Domine Deus meus in te speravi,* Noe exprimit, quem *Dominus in illa generatione iustum invenit,* et ideo *a persequentibus* aquis *salvum fecit. Domine Dominus noster* Sem congruit, quem Dominus *gloria et honore coronavit,* dum eum benedictione patris super fratres sublimavit. *Confitebor tibi* Heber innuit, quia *omnia mirabilia* Dei narravit, quando civitatem gigantium dissipavit. *In Domino confido* Thare depromit, qui *in Domino confidit,* quando eum impia gens ignem adorare coegit, cuius *pars calicis, ignis et sulphur* fuit. Hi quoque quaterni psalmi sub una *Gloria* canuntur, quia et illi patres, in quattuor virtutibus rutilantes, Trinitatem adorasse noscuntur. Antiphona vero modulationis, praefert devotionem illorum laudationis.

3

On the Second Hour

The second hour of this vigil lasted from Noah to Abraham, when Noah, Shem, Eber, and Terah stood guard, as the following psalms suggest. *Domine Deus meus in te speravi* represents Noah, whom *the Lord found just in his generation* and *saved from the pursuing* waters. *Domine Dominus noster* fits Shem, whom the Lord *crowned with glory and honor* when he raised him above his brothers through his father's blessing. *Confitebor tibi* points to Eber, who *related all the wonders* of God when he overthrew the city of giants. *In Domino confido* presents us with Terah, who *trusted in the Lord* when a wicked people forced him to worship fire, and *the portion of their cup was coals of fire and sulfur.* These four psalms are also sung under one *Gloria Patri,* because we know that these fathers who flashed brilliantly with the four virtues also worshiped the Trinity. The antiphon melody manifests their devoted praise.

4

De tertia hora

Tertia hora huius vigiliae, Abraham usque ad Moysen fuerat, in qua Abraham, Isaac, et Iacob et Ioseph vices vigilandi custodiebant, quod instantes psalmi proclamant. *Salvum me fac Domine* Abraham exprimit, quando *sanctus defecit,* cum videlicet ipse paene solus Deum coluit, et totus mundus idolatriae deditus fuit. *Usquequo Domine obliviscieris* Isaac innuit, cui Dominus *bona tribuit,* dum Christi figuram in omnibus praetulit. *Dixit insipiens* Iacob ostendit, quem insipiens Laban *sicut escam panis devoravit,* dum eum saepius defraudavit. Sed quia *Dominus spes eius* fuit, malum ab eo avertit, unde *exultavit Iacob, et laetatus est Israel. Domine quis habitabit* Ioseph demonstrat, qui *sine macula est ingressus* dum stuprum recusabat, *et operatus est iustitiam* dum populum a periculo famis liberabat. Hi quaterni sub una *Gloria Patri* clauduntur, quia hi vigiles, in quattuor virtutibus splendentes, Trinitatem coluisse leguntur. Antiphona melodiae, est laus ab eis exhibita Maiestati divinae. Sunt etiam istae antiphonae, quaedam vigilium cantilenae.

4

On the Third Hour

The third hour of the vigil ran from Abraham to Moses, when Abraham, Isaac, and Jacob took turns at the watch. The next psalms proclaim this. *Salvum me fac, Domine* points to Abraham, when *there was no saint,* which is to say when he was almost the only one who worshiped God and the whole world was wallowing in idolatry. *Usquequo Domine obliviceris* tells of Isaac, to whom the Lord *gave good things* when he appeared as a figure of Christ in all things. *Dixit insipiens* shows us Jacob, whom the fool Laban *devoured as bread* by deceiving him several times. But because *the Lord was his hope,* he turned away evil from him and so *Jacob rejoiced and Israel was glad. Domine quis habitabit* presents Joseph who *walked without blemish* when he refused to commit adultery and *worked justice* when he saved the people from the danger of famine. These four also conclude with one *Gloria Patri* because we read that these sentinels who shone with the four virtues also worshiped the Trinity. The melodic antiphon is the praise they gave to the Divine Majesty. For these antiphons are as songs sung by those on watch.

5

De versiculo

Versus qui sequitur, a vertendo dicitur, ideo quia se chorus vertit ad orientem, et quia se vertit de psalmis ad lectionem. Per orationem Dominicam quae secreto dicitur, secretum consilium regis intelligitur. Post *Pater noster* sacerdos versum aperte dicit, quasi rex mandatum legatis iniungit. Vicissitudines lectorum, sunt successiones legatorum. Qui *Domne iube benedicere* dicit, quasi licentiam eundi petit, benedictio vero sacerdotis, est licentia imperatoris. Ipsa autem lectio, est iniunctae legationis executio. *Tu autem Domine* reversionem legati exprimit, dum commisum mandatum reddit.

6

De lectionibus

Lectiones quoque praedicationem illorum patrum praeferunt, responsoria vitam eorum per quam praedicationi responderunt. Ideo autem post vigiliam Abrahae lectiones leguntur, quia ab eo primitus litterae post diluvium repertae

5

On the Versicle

A versicle follows. *Versus* comes from "turning," because the choir turns toward the east, and because it turns from the psalms toward the lesson. Then the Lord's prayer is said in silence, signifying the king's secret counsel. After the *Pater noster* the priest says the versicle out loud, like a king giving orders to his legates. The lectors' turns are the successions of legates. The one who says *Domne iube benedicere,* is as it were asking leave to go. The priest's blessing is the emperor's permission. The reading itself is the execution of the ordered legation. *Tu autem, Domine* indicates the legate's return, when he has fulfilled his commission.

6

On the Lessons

The lessons also display those fathers' preaching, the responsories their life that corresponded with their preaching. The lessons come after Abraham's vigil, because it is said that he was the first one after the Flood to discover

traduntur. Et ipse primus Chaldaeos astronomiam docuit, et Aegyptios mathematica imbuit. Ideo etiam peracta prima vigilia, lectiones leguntur, quia transacto primo tempore libri Legis ad doctrinam populi a Moyse eduntur.

7

De secunda vigilia et secundo nocturno

Secunda vigilia tempus legis accipitur, quod item quasi tribus horis discernitur, dum tribus interstitiis dividitur, scilicet uno a Moyse usque ad David, secundo a David usque ad Babyloniam, tertio a Babylonia usque ad Christum. Sive sacerdotibus, iudicibus, regibus, quod declarat psalmorum textus.

letters, and he was the first to teach the Chaldeans astronomy and train the Egyptians in astrology. The lessons come after the first vigil, because the books of the Law were published by Moses for the people's instruction at the end of the first time.

7

On the Second Watch and the Second Nocturn

The second vigil is taken to be the time of the Law, which is also as it were divided into a turn of three hours, since it consists of three parts, one from Moses to David, a second from David to Babylon, and a third from Babylon to Christ. Or to put it another way: priests, judges, and kings, as the text of the psalms declares.

8

De prima hora

Nam *Conserva me Domine* sacerdotes exprimit, quorum *Dominus pars hereditatis et calicis* fuit, qui prima hora huius vigiliae excubias servabant, dum Aaron et alii post eum legem Domini populum docebant. *Exaudi Domine iustitiam meam,* iudices innuit, quorum *iudicium de vultu Domini prodiit.*

9

De secunda hora

Hi secundae horae vigilandi curam susceperunt, dum Gedeon et alii populum secundum legem Dei iudicaverunt. *Diligam te Domine* reges ostendit, quos *Dominus caput gentium constituit,* qui tertiae horae vigilias custodiebant, dum David et alii populum ad iustitiam regebant.

8

On the First Hour

For *Conserva me Domine* represents priests, for whom *the Lord is their portion and their cup.* They kept their night watch at the first hour of this vigil, when Aaron and others after him taught the people the law of the Lord. *Exaudi Domine iustitiam meam* signifies the judges, whose *judgment came forth from the Lord's countenance.*

9

On the Second Hour

They chose to take the second hour's watch, when Gideon and others judged the people in accordance with God's Law. *Diligam te Domine* shows the kings, whom *the Lord made head of the gentiles,* and who kept watch during the third hour when David and others ruled the people in justice.

10

De *Gloria Patri* et
tertio nocturno

Singuli psalmi cum *Gloria Patri* psalluntur, quia singuli su-
pradicti ordines Trinitatem adorasse scribuntur, ideo etiam
et tres psalmi canuntur. Antiphonae ternae quibus psalmi
modulantur, sunt laudes quae ab illis iustis Trinitati exhibe-
bantur. Sequentes lectiones, sunt illorum vigilium praedica-
tiones. Responsoria vero illorum actiones, quibus hic *can-*
tabiles erant Dei iustificationes. Ideo autem lectiones post
vigiliam regum leguntur, quia illo tempore libri prophetarum scribuntur. Et ipsi tempore legis quasi secunda vigilia
populum docuerunt, et cantum bonorum operum personuerunt.

10

On the *Gloria Patri* and the Third Nocturn

Each of the psalms is sung with the *Gloria Patri*, because it is written that each of the aforementioned orders adored the Trinity, and for the same reason three psalms are sung. The three antiphon melodies are the praises tendered to the Trinity by these just men. The following readings are the preaching of these sentinels. The responsories are their actions, because here on earth God's *justifications were the subject of their songs*. The readings are done at the kings' watch because in that time the books of the prophets were written. They taught the people in the time of the Law, which is to say during the second watch of the night, and sang loud the song of good works.

II

De tertia vigilia et tertio nocturno

Tertia vigilia tempus gratiae extat, quae usque in finem mundi perdurat. Haec quasi in tres horas dividitur, dum tempore apostolicae praedicationis, tempore persecutionis, tempore pacis distinguitur.

Prima hora huius vigiliae apostoli vigilabant, quos demonstrat psalmus *Caeli enarrant gloriam Dei. Quorum voces omnis loquela et sermo audivit,* dum *eorum sonus in omnem terram exivit.* Secunda hora martyres vigilandi curam subibant, quos psalmus *Exaudiat te Dominus* denuntiat. Quos *nomen Dei in die tribulationis* protexit, et *omnis sacrificii* eorum *memor* fuit. Tertia hora excubias Constantinus dux pacis cum

2 fidelibus suscepit, quem psalmus *Domine in virtute tua laetabitur rex* innuit. Ipse enim rex *in virtute* Christi *est laetatus,* dum taurus in conventu totius orbis in nomine Christi per Silvestrum est resuscitatus. *Super salutem* Dei *vehementer exultavit,* dum maximam synodum in Nicaea congregavit, unde Ecclesia *coronam super caput eius posuit, gloriam et magnum decorem ei tribuit.* Huius vigiliae custodiam adhuc popu-

3 lus fidelium servat, cuius *rex in Domino sperat.* Ultimi versus psalmi, tangunt tempora Antichristi. Quem *Dominus clibanum ignis ponet,* in quo vasa sua examinat. In *tempore* vero

II

On the Third Vigil and the Third Nocturn

The third vigil is the time of grace, which lasts until the end of the world. This time is divided, as it were, into three hours, corresponding to the time of apostolic preaching, the time of persecution, and the time of peace.

During the first hour of this watch the apostles were on duty, as demonstrated by the psalm *Caeli enarrant gloriam Dei*. There were *no speeches nor languages where their voices were not heard,* when *their sound went forth into all the earth.* In the second hour the martyrs replaced the apostles at their watch posts, as the psalm *Exaudiat te Dominus* proclaims, for *the name of the Lord* protected them *in their tribulations,* and was *mindful of all* their *sacrifices.* Constantine, author of the peace, took the third hour's round with the faithful people, as we see in the psalm *Domine in virtute tua laetabitur rex.* He is the king who *rejoiced in* Christ's *strength* when in Christ's name Sylvester raised the bull from the dead in the midst of an international congress. He *rejoiced exceedingly in God's salvation* when he convened a great synod in Nicaea, for which the Church *set on his head a crown* of glory and *laid upon him great glory.* To this day the faithful people keep this watch and *their king hopeth in the Lord.* The last verses of the psalm touch upon the times of the Antichrist. The Lord *will make* him *as an oven of fire,* in which he tests his vessels. But *in the*

2

3

vultus tui id est in die iudicii eum cum omnibus iniquis *Do-minus in ira sua conturbabit,* cum *eos ignis devorabit.* Ecclesiam vero vigilem *in virtute sua Dominus* tunc *exaltabit,* quae *virtutes eius cantabit.* Hi psalmi singuli cum *Gloria Patri* terminantur, quia Trinitas ab his omnibus veneratur. Tres autem ideo sunt, quia in fide, spe, et caritate floruerunt. Antiphonae melodiae sunt gratiarum actiones Ecclesiae, et quaedam vigilum cantilenae.

12

De Paulo vigili

Paulus vigil suavem cantilenam in prima hora cantavit, dum pro gentium vocatione sic exultavit, "*Regi saeculorum immortali, invisibili, soli Deo honor et gloria in saecula saeculorum. Amen.*"

time of his anger, that is, on the day of judgment, the Lord *shall trouble them in his wrath* along with all the wicked, when *fire shall devour them.* But *the Lord* will *raise up* the watchful Church *in his strength,* and *she will sing his power.* Each of these psalms ends with the *Gloria Patri,* because all of these men venerated the Trinity. There are three psalms, because each of them flourished in faith, hope, and charity. The melody of the antiphon is the Church's thanksgiving and the song of the night watch.

12

On Paul the Sentinel

Paul the sentinel sang a sweet melody during the first hour of the watch, when he rejoiced at the calling of the gentiles, *"Now to the king of ages, immortal, invisible, the only God, be honor and glory for ever and ever. Amen."*

13

De Laurentio vigili

Laurentius vigil dulcem cantilenam in secunda hora est modulatus, dum in craticula sic est gratulatus, *"Gratias tibi ago Domine quia ianuas tuas ingredi merui."*

14

De Gregorio vigili

Gregorius vigil delectabilem harmoniam in tertia hora sonuit, dum musica arte Divinum Officium agi docuit. Per lectiones quae recitantur, doctrinae fidelium designantur. Responsoria quae cantantur, sunt eorum exempla quibus alii informantur, unde etiam "responsorium" vocabulum habet, quia vita doctrinae respondet. Per cantum versus, paenitentium conversatio intelligitur, cum quis de malo ad bonum convertitur, sicut enim laborat, qui versus solum cantat, ita paenitens laborem subit, dum pro errato satisfacit. Post versum autem cantus inceptio, est communis omnium pro

13

On Laurence the Sentinel

Laurence stood watch at the second hour, and he sang a lovely song when he gave thanks from the gridiron, "*I thank thee, O Lord, for I have deserved to enter into thy gates.*"

14

On Gregory the Sentinel

Gregory stood watch at the third hour and intoned a delightful melody when he instructed us to perform the Divine Office with the musical art. The lessons that are read signify the teachings of various Christians. The responsories that are sung are their good examples by which others are formed. Hence the name "responsory," for our life should correspond with what we are taught. The singing of the versicle signifies the life of penitents, when someone is converted from evil to good. The solo voice that sings the versicle is in travail, just like the penitent who undergoes suffering to satisfy for his transgression. The beginning of the chant that follows the versicle is a general thanksgiving for

converso gratulatio. Cui omnis per orationes succurrunt, sicut canenti subveniunt, quia et *angeli super uno peccatore paenitentiam agente gaudium in caelis ducunt.* Per hoc autem cantores, milites in excubiis imitantur, qui si aliquis ex sociis suis inter hostes aberraverit contristantur, si vero periculum

2 evadens ei congratulantur. Tertio responsorio semper *Gloria Patri* adnectitur, quia Trinitati omne praesens, praeteritum, et futurum subicitur. Ad tertiam vigiliam ideo Evangelium recitatur, quia in tertio tempore illud mundo praedicabatur, ideo et in tertio nocturno saepius in antiphonis Alleluia cantatur, quia in illo tempore laus et laetitia aeternae vitae praenuntiabatur. Haec universa ideo in Dominica nocte actitantur, quia omnes praedicti per fidem Resurrectionis Christi salvantur. Porro *Te Deum laudamus* gaudium et laetitiam nobis repraesentat, quo Ecclesia in die iudicii liberata exultat.

3 Forsitan aliquem movebit, cur tres tantum vigiliae a nobis ponantur, cum quattuor noctis vigiliae tradantur. Hic sciat cum ad noctem saeculi significatio refertur, tunc tres tantum vigiliae propter tria tempora ponuntur, pro quibus et tres nocturni psalluntur. Cum vero ad noctem temporis refertur, tunc quattuor vigiliae scribuntur, et pro quarta laudes canuntur. Et sciendum cum "nocturnus" dicitur, cantus intelligitur, cum autem "nocturna," tunc hora accipitur.

the converted. Everyone comes to his aid with prayers, just as they come to support the soloist, for *the angels rejoice in heaven upon one sinner that doth penance.* In this way the singers imitate soldiers on their night rounds, who are sorrowful when one of their comrades wanders into enemy territory. But if he returns and escapes danger, they are happy for him. The *Gloria Patri* is always appended to the third responsory 2 because everything present, past, and future is subjected to the Trinity. The Gospel is recited at the third watch because it was preached to the world in the third age. Further, the alleluia is sung rather often in the antiphons of the third nocturn, because in that time the praise and joy of eternal life was announced to the world. All of these things are enacted on Sunday night because all the aforementioned men are saved through faith in Christ's Resurrection. Furthermore, the *Te Deum laudamus* represents the joy and happiness of the Church, who rejoices in her liberation on the day of judgment.

Perhaps someone wants to ask why we have discussed 3 only three watches, when by custom we keep four watches in the night. Let the questioner know that, with respect to the night of this world, there are only three watches on account of the three times, and so we sing three nocturns. But with respect to the night reckoned as time, there are four, and so for the fourth watch we sing Lauds. Note too that when we use the masculine word *nocturnus* it refers to the chant, while *nocturna* refers to the hour.

15

De media nocte

Nocturnale autem officium ideo media nocte agimus, quia media nocte dormientes Aegyptios percussisse, et vigilantes Hebraeos liberasse legimus. Ideo etiam media nocte agitur, quia in media nocte in Bethlehem Dominus natus legitur, eique mox ab angelis laus concinitur. Qui etiam pastoribus cum lumine apparebant, *qui vigilias noctis custodiebant.* Ideo quoque in media nocte, et in Dominica nocte, quia Dominus media nocte, et in Dominica nocte, infernum devastavit, et populum hic vigilantem inde liberavit. Ideo nihilominus in media nocte, et in Dominica nocte, quia Dominus media et in Dominica nocte ad iudicium veniet, et dormientes a bonis *de civitate sua disperdet,* vigilantes vero in bonis, in locum exultationis adducet.

16

De auctoritate sanctorum

Auctoritatem vero a sanctis habemus, ut in nocte surgentes laudes creatori nostro cantemus. David namque et prophetae *media nocte ad confitendum nomini Domini* surge-

15

On the Middle of the Night

We perform the night office at midnight, because we read that at midnight the Lord struck the sleeping Egyptians and set free the watchful Hebrews. It is sung at midnight because that is when the Lord was born in Bethlehem and the angels sang their hymn to him, appearing also to *the shepherds who were keeping watch by night.* Likewise at midnight on Sunday, the Lord laid waste to hell and freed those who were keeping watch there. Again at midnight on a Sunday because the Lord will come in judgment on a Sunday at midnight and *will cast out* those who are asleep in good works *from his city,* but those watching through good works he will lead into the place of rejoicing.

16

On the Saints' Authority

When we rise in the night to sing praises to our creator, we are following the authority of the saints. For David and the prophets *rose at midnight to praise the name of the Lord,* and

bant, et Dominus in oratione pernoctabat, et Paulus atque Silas in carcere media nocte psallebant, quando ingens lumen divinitus ibi resplendebat. Hos qui imitantur, et praemiis participantur.

17

De dispositione Hieronimi

Hieronimus primum in Bethlehem ubi Dominus nasci voluit, nocturnale officium vel reliquas horas ut hodie canit Ecclesia disposuit. Sed Damasus papa per omnes ecclesias eodem ritu celebrari constituit. *Anti* dicitur contra, *phonos* vero dicitur sonus, antiphona inde nomen habet, quod contra tonum sonet, quia videlicet cum antiphona incipitur, secundum eius tonum psalmus canitur. Hunc cantum primitus Ignatius Antiochenus episcopus in caelo angelicum chorum alternare audivit, et secundum hanc formam suam ecclesiam cantare docuit, isque mos ad omnes ecclesias pertransiit. Responsorium a respondendo dicitur, quia choro canente versus ab uno respondetur, et huic iterum a choro per inceptionem respondetur. Hunc cantum in primis Ambrosius Mediolanensis episcopus composuit, et ab eo tota Ecclesia formam accepit. Hic etiam hymnos composuit quos adhuc Ecclesia in laude Christi canit.

the Lord himself spent the night in prayer, and Paul and Silas sang psalms all through their night in prison, when a great light shone from heaven. All who imitate these men will share in their reward.

17

On Jerome's Disposition of the Psalms

In Bethlehem, where our Lord wished to be born, Jerome first composed the night office and the other hours as the Church sings them today. Next Pope Damasus ordered it to be celebrated according to the same rite throughout all the churches. *Anti* means before, *phonos* means sound, and thus the antiphon is so called because it "sounds before," since after the antiphon has been intoned, the psalm is sung in its tone. In ancient times, Ignatius, bishop of Antioch, heard the angelic chorus alternating in heaven, and according to this form he taught his church to sing, and afterward this custom spread to all the churches. The word "responsory" comes from "responding," because when the choir has sung, one person responds with a verse, and the choir responds by repeating the beginning part. Ambrose of Milan first composed the responsory chant, and the whole Church received this form from him. He also composed hymns that the Church still sings in praise of Christ.

18

De vinea Domini

Nocturnale quoque officium est imitatio in vinea laborantium.

Cum in ecclesia ad servitium Dei noctu coimus, quasi in vineam ad operandum convenimus. Praesens enim vita nocti comparatur, quae tenebris ignorantiae obscuratur. Cum laudem Dei per *Domine labia mea* incipimus, quasi opus vineae inchoamus. Moxque divinum auxilium per *Deus in adiutorium meum* invocamus, quatenus inceptum opus perficiamus, per *Venite* vero alterutrum ad servitium Dei quasi operantes instigamus. Deinde hymnum Deo canimus, quod nocturnas illusiones superavimus, et illos per hoc imitamur, qui cantant dum operantur. Deinde dum alternatim psallimus, quasi certatim operi insistimus. Dum lectiones legimus, quasi nos ad opus instruimus. Dum etiam canimus, quasi pro peracto opere gratias agimus. Est etiam lectio, mentis refectio. Dum ergo lectiones legimus, quasi animas in divino opere lassas, velut vineae operarios reficimus. Dum responsoria canimus, quasi post refectionem laudes solvimus. Unde cum iterum psallimus, quasi refecti ad laborandum surgimus. Diversae nocturnae variae horae sunt, quibus operarii in vineam Domini introierunt. Ut autem labor huius vineae levigetur, priorum patrum in hac vinea pondus

18

On the Lord's Vineyard

The night office is also an imitation of the laborers in the vineyard.

When we gather at night in the church for God's service, it is as if we are gathering in the vineyard to work. For the present life may be compared to a night sunk in the darkness of ignorance. When we begin God's praise through *Domine labia mea,* we begin to work. Soon we invoke the divine aid through *Deus in adiutorium meum,* so that we may finish the work we have begun. Then through the *Venite* we exhort our fellow laborers to carry out God's service. Then we sing a hymn to God because we have overcome the deceits of the night. In doing so, we imitate laborers who sing while they work. Then when we sing alternately, we lay into our work with a competitive spirit. When we read the readings, we instruct ourselves how to work. When we continue on singing the responsories, we give thanks for the work we have done. For reading is mental recreation. When we read, we rest our souls made weary by the divine work, like workers in the vineyard. When we sing the responsories, we give thanks after our recreation. When we begin the psalms again, we rise refreshed to go back to work. The various nocturns are the various hours when the workmen entered the Lord's vineyard. So that the difficulty of our labor may be made lighter, the psalms and readings show us the example

diei et aestus portantium exemplum per psalmos et lectiones praebetur.

19

De sacerdote

Sacerdos itaque qui incipit, figuram patrisfamilias gerit, qui operarios in vineam conducit. Cantor qui *Venite* cantat, praefert procuratorem, qui ad vineae culturam invitat. Porro hymnus illum cantum representat quem post peractum opus alacriter inchoant. Psalmi diversorum sanctorum opera nobis insinuant, qui in hac vinea laborabant. Primi namque quaterni psalmi mane, scilicet ab Adam usque ad Noe demonstrant, secundi quaterni horam tertiam, scilicet a Noe usque ad Abraham indicant, tertii quaterni sextam horam, scilicet ab Abraham usque ad Moysen denuntiant.

of our more ancient fathers bearing the first heat and labor of the day in the vineyard.

19

On the Priest

Now the priest who begins the office stands for the paterfamilias who hires the laborers to work in the vineyard. The cantor who sings the *Venite* stands for the foreman who invites them to the vineyard. The hymn represents the song they sing lustily after the work is complete. The psalms teach us the works of the saints who labored in this life. The first four psalms show the morning, from Adam to Noah. The second four point to the third hour, from Noah to Abraham. The third set of four proclaims the sixth hour, from Abraham up to Moses.

20

Mane Abel

Mane itaque primus Abel huius vineae laborem subiit, quem primus psalmus *Beatus vir* exprimit, qui nos *in lege Domini die ac nocte* meditari, quasi in vinea operari docuit, dum ipse protomatyr *tamquam lignum fructiferum fructum* martyrii primus *obtulit.* Post hunc Enos hanc vineam excoluit, quem psalmus *Quare fremuerunt* innuit, qui nos in hac vinea *Domino in timore* servire instituit, quando *gentes* ex Cain in malitia *fremuerunt,* et *adversus Dominum inania meditati sunt.* Deinde Enoch huius vineae cultor extitit, quem psalmus *Domine quid multiplicati* depromit, qui nos *a somno exurgere, et voce nostra ad Dominum clamare* monuit. Quem quia *multitudo populi maligni circumdedit, Dominus eum suscepit.* Lamech quoque ad laborem introiit, quem psalmus *Domine ne in furore* innotescit, qui nos *per singulas noctes lectum nostrum lacrimis lavare* instruit, ne cum his pereamus, quos *Dominus in furore suo arguit.*

20

Abel in the Morning

Now Abel was the first to begin work in the vineyard in the morning, as the first psalm *Beatus vir* makes plain, and he taught us to *meditate on the Law of the Lord day and night,* or rather to work in the vineyard, since as the Protomartyr, *like a fruitful tree,* he was the first *to offer up the fruit* of martyrdom. After him, Enos worked this vineyard, as told in the psalm *Quare fremuerunt,* which taught us to *serve the Lord in fear* in this vineyard, when the *peoples* of Sham *raged* in their wickedness and *devised vain things against the Lord.* Next Enoch came to tend the vineyard, as presented in the psalm *Domine quid multiplicati,* which teaches us to *rise up from our sleep* and *cry to the Lord with our voice.* When *a multitude of evil peoples surrounded him, the Lord lifted him up.* Lamech too entered into service, as we learn in the psalm *Domine ne in furore,* which teaches us *every night to wash our bed with tears,* lest we perish along with those whom *the Lord rebukes in his indignation.*

21

Tertia hora Noe

Domine Deus meus in te speravi Noe ostendit, qui quasi hora tertia hanc vineam excoluit, et primus vites plantare nos docuit. Qui quia *in Domino speravit, eum* in undis *liberavit. Domine Dominus noster* Sem denuntiat, qui post diluvium in hac vinea *nomen* Domini *mirabile in universa terra* nuntiabat, qui omnes se laudantes *gloria et honore coronabit,* qui *ex ore infantium et lactentium laude perfecit. Confitebor tibi Domine* Heber cultorem huius vineae insinuat, qui nos admonet *psallere Domino qui in Sion habitat. In Domino confido* Thare indicat, qui cultor huius vineae *in Domino confidebat,* et Domino *in Templo sancto suo* nos servire monebat.

22

Sexta hora Abraham

Sexta hora Abraham hanc vineam intrabat, quem psalmus *Salvum me fac* declarat, quando *sanctus defecit,* cum mundus

21

Noah at the Third Hour

The psalm *Domine Deus meus in te speravi* tells us of Noah, who, so to speak, tended this vineyard at the third hour and was the first to teach us to plant vines. Because *he put his trust in the Lord, he was saved* from the Flood. *Domine Dominus noster* proclaims Shem, who after the Flood announced in the vineyard *how admirable the Lord's name was in all the earth,* the Lord who *will crown with glory and honor* all those who praise him and who *hast perfected praise out of the mouths of infants and of sucklings. Confitebor tibi Domine* shows us Heber's work in this vineyard. He teaches us to *sing to the Lord who dwells in Zion. In Domino confido* deals with Terah, who *put his trust in the Lord* when he tended this vineyard and taught us to *serve the Lord in his holy Temple.*

22

Abraham at the Sixth Hour

The psalm *Salvum me fac* tells of how Abraham entered the vineyard at the sixth hour, when *there was no saint,* in the

idola coluit. *Usquequo Domine oblivisceris me,* Isaac in hac vinea laborantem exprimit, cuius *Dominus oblitus* non fuit, dum arietem pro eo mactandum posuit. Qui nos *cantare Domino* et *psallere nomini* eius monuit, qui omnia *bona* nobis *tribuit. Dixit insipiens* Iacob innuit, qui apud *insipientem* Laban pondus diei et aestus portavit, et nos *Dominum invocare* docuit. *Domine quis habitabit* Ioseph depromit, qui in hac vinea *sine macula* desudavit, et nos *Dominum glorificare* monuit.

23

De versu

Quod intermissa psalmodia versus dicitur, designat quod intermisso opere multitudo ad refectionem expeditur. Lectiones quae leguntur, sunt diversa fercula quibus operarii ad sextam reficiuntur. Benedictiones quae praecedunt, religiosorum benedictiones praeferunt, qui cibum benedicunt. Responsoria, quae post lectionem canuntur, sunt laudes quae sumpto cibo solvuntur.

time when the world worshiped idols. *Usquequo Domine obliviscéris me* tells of Isaac's work in the vineyard. *The Lord did not forget him* when he gave a ram to be sacrificed in his place. This psalm instructs us to *sing to the Lord* and *sing to his name,* because *he hath given us good things. Dixit insipiens* is about Jacob, who bore the heat of the day when he stayed with that *fool* Laban and taught us *to call upon the Lord. Domine quis habitabit* shows us Joseph, who labored *without blemish* in the vineyard and taught us *to glorify the Lord.*

23

On the Versicle

The versicle that interrupts the psalmody here shows us the laborers who break off their work for a rest. The lessons are the various dishes the workers eat at the sixth hour. The blessings that precede signify the blessings of religious men, by whom the food is blessed. The responsories sung after the readings are the thanksgiving offered after the food has been consumed.

24

Nona hora Moyses

Secunda nocturna est hora nona. Hac Moyses et Aaron aliique legis sacerdotes vineam Domini excolebant, qui in psalmo *Conserva me Domine* Dominum partem suam et calicem dicebant, et nos *Dominum qui tribuit intellectum* benedicere docebant. In hac etiam iudices laborabant, quos psalmus *Exaudi Domine iustitiam,* denotat, qui iudicium suum de vultu Domini prodire rogabant, et nos in nocte ad Dominum clamare monebant. In hac reges quoque desudabant, qui se in psalmo *Diligam te Domine in caput gentium constitutos* proclamant. Qui nos *laudando Dominum invocare* instruebant. Versus modulatio est ab opere separatio. Lectiones sunt operariorum refectiones. Responsoria sunt illorum laudationes.

25

Undecima hora apostoli

In tertia nocturna repraesentatur hora undecima. In hac apostoli humeros oneri supponebant, quos canit psalmus

24

Moses at the Ninth Hour

The second nocturn is at the ninth hour, when Moses and Aaron and the other priests of the Law worked the Lord's vineyard. These men called the Lord *their portion and their cup* in the psalm *Conserva me Domine,* and taught us to *bless the Lord who hath given us understanding.* In this hour the judges also labored, as noted in the psalm *Exaudi Domine iustitiam,* and they pleaded for their *judgment to come from the Lord's countenance,* and warned us *to cry to the Lord* in the night. The kings also toiled in this hour, proclaiming that they would be *made the head of the gentiles* in *Diligam te Domine.* They showed us how *to call upon the Lord in praise.* The versicle is the laborers' ceasing from work. The Lessons are their refreshments. The responsories are their praises.

25

The Apostles at the Eleventh Hour

The third nocturn represents the eleventh hour. In this hour the apostles took the work upon their shoulders, as the

Caeli enarrant, qui nos *iustitias Domini* edocebant. In hac martyres, ut in magno aestu grave pondus portabant, quos loquitur psalmus *Exaudiat te Dominus,* qui nos *Dominum in die tribulationis invocare* monebant. In hac et confessores operati sunt, qui in psalmo *Domine in virtute* expressi sunt, qui *voluntate labiorum suorum fraudati non sunt,* et nos *cantare et psallere virtutes Domini* persuaserunt. Per versum qui sequitur et Evangelium quod legitur, conversio gentilium intelligitur. Qui quasi responsorium cantant, quod per Evangelium in vineam Domini conducti sunt, qui *tota die in foro* infidelitatis *otiosi steterunt.* Per *Te Deum laudamus,* illorum gaudium accipitur, quibus peracto opere denarius in sero, id est in vita aeterna *in consummatione saeculi* traditur. Hos ideo in nocturnali officio imitamur, ut cum eis denarium vitae Christum mereamur, et quia haec cuncta per Christi Resurrectionem sperantur, ideo in nocte Dominicae resurrectionis tali modo cantatur.

26

De versibus

Antiqui patres in omni opere Deum invocabant, sed et gentiles Deum in minimis etiam rebus invocandum

psalm *Caeli enarrant* sings. They taught us *the justices of the Lord*. The martyrs bore a great weight, as of the day's heat, and the psalm *Exaudiat te Dominus* speaks of them, who taught us *to call upon the Lord in the day of tribulation*. The confessors take their shift in the same nocturn. They are given voice in *Domine in virtute*, from whom the Lord *has not withholden the will of their lips*, and who persuaded us to *sing and praise the Lord's power.* Through the versicle and Gospel 2 that follow, we understand the conversion of the gentiles, who sing, as it were, a responsory because they were hired for the Lord's vineyard through the Gospel after *they had stood all day idle in the marketplace* of unbelief. The *Te Deum laudamus* signifies the joy of those who receive a penny when the work is done late in the day, or eternal life *at the consummation of the world.* We imitate them in the night office so that with them we may earn the penny of life, who is Christ. Because we hope for all these things through Christ's Resurrection, so we sing in this way on the night of the Lord's Resurrection.

26

On the Versicles

Our forefathers called upon God in all their works, and the pagans also believed that they ought to call upon God in

censebant. Ideo nos omnes horas per versum *Deus in adiuto-rium* incipimus, ut in omni actione divinum auxilium invo-cemus. Versus *Memor fui in nocte* tempus ante legem designat, quo patriarchae *in nocte* ignorantiae *nominis Domini memores erant.* Sed et Dominum exprimit, qui pro nobis in nocte ora-vit, ut et Ecclesia nominis eius in nocte memor sit. Versus *Media nocte surgebam* tempus legis denotat, quo prophetae de nocte ignorantiae ad lucem scientiae surgebant. Sed et Do-minum demonstrat qui *media nocte* de mortuis *surgebat,* ut et Ecclesia *media nocte ad confitendum nomini eius surgat.* Per versum *Exaltare Domine* tempus gratiae designatur, quo *Do-minus in virtute sua* scilicet in dextera Patris *exaltatur.* Et si Ecclesia *virtutes eius* in nocte *cantabit,* eam quoque in gaudio *exaltabit.*

2   *Exaudi Domine preces servorum tuorum* ex libro Paralipo-menon assumptum, patriarchis convenit, quos primus noc-turnus exprimit. *Ostende nobis Domine* vel quodcumque aliud pro tempore de psalterio vel prophetia alia sumptum pro-phetis congruit, quos secundus nocturnus innuit. *Precibus et meritis beatae Mariae omniumque sanctorum* sanctae Mariae et apostolis convenit, quos tertius nocturnus concinit. *Domne, iube* ad Dominum dicitur, ad quod *Tu autem Domine* conti-nuatur, quod de psalmo *Beatus qui intelligit* assumitur. Sacer-dos autem, qui tenet Domini vicem, dat benedictionem.

even the smallest things. Wherefore we begin all the hours with the verse *O God, come to my assistance,* so that the divine assistance be invoked in every action. The versicle *Memor fui in nocte* refers to the time before the Law, when the patriarchs *remembered the Lord's name throughout the night* of ignorance. It also portrays our Lord, who prayed for us during the night so that the Church would be mindful of his name during the night. The versicle *Media nocte surgebam* denotes the time of the Law, when the prophets rose from the night of ignorance to the light of knowledge. But it also represents our Lord who *rose* from the dead *at midnight* so that the Church would *rise at midnight to give praise* to his name. The versicle *Exaltare Domine* refers to the time of grace, when *the Lord is exalted in his strength,* that is to say at the right hand of the Father. And if the Church *sings of his strength* in the night, *he will* also *exalt* her with bliss.

Exaudi Domine preces servorum tuorum, taken from the 2 book of Chronicles, pertains to the patriarchs, who were expressed in the first nocturn. *Ostende nobis Domine,* or some other versicle according to the season taken from the psalter or from another prophecy, refers to the prophets, signified in the second nocturn. *Precibus et meritis beatae Mariae omniumque sanctorum* pertains to Mary and the apostles, about whom we sing in the third nocturn. *Domne iube* refers to the Lord, followed by *Tu autem Domine* which is taken from the psalm *Beatus qui intelligit.* The priest, who is the Lord's representative, gives the blessing.

27

De festivitate sanctorum

In festis sanctorum ita nocturnale officium ut in nocte Dominica agimus, quia eos per Christi Resurrectionem gaudia consecutos credimus. Ideo autem cum novem psalmis et totidem lectionibus et responsoriis celebramus, quia eos in consortio novem ordinum angelorum esse praedicamus.

28

De nocturnis monachorum

Porro Divinum Officium a beato Benedicto ordinatum paene idem significat, praesertim cum ad idem videlicet ad laudem Dei et ad iustorum praeconia tendat. Hoc ideo ab Ecclesia est receptum, quia ab illo qui *omnium iustorum spiritu plenus fuit* est prolatum, et ab apostolici pontificis Gregorii auctoritate roboratum.

Siquidem patet quod idem vir Deo plenus in vinea laborantes et in vigiliis excubantes attenderit, dum tali modo psalmos distribuerit, et Dominicam noctem tribus

27

On the Feasts of Saints

On saints' feast days we do the night office as on Sunday night, because we believe that they have reached the joys of heaven through Christ's Resurrection. We celebrate it with nine psalms and as many readings and responsories, which teaches us that they are in the company of the nine orders of angels.

28

On Monastic Matins

Now, the Divine Office as arranged by Saint Benedict signifies nearly the same thing, since its intention is the same, namely to praise God and to celebrate the deeds of the just. The Church has received this office because it came from a man who *was filled with the spirit of all the just* and was approved by the authority of the apostolic pontiff Gregory.

It is certainly obvious that this man full of God had in mind the laborers in the vineyard and the sentinels on night watch when he distributed the psalms in this manner and

vigiliis per tres nocturnos distinxerit, licet ipse psalmos senario, lectiones vero quaternario numero assignaverit. Quia videlicet per senarium activae vitae actio designatur, propter sex opera Evangelii quibus in istis sex diebus quasi in vinea laboratur. Per quaternarium autem contemplativae vitae perfectio propter quattuor Evangelia figuratur, quibus contra hostes animarum scilicet vitia et daemones iugiter vigilatur. Per sex ergo psalmos in vinea Domini laborantes declarantur, per quattuor lectiones in castris Domini vigilantes demonstrantur. Per responsoria alacritas laborantium denotatur.

2   Notandum quod hic divini servitii ordinator a psalmo *Domine in virtute* qui de pace Ecclesiae constat incepit, et reliquos qui de Passione Domini sonant in hoc officio conclusit. Dominus enim in Cruce pendens, a *Deus Deus meus* incepit, et ita decem psalmos cantans in versu "*In manus tuas commendo spiritum meum*" finivit. Hoc idcirco in nocte Dominicae Resurrectionis instituit, quia nimirum Christus per Passionem ad Resurrectionis pacem pervenit, et Ecclesiae pacem per Passionem suam contulit. Et nos in pace degentes si Passionem Christi in vigiliis nos cruciando imitabimus, in resurrectione pace aeterna per Christum ditabimur.

divided Sunday night into three watches through the three nocturns. He assigned six psalms and four readings because the number six signifies the work of the active life, on account of the six works of mercy in the Gospel, by means of which man works for six days in the vineyard. The number four is a figure for the perfection of the contemplative life, because of the four Gospels by which a ceaseless watch is kept against the enemies of souls, namely the vices and the demons. Thus, the six psalms proclaim the laborers in the Lord's vineyard, the four readings those keeping watch in the Lord's camp, and the responsories the eagerness of the laborers.

Observe how this author of the divine service began with 2 the psalm *Domine in virtute,* which is about the peace of the Church, and concluded the office with others that signify Christ's Passion. For while our Lord hung on the Cross he sang ten psalms, beginning with *Deus Deus meus* and ending with the verse "*Into thy hands I commend my spirit.*" Benedict obviously instituted the office in this way on the night of our Lord's Resurrection because Christ went through his Passion to the peace of his Resurrection, and conferred peace on the Church through his Passion. If we who are now at peace imitate Christ's Passion by doing violence to ourselves in these watches, we will be granted peace through Christ at the Resurrection.

29

De tertio nocturno

Tertium nocturnum idem vir Dei tribus canticis attribuit, quia Trinitatem in fide, spe, caritate, laudari voluit. Unde eadem cantica cum alleluia cantari instituit, quia laudatores Trinitatis ad canticum caelestis laetitiae vocari docuit. Deinde, quattuor lectiones de Evangelio legi praecepit, quia Christi vigiles per doctrinam quattuor Evangeliorum in quattuor virtutibus munitos monuit. Ut videlicet in divinis et humanis sint prudentes, in adversis et prosperis fortes, in Dei servitio solvendo et praelatis obediendo iusti, in omnibus actibus suis temperati. His quattuor responsoria subiungunt, si haec omnia alacriter peragunt. Post haec constituit Deo dilectus cantari *Te Deum laudamus,* quatenus nil sibi in his omnibus adscribant, sed cuncta divinae laudi attribuant, se vero *inutiles servos* dicant. Per *Te Deum laudamus* etiam ille cantus intelligitur, qui peracto opere ab operariis prae gaudio canitur. Deinde Evangelium legi praecipitur, per quod vita aeterna promittitur, quod denarius intelligitur qui operariis post laborem dabitur. Per hymnum *Te decet laus* qui ad extremum canitur, illa ultima gratulatio accipitur. Quando percepto vitae denario in Domino exultant, quod de labore ad requiem de vinea ad patriam eis ire liceat.

29

On the Third Nocturn

The same man of God gave the third nocturn three canticles, for he wanted the Trinity to be praised in faith, hope, and charity. He ordered the same canticles to be sung with the alleluia, teaching us that those who praise the Trinity are called to join heaven's gladness. Next he ordered four readings from the Gospel, showing that Christ's watchmen are defended by the four virtues through the doctrine of the four Gospels, so they may be prudent in human and divine things, strong in good and bad times, temperate in discharging the divine service, and obedient in all things to the will of their superiors. They add four responsories if they perform all these things readily. Next, that man beloved of God decided the hymn *Te Deum laudamus* should be sung, so that in all these things they do not ascribe anything to themselves, but everything to the divine praise, holding themselves to be *unworthy servants*. In the *Te Deum laudamus* we may also understand the song of joy sung by the workers when the work is done. Next the Rule ordains that the Gospel be read, in which we are promised eternal life. It is the penny the laborers receive for their work. The hymn *Te decet laus* sung at the very end is their final thanksgiving when, having received the penny of life, they rejoice in the Lord who permits them to pass from work to rest, from the vineyard to the homeland.

30

De inclinationibus

Cum ecclesiam ingredientes ad altare inclinamus, quasi regem milites adoramus. Aeterni quippe Regis milites sumus, cui semper in procinctu specialis militiae adsumus. Cum autem ad orientem et occidentem inclinamus, Deum ubique praesentem nos adorare monstramus. Quem ita rationali motu *ab ortu* nostrae nativitatis *usque ad occasum* mortis sequi debemus. Sic caelum ab oriente in occidentem naturali revolutione ferri videmus. Quod monachi expressius designant, qui se toto corpore ab oriente in occidentem girant.

31

De matutinis Laudibus

Apud gentiles dii infernales dicebantur manes, eo quod mane diem terris emitterent, quem tota nocte quasi inclusum retinerent. A manibus ergo mane, id est bonum dicitur,

30

On Bowing

When we bow to the altar upon entering the church, it is as if we are soldiers paying homage to a king. For we are warriors of the eternal King, always standing at the ready for a special military deployment. When we bow to the east and west, we show that we pay homage to the omnipresent God, whom we must follow in a rational motion *from the rising* of our birth *to the setting* of our death, just as the heavens move in a natural revolution from east to west. The monks show this more expressively by turning their whole bodies around from east to west.

31

On Morning Lauds

Among the pagans the gods of the underworld were called *manes,* because in the morning they would send upon the earth the day which they had held captive, as it were, during the night. From *manes,* therefore, we have *mane* (morning), meaning good, because we value nothing more

eo quod nil melius luce videatur. A mane autem dicitur matutina, quasi laus Deo pro luce exhibita.

32

De prima causa

Hanc horam ea de causa canimus, quod hac hora mundum creatum credimus. Hac hora *astra matutina* exorta, cum iucunditate luxerunt, et *Deum* qui fecit ea dulci harmonia *laudaverunt*. Scilicet angeli ea hora creati sunt, qui et *filii Dei* nominati sunt, qui mox pro creatione mundi magna voce suavi concentu conditori *iubilaverunt*. Quos nos hac hora canentes imitamur, qui astra vespertina appellamur, quatenus si solem Christum pro nobis occidentem laudibus sequamur, per eum ad ortum lucis videlicet in resurrectione ad astra matutina perducamur.

highly than light. From *mane* we have "morning Lauds," the praise rendered to God for his gift of light.

32

On the First Reason

We sing this hour because we believe that it is the time when the world was created. At this hour *the morning stars* arose, shining merrily, and *praised God* their maker in sweet harmony. That is to say, at this hour the angels, also called the *sons of God,* were created, and soon *broke out in* charming concert and *loud jubilation* to their creator for the creation of the world. We, who are called evening stars, imitate them when we sing at this hour. Insofar as we follow, by our praises, Christ the sun as he sets before us, we are led to the sunrise, which is to say to the morning stars in the general resurrection.

33

De secunda causa

Hac hora Dominus populum suum per Mare Rubrum transduxit, et hostes illorum submersit, sicut scriptum est, *"Factum est in vigilia matutina, Dominus per nubem respexit et Aegyptios interfecit."* Ea hora qua illi sunt in mari et in nube baptizati, sunt illi in fluctus praecipitati.

34

De tertia causa

Hac hora Christus victor a morte resurrexit et diem nobis ab inferis revexit, et populum sanguine redemptum a regno tyranni reduxit, et hostes eorum barathro immersit.

33

On the Second Reason

Also at this hour, the Lord led his people across the Red Sea and drowned their enemies, as it is written, "*It happened at the morning watch that the Lord looked down through the cloud and killed the Egyptians.*" In the same hour when Israel was baptized in the sea and cloud, the Egyptians were cast headlong into the waves.

34

On the Third Reason

Also at this hour Christ the victor rose from the dead, carried the light back from the underworld, led the people he had redeemed by his blood back from the tyrant's realm, and drowned their adversaries in the abyss.

35

De quarta causa

Hac hora in fine mundi *iusti* a somno mortis *evigilabunt,* dum de nocte huius mundi ad lucem aeternae claritatis transmigrabunt. Tempus igitur *noctis,* quod ante nocturnam *praecedit,* praefert illud tempus mortis, quod ante legem praecessit. Nocturna vero illud tempus exprimit, quo populus sub lege Dominum coluit. Matutinalis autem hora cum *lux appropinquat,* tempus a Christi Resurrectione usque in finem mundi demonstrat, quo Ecclesia dilecto suo canticum cantat. Psalmi namque qui hic cantantur utrumque exprimere conantur, et tempus legis quod velut *umbra praecessit,* et tempus gratiae, quod ut *lux* veritatis postea *fulsit.*

36

Dominus regnavit

Primus itaque psalmus, illud tempus umbrae legis innuit, quo Dominus post liberationem populi sui super eundem populum regnavit, et ei quasi rex legem servandam constituit. *Decorem induit,* dum in *mirabili* tabernaculo coli voluit.

35

On the Fourth Reason

At this hour at the end of the world *the just shall awaken* from the sleep of death and pass on from the night of this world to the light of eternal glory. The *night that comes before* the nocturn signifies that time of death that came before the Law. The nocturn expresses that time when the people worshiped the Lord under the Law. But the morning hour, prayed as *the light is dawning,* shows the time from Christ's Resurrection to the end of the world, when the Church sings to her beloved. For the psalms that are sung now express both the time of the Law, which came before as a shadow, and the time of grace, which *shone* afterward like a *light* for our eyes.

36

Dominus regnavit

Thus the first psalm signifies that dark time of the Law, when the Lord ruled over his people after their liberation and like a king gave them a Law to observe. He *was clothed in beauty* when he desired to be worshiped in a *marvelous*

Tempus quoque gratiae exprimit, quo Dominus post redemptionem populi sui a morte resurgens per mundum regnavit, et *decorem* immortalitatis *induit.*

37

Iubilate

Secundus psalmus illud tempus umbrae ostendit, quo populus Domini et *oves pascuae eius portas eius,* id est terram repromissionis *in confessione* intravit, et *ei omnis terra iubilavit, eique in laetitia servivit.* Tempus etiam gratiae depromit, quo Ecclesia fidem Christi recepit. Et ad praedicationem apostolorum *iubilavit omnis terra,* et *Domino servivit in laetitia.*

tabernacle. It also expresses the time of grace, when rising from the dead after his people's redemption, *the Lord reigned* throughout the whole world and *was clothed in the beauty* of immortality.

37

Iubilate

The second psalm shows the time of darkness when *the Lord's people and the sheep of his pasture went into his gates,* or as it were into the land of the promise, *with praise,* and *all the earth sang joyfully to the Lord* and *served him with gladness.* It also signifies the time of grace, when the Church received faith in Christ and *all the earth sang joyfully* in the apostles' preaching, and *served the Lord with gladness.*

38

Deus Deus meus et *Deus misereatur nostri*

Tertius psalmus illud tempus umbrae indicat, quo devictis hostibus sub Salemone populus in pace tripudiabat,
quando *in velamento* Templi exultabat, et *rex omnisque populus
in Deo iurans eum laudabat.* Huic psalmo alius sub una *Gloria
Patri* copulatur, quia regnum Iuda et regnum Israel in una
lege sociatur.

39

Item de *Deus Deus meus* et
Deus misereatur nostri

Tempus etiam gratiae exprimit, quo sedata persecutione
Ecclesia pacem recepit. Ideo *ad Deum de luce vigilat,* et *in
matutinis in eo meditatur,* quia *ei adiutor extiterat. Rex vero* Constantinus *in Deo laetatur,* per quem omnis Ecclesia *in Christo
iurans* pace gratulatur, dum *os* haereticorum *iniqua loquen-
tium obstruitur.* Alius psalmus huic sub una *Gloria* adiungitur,
quia Iudaicus populus Ecclesiae adhuc in una fide associabi-
tur.

38

Deus Deus meus and *Deus misereatur nostri*

The third psalm indicates that time of darkness when, after Solomon had defeated his enemies, the people rejoiced in the peace. They rejoiced *in the covert* of the Temple, and *the king and all the people who swear by God praised him.* Another psalm is added to this one under one *Gloria Patri* because the kingdoms of Judah and Israel are joined by one Law.

39

More on *Deus Deus meus* and *Deus misereatur nostri*

It also expresses the time of grace when persecution ceased and the Church was at peace. The Church *watches for the Lord at the break of day* and *meditates on him in the morning* because *he was her helper. But the king* Constantine *rejoices in God,* since through him the whole Church who *swears by Christ* gives thanks for peace when *the mouth of them that speak evil things,* namely heretics, *is stopped.* Another psalm is added under one *Gloria Patri,* because the Jewish people will one day join the Church in one faith.

40

Benedicite omnia opera Domini Domino

Canticum *Benedicite* quod sibi quintus locus adscribit, illud tempus umbrae innuit, quod quinta aetate Nabuchodonosor tres pueros in caminum ignis misit, in quo angelus eos resolvens eundem hymnum cum eis cecinit. Illud quoque tempus exprimitur quod Antichristus tres mundi partes, Asiam, Africam, Europam, a tribus filiis Noe genitas, in caminum tribulationis missurus dicitur. Unde et sine *Gloria Patri* canitur, quia tunc omnis laus Ecclesiae clauditur.

41

Laudate Dominum de caelis et *Cantate* et *Laudate* sub uno *Gloria Patri*

Laudate Dominum illud tempus umbrae denuntiat, quo populus a Babylone reversus Templum Domino reaedificabat, et illud tempus ostendit, quo Ecclesia occiso Antichristo, Deum laudabit et per terrorem lapsos in domum

40

Benedicite omnia opera Domini Domino

The canticle *Benedicite,* assigned the fifth place, signifies
that time of darkness when in the fifth age Nebuchadnezzar
cast the three children into the furnace of fire, where an angel freed them and sang the same hymn with them. It also
expresses that time when the Antichrist will cast the three
parts of the world—Asia, Africa, and Europe, all born from
the three sons of Noah—into the furnace of tribulation.
Hence no *Gloria Patri* is added, because the praise of the
Church is concluded.

41

Laudate Dominum de caelis, Cantate, and *Laudate* under One *Gloria Patri*

Laudate Dominum proclaims that time of darkness when
the people returned from Babylon and rebuilt the Lord's
Temple, and the time after Antichrist has been slain when
the Church will praise the Lord and anyone who fell away
through fear will be put back into God's house by means of

Dei paenitentia restaurabit. Hi tres psalmi ideo sub una *Gloria Patri* psalluntur, quia tunc Christiani, Iudei, gentiles, in una religione Deum laudare noscuntur.

42

De hymno

Hymnus illud tempus umbrae exprimit, quo Iudas Machabeus dedicato Templo pro victoria hymnum Domino cum populo cecinit, et illud tempus innuit quo Ecclesia pro victoria de Antichristo hymnum Domino canit.

43

De capitulo

Capitulum quod a sacerdote dicitur, est angeli legatio qua Praecursor Christi Zachariae repromittitur. Et ultimam horam denuntiat, qua *novissima tuba* angeli mortuos ad vitam excitat. Versus qui sequitur *Dominus regnavit,* declarat quod

penance. These three psalms are sung under one *Gloria Patri,* because at that time Christians, Jews, and gentiles will be seen to praise the Lord in one religion.

42

On the Hymn

The hymn expresses that time of darkness when, after the Temple's dedication, Judah Maccabee sang a victory hymn to the Lord along with the people. It also indicates that time when the Church will sing a hymn to the Lord in thanks for her victory over Antichrist.

43

On the Chapter

The chapter said by the priest is the angel's legation, when Christ's Precursor is promised to Zachary. It also proclaims that final hour, when the angel's *last trumpet* will quicken the dead to life. The following versicle *Dominus regnavit* declares

sicut Christus post Resurrectionem in Ecclesia *regnavit,* ita post generalem resurrectionem in omnibus electis regnabit. A quibusdam versus *In matutinis Domine* dicitur, et Ecclesiae resurrectio exprimitur.

44

De cantico *Benedictus Deus*

Per canticum autem *Benedictus,* quod illucescente die cantatur, adventus *verae lucis* Christi *in hunc mundum* designatur, quod Zacharias *ei in obviam* cantavit, quando *plebem suam* in hoc mundo *visitavit,* et *sedentes in tenebris et umbra mortis* inferni *illuminavit.* Et illud tempus repraesentat, quo in ultimis Christus splendor lucis aeternae et sol iustitiae adventus sui ortu orbem illustrat, et Ecclesia *ei obviam rapta* laetabunda laudes iubilat, quod eam sponsus suus visitat, et diu *in tenebris* huius mundi *sedentem sua claritate illuminat.*

that just as Christ *reigned* in the Church after his Resurrection, so after the general resurrection he will rule over all the elect. Some say the versicle *In matutinis Domine,* and this signifies the Church's resurrection.

44

On the Canticle *Benedictus Deus*

In the canticle *Benedictus,* which we sing as the day is breaking, we proclaim the advent of Christ *the true light into this world.* Zachary sang it at Christ's *royal entry,* when he *visited his people in this world* and *enlightened those who sat in darkness and the shadow of the death* of hell. It represents that time when, on the last day, Christ, the splendor of eternal light and the sun of justice, illuminates the globe with the rising of his advent, and the joyful Church *caught up to meet him* thrills with his praises, because her spouse visits her and *his brightness shines upon her who was sitting in the darkness* of this world.

45

De oratione et suffragiis

Oratio quae sequitur, illa ultima benedictio, "*Venite bene-dicti Patris mei*" intelligitur. Suffragia sanctorum quae postea canuntur, sunt *multae mansiones in domo Patris* in quas singuli pro meritis tunc introducuntur. Ideo in Dominica die hae laudes canuntur, quia per fidem Resurrectionis Christi haec gaudia iustis in resurrectione dabuntur. Ideo etiam infra Pascha frequentantur, quia Resurrectionis Christi et nostrae tempus per eas repraesentatur. Ideo vero hae in festis sanctorum cantantur, quia sancti nunc in gaudio quod in resurrectione dupliciter percepturi sunt gratulantur. Hanc eandem significationem et sanctus Benedictus in ordinatione sui officii expressit, hoc solo mutato, quod *Deus misereatur* in primis ad honorem sanctae Trinitatis cantari iussit.

45

On the Collect and Suffrages

The Collect that follows is that final blessing, *"Come, ye blessed of my Father."* The Suffrages of the saints sung just after are *the many rooms in the Father's house,* into which each one will be inducted at that time according to his merits. These praises are sung on Sunday, because through faith in Christ's Resurrection these joys will be given to the just on the day they rise from the dead. We sing them also during Eastertide, because they represent the time of Christ's Resurrection and our own. We sing them on the feast days of saints, because the saints who are now in bliss are giving thanks that they will receive it twofold at the general resurrection. Saint Benedict conveyed the same signification in his arrangement of the Office with this one difference, that *Deus misereatur* is sung first in honor of the Holy Trinity.

46

De privatis noctibus

In Dominica nocte celebravimus nostram liberationem, et angelorum coaequalitatem, in privatis noctibus commemoravimus nostri exilii servitutem. A quo enim quis superatur, illius et servus vocatur. Diabolus autem humanum genus in primo parente devicit, et durae servituti subiecit. Ut ergo ab hac servitute liberi fiamus, divino servitio nocturnis horis insudamus, et ut a nocte huius vitae ad aeternam lucem perveniamus. Verumtamen quia nostram servitutem per sex aetates mundi extendi deploramus, ideo sex noctibus hebdomadae hoc officium celebramus.

47

De duodecim horis

Et quia nocti duodecim horas adscribimus, ideo duodecim psalmos canimus, quatenus qui duodecim mensibus anni servitute detinemur, per doctrinam duodecim apostolorum liberati donemur.

46

On Ferial Weeknights

On Sunday night we have celebrated our liberation and our being made equal to the angels. On weeknights we have commemorated our servitude in exile. For if a man is vanquished by another, he is called his slave. The devil defeated the human race in our first parent and subjected it to a bitter slavery. So that we might be freed from this slavery, we sweat away at the divine service through the night hours, so that we may leave the night of this life and reach the eternal light. Now as we deplore a slavery that has lasted through six ages of the world, so we celebrate this office on six nights of the week.

47

On the Twelve Hours

Now because we ascribe twelve hours to the night, so we sing twelve psalms, so that we who are bound to our servitude through the twelve months of the year may be granted freedom through the teaching of the twelve apostles.

48

De sex antiphonis super nocturnam

Ideo autem sex antiphonas cantamus, ut per sex opera Evangelii de nocte mortis ad lucem Christum transeamus. Quae sex opera sunt esurientem cibare, sitientem potare, nudum vestire, hospitem colligere, infirmum visitare incarceratum redimere.

49

De viginti quattuor horis

Sol quoque totum mundum superius et inferius inter diem et nocte, hoc est viginti quattuor horis perlustrat, et praesentes sibi quidem stellas in die lumine suo obscurat, absentes vero in nocte illuminat. Qui solem iustitiae Christum praefigurat, qui hunc mundum superius quasi in die illustrabat, dum praesentia sua doctrinis et miraculis illum illuminabat. Inferius vero quasi in nocte eum irradiavit, dum morte sua *sedentes in tenebris et umbra mortis visitavit*. Qui stellas praesentes in die velat, dum sanctos in gloria suae prae-

48

On the Six Antiphons in the Nocturn

We sing six antiphons so that through the six works of the Gospel we may pass from the night of death into Christ the light. These six works are to feed the hungry, give drink to the thirsty, cloth the naked, give shelter to travelers, visit the sick, and redeem the imprisoned.

49

On the Twenty-Four Hours

The sun traverses the whole world, the upper part and the lower, within the space of a day and night, a span of twenty-four hours. During the day, the sun's light obscures the stars around it, but at night illumines those that are far away. The sun prefigures Christ, the sun of justice, who shone in the daytime of this upper world, illuminating it through his teachings and miracles while he was present. His light also pierced the night of the lower world when after his death he *visited those sitting in the darkness and shadow of death.* He veils the stars during the day when he shields the saints from the

sentiae a mundi tenebris celat. Stellas vero in nocte absentes illuminat, quia iustos in nocte huius vitae illustrat.

50

De duodecim psalmis

In nocte ergo duodecim psalmos et in die totidem psallimus, quot horis stellas a sole undique versum illuminari diximus, quatenus nos Christiani in baptismate stellae facti ab aeterno sole in omni hora illuminemur, si Dominum *in omni tempore benedicentes* veneremur. Et quia peccato devicti servituti sumus addicti, et *in sudore vultus nostri oportet nos pane vesci,* ideo solemus in die necessaria operari, in nocte vero quando nemo potest operari in vigiliis Domini excubamus, ut eo revertente a nuptiis cum illo ad libertatis iura redeamus.

2   Ideo etiam tres lectiones legimus, quia tres vigilias posuit Dominus, "*Si,*" inquit, "*in prima, si in secunda, si in tertia vigilia venerit, et ita invenerit, beati sunt servi illi.*" Quae tres vigiliae tres aetates saeculi scilicet pueritia, iuventus, senectus intelliguntur, in quibus cuncti Dominum in bonis operibus pervigiles praestolari iubemur. Tres ergo lectiones legimus, cum

darkness of the world with the glory of his presence. He shines upon the stars of the night when he illumines the just in the night of this life.

50

On the Twelve Psalms

We sing twelve psalms in the night and as many again in the day, as many hours as we said the stars are entirely illuminated by the sun, so that, as Christians who have become stars through baptism, we may be illuminated by the eternal sun at every hour by worshiping the Lord and *blessing him at all times*. Because we stand vanquished by sin and bounden to our servitude, and *must eat bread by the sweat of our brow*, so we must do necessary tasks during the daytime. But at night when no one can work, we keep watch in vigils, so that when he returns from the wedding feast, we may regain the rights of free men with him.

We read three lessons because the Lord established three watches, saying, "*If he shall come in the second watch, or come in the third watch, and find them so, blessed are those servants.*" These three watches signify the three ages of life: boyhood, youth, and old age, through all of which time we are commanded to wait expectantly for the Lord in good works. Therefore, we read three lessons when in these three ages

in fide Trinitatis in tribus aetatibus alterutrum divinum opus instruimus. Tria responsoria cantamus, cum Trinitatem in fide, spe, caritate glorificamus. Psalmi quoque pro prima vigilia, lectiones pro secunda, responsoria pro tertia, matutinae Laudes pro quarta vigilia noctis quasi pro debito solvuntur. Sanctus etiam Benedictus in eadem significatione duodecim psalmos et tres lectiones in privatis noctibus instituit, hoc tantum mutato, quod lectiones psalmis interposuit, quia hoc videlicet media nocte agi voluit.

51

De privatis noctibus et de matutinis Laudibus cum cantamus *Miserere mei Deus*

*N*ox quae *praecessit* vitam nostram in peccatis expressit, nocturnale autem officium nostri exilii servitium. In matutinis Laudibus iam ad libertatem per paenitentiam tendimus dum cantamus psalmum *Miserere mei* et quia per paenitentiam de tenebris mortis ad lucem vitae transitur, ideo in secundo psalmo per singulas ferias "mane" concinitur, ut in *Verba mea:* "*Mane astabo*" et "*Mane exaudies.*" In *Iudica me:* "*Emitte lucem tuam.*" In *Te decet hymnus:* "*Exitus matutini.*" In

we teach one another the divine work in Trinitarian faith. We sing three responsories when we glorify the Trinity in faith, hope, and charity. As payment of our debt, we offer up the psalms in place of the first watch, the readings for the second, the responsories for the third, and morning Lauds for the fourth watch. Saint Benedict instituted the twelve psalms and three lessons for ferial weeknights with the same signification, with this exception, that he placed the lessons in between the psalms, since he wanted this office done in the middle of the night.

51

On Weeknights and on Morning Lauds When We Sing *Miserere mei Deus*

The night that has passed expresses our life in sin, the night office our servitude in exile. In morning Lauds we already tend toward our freedom through penance when we sing the psalm *Miserere mei*. Because we go from the shadows of death to the light of eternal life through penance, so on all ferial days the word "morning" is found in the second psalm. On Monday in *Verba mea* we find, "*In the morning I will stand before thee,*" and "*In the morning thou shalt hear my voice.*" On Tuesday in *Iudica me,* we find, "*Send forth thy light.*" On Wednesday in *Te decet hymnus* we find, "*Thou shalt make*

Domine refugium: "*Mane floreat*" et "*Mane repleti sumus.*" In
Domine exaudi: "*Auditam fac mihi mane misericordiam tuam.*"
In *Bonum est confiteri:* "*Ad annuntiandum mane.*"

52

Deus Deus meus

Quia vero per caritatem remissio peccatorum tribuitur,
tertius psalmus de dilectione Dei canitur, *in quem sitit anima
nostra,* cuius nos paenitentes *suscepit dextera.*

53

Deus misereatur nostri

In sequenti psalmo, dilectio proximi subiungitur, in quo
vultus Dei super nos illuminari, et *salutare Dei in omnibus gentibus cognosci* poscitur. Hi duo psalmi, ideo sub una *Gloria*

the outgoings of the morning and of the evening to be joyful." On
Thursday in *Domine refugium,* we find, "*In the morning he shall
flourish*" and "*We are filled in the morning with thy mercy.*" On
Friday in *Domine exaudi,* we find, "*Cause me to hear thy mercy
in the morning.*"

52

Deus Deus meus

Because remission of sins is granted through charity, the
third psalm sings of the love of God, for whom *our soul
thirsts,* whose *right hand receives* us in our penitence.

53

Deus misereatur nostri

In the following psalm, the subject is the love of neighbor.
In it we ask that the *countenance* of God may *shine upon us* and
his salvation be known in all the nations. These two psalms are
sung under one *Gloria Patri* because the twofold precept of

psalluntur, quia praecepta geminae dilectionis in una Christiana professione peraguntur. In psalmo quoque *Deus Deus meus ad te* exprimitur Christi deitas, cuius *misericordia melior est super vitas.* In *Deus misereatur* eius humanitas, per quam illuminatur nostra fragilitas. Et quia hae duae substantiae in una persona Christi venerantur, ideo hii duo psalmi sub una *Gloria* cantantur, et quia in fide huius nominis paenitentes salvantur. Per hos etiam duos psalmos fides et operatio intelliguntur, per quas conversi libertatem veniae consequuntur. Et quia per sex opera misericordiae servi peccati libertatem spiritus adipscuntur, ideo sex cantica victoriae per sex dies canuntur.

In primo cantico cum Isaia exultamus, quia sicut ille infidelem populum, ita nos peccata superavimus. Et Dominus qui propter peccata nobis *erat iratus,* propter paenitentiam *est nos consolatus.*

In secundo cum Ezechia gaudemus, quia sicut ille mortem corporis, ita nos mortem animae evasimus, ideo gratulando canimus, *"Vivens vivens confitebitur tibi sicut et ego hodie."*

In tertio cum Anna tripudiamus, quia sicut illa aemulam suam ita nos carnem nobis adversantem devicimus, unde gaudendo dicimus, *"Exultavit cor meum in Domino,"* qui *carnem in vitiis mortificat,* et animam in virtutibus *vivificat.*

In quarto cum populo Israel laetamur, quia sicut ille Pharaonem et Aegyptios per Moysen, ita nos diabolum et daemones per Christum subterfugimus. Unde laetabundi exultamus, *"Cantemus Domino."*

In quinto cum Habacuc gratulamur, quia sicut ille cum

charity is carried out in the one Christian religion. Also, the psalm *Deus Deus meus ad te* puts across Christ's divinity, whose *mercy is better than lives,* and the psalm *Deus misereatur* his humanity, which shines upon our fragility. Because these two substances are worshiped together in the one person of Christ, so these two psalms are sung under one *Gloria Patri*. Because those who repent are saved by faith in this name, these two psalms refer to faith and works, by which those who are converted will obtain the free status of pardon. Now those who are slaves to sin attain spiritual freedom by the six works of mercy, and so they sing six victory canticles throughout the six days of the week.

In the first canticle, we rejoice with Isaiah, because just as he won over an unfaithful people, so we have conquered our sins, and the Lord who *had been angry with us* on account of our sins *comforted us* on account of our penance.

In the second, we share Hezekiah's joy, because as he escaped bodily death, so we have escaped death of the spirit. And so we gladly sing our thanksgiving: "*The living, he shall give praise to thee, as I do this day.*"

In the third, we jump for joy with Hannah because as she defeated her rival, so we have defeated our enemy the flesh. Thus we joyfully say, "*My heart has rejoiced in the Lord,*" who *mortifies the flesh in its vices,* and *gives life* to the soul in the virtues.

In the fourth, we celebrate with the people of Israel, because as they escaped from Pharaoh and the Egyptians through the hand of Moses, so we have escaped the devil and his demons through Christ. And so we leap for joy, "*Let us sing to the Lord.*"

In the fifth, we give thanks with Habakkuk because, as he

populo Babylonem, ita nos peccatorum confusionem evasimus, et diabolum per *cornua* Crucis superatum exultamus —
qui *ante pedes* Domini *est egressus.*

In sexto cum Moyse hilarescimus, quia sicut ille devictis
hostibus terram repromissionis, ita nos devictis vitiis et peccatis, promissam indulgentiam recepimus. Et Domino car-
men canimus, qui *vindictam in hostes retribuit, et propitius erit
terrae populi sui.*

Porro in septimo cum tribus pueris triumphamus, quia
sicut illi Nabuchodonosor et caminum ignis, ita nos diabolum et inferni incendium evasimus. Ideo cum omni creatura
Deum benedicimus, quia in resurrectione aeternas flammas
superabimus.

2   Deinde *Laudate Dominum* canimus, quia triumphum per
hymnum exprimimus. Capitulum vero nos consolatur, dum
sacerdos in persona Domini nos *vigilare et stare in fide* horta-
tur. De qua consolatione nos plaudimus, dum versum "*Repleti sumus mane misericordia tua*" dicimus. Sic iam libertate
recepta in gaudium prorumpimus, et liberatori nostro grates
referimus ita dicentes, "*Benedictus Dominus Deus Israel,* quia
nos in peccatis *visitavit, redemptionem* per paenitentiam *fecit,
de manu* inimicorum *liberavit, scientiam salutis in remissionem
peccatorum per viscera misericordiae dedit,* de morte *illuminatos
in viam pacis direxit.*" Oratio quam sacerdos dicit est indul-
gentia quam Dominus ad se reversis tribuit.

3   Sanctus quoque Benedictus servos peccatorum per paenitentiam libertatem et victoriae laetitiam adipisci docuit,

escaped Babylon along with the people, so we have escaped the confusion of sinners and rejoice in the devil's defeat through the *beams* of the Cross—he who *went forth before* the Lord's *feet*.

In the sixth, we make merry with Moses, because as he received the promised land after defeating his enemies, so we have received the promised forgiveness after overcoming our sins and vices, and we sing a song to the Lord who *rendered vengeance on our enemies* and *will be merciful to the land of his people*.

In the seventh, we triumph with the three young men, because as they escaped Nebuchadnezzar and the fiery furnace, so we have evaded the devil and the fires of hell. And so with all creation we bless God, because in our resurrection we shall overcome the everlasting fires.

Then we sing *Laudate Dominum,* conveying our triumph 2 with a hymn. The chapter consoles us, when in the person of the Lord the priest exhorts us to *watch and stand fast in the faith*. We voice our satisfaction with this consolation when we say the versicle, "*We are filled in the morning with your mercy.*" And so we break out in joy for our liberation, giving thanks to our Liberator in these words: "*Blessed be the Lord God of Israel,* because *he looked favorably on us* in our sins, *redeemed us* through penance, *delivered us from the hands* of our enemies, *gave knowledge of salvation unto the remission of our sins through the bowels of his mercy,* and *directed our feet into the way of peace,* having *enlightened us* in our death." The Collect the priest says is the forgiveness the Lord gives to those who have returned to him.

Saint Benedict also taught those who are enslaved to 3 their sins to seek their freedom and the happiness of victory

qui paene eosdem tamen totidem psalmos et eadem cantica per easdem ferias in eadem significatione instituit.

Septem cantica in hebdomada canuntur, quia per septem dona Spiritus sancti mundus salvatur.

Dominica die canitur *Benedicite omnia opera,* quia prima aetate creavit Deus omnia, et eadem die per Resurrectionem Christi innovata sunt omnia. Prima die creavit Deus lucem, et hac die omnia ad laudem Dei admonentur, quia omnia illustrata sunt a luce.

Secunda aetate contigit diluvium, quod significat baptismum. Secunda die canitur canticum de baptismate, ut ibi *Haurietis aqua*s, et feria secunda Christus baptizatus traditur. Secunda die creavit Deus caelum et *separavit aquas ab aquis,* ita per baptismum incredulos a fidelibus.

Tertia aetate liberatus est Isaac de morte, et tertia feria cantatur canticum quod cantavit Ezechias quando liberatus est a morte, quia verus Isaac, id est Christus, liberavit populum suum a morte per fidem sanctae Trinitatis. Tertia die segregavit Deus terram a mari, hoc est Ecclesiam a Synagoga.

Quarta aetate est Anna amata, aemula eius repudiata. Ideo quarta feria psallitur eius canticum, quia per quattuor Evangelia est Ecclesia electa, Synagoga abiecta. Quarta die factus est sol et luna et sidera. Christus est sol, Ecclesia luna, sancti sunt stellae.

Quinta aetate liberavit Dominus populum a Babylone. Ideo quinta feria recitatur canticum, quod cecinerunt filii

through penance, and he instituted, not exactly the same, but still the same number of psalms, and the same canticles on the same weekdays with the same signification.

The number of canticles sung during the whole week is seven because the world is saved by the seven gifts of the Holy Spirit.

On Sunday we sing *Benedicite omnia opera,* because in the first age God created all things, and on the same day *all things were made new* through Christ's Resurrection. On the first day God created light, and on this day all things are enjoined to praise God, because the light illumines all things.

In the second age came the Flood, which signifies baptism. On the second day a canticle about baptism is sung, *Haurietis aquas,* and on the second feria Christ is said to have been baptized. On the second day, God created the heavens and *separated the waters above from the waters below,* just as baptism separates the faithful from the unfaithful.

In the third age Isaac was rescued from death, and on the third day we sing the canticle that Ezekiel sang when he was rescued from death, because the true Isaac, who is Christ, delivered his people from death through faith in the Holy Trinity. On the third day God separated the land from the sea, that is, the Church from the Synagogue.

In the fourth age Hannah was cherished and her rival defeated. Her canticle is sung on the fourth feria, because through the four Gospels the Church was elected, the Synagogue rejected. On the fourth day, the sun and moon and stars were made. Christ is the sun, the Church the moon, and the saints are the stars.

In the fifth age, the Lord freed his people from Babylon. On the fifth feria we sing the canticle that the sons of Israel

Israel, cum liberati sunt a Pharaone in Mari Rubro post paschalem agnum. Feria quinta tradidit Dominus corpus suum, quo liberavit populum suum de diabolo. Quinta die fecit Deus de aquis volucres et pisces. *Volucres in aera sustulit, pisces in aquis dereliquit,* quia per quinque vulnera sua iustos ad alta levat, impios in ima damnat.

Sexta die creavit Deus hominem, sexta aetate etiam crucifixus est Christus, ideo sexta feria cantatur canticum de Passione, ubi dicitur *"Cornua in manibus eius,"* id est bracchia Crucis, quia eadem die passus est Dominus.

Sabbato requievit Deus ab operibus suis, ideo Sabbato canitur canticum *Audite caeli,* quod datum est filiis Israel post laborem itineris, cum iam intrarent terram repromissionis. Ita septima aetate post laborem huius mundi dabit Dominus requiem sanctis.

4 Propinquante luce *Benedictus* ad Laudes cantatur, quia per illud canticum nobis vera lux nuntiatur. Ad Vesperum *Magnificat,* scilicet in fine diei canitur, quia in fine mundi Deus *superbos disperdet, et humiles exaltabit.* Ad Completorium *Nunc dimittis* cantatur, quia post Iudicium sancti in pacem introducuntur.

Septem horas canonicas in die, quasi ex debito canimus, pro septem gradibus, quos a septiformi Spiritu suscepimus, formam autem a prophetis et aliis sanctis habemus, ut *septies in die* creatorem nostrum *laudemus,* quatenus *in domo eius* cum angelis eum *in saeculum saeculi laudare* valeamus.

sang when they were delivered from Pharaoh in the Red Sea after the paschal lamb. On the fifth day, the Lord gave up his body, by which he delivered his people from the devil. On the fifth day, God made birds and fishes out of the waters. *The birds he raised into the air, the fish he left in the waters,* because through his five wounds he raises the upright on high and casts the impious into the depths.

On the sixth day, God created man, and in the sixth age he was crucified. On the sixth day the canticle sung is about the Passion, where it says *"Horns are in his hands,"* referring to the beams of the Cross, because the Lord suffered his Passion on the same day.

On the Sabbath, God rested from his works. Therefore, on the Sabbath we sing the canticle *Audite caeli,* which was given to the sons of Israel after the travails of their journey, as they were about to enter the promised land. So in the seventh age, after the labor of this world, the Lord will give rest to his saints.

As the light approaches the *Benedictus* is sung at Lauds, 4 because through this canticle the coming of the true light is announced to us. The *Magnificat* is sung at Vespers at the end of the day, because at the end of the world God will *scatter the proud and lift up the humble.* The *Nunc dimittis* is sung at Compline, because after the Judgment the saints are led into eternal peace.

We sing the seven canonical hours in the daytime as a sort of debt of gratitude for the seven grades of orders we have received from the sevenfold Spirit. But their form we have from the apostles and other saints: to *sing praises* to our creator *seven times a day,* so that we may *praise him in his house* along with the angels *unto the ages of ages.* Each day

Quilibet autem dies repraesentat nobis saeculi tempus, in quo quasi diversis horis in vinea Domini laboramus. Matutina illud tempus nobis memorat, quo primi parentes Deum in paradiso laudabant. Prima illud tempus indicat, quo Abel et Enoch, et alii iusti Deo laudes solvebant. Tertia illud tempus insinuat, quo Noe et alii iusti de arca egressi Deum benedicebant. Sexta illud tempus denuntiat, quo Abraham et alii patriarchae Deum glorificabant. Nona illud tempus demonstrat, quo prophetae sub lege Deum magnificabant. Vespera illud tempus revocat, quo apostoli et illorum sequaces Deo hymnizabant. Completorium illud monet, quo novissimo sub Antichristo Deo iusti gratias referent.

54

De horis et aetatibus

Dies etiam repraesentat nobis vitam uniuscuiusque qui diversis aetatibus, quasi diversis horis docetur *in lege Domini* quasi in vinea laborare.

Ergo per matutinam commemoramus infantiam, in qua quasi de nocte ad diem exorti sumus, dum de matribus in hunc mundum nati sumus. Iuste itaque in hac hora Deum laudamus, qua de nocte erroris ad lucem veritatis in baptismo nos renatos exultamus. Per Primam pueritiam recolimus, qua aetate libros discere cepimus. Merito ergo in hac

represents for us the whole time of this world, during which we labor in the Lord's vineyard at different hours. Lauds puts us in mind of the time when our first parents praised God in paradise. Prime indicates that time when Abel, Enoch, and the other just men offered their praises to God. Terce points to that time when Noah and the others blessed God after leaving the ark. Sext proclaims that time when Abraham and the other patriarchs glorified God. None shows us that time under the Law when the prophets gave glory to God. Vespers calls to mind that time when the apostles and their followers sang hymns to God. Compline reminds us of that time at the end of the world, under the Antichrist, when the just will give thanks to God.

54

On the Hours and the Ages

The day also enacts the life of each person, who is taught through several life stages—the various hours—to work *in the Law of the Lord,* as if in a vineyard.

So at morning Lauds we commemorate our infancy, when we rose from night to day and were born into this world from our mothers. Justly do we praise God at this hour, rejoicing that we have been reborn in baptism from the night of error into the light of truth. At Prime we recall our childhood, the age when we began to study books. It is

hora laudes Deo solvimus, qua eius servitio imbuti sumus. Per Tertiam adulescentiam recolligimus, qua ordines suscepimus. Iuste in hac hora Deum glorificamus, qua eius ministris associati sumus. Per Sextam iuventutem innuimus, qua ad diaconatus vel presbyteratus gradum promoti sumus. Et in hac ergo hora non incongrue Deum benedicimus, qua duces et magistri populorum electi sumus. Per Nonam senectutem notamus, qua plerique ex clero ecclesiasticas dignitates, quasi graviora vineae pondera subimus. Convenit itaque nos in hac hora Deum magnificare, qua nos voluit super plebem suam exaltare. In Vespera decrepitatem reducimus ad memoriam, qua plurimi ex nobis ad melioris vitae conversationem in primis venimus, qui quasi *tota die in foro otiosi stetimus,* dum tota vita in vanitate viximus. In hac hora decet nos Deum laudibus extollere, qua nos dignatus est suis laudatoribus adiungere. Per Completorium finem vitae nostrae retractamus, qua per confessionem et paenitentiam salvari speramus.

55

Item de horis diei

Per diurna quoque et nocturna officia, celebrat Ecclesia Christi mysteria.

In nocte est Christus pro nobis comprehensus, ideo in

fitting for us to praise God at this hour, when we were being trained for his service. At Terce we recollect our adolescence, when we took orders. It is right to glorify God at this hour, when we joined the ranks of his ministers. Sext intimates our youth, when we were elevated to the diaconate or priesthood. Wherefore it is not unfitting to bless God at this hour, when we were chosen as leaders and teachers of peoples. None is our old age, when most clergy take on ecclesiastical dignities, which are as the heavier burdens of the vineyard. We magnify God, therefore, in this hour when it pleased him to place us over his people. At Vespers we recall our decrepitude, when many of us begin to live a better life, especially those of us who *stood idle in the marketplace all day* by living our whole lives in vanity. It is proper to render God praises at this hour, when he saw fit to join us to those who praise him. At Compline we ponder the end of our life, when we hope to be saved by confession and penance.

55

More on the Hours of the Day

Through both her day and night offices, the Church celebrates the mysteries of Christ.

At night Christ was arrested for us, and so we sing Matins

nocte nocturnam psallimus. Mane est illusus, ideo Matutinam canimus. Prima hora est gentibus traditus, ideo Primam cantamus. Tertia hora est flagellatus, ideo tertia psallimus. Sexta hora est crucifixus, propterea Sextam canimus. Nona est mortuus, ideo Nonam cantamus. In vespere est de Cruce depositus, idcirco Vesperam psallimus. In fine diei est sepultus, idcirco Completorium canimus.

56

De horis diei et noctis

Nocturna etiam hora Dominus infernum spoliavit, matutina victor de morte remeavit. Prima Mariae apparuit. Tertia duabus a monumento euntibus obviavit. Sexta Iacobo, Nona Petro, Vespera duobus ambulantibus in Emmaus se manifestavit, Completorio cum apostolis manducavit.

in the night. In the morning he was mocked, so we sing Lauds. At the first hour he was handed over to the pagans, and so we sing Prime. At the third hour he was scourged, so we sing Terce. At the sixth hour he was crucified, therefore we sing Sext. At the ninth hour he died, so we sing None. In the evening he was taken down from the Cross, so we sing Vespers. At the end of the day he was buried, so we sing Compline.

56

On the Hours of the Day and Night

Our Lord harrowed hell at the hour of Matins, and came back out from it at Lauds as the victor over death. At Prime he appeared to Mary. At Terce he met the two coming from the tomb. He showed himself at Sext to James, at None to Peter, and at Vespers to the two disciples on the road to Emmaus. At Compline he ate with the apostles.

57

Item de horis diei et noctis

In nocte nihilominus Petrus pro negatione ploravit, qui postea tota nocte in piscatione laboravit. In mane Christus in littore stetit, rete piscibus implevit. Prima hora cum septem comedit, Petro oves suas commisit. Tertia hora super credentes Spiritus sanctus descendit. Sexta cum undecim Dominus recubuit. Nona eis videntibus caelos ascendit. In vespera ante Passionem cum eis cenavit, corpus suum tradidit. Completorio pro eis Patrem oravit.

58

De prima Dominicis diebus

In Dominica die novem psalmos ad Primam psallimus, quatenus cum novem ordinibus angelorum in gaudio resurrectionis Trinitatem laudare possimus. In primis quinque psalmos de Passione Christi cantamus, quia Christum per quinquepertitam Passionem ad resurrectionis gloriam pervenisse significamus. Quem si nunc imitari volumus, in

57

More on the Hours of Day and Night

In the night, moreover, Peter mourned his denial and then fished all night without luck. In the morning Christ stood on the shore and filled the net with fish. At the first hour he ate with the seven and committed his sheep to Peter. At the third hour the Holy Spirit came down upon the believers. At the sixth he reclined with the eleven. At the ninth he ascended into heaven before their very eyes. At Vespers before his Passion he ate with them and gave them his body. At the hour of Compline he prayed the Father on their behalf.

58

On Prime on Sundays

On Sunday we sing nine psalms at Prime, so that we may be able to praise the Trinity in the joy of the resurrection with the nine orders of angels. In the first five psalms we sing about the Passion of Christ, signifying that Christ entered into the glory of his Resurrection through his fivefold Passion. If we imitate him now, we will reign with him in the

resurrectione ei conregnabimus. Deinde quattuor subiungimus, quia Ecclesiam in quattuor partibus mundi per quattuor Evangelia Deum laudare praedicamus. Per *Deus in nomine* erroris desertionem, per *Confitemini* laudis confessionem, per *Beati immaculati,* legis operationem, per *Retribue,* animae vivificationem exprimimus. Per *Quicumque vult* autem fidem nostram depromimus, in qua reliqua omnia concludimus, per quam angelis associari credimus.

59

De fide quattuor temporibus edita

Fidem Catholicam quattuor temporibus editam immo roboratam Ecclesia Catholica recepit, et in quattuor mundi climatibus inviolabiliter custodit. Primo symbolum apostolorum scilicet *Credo in Deum* fundamentum sibi ponit, dum hoc cottidie in principio diei et in principio horarum scilicet ad Primam canit. Per hoc opera sua consummat, dum hoc ad Completorium recitat. Deinde fidem *Credo in Deum Patrem* legimus, quem Nicaena synodus edidit. Tertio fidem *Credo in unum,* in conventu populi ad Missam modulatur, quae per Constantinopolitanum Concilium propalatur. Quarto fidem *Quicumque vult* cottidie ad Primam iterat, quem Athanasius Alexandrinus episcopus rogatu Theodosii imperatoris ediderat. Per reliquas horas colitur sancta Trinitas.

resurrection. Then we add four more psalms proclaiming that the Church praises God in all four regions of the world through the four Gospels. *Deus in nomine* signifies rejection of error; *Confitemini* our confession of praise; *Beati immaculati* following God's Law; *Retribue* the soul's new life; *Quicumque vult* our faith, which contains everything else, and by which we believe we join the company of the angels.

59

On the Four Creeds

The Catholic Church receives the Catholic faith as expressed and defended in four creeds, and safeguards it inviolate across the four regions of the world. First she lays her foundations in the Apostle's Creed, *Credo in Deum,* when she sings it daily at the beginning of the day and the beginning of the hours, namely at Prime. She brings all her works to completion through the Creed when she recites it at Compline. Next, she reads the creed *Credo in Deum Patrem,* which was issued by the Synod of Nicaea. Third, the creed *Credo in unum,* promulgated by the Council of Constantinople, is sung at public Masses. Fourth, daily at Prime she repeats the creed *Quicumque vult,* which Athanasius, bishop of Alexandria, issued at the behest of the emperor Theodosius. Throughout the other hours the Holy Trinity is worshiped.

60

De Prima in privatis diebus

In privatis diebus imitamur in diurno officio operarios in vinea laborantes, et diversis horis ad excolendam vineam intrantes.

Porro sacerdos qui incipit, imitatur opilionem, oves tota nocte inclusas, mane in pascua eicientem. Grex ovium est plebs Christiana, pascua Domini mandata. Itinera vero obsident bestiae, gregis Dei inimicae. In una namque parte *leo rugiens circuit, quaerens quem devoret.* In altera draco insidians deviantes veneno interimit, aberrantes avide degluttit. Hinc lupus irruens rapit, et oves dispergit. Inde ursus invadens lacerat, gregem dissipat. Unde pastor *"Deus in adiutorium"* clamat, quatenus ovile hoc periculum evadat. Oves autem pascuae Domini, in hymno summum Pastorem invocant, ut eas in *diurnis actibus a nocentibus custodiat.*

60

On Prime on Ferial Weekdays

During the day office on ferial weekdays, we imitate laborers in the vineyard, entering the vineyard for work at different times.

Additionally, the priest who begins imitates the shepherd, who drives the sheep out for morning pasture after they have been in the fold all night. The flock of sheep is the Christian people, the pasture our Lord's commandments. But wild beasts lurk along the path, menacing God's flock. On one side, *a roaring lion goeth about seeking whom he may devour;* on the other lurks a dragon, slaying the strays with his venom and greedily gulping up those who lose their way. Here a wolf pounces and carries one off, scattering the flock. There a bear charges, rips through the flock and disperses it. Thus our shepherd cries, *"O God, come to my assistance!"* praying that the flock may escape these dangers. The sheep of our Lord's pastures call upon the supreme Pastor in a hymn, that *he from harm may keep them free in all the deeds this day shall see.*

61

De horis minoribus

Deinde per psalmum *Deus in nomine* iter arripiunt, et Deum *in virtute sua* se a periculo liberare petunt, *quoniam alieni* eis *insurrexerunt, et fortes animas* earum *quaesierunt,* ut Deus *in virtute sua* illos dispergat, et eas *ex omni tribulatione eripiat.*

2 Per *Beati immaculati* vineam quod est Christiana religio ingrediunt, et in pascua vitae scilicet *in lege Domini* pascuntur. In qua impigre operantur, dum *testimonia* Dei *scrutantur.* In hac fortiter laborant, dum in *Retribue mirabilia de lege* Dei considerant. Hanc summopere excolunt, dum fidem suam in *Quicunque vult* exponunt. Per legem Domini, id est dilectionem, ad patriam revertimur, per psalmum *Deus in nomine* ad iter praecingimur, per psalmum *Beati immaculati* dilectio Dei, per *Retribue* dilectio proximi accipitur. *Quicumque vult* id est fides, cursum nostrum exprimit. Per fidem enim ambulamus, ut ad speciem perveniamus. In capitulo paterfamilias operarios consolatur, quia *omnis qui nomen Domini invocaverit, salvus erit.* Unde alacres in responsoriis fidem iterant, et cum Petro Christum *Filium Dei vivi* invocant, quem in versu *Exurge Domine* se adiuvare in incepto opere postulant.

3 *Kyrieleyson* et *Christeeleyson* quod sequitur, ob tres causas dicitur. Primo ut superflua cogitatio quae psallentibus

61

On the Minor Hours

Next, they call a halt to their journey with the psalm *Deus in nomine* and beg our Lord *in his might* to free them from danger, *because strangers have risen up against them* and *the mighty have sought after their soul.* They ask God in his might to scatter their enemies and *deliver them out of every trouble.*

With the psalm *Beati immaculati,* they enter the vineyard 2 that is the Christian religion, and graze in the pasture of life, that is, *in the Law of the Lord.* Here they sedulously work when they *search his testimonies.* In the vineyard they work diligently when in *Retribue* they behold the *wondrous things of God's Law.* They cultivate it above all when they expound their faith in *Quicunque vult.* Through the Law of the Lord, which is love, we return to the homeland. Through the psalm *Deus in nomine,* we prepare for the journey. Through the psalm *Beati immaculati,* we understand love of God. Through *Retribue,* love of neighbor. The *Quicumque vult,* which is faith, shows us our course; for we walk through faith to arrive at vision. In the chapter the paterfamilias comforts the workers, because *all who invoke the Lord's name will be saved.* Hence in the responsories they are quick to repeat their faith, and along with Peter they call upon Christ *the Son of the living God,* whom they ask for help in their labors in the versicle *Exurge Domine.*

The *Kyrie eleison* and *Christe eleison* that follows is said for 3 three reasons. First, to put aside any superfluous thoughts

obrepsit dimittatur, secundo ut sequens oratio sacerdotis exaudiatur, tertio ut oratio Dominica quasi quadam praefatiuncula ornata attentius dicatur. Quae ideo silenter dicitur, quia Deo in ea loquimur, qui non verba sed cor intuetur. Cuius ultima pars ideo aperte dicitur, ut ab omnibus confirmetur. Per duos versus, scilicet *Vivet anima mea* et *Erravi sicut ovis* paenitentes intelliguntur, qui per pastorem velut oves errantes ad gregem reducuntur. Qui mox symbolum recitant, quia fide corda sua purificant, quae per prava opera maculaverant. Ideo autem *Credo in Deum* occulte dicitur, quia occulta paenitentia occulte paenitentibus iniungitur. Idcirco et preces et confessio et oratio sequuntur, quia per tales fructus paenitentes in communionem recipiuntur. Ob hanc etiam causam septem paenitentiales psalmi ac litaniae canuntur.

4   Solent pastores loca mutare, et greges ad alia pascua minare. Hos religiosi imitantur, dum praelatum de ecclesia sequentes in capitolium congregantur. Ibi Dei animalibus sal ad lambendum datur, dum eis in Martyrologio passio vel vita sanctorum pronuntiatur. Opilio vero eis quasi pabulum ponit, dum per versum *Pretiosa* patientiam sanctorum proponit. Deinde divinum auxilium ter per *Deus in adiutorium* invocat, ut grex Dei periculum animae evadat. Deinde quasi ovile benedicit, dum eos *dirigi et sanctificari in lege Dei* poscit. Post haec lectione reficiuntur, et tunc singuli *in opera* quasi vineae cultores *diriguntur.*

5   Dum Tertia cantatur, quasi a novis operariis in vinea

that may have arisen among the choir members while singing. Second, so that God may hear the prayer of the priest that follows. Third, so that the Lord's Prayer, furnished with a brief sort of preface, may be said with more fervor. We say it silently, because in it we speak to God, who hearkens not to words but to the heart. The last part is said out loud, so that all may affirm it. The two versicles *Vivet anima mea* and *Erravi sicut ovis* are understood as the repentant, who are led back to the flock by their shepherd like straying sheep. They now recite the Symbol, because through faith they purify their hearts, which they had stained through their wicked works. *Credo in Deum* is said in secret, because those who repent in private are given a private penance. The *preces,* a *Confiteor,* and the Collect follow, because the penitent are received back into communion on the basis of such fruits. For the same reason the seven penitential psalms and the litany are sung.

Shepherds are used to move about and lead their flocks 4 to other pastures. The religious imitate this practice when they follow their superior from the church and gather in the chapterhouse. There God's animals are given licking salt when a passion or life of the saints is read to them from the Martyrology. The shepherd gives them a sort of feed when he commends the patience of the saints in the versicle *Pretiosa.* Then he invokes the divine help three times through *Deus in adiutorium,* that God's flock might escape all spiritual dangers. Then he blesses the flock when he asks that they may be *guided and sanctified in God's Law.* After all these things they are fed by the reading, and then all of them *are assigned tasks* as workers in the vineyard.

When Terce is sung, it is as if new workers are taking their 5

laboratur. Dum Sexta canitur, quasi ab aliis labor suscipitur.
Dum Nona psallitur, quasi iterum ab aliis onus subitur. In
Vespera denarius recipitur. Tertia et Sexta et Nona ideo trini
psalmi celebrantur, quia in his tribus horis Trinitas veneratur. Sed quaeritur cum Prima dicatur, cur Tertia et non pot-
ius "Secunda" sequatur. Item cum Tertia ponatur, cur deinde
Sexta et non "Quarta" vel "Quinta" dicatur. Itemque cur
Sextam Nona, et non magis "Septima" et "Octava" perse-
quatur. Sciendum est quod dies in duodecim horas dividitur,
et pro unaquaque hora unum caput de psalmo *Beati immaculati* concinitur pro prima hora *Beati immaculati,* pro secunda
Retribue, pro tertia *Legem pone,* pro quarta *Memor esto,* pro
quinta *Bonitatem fecisti,* pro sexta *Defecit in salutare,* pro septima *Quomodo dilexi,* pro octava *Iniquos odio,* pro nona *Mirabilia* tua, pro decima *Clamavi,* pro undecima *Principes persecuti.*

6   Per hunc psalmum lex Dei id est caritas nobis pronuntiatur, in qua operarii pro aeterna vita cottidie operantur, unde
et in singulis capitulis aliquid de lege memoratur, quia per
hanc solam quasi per regiam viam superna patria intratur.
In *Beati immaculati* dicitur, "*Qui ambulant in lege Domini.*" In
Retribue: "*Considerabo mirabilia de lege tua*" et "*De lege tua miserere mei.*" In *Legem pone:* "*Scrutabor legem tuam.*" In *Memor esto:*
"*A lege tua non declinavi*" et "*Dixi custodiam legem tuam.*" In
Bonitate: "*Bonum mihi lex oris tui.*" In *Defecit:* "*Non ut lex tua.*"
In *Quomodo:* "*Dilexi legem tuam.*" In *Iniquos:* "*Legem tuam
dilexi.*" In *Mirabilia:* "*Non custodierunt legem tuam.*" In *Cla-
mavi:* "*Legem tuam non sum oblitus.*" In *Principes:* "*Legem autem
tuam dilexi*" et "*Lex tua meditatio mea est.*"

turn in the vineyard. When Sext is sung others begin working. When None is sung, still others take up the labor. At Vespers they receive their penny. Terce, Sext, and None are celebrated each with three psalms, because the Trinity is worshiped in these three hours. But someone may ask why Prime is not followed by "Second," and why after Terce we have Sext and not "Fourth" or "Fifth," and why it is None that follows Sext instead of "Seventh" or "Eighth." One should know that the day is divided into twelve hours, and one section of the psalm *Beati immaculati* is sung for each hour. For the first hour *Beati immaculati;* for the second, *Retribue;* for the third, *Legem pone;* for the fourth, *Memor esto;* at the fifth *Bonitatem;* for the sixth, *Deficit in salutare;* for the seventh, *Quomodo dilexi;* for the eighth, *Iniquos odio;* for the ninth, *Mirabilia;* for the tenth, *Clamavi;* for the eleventh, *Principes persecuti.*

This psalm proclaims God's Law, that is, charity, in which 6 the laborers work every day for eternal life. Thus each section mentions something about the Law, because only through it, as a sort of imperial highway, may we enter into the heavenly homeland. In *Beati immaculati* it says, "*Who walk in the Law of the Lord*"; in *Retribue,* "*I have considered the wonderful things of thy Law*" and "*Out of thy law have mercy on me.*" In *Legem pone,* it says "*I will search thy Law.*" In *Memor esto,* it says "*I declined not from thy Law*" and "*I have said, I will keep thy Law.*" In *Bonitatem,* it says "*The Law of thy mouth is good to me.*" In *Deficit,* it says, "*Not as thy Law.*" In *Quomodo,* it says, "*I have loved thy Law.*" In *Iniquos,* it says, "*I have loved thy Law.*" In *Mirabilia,* it says "*They have not kept thy Law.*" In *Clamavi,* it says "*I have not forgotten thy Law.*" In *Principes,* it says, "*But I have loved thy Law*" and "*Thy Law is my meditation.*"

Semper in tertia hora officium solvitur, quia Trinitas in omnibus colitur.

62

De Vespera

Vesperam ideo Ecclesia sollemniter celebrat, quia Abraham et alii patriarchae ante legem, sacerdotes et prophetae sub lege sacrificia ad vesperam offerebant, et Dominus in vespera cenans, corpus suum discipulis tradebat. Quinque autem psalmi huius horae quinque vulnera Christi significant, qui se in vespera mundi pro nobis sacrificabat. Hoc et versus insinuat: *Dirigatur oratio mea sicut incensum in conspectu tuo, elevatio manuum mearum sacrificium vespertinum.* Duodecima hora dies clauditur, et operariis iam peracto opere denarius dabitur. Finis autem uniuscuiusque intelligitur, cum pro transacta vita merces cuique redditur. Ideo quinque psalmi canuntur, quia pro labore quinque sensuum remunerabuntur.

2 Hymnus qui subiungitur, laus victoriae accipitur, quia sicut illi post laborem adepta mercede gratulantur, ita isti post devictum mundum pro aeterna gloria iucundantur. Hos capitulum excitat, ut surgentes venienti Domino occurrant. Qui post versum qui sequitur, quasi ostium pulsant, et si

There is always an office at the third hour, because the Trinity is worshiped in all the offices.

62

On Vespers

The Church celebrates Vespers with great festivity, because Abraham and the other patriarchs before the Law, and the priests and prophets under the Law offered sacrifices in the evening, and our Lord while dining in the evening gave his body to his disciples. The five psalms of this hour signify the five wounds of Christ, who sacrificed himself for us in the evening of this world. The versicle indicates this meaning: *Let my prayer rise to your presence as incense, the lifting up of my hands as an evening sacrifice.* With the twelfth hour the day comes to a close, and when the work is done the laborers receive their penny. Further, it may be understood as the end of each person's life, when each will be given wages for the life he led. Five psalms are sung, because the five senses will be rewarded for their labor.

The hymn that follows is a victory song, because just as the laborers in the Gospel gave thanks after receiving their reward, so the saints will be glad in eternal glory after they have vanquished the world. The chapter spurs them to rise and meet the coming Lord. In the verse that follows, it is as 2

aperiri postulant, accensis autem bonorum operum lampa-
dibus *gaudium Domini sui intrant* cum quinque virginibus.
Unde cum cantico sanctae Mariae *anima* illorum *Dominum
magnificat,* et *spiritus* illorum *in Deo exultat,* qui *fecit* eis *magna,
cuius misericordia est in saecula.* Oratio quae postea dicitur, est
benedictio qua quisque a Domino benedicitur.

3   Cum Vespera de praecedenti die cantatur, tunc praesen-
tis vitae tempus denotatur. Quia ab initio mundi dies praecessit, nox sequebatur, significans quod gaudium paradisi
praecessit, mors hominem—heu!—sequebatur. Cum vero
de sequenti die celebratur, tunc futurae vitae laetitia designatur. Quia a Christi Resurrectione *nox praecedit,* dies sequitur, designans quod post mortem carnis dies vitae credentibus dabitur.

63

De cursu sanctae Mariae

Cursus de sancta Maria vel de omnibus sanctis nulla lege
constricti, sed ob devotionem canimus, ut quia *servi inutiles*
debitum servitium negligenter persolvimus, munera amicis
Domini nostri offerimus, ut per eos obsequium nostrum

if they knock on the door and ask to be let in. Having lit the lamps of good works, they *enter into the joy of their Lord* with the five virgins. Thus their *souls do magnify the Lord* with the canticle of the blessed Virgin Mary, and their *spirit rejoices in God who has done great things for them, whose mercy endures forever.* In the Collect that follows each one receives the Lord's blessing.

When Vespers of the preceding day is being sung, it denotes the time of the present life, because at the beginning of the world the day preceded and the night followed, signifying that the joy of paradise came first and that—alas!—death has pursued man ever since. But when it is Vespers of the following day, it signifies the happiness of the life to come, because ever since Christ's Resurrection *night has passed* and the day follows, signifying that after their death in the flesh believers will be granted the day of eternal life.

3

63

On the Little Office of Our Lady

We sing the Offices of Our Lady and of All Saints out of devotion, not because any law obliges us, but rather because we are *worthless servants* who have carelessly discharged the service we owe. And so we offer gifts to the friends of our Lord, so that through them we might render our service

acceptabile faciamus, et gratiam Domini nostri Iesu Christi obtineamus. Consuetudo cibum benedicendi, vel post cibum gratias agendi, ab ipso Domino coepit, qui quinque panes benedixit, et post cenam hymnum dixit. Legere autem ad mensam, sanctus Augustinus instituit, qui mentes cum corporibus refici voluit, quia *non in solo pane, sed in omni verbo Dei homo vivit.* Quod religiosi ad collationem veniunt, hoc a sanctis patribus acceperunt, qui in vesperis solebant inunum convenire, et de scripturis insimul conferre. Et quae ipsi tunc invicem contulerunt, "collationes" dicuntur, et haec vel his similia ad collationem leguntur.

64

De Completorio et de confessione sero et mane

Ad Completorium ideo confessionem facimus, ut quicquid in die deliquimus diluamus. Ad Primam vero idem facimus, ut quicquid in nocte peccavimus, puniamus. "Completorium" inde dicitur, quod diurna servitus nostra per hoc completur. Et quia corpus nostrum in nocte ab humanis sensibus destituitur, ideo per hanc horam intentius Deo committimus. Ideo autem quattuor psalmos canimus, quia ex quattuor elementis subsistimus. Per hymnum victoriam de nocturnis illusionibus rogamus. Per versum nos sub

acceptable and obtain grace from our Lord. The custom of blessing food and giving thanks after a meal began with our Lord, who blessed five loaves and said a hymn after the Last Supper. Table reading was instituted by Augustine, who desired that our minds should be refreshed along with our bodies, because *man lives not by bread alone, but by every word of God.* That religious gather for the collation is a custom they take from the holy fathers, who used to come together in the evening to discuss the scriptures. The discussions they had were called "collations," and thus these texts, or others like them, are read at the collation.

64

On Compline and the Evening and Morning Confession

We make the confession at Compline to wash away whatever sin we have committed during the day. We do it at Prime to punish whatever sins we committed during the night. The name "Compline" comes from the fact that it brings our daytime service to completion. During the night our body is bereft of the human senses, and so in this hour we commit it more earnestly to God. We sing four psalms, because we are composed of the four elements. In the hymn we ask for victory over the fantasies of the night. In the

signaculo divinae custodiae *quasi pupillam oculi* sigillamus.
Per *Nunc dimittis,* pacem et lumen Dei optamus. Per Dominicam orationem et symbolum fidei nos ab hostibus firma-
2 mus. Ad Primam ideo *Pater noster* et *Credo in Deum* dicimus,
quia *cuncta opera* per Christum *incipimus,* in quem credimus.
Ad Completorium eadem dicimus, quia *cunctas operationes* in
eo concludimus. Per Completorium etiam quod nunc canitur cum dies a nocte excipitur, illud tempus nobis ad memoriam reducitur, cum vita nostra a morte praeripitur. Ideo per
Converte nos inchoamus, ut a malis convertamur, et *ira* Dei *a
nobis avertatur.* Et quia de meritis desperamus, Deum per
versum *Deus in adiutorium* invocamus. Tunc psalmum *Cum
invocarem,* qui in Sabbato sancto de morte Domini psallitur
cantatur, quatenus in morte dormientes, *in pace* qui est
3 Christus *quiescamus.* Deinde *In te Domine* canimus, quem
Dominus in Cruce cantavit, cum iam expirans *spiritum in
manus Patris commendavit,* ut tunc spiritum nostrum suscipere velit. Huic *Qui habitat* subiungimus, quem de tentatione vel Passione Domini canimus, quatenus *a timore nocturno* ab *aspidis et basilisci* tentatione Dominus nos eruat, et *a
leonis et draconis* incursione eripiat. Et deinde *Ecce nunc* psallimus, quatenus *in domo Domini* benedici possimus. In hymno,
capitulo, versu, victoriam poscimus, ut in Christo qui vincit
mundum triumphemus. In cantico Simeonis pacem rogamus, ut sicut Simeon postquam lumen Christum vidit,
pacem vitae intravit, ita nos post lumen fidei, intremus in
pacem requiei.

versicle we seal ourselves *as the apple of his eye* with the sign of divine protection. In the *Nunc dimittis* we wish for God's peace and light. In the Lord's prayer and the symbol of faith we make ourselves secure from our enemies. We say the *Pa-* 2 *ter noster* and *Credo in Deum* at Prime, because *we begin all our works* through Christ in whom we believe. We say the same prayers at Compline, because we conclude *our daily works* in him. Compline, which is sung at the time when day is overtaken by night, recalls to our mind the time when our life is cut off by death. We begin with *Converte nos* that we may be converted from evil and God's *wrath be turned away from us.* And because we put no trust in our own merits, we call upon God through the versicle *Deus in adiutorium.* Then we chant the psalm *Cum invocarem,* which is also sung on Holy Saturday for the Lord's death, that when we *sleep* in death *we may rest in the peace* that is Christ. Next we sing *In te Domine* 3 which our Lord sang from the Cross, when he breathed his last and commended his spirit into his Father's hands, so that he may be pleased to receive our spirit when we die. Next we add *Qui habitat,* in which we sing of the temptation and Passion of our Lord, so that the Lord may save us from *the terror of the night,* from the temptation of *the asp and the basilisk,* and deliver us from the attacks of *the lion and the dragon.* Next we sing *Ecce nunc,* that we may be blessed *in the house of the Lord.* In the hymn, chapter, and versicle we ask for victory, that we may triumph in Christ who has conquered the world. In the canticle of Simeon we ask for peace, so that just as Simeon entered the peace of eternal life after he saw Christ the light, so after the light of faith we may enter into the peace of eternal rest.

65

De cursu monachorum

Quaeritur cur sanctus Benedictus aliter monachis horas ordinaverit, quam mos Ecclesiae habuerit, vel cur praecipuus apostolicorum Gregorius hoc sua auctoritate probaverit. Sed sciendum est hoc sapientissima dispositione provisum, utputa a *viro pleno spiritu omnium iustorum,* scilicet ut contemplativa vita sicut habitu, ita etiam officio ab activa discerneretur, et monasticae disciplinae religio hoc privilegio commendaretur. Unde beatus Gregorius omni sapientia praeditus, perpendens *virum Deo plenum* cuncta sub praedicta significatione ordinasse, iure legitur ea sua auctoritate roborasse. Licet enim psalmos permutaverit, cuncta tamen sub eadem significatione posuit: Nempe quia sex diebus in hac vita, quasi sex aetatibus in vinea Domini laboratur, ut sicut in Dominica requies, ita in septima aetate denarius vitae recipiatur. Ideo sex diebus psalmos de illis iustis ad Primam instituisse consideratur, qui sex aetatibus quasi diversis horis in vinea Domini laborasse memoratur.

65

On the Monastic *Cursus*

One may ask why Saint Benedict ordered the hours for monks otherwise than the custom of the Church, and why the most eminent of popes, Gregory, used his authority to approve it. Know that it was ordered with a most wise intention, as one would expect from a *man full of the spirit of the saints*. Namely, that the contemplative life should have not only a distinct habit, but also an office that distinguishes it from the active life, so that in this way the monastic way of life should appear more worthy. Thus it is written how Saint Gregory, a man endowed with all wisdom, wisely perceiving that this man full of God had ordered his whole office according to the aforesaid signification, duly confirmed it by his own authority. For though Benedict chose different psalms, he wrote the office with the same meaning in mind, namely: We work for six days in this life, just as mankind has worked for six ages in the vineyard, so that just as we rest on the Lord's day, so in the seventh age we may receive the penny of eternal life. Thus he is thought to have chosen psalms for Prime over the six days of the week that tell of the just men who worked in the Lord's vineyard throughout six ages of the world, as if at various hours of the day.

66

De horis minoribus

Prima quippe die *Beatus vir* cum reliquis instituit, qui Abel et alios iustos designant, qui prima aetate, quasi mane vineam Domini intrabant. Secunda die *Domine Deus meus* cum aliis cantari censuit, qui Noe et alios sanctos preferunt, qui secunda aetate, quasi tertia hora in vinea Domini laboraverunt. Tertia die *Exurge Domine* canitur, in quo Nemrod, qui primus idolatriam instituit intelligitur, per quem Antichristus exprimitur, qui supra omne quod dicitur deus extollitur. Canitur etiam *In Domino confido* qui Thare, et *Salvum me fac,* qui Abraham demonstrat, qui tertia aetate in hac vinea desudabant. Quarta die *Usquequo Domine* cum reliquis instituit, qui Ioseph et filios Israel in Aegypto peregrinantes insinuant, qui quarta aetate velut sexta hora pondus diei et aestus portabant. Quinta die *Conserva me* cum aliis decantari voluit, qui sacerdotes, iudices, reges exprimunt, qui quinta aetate quasi hora nona sub lege huius vineae operi institerunt. Sexta die *Cum sancto sanctus eris* canitur, in quo Iohannes baptista intelligitur, et *Caeli enarrant* qui apostolos, et *Exaudiat* qui martyres designat, qui sexta aetate quasi hora undecima hanc vineam excolebant.

3   Ad tres horas, scilicet Tertiam, Sextam, Nonam, psalmos

66

On the Minor Hours

For instance, on Monday he assigned *Beatus vir* along with the others, because it signifies Abel and the other just men who entered the Lord's vineyard in the first age, as if in the morning. On Tuesday he chose *Domine Deus meus* to be sung along with the others, because it tells of Noah and the other saints who worked in the Lord's vineyard in the second age, as if at Terce. On Wednesday, *Exurge Domine* is sung, in which Nimrod, the founder of idolatry, is understood. Nimrod stands for the Antichrist who is praised above all the false gods. *In Domino confido* is also sung, which portrays Terah, and *Salvum me fac,* which portrays Abraham, who toiled in the vineyard during the third age. He assigned *Us-* 2 *quequo Domine* along with the rest to Thursday, for they signify Joseph and the sons of Israel wayfaring in Egypt, who bore the weight of the day and heat in the fourth age, as it were during Sext. He wanted *Conserva me* and the rest to be chanted on Friday, because they express the priests, judges, and kings who in the fifth age, as it were at None, laid into their work in the vineyard under the Law. On Saturday, *Cum sancto sanctus eris* is sung, in which John the Baptist is understood, and *Caeli enarrant,* which signifies the apostles, and *Exaudiat,* which signifies the martyrs, who in the sixth age, as at the eleventh hour, tended the vineyard.

Saint Benedict chose to have the fifteen gradual psalms 3

JEWEL OF THE SOUL

de quindecim gradibus cantari statuit, quia per quindecim gradus caritatis Trinitatem adiri docuit. Vesperas quaternis psalmis celebrari decrevit, quia per quattuor Evangelia denarium adipisci monuit. Completorium duobus psalmis sicut alias horas terminari censuit, quia cuncta in fide, spe, et caritate compleri voluit. Hunc autem ordinem psalmorum traditur a beato Ambrosio accepisse. Porro in Dominica die de illo psalmo horas instituit, qui legem Dei, scilicet caritatem innuit, qui in resurrectione Deus qui est caritas omnibus hic pie in lege per caritatem laborantibus praemium et requies erit. Ad Primam autem quaterna, ad reliquos vero horas novena capitula psalluntur, quia per quattuor virtutes ad novena angelorum agmina hic in Christo laborantes perducuntur.

67

De nocturnis

Sicut olim dies a paganis erant idolis dedicati, ita sunt nunc singuli a Christianis Christo Deo dicati. Dominica quippe est ipse conceptus, ideo illa die nocturnam *Beatus vir* psallimus, quia ipse in consilio Patris in uterum virginis abiit, et *tamquam sponsus de thalamo suo* processit. In nocturna cantatur "*Filius meus es tu ego hodie genui te.*" In Vespera

sung at the three hours of Terce, Sext, and None to teach that one approaches the Trinity through the fifteen grades of charity. He wanted Vespers to be celebrated with four psalms to teach that one obtains the penny through the four Gospels. He gave Compline three psalms, because all things reach their consummation in faith, hope, and charity. Some say he took this order of psalms from Saint Ambrose. Moreover, on Sunday he designed the hours based on the psalm that signifies God's Law, that is, charity, because in the resurrection, God, who is charity, shall be rest and reward to all those who labor in this world in obedience to his law through charity. Four parts of this psalm are chanted at Prime, but nine over the other hours, because those who labor in Christ here below are ushered into the ninefold ranks of the angels through the four virtues.

67

On the Nocturns

Formerly, the pagans dedicated the days to their idols. Now just so, Christians dedicate the days to our God, Christ. On Sunday he was conceived. Hence on that day we sing the nocturn *Beatus vir,* because in the Father's plan he went into the Virgin's womb and came out *like a bridegroom from his bridal chamber.* In the nocturn we sing, "*Thou art my son, this day have I begotten thee,*" and at Vespers "*Before the day*

2 autem "*Ante luciferum genui te.*" Secunda die est baptizatus,
ideo ea die nocturnam *Dominus illuminatio* cantamus, in
qua dicitur, "*Vox Domini super aquas,*" dum Pater voce, Filius
tactu, Spiritus sanctus specie sanctificabat illas. In Vespera
autem "*Placebo Domino*" Filius dicit, et Pater "*Hic est Filius*

3 *meus dilectus in quo mihi bene complacui*" sonuit. Tertia die est
natus, ideo tertia feria nocturnam *Dixi custodiam vias meas*
cantamus, in qua dicitur "*Holocaustum et pro peccato non postu-*
lasti," ideo "*Ecce venio*" Filius dicit, et Pater, "*Eructavit cor*
meum verbum bonum." In Vespera autem "*Fiat pax in virtute*
tua," quia pax magna in mundo fuit, dum Christus pax nos-

4 tra venit, qui nobis veram pacem fecit. Quarta die est a Iuda
proditus, ideo feria quarta nocturnum *Dixit insipiens* canimus, quia *insipiens* Judas dixit "*Non est Deus,* sed magus." De
quo ipse in eadem nocturna, "*Tu vero homo unanimis, dux meus*
et notus meus, qui simul mecum dulces comedi cibos." De Iudaeis
quoque: *exacuerunt ut gladium linguam suam, intenderunt arcum*
rem amaram. In Vespera autem: *Saepe expugnaverunt,* "*Supra*

5 *dorsum meum fabricaverunt peccatores.*" Quinta die novam legem inchoavit, corpus suum tradidit, ideo feria quinta psallimus nocturnam *Salvum me fac,* in qua canimus "*Panem ange-*
lorum manducavit homo." Ea etiam nocte est comprehensus,
ideo canimus: "*Deus dereliquit eum, persequimini et comprehen-*
dite eum." In Vespera autem "*Oculis suis somnum* non dedit,
donec tabernaculum Deo," scilicet Ecclesiam per Crucem in-

6 venit. Sexta die est crucifixus, ideo feria sexta nocturnam
Exultate Deo canimus, in qua dicitur quod *inimici* eius *sonave-*
runt, qui eum *in lacu inferiori posuerunt,* quando est traditus,

star I begot thee." On the second day he was baptized, so on   2
that night we sing the nocturn *Dominus illuminatio mea,* in
which is said, "*The voice of the Lord is upon the waters,*" for the
Father sanctified the waters by his voice, the Son by his
touch, and the Holy Spirit by his appearance. At Vespers the
Son says, "*I will please the Lord,*" and the Father boomed,
"*This is my beloved Son, in whom I am well pleased.*" On the   3
third day he was born, so on Tuesday we sing the nocturn
Dixi custodiam vias meas, where we read, "*Burned offering and
sin offering thou didst not require,*" and so the Son says, "*Behold,
I come,*" and the Father responds, "*My heart hath uttered a
good word.*" At Vespers, we sing "*Let peace be in thy strength,*"
because great peace came upon the world when Christ our
peace came and brought true peace. On the fourth day Judas   4
betrayed him, so on Wednesday we sing the nocturn *Dixit
insipiens,* because Judas was *the fool* who said, "*He is not God,*
but a wizard." The same nocturn also has this verse, "*But
thou a man of one mind, my guide, and my familiar, who didst take
sweetmeats together with me.*" It also speaks of the Jews, who
*have whetted their tongues like a sword; they have bent their bow
a bitter thing.* In Vespers we have *Saepe expugnaverunt,* with
the verse, "*The wicked have wrought upon my back.*" On the   5
fifth day he initiated the New Law and gave over his body, so
on Thursday we sing the nocturn *Salvum me fac,* in which we
sing, "*Men ate the bread of angels.*" On the same night he was
arrested and so we sing, "*God hath forsaken him, pursue and
take him.*" At Vespers, "*He gave his eyes no sleep until he had
found a tent for God,*" namely the Church, through the Cross.
On the sixth day he was crucified, so on Friday we sing the   6
nocturn *Exultate Deo,* in which it says that *his enemies have
made a noise.* They *laid him in the lower pit* when he was

et *sicut homo sine adiutorio inter mortuos* aestimatus. In Vespera autem *"Linguas suas sicut serpentes acuebant, tota die proelia*
7 *in die belli constituebant."* Septima die iacuit sepultus, ideo Sabbato nocturnam *Cantate Domino* psallimus, in qua dicitur quod *percussus sicut fenum aruerit,* et sicut pellicanus a parente occisus emarcuerit. In Vespera autem *"Vanitati similis factus*
8 *est, dies eius sicut umbra praetereunt."* In octava die resurrexit, ideo Dominica canimus: *"Ego dormivi et exurrexi, et Dominus me suscepit,* et *animam meam in inferno* non dereliquit, et *in caput gentium me* constituit." In Vespera autem, *"De torrente in via bibet, propterea caput exaltabit,"* quia Dominus de pulvere inopem suscitavit.

68

De officio monastico

Eadem in officio sancti Benedicti notantur.
    In Dominica conceptio, ut ibi, *"Tollite portas principes vestras et elevamini portae aeternales, et introibit rex gloriae."* In
2 Vespera, ut ibi, *"Habitare facit sterilem in domo, matrem."* In feria secunda baptismus, ut ibi, *"Verbo Domini caeli firmati sunt, et spiritu oris eius omnis virtus eorum, congregans sicut in utrem aquas."* In Vespera ut ibi, *"Iordanis conversus est retrorsum."*

betrayed and, *as a man without help, counted free among the dead.* At Vespers, however, "They *sharpened their tongues like a serpent* and *all the day long they designed battles on the day of war.*" On the seventh day he lay in the tomb, so on Saturday 7 we sing the nocturn *Cantate Domino,* in which it says that he *withered, smitten as grass* and wasted away like a pelican killed by its mother. At Vespers, "He is *like to vanity, his days pass away like a shadow.*" On the eighth day he rose, so on Sunday 8 we sing, "*I have slept, and I have risen up, and the Lord hath protected me* and he did not *leave my soul in hell,* and *he made me the head of the gentiles.*" At Vespers, "*He drank of the torrent in the way, therefore shall he lift up the head,*" because he raised the poor man from the dust.

68

On the Monastic Office

We find the same in the office of Saint Benedict.

On Sunday it is the conception, as when we say, "*Lift up your gates, O ye princes, and be ye lifted up, O eternal gates, and the King of Glory shall enter in*"; and at Vespers, "*Who maketh a barren woman to dwell in a house, the joyful mother of children.*" Monday is the baptism, as when we say, "*By the word of the* 2 *Lord the heavens were established; and all the power of them by the spirit of his mouth, gathering together the waters of the sea as in a vessel*" and at Vespers, "*The Jordan was turned back.*"

3   In feria tertia Nativitas, ut ibi, "*Dominus virtutum nobiscum,*" et ibi, "*Sicut audivimus sic vidimus in civitate Domini,*" et iterum, "*Suscepimus Deus misericordiam tuam in medio Templi tui.*" In Vespera ut ibi, "*De fructu ventris tui ponam super sedem*

4   *tuam.*" In feria quarta traditio, ut ibi, "*Pretium meum cogitaverunt repellere,*" et ibi, "*Adversum me loquebantur qui sedebant in porta, in me psallebant qui bibebant vinum.*" In Vespera ut ibi, "*Filia Babylonis misera, beatus qui retribuet nobis,*" et "*Dominus*

5   *retribuet pro me.*" In quinta feria corporis eius commestio, ut ibi, "*Panem caeli dedit eis.*" In Vespera, ut ibi, "*Dirigatur oratio mea sicut incensum in conspectu tuo, elevatio manuum mearum*

6   *sacrificium vespertinum.*" In feria sexta Passio, ut ibi, "*Deus iniqui insurrexerunt super me, et synagoga populorum quaesierunt animam meam, et non proposuerunt te in conspectu suo,*" et ibi, "*Non es auxiliatus ei in bello.*" In Vespera ut ibi, "*Considerabam ad dexteram, et videbam, et non est qui cognosceret me, periit fuga a*

7   *me.*" In Sabbato sepultura, ut ibi, "*Sol cognovit occasum suum.*" In Vespera ut ibi, "*Exibit spiritus eius et revertetur in terram*

8   *suam.*" In Dominica Resurrectio, ut ibi, "*Anima mea illi vivet.*" In Vespera ut ibi, "*Exortum est lumen.*" Quod quibusdam psalmis *Gloria Patri* interposuit, hoc secundum Hebraeos fecit, qui quibusdam diapsalma interponunt, ubi altiorem sensum intelligunt.

On Tuesday is the Nativity, as when we say, "*The Lord of* ₃ *armies is with us,*" and, "*As we have heard, so have we seen, in the city of the Lord of hosts,*" and "*We have received thy mercy, O God, in the midst of thy Temple,*" and at Vespers, "*Of the fruit of thy womb I will set upon thy throne.*" On Wednesday is the be- ₄ trayal, as when we say, "*They have thought to cast away my price,*" and "*They that sat in the gate spoke against me, and they that drank wine made me their song,*" and at Vespers, "*O daughter of Babylon, miserable, blessed shall he be who shall repay thee,*" and "*The Lord will repay for me.*" On Thursday it is the eating ₅ of his body, as where we say, "*He had given them the bread of heaven,*" and at Vespers, where we say, "*Let my prayer be directed as incense in thy sight; the lifting up of my hands, as evening sacrifice.*" Friday is his Passion, as where we say, "*O God, the* ₆ *wicked are risen up against me, and the assembly of the mighty have sought my soul, and they have not set thee before their eyes*" and "*Thou hast not assisted him in battle,*" and at Vespers, where we say, "*I looked on my right hand, and beheld, and there was no one that would know me, flight hath failed me.*" Saturday is his ₇ burial, as here, "*The sun knoweth his going down,*" and at Vespers, as here, "*His spirit shall go forth, and he shall return into his earth.*" Sunday is the day of his Resurrection, as where we ₈ say, "*To him my soul shall live,*" and at Vespers, where we say, "*A light is risen up.*" The fact that he interposed a *Gloria Patri* in certain psalms comes from the Hebrews, who put a *diapsalma* in certain psalms where they perceive a deeper meaning.

Abbreviations

ARP = *Acta Romanorum pontificum a s. Clemente I ad Coelestinum III* (Rome, 1943)

Cantus ID = Debra Lacoste, Terence Bailey, Ruth Steiner, and Jan Koláček, *Cantus: A Database for Latin Ecclesiastical Chant—Inventories of Chant Sources,* http://cantus.uwaterloo.ca/ (accessed March 22, 2022)

CAO = R. J. Hesbert, ed., *Corpus antiphonalium officii,* 6 vols. (Rome, 1963–1979)

CCCM = *Corpus Christianorum continuatio mediaevalis*

CCSL = *Corpus Christianorum series Latina*

CO = Eugenius Moeller, Johannes Maria Clément, and Bertrand Coppieters 't Wallant, eds., *Corpus orationum,* 15 vols., CCSL 160–160M (Turnhout, 1992–2004)

CT III = Gunilla Björkvall, Gunilla Iversen, and Ritva Jonsson, eds., *Corpus Troporum III: Tropes du propre de la messe,* vol. 2, *Cycle de Pâques,* Studia Latina Stockholmiensia 25 (Stockholm, 1982)

MGH = *Monumenta Germaniae historica*

MS = Joseph Jungmann, *The Mass of the Roman Rite: Its Origin and Development (Missarum sollemnia),* 2 vols., trans. Francis Brunner (New York, 1951)

OR = Michel Andrieu, ed., *Les Ordines Romani du haut moyen âge,* 5 vols. (Louvain, 1931–1961)

PL = J. P. Migne, ed., *Patrologia Latina cursus completus* (Paris, 1844–1865)

PRG = Cyrille Vogel and Reinhard Elze, eds., *Le Pontifical romano-germanique du dixième siècle,* Studi e Testi 226, 227, 269 (Rome, 1963–1972)

Note on the Text

No critical edition yet exists of the *Jewel of the Soul,* which is found in at least seventy-two manuscripts. The sole published edition (Leipzig, 1514) was edited by Melchior Lotter and reprinted in *Patrologia Latina* 172:541–738.

In this edition, we supply a fresh text based on a mid-twelfth-century manuscript, Admont Benediktinerstift, Cod. 366, chosen for temporal and geographical proximity to the place of composition and for the quality of its text. The manuscript's text is reproduced—normalized to conform to classical orthography—except where omissions and obvious corruptions required correction, which we have made based on a handful of geographically dispersed manuscripts, including Lambach, Benediktinerstift, Cml XXXV; Saint-Omer, Bibliothèque Municipale, Ms. 304; London, British Library, Cotton MS Tiberius C III; and Vatican, Biblioteca Apostolica Vaticana, Reg. lat. 328.

Since the Admont text exhibits an unusual organization and inadequate division of the text, and in order not to disturb the conventional scholarly system of reference, we have retained the *Patrologia Latina*'s chapter divisions, numbers, and titles in most cases.

Appendices

The Admont manuscript contains several pages of material interspersed between the final chapters of the text proper: brief comments, unmistakably in Honorius's style, supplementing identifiable passages in all the previous books. The same material appears almost identically in the Lambach manuscript. Some of it has already been worked into the text verbatim. It is possible that these appendices are notes made in view of a final recension. Curiously, in Sicard of Cremona's *Mitrale,* which drew heavily on the *Jewel,* much of this end material is found inserted into the text precisely where one might have expected Honorius to do so; see Gábor Sarback and Lorenz Weinrich, eds., *Sicardi Cremonensis episcopi Mitralis de officiis,* CCCM 228 (Turnhout, 2008). Either Sicard incorporated the notes himself, or there is a yet-undiscovered later recension of the *Jewel* that did so.

We include this material because it is clearly written by Honorius, its inclusion in the *Mitrale* makes it a valuable part of that work's transmission history, and it supports our contention that the Admont manuscript is a valuable early witness, since the later tradition (as we know it) does not transmit this provisional material.

Appendix A contains unfinished hagiographical material appearing in Admont 366 between 4.115 and 4.116. They may be Honorius's notes toward an unfinished commentary on the sanctoral cycle. Appendix B contains reflections on the imperial *adventus* ceremony and other ceremonial events. This material appears in Admont 366 between 4.116 and 4.117. Appendix C appears as the final element of the Admont text, just after the valediction.

Admont = Admont, Benediktinerstift, Cod. 366

Lambach = Lambach, Benediktinerstift, Cml XXXV

Amalar = Amalar of Metz, *Liber officialis,* ed. and trans. Eric Knibbs, *On the Liturgy,* 2 vols., Dumbarton Oaks Medieval Library 35 and 36 (Cambridge, MA, 2014)

Beleth = Heribert Douteil, ed., *Iohannis Beleth Summa de ecclesiasticis officiis,* CCCM 41 (Turnhout, 1976)

Flint = Valerie I. J. Flint, "Place and Purpose of the Works of Honorius Augustodunensis," *Revue Bénédictine* 87 (1977): 97–127

PL = Honorius Augustodunensis, *Gemma animae,* ed. Melchior Lotter, *PL* 172 (Paris, 1854), cols. 541–738

Sacramentarium = Honorius Augustodunensis, *Sacramentarium,* ed. Bernard Pez, PL 172 (Paris, 1854), cols. 737–806

Sicard = Gábor Sarback and Lorenz Weinrich, eds., *Sicardi Cremonensis episcopi Mitralis de officiis,* CCCM 228 (Turnhout, 2008)

Notes to the Text

DEDICATORY LETTERS

1   Fratres solitario *Admont*: Fratres Honorio solitario *PL*
2   Responsio solitarii *Admont*: Responsio Honorii *PL*

PREFACE

1   Incipit praefatio libri *Admont*: Honorii praefatio in Gemmam animae *PL*

BOOK I

1   Incipit Gemma Animae *Admont*: Dicendorum summa libris quatuor *PL*
5.1   . . . corporaliter retulerunt. <Sapientia id est subdiaconi vadunt in medio iuvencularum tympanistriarum, ut doceant quem tympanistriae laudare debeant. Timpanistriae sunt cantores laudes resonantes, adolescentulae sunt novae ecclesiae Deum laudantes edomita carne.> *Lambach and others*
6.3   <Porro . . . collaudatur> *Lambach*
26   ad Ierusalem passuro *Lambach*: ab Ierusalem passuro *Admont*
27   hi qui spiritum suum *Lambach*: hi qui Spiritum Sanctum *Admont*
54   Omnia bona creas, sanctificas *Lambach*: Omnia benedicis, creas, sanctificas *Admont*
59   Unde et memores nos servi tui *Lambach*: Unde et memoriam d. n. t. f. *Admont*
75   turbarum clamore *Lambach*: tubarum clamore *Admont*
78   ab Iesu qui et Iosue *Lambach*: ab Iesu et Iosue *Admont*

83.2 per duellum prostrato *Lambach*: perduello prostrato *Admont*

85 Amalarius de Missa *editors*: Rabanus Maurus de Missa *PL*, Item de Missa Rabanus *Admont*

87 Pax vobiscum de Novo id est *Lambach*: Pax vobiscum denuo idem *Admont*

98 ante ostium pugnae *Lambach*: ante hostium pugnam *Admont*

106.1 calix est in ministerio *Admont*: calix est in mysterio *Sicard* (3.6.567), *PL*

106.2 Sacrificium patriarchae nostri Abrahae *Lambach*: Sacrificavit patriarcha Abraha *Admont*

106.3 iube haec perferri *Lambach*: iube hoc perferri *Admont*

sancti angeli tui in sublime altare *Lambach*: sancti angeli in sublime altaris *Admont*

111.2 Deum pro omnibus *Lambach*: Deum prae omnibus *Admont*

112 ad Offertorium *Lambach*: ad officium *Admont*

114.1 quia et Romani hoc *Lambach*: quia et Romani haec *Admont*

114.2 Section lacking in *PL, Lambach*

115 in duobus etiam *Lambach*: in duobus et *Admont*

117.2 Genuum autem flectio *Lambach*: Genu autem flexo *Admont*

120 Quia per incarnati verbi *Lambach*: Quia per incarnationem *Admont*

Dominicis in Quadragesima *Admont*: de Quadragesima *Lambach, PL*. See *Notes to the Translation*.

143 qua praedicatores *Lambach*: quia praedicatores *Admont*

tractu funis *PL*: tactu funis *Admont, Lambach*

151 capita percussit *Admont*: cambuta percussit *Lambach, PRG*

principes tenebrarum *Lambach*: princeps tenebrarum *Admont*

161 et psalmum Iudica me Deus *Lambach*: et post *Admont;* cum psalmo Iudica me Deus *PRG*

165 qui ornatui Ecclesiae *Lambach*: qui ornatu Ecclesiae *Admont*

Diversae antiphonae <quae> *Lambach*

175 <et templum Dei quod ipsi sunt virtutibus aperiant, vitiis claudant> *Lambach*

183 undique prospicit *Lambach*: undique prospiciens *Admont*

192b Potestates saecularium . . . psalmistae *Admont, Sicard (2.4), Beleth (14a–b), Lambach end material, PL omits*

197 Per mensam in qua *Lambach* : Per mensam quoque *Admont*

207.2 \<In pectore duplicatur\> . . . \<Inter humeros duplicatur . . . supportantur\> *Lambach*

208 coram Deo gratiam inveniat *Lambach*: coram Deo gratiam inveniet *Admont*

225 a Nino primum *Lambach*: anno primo *Admont*

230 pii laboris exercitium *Lambach*: proprii laboris exercitium *Admont*

Book 2

23 qui cibum benedicunt *Lambach*: quibus cibum benedictum *Admont*

24 Secunda nocturna est hora nona *Lambach*: Secunda nocturna est hora undecima *Admont*

28 De Nocturnis Monachorum: De Matutinis Monachorum *PL*

42 pro victoria hymnum Domino cum populo cecinit *Lambach*: pro victoria de Antichristo hymnum Domino cum populo cecinit *Admont*

44 quo in ultimis Christus *Lambach*: quod in ultimis Christus *Admont*

47 nocti duodecim horas *PL*: noctem duodecim horis *Admont, Lambach*

53.3 sexta aetate crucifixus \<est Christus\> *Lambach*

61.3 quia \<per\> tales fructus paenitentes *Lambach*

62 Vesperam ideo *Lambach*: Responsum ideo *Admont*

67.3 ideo Ecce venio \<Filius dicit\> *our addition*

Notes to the Translation

DEDICATORY LETTERS

1   *Solitary*: In the twelfth century, a solitary was a charismatic her-
     mit often sought for his teaching. On the role of solitaries in
     the Gregorian Reform movement, see Henrietta Leyser, *Her-
     mits and the New Monasticism* (New York, 1984), 69–77.

     A company on campaign: The word *excubans* (literally, "sleeping
     outdoors") refers to watch duty, but also to the night offices of
     the Church (see 2.1.1). Clerical authors frequently compare
     their life to military service. See Giles Constable, "Metaphors
     for Monastic Life in the Middle Ages," *Revue Mabillon* n.s. 19
     (2008): 231–42.

     instructor in the arts of war: A pun on Honorius's profession as a
     teacher of the liberal arts, often allegorized as "weapons." The
     troops in question lack the tools of war (books) necessary to
     fight the battle of Christian life, and Honorius is a good sup-
     plier. A bookcase was called an *armarium*.

2   *literature's open main*: On the tradition of scripture as an ocean,
     which Honorius here applies to secular literature, see, among
     many others, Gregory the Great, *In librum primum Regum*, pro-
     emium 4, ed. P.-P. Verbraken, CCSL 144 (Turnhout, 1963), and
     Homiliae in Hiezechielem prophetam 1.1.19, ed. M. Adriaen, CCSL
     142 (Turnhout, 1971).

     Summa totius: Honorius refers to his *Summa totius de omnimoda
     historia* (PL 172:187), an encyclopedic literary history written
     just before the *Jewel of the Soul*.

voyage: Drawing on this ancient nautical metaphor, Honorius describes monastic life as a safe harbor also in *De vita claustrali* (*PL* 172:1247).

PREFACE

1   *What profit . . . brutal sway*: He means the *Iliad,* Plato's dialogues, and the works of Virgil (Publius Vergilius Maro) and Ovid (Publius Ovidius Naso). Virgil and Ovid in particular formed an integral part of monastic education. Like Christian authorities before him, Honorius does not condemn the study of classical authors, but a misguided enthusiasm that leads students to neglect scripture. In fact, his commentary boldly appropriates pagan antiquity to explain Christian ritual. See his *De animae exilio et patria* (*PL* 172:1241) on liberal education, where the poets are imagined as houses in the city of knowledge. On medieval liberal education, see Rita Copeland, *Medieval Grammar and Rhetoric: Language Arts and Literary Theory, AD 300–1475* (Oxford, 2012), and Paul Abelson, *The Seven Liberal Arts: A Study in Mediaeval Culture* (New York, 1906).

2   *God's Wisdom*: An epithet for Christ (1 Corinthians 1:24).

BOOK I

1   *the Mass*: For an introduction to the Mass and the experience of worship in the Middle Ages, see James Monti, *A Sense of the Sacred: Roman Catholic Worship in the Middle Ages* (San Francisco, 2012).

     dues of our servitude: Feudal vassals' obligations to their lords were called "dues" *(debitum)*. Priests and religious were specially called God's servants *(servi),* bound to render him the "sacred service" *(servitium, officium)* of the Divine Office and sacrifice. See *Rule of Saint Benedict,* 16.2, 16.49.

2   *legal causes*: Apart from the basic sense of "cause" or "reason," *causa* also has legal connotations. Since all four reasons envision the Mass in relation to legal formalities, we have brought

this out in the translation. There is further discussion of the Mass as a judicial procedure in 1.80.

legation: The notion of divine legation is Pauline. See 2 Corinthians 5:20 and Amalar of Metz, *Liber officialis* 3.36.2–5.

who are obliged . . . Vespers and Lauds: Laymen were generally expected to attend Lauds and Vespers as well as Mass on Sundays and great feasts *(festa ferianda),* when servile labor was prohibited.

3.1   *seven offices:* The basic meaning of *officium* is "duty." Here it is a ritual action performed by the clergy as an obligation of their state. It can refer to the whole of the Mass *(Missae officium)* or to the Divine Office *(Divinum Officium),* but here it refers to a discrete part of the liturgical act, perhaps as "rite" or "ritual" is used today (entrance rite, sprinkling rite, etc.).

Moses: Moses plays a central role in Honorius's commentary. As the great priestly author of the Pentateuch who spoke with God face to face, Moses had complete knowledge of God's plan to save mankind. See Honorius's *De neocosmo (PL* 172:265–70).

god of Pharaoh: See Exodus 7:1.

3.2   *who prefigure the pastors of the Church:* In the Christian view, history is God's gradual communication of himself to humankind, culminating in the person of Christ. All events and persons of the Old Testament pointed to and prophesied his coming, bearing his image as wax "stamped" with a seal. Any event so interpreted "bears the stamp" *(typum gerit),* or, in another metaphor, a "shadow" *(umbram gerit),* because in some way it dimly reveals the contours of Christ. The liturgical commentator seeks these types in the liturgy, as the exegete finds them in scripture. Compare Amalar of Metz, *Liber officialis,* proem 6–7 and 4.23.23. For an introduction to Carolingian biblical exegesis, see Celia Chazelle and Burton Van Name Edwards, eds., *The Study of the Bible in the Carolingian Era* (Turnhout, 2003), and Henri de Lubac, "The Interpretation of Scripture," chap. 6 in *Catholicism: Christ and the Common Destiny of Man* (San Francisco, 1988), 165–216.

4.1   *Seven acolytes*: In large churches on major feasts, the pontifical liturgy was officiated by a bishop and seven acolytes, subdeacons, deacons, and priests. Lesser churches or lesser feast days required fewer ministers.

plenaries: The meaning of this term is ambiguous. In his entry on *plenarium* in *Dictionnaire latin-français des auteurs chrétiens* (Turnhout, 1954), 696, Albert Blaise, citing this passage, defines it as a reliquary case. However, Joseph Braun, "Buchreliquiar," in *Reallexikon zur deutschen Kunstgeschichte,* ed. Otto Schmitt, vol. 3, (Stuttgart, 1954), 1–3, states that the term refers to a lectionary, encrusted with relics, that contains the Epistle and Gospel texts. Both types were commonly borne in solemn processions and placed on the altar for decoration and veneration.

5.1   *pontiff*: We translate *pontifex* (high priest) as "pontiff," even when the bishop is meant, to preserve symmetry between the titles of Aaron, Christ, and the pope, all called *pontifex.*

as a bridegroom coming from his bridal chamber: Psalms 18:6.

past and future coming: See note to 1.6.1.

all the fullness . . . corporeally: See Colossians 2:9. There is wordplay on *plenarium* (plenary, see above, note to 1.4.1) and *plenitudinem* (fullness). The Gospel book represented Christ, who "took flesh" in the visible word.

5.2   *officers*: The *presbyteri priores* were priests with an official dignity or prelature, such as the provost or dean of a chapter. The term originally referred to the senior presbyters of Rome's titular churches, later also called *prebysteri cardinales.* See Stephan Kuttner, "*Cardinalis*: The History of a Canonical Concept," *Traditio* 3 (1945): 129–214.

prepares the way for us: See Mark 1:3 and Matthew 3:3.

5.3   *introduced*: Literally, "carried in," as on a triumphal chariot.

6.1   *the chariot of God . . . ten thousands*: Psalms 67:18, which describes a majestic victory procession with prisoners and costly objects. The entrance rite, which often included the *laudes regiae* (hymns in praise for the emperor), is treated as a royal reception of Christ in the person of the bishop, recalling his reception at several "comings." See the Einsiedeln Customary in

P. Odilo Ringholz, *Geschichte des Fürstlichen Benediktinerstiftes U. L. Fr. zu Einsiedeln* (Einsiedeln, 1888), 675; and the Saint Emmeram *Cantatorium* (Munich, Bayerische Staatsbibliothek, Clm 14322, fols. 98v–99v). See Maureen Miller, "The Florentine Bishop's Ritual Entry and the Origins of the Medieval Episcopal *Adventus,*" in *Revue d'histoire ecclésiastique* 98 (2003): 5–28, and David Werner, "Ritual and Memory in the Ottonian Reich: The Ceremony of Adventus," *Speculum* 76, no. 2 (2001): 255–83. See also Honorius's treatment of the chariot in *Expositio in Cantica canticorum* (PL 172:352–53).

6.2   *Two choirs*: The clergy in the sanctuary are divided into two facing choirs who sing the ceremony.

The Introit . . . gentiles: Because the Introit is often from the Old Testament, and *Kyrie eleison* is Greek. By "Church of the Jews," Honorius means Christian converts from Judaism.

a dignity equal to the angels': See Luke 20:36 and Matthew 22:30, and Honorius's *Liber XII quaestionum* 5 (PL 172:1180), where he argues that saints from the nine orders of the Church will replace the members fallen from the nine choirs of angels.

6.3   *prophetic verse*: A verse taken from the psalms, written by David, called the Prophet.

various tongues: Because the text is Greek.

7.1   *Making his confession . . . the entire people*: The celebrant makes his confession at the foot of the altar to the assisting ministers (here figured as Peter and the thief), who then themselves confess and ask and obtain his pardon.

7.2   *by Christ the cornerstone . . . one faith*: See Ephesians 2:20. The two walls are the Jews and the gentiles.

Christ preached peace to those far off and nigh: See Ephesians 2:17.

in the bond of peace: Ephesians 4:3.

those coming from east and west: Luke 19:29.

the smoke of spices . . . sight of God: See CAO 1491, 6124; Revelation 8:4.

angel of great counsel: Introit *Puer natus,* Isaiah 9:6, Cantus ID g00553 (*Cantus: A Database for Latin Ecclesiastical Chant,* http://cantus.uwaterloo.ca/ [accessed March 22, 2022]).

offered himself up for us: See Ephesians 5:2.

a fragrant odor: Ephesians 5:2. Perhaps better rendered "pleasing or appeasing odor," the phrase is applied to sacrifices that are pleasing to God. See Genesis 8:21, Numbers 15:3, 2 Corinthians 2:14–15, and Ephesians 5:2.

the prayers of the saints . . . golden altar: See Revelation 8:3.

like burning coals: 2 Samuel 22:9. These *burning coals* are "human hearts inflamed by the Holy Spirit" *(Corda hominum inflammata a Spiritu sancto)* according to an interlinear gloss to 2 Samuel 22:9, in *Glossa ordinaria,* ed. Martin Morard, CNRS-Paris, 2017, http://gloss-e.irht.cnrs.fr.

7.3   *restored to mankind the glory of the angels*: Augustine (*De civitate Dei* 22, *Enchiridion* 29) and Anselm (*Cur Deus homo* 18) famously argued that the elect make up for the number of rebellious angels expelled from heaven.

has already crossed from death to life: See John 5:24.

sitting at the right hand of the Father: See Mark 16:19. In medieval churches the bishop's chair was often located at the Gospel side of the altar, or on the right, from the point of view of one looking down the nave from the sanctuary.

8   *As the bishop goes up . . . to the altar*: During the bishop's confession, the candles were placed in a horizontal line parallel to the altar. Here, the line is pivoted around the first candle to make a line perpendicular with the altar.

9.1   *followed in Christ's footsteps*: 1 Peter 2:21.

sent the disciples . . . every town: Luke 10:1.

Peace to this house: Luke 10:5.

9.2   *the apostles chose seven deacons*: See Acts 6.

seven columns in the house of wisdom: See Proverbs 9:1.

seven lamps: See Exodus 25:37 and Revelation 4:5.

seven candelabras: See Revelation 1:12.

9.3   *the damsel's resuscitation*: See Mark 5.

9.4   *James*: See Mark 14. Tradition holds that the youth mentioned in the Gospel was John, and many manuscripts read *Iohannem* here. Some writers claimed it was James the Greater, the brother of Jesus, however, so either reading may be correct.

dying alone: Acts 7:54–60. Stephen was seized and stoned to death by an angry mob while preaching the Gospel. He was thus "alone" at his death.

11   *Christ . . . every soul*: See John 1:9.

an odd number . . . delight: Virgil, *Eclogae* 8.75. See also Amalar of Metz, *Eclogae* 3.2.

12.1   *thurible*: The thurible (from *thus*, "incense") is a metal censer suspended on one or more chains used to burn incense during sacred functions. They were often designed to look like a model city, with the base formed as the earth and the lid as walls and spires, through whose windows the incense escapes. In this way the instrument evoked the angel in the heavenly Jerusalem in Revelation 8:3.

A fifth chain: The chain that raises and lowers the lid.

12.2   *laid down his soul in death for the sheep*: See John 10:11.

free one among the dead: Psalms 87:6.

13   *pulpit*: The words *pulpitum, ambo, analogium, tribunal, suggestus,* and *pyrgus* all refer to a raised reading platform, either separate from or (later) incorporated into the rood screen, forming an essential part of ecclesiastical architecture and ritual. By synecdoche, the rood screen itself is often also called by these names. See A. W. N. Pugin, *A Treatise on Chancel Screens and Rood Lofts* (London, 1851), and Richard Hayman, *Rood Screens* (London, 2018).

watch over: The Greek word *episkopos* means "overseer" or "superintendent," as well as "bishop."

14   *exult in the living God*: See Psalms 83:3.

with organum: An early form of polyphony involving at least one additional voice, usually singing in parallel. The practice of organum in twelfth-century Germany is poorly attested. Honorius may have encountered it in England but seems to assume that his German audience knows what it is.

jubilus: The Alleluia verse developed a florid concluding melismatic phrase called a jubilus (from *iubilare*, to shout out joyfully). A melisma is a melodic phrase in which one syllable is sustained over several or many notes. See Richard Taruskin,

"New Styles and Forms," chap. 2 in *The Oxford History of Western Music* (Oxford, 2005).

16   *will go from virtue to virtue*: Psalms 83:8.

will praise the Lord unto the ages of ages: Psalms 83:5.

17.1   *the Gospel*: See Luke 17:7–10.

the plowing servant: Compare Amalar, *Liber officialis* 3.11, and 1 Corinthians 9.

fruit of justice: James 3:18.

precentor: The precentor's duty was to "rule" the choir, giving musical direction.

17.2   *Schola means a summoning*: It actually means *vacatio,* "being at leisure." Honorius misremembers or massages the truth for effect.

lofty trumpet: In Isaiah 58:1, God tells the prophet to cry out like a trumpet.

18   *remains seated during three parts*: See *OR* 5.27.

At this point in the Mass: Ordinations normally took place right before the Gospel. Honorius interprets this placement as an allegory, symbolizing that the clergy are ordained to preach the Gospel, just as Christ sent out the seventy-two to preach in Judaea.

19   *a sermon*: In *Speculum Ecclesiae* (PL 172:827–30), Honorius gives a template of a festive sermon that ends with a shout of *Kyrie eleison.*

the people . . . and the clergy: Honorius may be referring to vernacular *Credo*-songs sung by the laity in lieu of the Latin *Credo,* to the refrain *Kyrie eleison.* Berthold of Regensburg (d. 1272) mentions several places where the people joined the *Credo* with a German song: "Ich gloube an den Vater, ich gloube an den Sun miner frouwen sant Marien, und an den Heiligen Geist. Kyrieleys." See *MS* vol. 1, p. 472.

20   *having called . . . kingdom of God*: See Luke 9:1–5.

the Law . . . Jerusalem: See Isaiah 2:3.

going forth . . . the whole world: See Mark 16:15.

the Lord will come from the south: Habakkuk 3:3.

21   *the two precepts of charity*: The two "great commandments" of

Christ were love of God and love of neighbor. See Matthew
22:35–40, Mark 12:28–34, and Luke 10:27.

Moses and Elijah . . . the mountain: See Matthew 17, Mark 9, and
Luke 4.

fragrant odor: Ephesians 5:2.

22   *light of life*: See John 8:12.

According to the Roman order: Honorius is paraphrasing Bernold
of Constance's *Micrologus de ecclesiasticus observationibus* 9 (*PL*
151:982). Bernold himself may be referring to the *OR* 5.36.

the north: For a discussion of the complicated question of reading orientation, and medieval attempts to explain it with allegory, see *MS* vol. 1, pp. 413–17.

23   *A continuation of this or that Gospel*: The deacon announces the
Gospel with the words *Sequentia* or *Initium sancti Evangelii secundum (Matthaeum, Marcum . . .)*, "A continuation" or "A beginning of the holy Gospel according to (Matthew, Mark . . .)."

whoever . . . before the Father and the angels: See Luke 9:26.

the mouth makes confession unto salvation: Romans 10:10.

24.1   *anyone holding a staff puts it down*: In church, staves were carried
by bishops, abbots, and cantors, as signs of their office and
tools for conducting the choir. Laymen also used staves to lean
upon. See "Staff" in Augustus Pugin, *Glossary of Ecclesiastical
Ornament and Costume* (London, 1868), 215–16.

Head coverings: The priest kept his head covered by the amice
during Mass when not officiating at the altar.

face to face . . . dark manner: 1 Corinthians 13:12.

24.2   *the devils . . . his name*: See Luke 10:17.

25   *the people sing . . . has preached*: See note to 1.19 above.

the odor of life: See 2 Corinthians 2:15–16.

26   *act of sacrifice*: The word *actio* refers implicitly to the Canon of
the Mass, the *Canon actionis*. We have translated it as "act of
sacrifice" to bring out this connotation.

the people of Israel . . . tabernacle: See Exodus 35.

27   *sent their oblations . . . Paul and Barnabas*: See Acts 11:27–30.

in a sacrifice of praise to the Lord: See Hebrews 13:15.

those who lay down their lives for their brothers: See John 15:13.

28   *strong in Christ*: See 1 Corinthians 4:10.
      living sacrifice: See Romans 12:1.

29   *rite of the Synagogue . . . religion of the Church*: Beginning with the
      Gospels and Epistles, Christian writers stressed the continuity
      between Jewish and Christian sacred orders. Thus in Clem-
      ent's *First Letter,* the basic hierarchy remains unchanged: high
      priest (bishop), priests (presbyters), and Levites (deacons).

31   *bread of life . . . bread of angels*: See John 6 and Psalms 77.
      Just so, Christ, the noble grain: This mystical view led, in places, to
      the production of the Eucharistic species being surrounded
      with great care and symbolism, analogous to the Byzantine
      proskomedia or Liturgy of Preparation. See William of Hirsau,
      Constitutiones Hirsaugienses 2.32, ed. Candida Elvert and Pius
      Engelbert, Corpus consuetudinum monasticarum 15 (Siegburg,
      2010).
      with swords and clubs: Luke 22:52.

32   *scrutiny*: A sequence of oral examinations of candidates for bap-
      tism, conducted by the bishop during Lent (see 3.53–69). For a
      discussion of these ancient rites and their reception in the
      early Middle Ages, see Bryan Spinks, "The Western Rites: From
      John the Deacon to Anglo-Saxon England," chapter 6 in *Early
      and Medieval Rituals and Theologies of Baptism: From the New Tes-
      tament to the Council of Trent* (Ashgate, 2006), 109–33.
      they will not die forever: John 11:26.

33   *as if in a winepress*: The *torculus Christi,* or mystical winepress, a
      motif developed by Augustine (*Enarrationes in Psalmos* 8), Greg-
      ory the Great, and others out of a web of scriptural texts, espe-
      cially Isaiah 63:3 and Revelation 19, was a favorite mystical al-
      legory for the Middle Ages, expressed in many art media. An
      altar by Nicholas of Verdun (1181) in Klosterneuburg is a fine
      example.

34   *the waters were the people*: See Revelation 17:15. The commingling
      of water and wine was understood to represent the union of
      Christ (wine) and his people (water), an extension of the incar-
      national union mentioned in the prayer of the commingling,
      Deus qui humanae substantiae. This doctrine is well articulated

by, among others, Saint Cyprian in Letter 62 to Caecilius and session 22, chapter 7 of the Council of Trent.

35   *stamped in this bread*: The altar bread was stamped with a simple cross or more elaborate design. The stamping device was called a *ferrum* or *ferramentum,* the English terms for which were "bult" or "singing iron."

  in the book of life: Revelation 20:15.

36   *for them to imitate*: As in the Collect for Palm Sunday, *Omnipotens . . . qui humano generi,* CO 1699.

37   *the chalice his Passion*: See Matthew 20:22 and 26:39.

  Christ our subdeacon: Honorius often operates in the tradition of the Ordinals of Christ, an early medieval ordering of the ecclesiastical grades that showed how Christ had performed each role in his life. See Roger E. Reynolds, *The Ordinals of Christ from Their Origins to the Twelfth Century* (Berlin, 1973). Honorius gives his own complete Ordinal in *Sacramentarium* 24 (*PL* 172:759–60). See also 1.44, 1.72, 1.156, 1.194, 3.76, and 3.89, among others.

38   *One cantor . . . in the wine*: The cantors' offering is an ancient feature of the Roman rite, attested in *OR* 1.80. See Amalar of Metz, *Liber officialis* 3.19.30.

  Enoch and Elijah: On Enoch and Elijah's coming at the end of time, see Augustine's interpretation of Malachai 4:5 in *De civitate Dei* 20.29.

41   *Thrice three times divided*: According to Christian tradition, there are nine orders of angels, divided into three groups of three: seraphim, cherubim, and thrones; dominions, virtues, and powers; principalities, archangels, and angels.

42.1   *resound with organs*: Or perhaps "resound with organum," referring to singing polyphonically (see note to 1.14). See Gunilla Iversen, "The Mirror of Music: Symbol and Reality in the Text of *Clangat hodie,*" *Revista de musicología* 16, no. 2 (1993): 786.

  the people join in . . . lively voice: The laity sang the *Sanctus,* as attested by a number of *ordines* and capitularies. See *MS* vol. 2, p. 130 for documentation.

42.2   *partly by angels, partly by men*: The *Hosanna in excelsis* is sung

by the angels in Isaiah's vision (Isaiah 6) and the *Benedictus* by
the crowds welcoming Christ into Jerusalem on Palm Sunday
(Matthew 21).

sign of contradiction: Luke 2:34.

43   *the first age*: For Augustine's division of history into ages, see *De
civitate Dei* 22.30.5, where he draws on a passage beginning with
Luke 22:39 and on Matthew 1:1–17, 20:1–19. See Henri de Lubac, *Catholicism* (San Francisco, 1988), 148–56.

the blessed shall praise the Lord forever and ever: See Psalms 83:5.

44   *veiled . . . cherubim*: The Canon was shrouded by a veil of silence—nearly the whole Canon was recited by the priest in a
low voice—and often by real veils drawn across the front of the
chancel screen or around the sides of the ciborium.

Joshua, who is Jesus: In Hebrew, Latin, and Greek, Joshua's name
is spelled the same as Jesus's, partly explaining the long tradition, beginning with Origen, of reading the book of Joshua as
an allegory of Christ's redemptive work. See Origen, *Homilies
on Joshua*.

with hands outstretched . . . gainsaying people: See Romans 10:21 and
Isaiah 65:2.

45   *return joyfully homeward*: See Tobit 5:27.

46.2   *bowing his head, Christ gave up his spirit*: See John 19:30.

Indeed this was the Son of God: See Matthew 27:54.

47   *symbolizes Joseph of Arimathea*: The identification of the various
ministers with characters in Christ's Passion fits the general
allegorical scheme, but also corresponds to the roles these
ministers played in Passion dramas.

The chalice represents the tomb: In Honorius's day, the corporal was
a full-length altar cloth spread by the deacon at the offertory.
During the Mass, the chalice was covered with the back part of
the corporal. It was common to call the altar the tomb *(sepul-
crum)*. This sensibility was illustrated in many artworks depict-
ing Christ rising from the altar.

48.1   *the acolyte holds the wrapped paten*: Later this became the role of
the subdeacon, but in the *OR* 1.17 the acolyte, standing next to
the subdeacon, held the paten.

48.2   *the deacons stand bowed*: In the ancient papal stational liturgy, the assisting ministers remained in a profound bow during the Canon, until called to their functions (*OR* 1.16).

49   *This sacrament . . . only by the Cross*: Some twelfth-century writers speculated that the gifts were transformed by the sign of the Cross, among them, Odo of Cambrai, *Expositio in canone missae* (*PL* 160:1062). See Honorius's *Speculum Ecclesiae* (*PL* 172:941) and *Dialogus de laudibus sanctae crucis* (Munich, Bayerische Staatsbibliothek, Clm 14159, from Prüfening Abbey near Regensburg, ca. 1170–1180) for striking depictions of the Cross's role in history.

    There are six orders of crosses: Liturgical manuals such as *OR* 7.6–26 indicated six places where the priest was to make signs of the Cross over the offerings. Carolingian commentators assigned mystical reasons to what were originally merely rhetorical gestures indicating the objects mentioned in prayers.

    all the ages . . . united to Christ by the cross: Developing Paul's doctrine that Christ is a new Adam, Augustine said that Adam, who stands for the human race, was scattered in pieces throughout the world, but redeemed and welded back together by Christ with the fire of charity. See especially Augustine, *Enarrationes in Psalmos* 95, and Augustine, *In Iohannis Evangelium tractatus* 9.14 and 10.10–13. Compare Honorius Augustodunensis, *Speculum Ecclesiae* (*PL* 172:945).

50   *just men . . . had faith in the Trinity*: Honorius describes the just men's sufferings as *cruciatus* (torments, sufferings), using a word derived from *crux* (cross). This cleverly illustrates his point that "all the ages . . . are united to Christ by the Cross" (1.49) and that "the just of the Old Testament were participants in this sacrament" (1.57). Whether by *supplicia, tormenta,* or *cruciatus* (all words he employs for "tortures"), all participate in Christ's Passion in the Eucharistic moment of faithful suffering. This section should be read together with 1.106–8.

    suffered the crosses . . . gentiles: See Genesis 14:18–20, though the biblical story does not say Melchizedek was involved in the battles.

NOTES TO THE TRANSLATION

52   *Simon received . . . with great joy*: See Luke 2:25–35. The wording
      recalls the narrative of consecration: "He took bread in his
      holy and venerable hands" (*Accepit panem in sanctas et venerabiles
      manus suas*). Greek and Latin depictions of the Presentation
      depict Simeon taking the baby Jesus with a cloth, as if touching
      the host or a holy vessel. Much of the imagery of the whole
      Christmas-Epiphany cycle is sacrificial, anticipating Christ's
      role as priest and victim of his own sacrifice.

      whenever our Lord's words . . . body and blood: As in 1.103.2, Hono-
      rius's remarks reflect an almost magical account of the pow-
      ers of the words of consecration. The same word *commutare*
      (change) described the transformation of the Old Law into the
      New in 1.38.

56   *God breathed the breath of life into his face*: See Genesis 2:7.

      through whom, with whom, and in whom: Formed in analogy with
      the prayer *Per ipsum et cum ipso et in ipso* ("Through him and
      with him and in him") at the achievement of the Canon.

57   *with three fingers*: The Latins and Greeks attached great impor-
      tance to the proper way of signing the Cross. The Latin prac-
      tice is described by Innocent III, *De sacro altaris mysterio* 2.45.

      seventy-two languages: Seventy-two is the number of nations enu-
      merated in Genesis 10, cursed and scattered at the Tower of
      Babel. Moses and Jesus choose seventy-two elders (Numbers
      11:25) and disciples (Luke 10:1) to share in their ministry, sym-
      bolically reuniting the human race after its scattering at Babel.

58.2 *crucified . . . concupiscence*: Galatians 5:24.

58.3 *the sacrifice of the penitents*: Christians who had entered the ca-
      nonical penitential system of the Church after confessing a
      grave sin. For a short period (usually during Lent), they were
      excluded from the community, required to stand outside or in
      the vestibule during Mass until their public reconciliation dur-
      ing Holy Week. Honorius discusses public penance in more
      detail in Book 3.

59   Compare Bernold of Constance, *Micrologus* 13 (PL 151:986).

      the Church is composed . . . the married: A traditional division made
      by Gregory the Great (*Homiliae in Ezechielem* 2.7), developed by

Bede (*In evangelium sancti Ioannis* 2) and Haymo of Halberstadt (*Commentaria in Cantica canticorum* 6, *PL* 117:337).

60.1   *the bishop blesses the people*: The pontifical blessing before communion was a feature from the Gallican rite that resisted many Roman attempts to expunge it, before finally making its way into the solemn Roman service. Matching the great priestly blessing of Numbers 6:22–26, each blessing usually had three sections: a response, an Amen, and a concluding clause. See *MS* vol. 2, p. 296.

       Moses . . . Joshua: See Deuteronomy 31.

       Jacob . . . inheritance: See Genesis 49.

       sitting in the darkness . . . heavenly fatherland: See Luke 1:79.

60.2   *cause them to inherit a blessing:* 1 Peter 3:9.

       be fruitful and multiply: See Genesis 1:28.

       He blessed mankind a second time: See Genesis 9.

       God blessed the world through Abraham: See Genesis 18.

       He blessed the world a fourth time: See Luke 24.

       Come . . . for you: Matthew 25:34.

62   *Peace be to you*: Luke 24:36; John 20:19, 20:21, 20:26.

       eating and drinking condemnation on themselves: See 1 Corinthians 11:29.

63.1   *The host is broken*: The elaborate ceremonies of the fraction and the communion in the ancient papal rite were simplified and confused during their transmission to the Frankish kingdoms, such that there was much debate on how they ought to be performed. For a discussion of these problems, see *MS* vol. 2, pp. 303–21.

63.2   *The pope . . . places the rest in the chalice*: *OR* 1.107.

       took a bite out of hell: See Hosea 13:14, where the prophet anticipates Israel's resurrection from national death. Following Saint Paul (1 Corinthians 15:55), exegetes read this verse as a prophecy about the Harrowing of Hell: for example, Gregory the Great, *Moralia in Iob* 33.14, and Rupert of Deutz, *Commentarius in Oseam prophetam* (*PL* 168:196–97). Faced with a strange feature of the papal rite, Honorius justifies it as a representation of the Harrowing. See also the antiphon *O mors* (CAO 4045),

sung on Holy Saturday. Compare his treatment of this allegory in *Speculum Ecclesiae,* "De Paschali die" (*PL* 172:936–38).

The subdeacon . . . for the people: In the papal station rite, the Eucharistic bread was given by the subdeacons to the bishops for the general fraction (*OR* 1.102). Of course, this presumes the use of bread loaves, a form of Eucharistic species largely displaced by the denarius wafer throughout the twelfth century. For Honorius's explanation of the denarius wafer, see 1.66 below.

63.3   *our Lord broke . . . Emmaus*: See Luke 24.

64   *Christ's body is threefold*: See Gratian, *Decretum,* part 3 *(De consecratione),* 2.22, ed. Emil Albert Friedberg, *Decretum magistri Gratiani,* vol. 1 of *Corpus iuris canonici,* 2nd ed. (Leipzig, 1879). On the Amalarian doctrine of the *corpus triforme* ("threefold body," *Liber officialis* 3.35.1–2), see Enrico Mazza, *The Celebration of the Eucharist: The Origin of the Rite and the Development of Its Interpretation* (Collegeville, 1999), 169–71.

65.1   *Christ ate . . . left over*: See Luke 24.

     went away to Jerusalem . . . in the Temple: See Luke 24:52–53.

65.2   *the blessing . . . after Mass*: The *Oratio super populum.*

     he filled the faithful with every spiritual blessing: See Ephesians 1:3.

66   *it was decided . . . thrice in the year*: Compare Gratian, *Decretum,* part 3 *(De consecratione),* 2.16, which specifies Easter, Pentecost, and Christmas.

     coins: The ancient rule was that none should communicate without offering something; Gratian, *Decretum,* part 3 *(De consecratione),* 1.69. Honorius argues that the bread is made as a penny *(denarius)* to fit this ancient principle: people give a penny and receive one back. Drawing on three scriptural moments (Matthew 10:1–16, 22:20–21, 26:15), Honorius repeatedly points out the wafer-shaped host's relation with coinage. See also his *Speculum Ecclesiae* (*PL* 172:1052) and *Eucharistion* (*PL* 172:1256). He is one of the earliest authorities to mention that wafers for communion were made in the shape of a coin, a development that is, therefore, usually dated to the late eleventh century.

67   *Prayer over the People*: The appearance in liturgical books of the

Prayer over the People *(Oratio super populum)* during the Masses of Lent has puzzled commentators medieval and modern. The reason for its disappearance except during Lent is unclear, though the tendency to greater conservatism during penitential seasons may explain its survival in Lent. Joseph Jungmann suggests that the institutions of public ecclesiastical penance contributed to its survival as well (*MS* vol. 2, pp. 427–32).

68   *For the people went ... emblems before them*: See Numbers 10.

69   *reliquary capsules ... feretory of relics.* The deacons' *capsae* are probably small handheld reliquary capsules or chests placed for display on the altar (see 1.134). The *scrinium* is a larger shrine or chest containing one or many relics, and a *feretrum* is strictly speaking a bier, but because large shrines were so often carried on these biers, they came to be called by this name. Both of the latter were sometimes called an ark *(arca)*.

    pontifical vestments: The term *infula* "was classically used to denote the wearing of a sort of woolen headband, either by Roman priests or their sacrificial victims, but in Christian parlance was deployed to describe raising a prelate to his 'dignity' or, more literally, assuming the special vestments and insignia (particularly the miter) worn by bishops"; Maureen Miller, "Reform, Clerical Culture, and Politics," in *The Oxford Handbook of Medieval Christianity,* ed. John H. Arnold (Oxford, 2014), 305. See also 1.214.

70   *crucifies himself ... concupiscences*: See Galatians 5:24, 6:14.

72.1   *heavenly commonwealth*: On this notion, see Augustine, *De civitate Dei* 2.19, 2.21.

    he might ... angels: See Matthew 26:53.

72.2   *like an emperor and his army*: The contemporary background of the Crusades gives added color to these chapters.

73   *sancta*: The word *sancta* in *OR* 1.48 refers to the sacrament, specifically the particles of consecrated bread reserved during a previous papal Mass for use in the next stational liturgy as a symbol of sacrificial continuity.

    our station: Honorius alludes to the penitential stational liturgy of Rome, when the pope, clergy, and faithful processed to a

designated church, called the *statio*, for Mass. The custom was imitated north of the Alps. This use of the word *statio* goes back to the time of Tertullian (*De oratione* 19), who uses the word to describe special services held on Wednesday and Friday, and notes the military connotations of the expression. Compare Isidore, *Etymologiae* 6.19.66–67.

74   *tablets*: Tablets, often of ivory, on which a musical score is written.

75   *not against enemies . . . heavenly places*: See Ephesians 6:12.

76   *Moses prayed . . . on the mountain*: See Exodus 17.

77   *with voice and organum*: See note to 1.14.

78   *milk pail*: The Vulgate mentions only the shepherd's knapsack (*pera pastorali*), while Greek and Hebrew texts also mention a bucket (*kadiōi*) or vessel. A note in the *Glossa ordinaria*, however, does mention a milk bucket (*vase pastorali*). The point is essential for his allegory in the next chapter.

a stone to the thirsty people: See Exodus 17:1–7.

the cornerstone: See Psalms 118:22 and Matthew 21:42.

79   *Saul . . . arming David*: See 1 Samuel 17.

80   *The Mass also resembles a sort of trial*: For the way medieval people imagined God's "case" against Satan, see G. R. Evans, *Law and Theology in the Middle Ages* (New York, 2002), 7–10. Since medieval law viewed trial as an adversarial contest (*litis contestatio*) in which the defendant "battles" to defend himself against an accusation, there is deep affinity between the Mass as battle (1.72) and the Mass as trial here. See again Evans, *Law and Theology,* especially 100–102.

actio: In Roman legal Latin, an *actio* was a trial, a plea, or an accusation, depending on the context. In the Middle Ages, a *placitum* was a public judicial assembly.

tribunal: There is wordplay here on the Latin *tribunal,* a name for the sanctuary where the priest officiated, and also for the pulpit or rood loft where liturgical readings, sermons, and decrees of all sorts were read before the people in the nave.

judicial duel: On the judicial duel, see Evans, *Law and Theology,* 141. The concept appears in the Easter Sequence *Victimae pas-*

chali laudes, Cantus ID 508002: *Mors et vita duello conflixere mirando* ("Death and life clashed in an awful duel").

81   *He is guilty of death:* Matthew 26:66.

82   *the spiritual forces . . . heavenly places:* Martial allegory permeates the priest's vesting prayers, which draw on Paul's imagery of the armor of faith in Ephesians 6:10–17.

subcingulum: See 1.206.

throws his chasuble over his shoulder: To use his hands, the priest and deacon had to roll the chasuble's long folds up to the elbows or shoulders. A more efficient solution was to remove the chasuble, roll it, throw it over the right shoulder and tie it at the waist on the left side (folded chasuble). The deacon wore it like this from the Gospel to the end of the ablutions.

83.1   *tragedy in the theaters:* In Honorius's conception, tragedy is about war *(bella tractant); De animae exsilio et patria* 2 (PL 172:1243).

83.2   *By extending his arms:* During the Canon in many medieval rites, the priest extended his arms straight out on each side after the consecration, representing Christ's arms outstretched on the Cross.

Christ sang ten psalms: The Gospels record Christ saying the first words of Psalm 21—a song about the persecution of a just man—and "Father, into your hands I commend my spirit," taken from Psalm 31.

our accuser: The Greek *diabolos* means "accuser" as well as "devil."

champion: The *agōnothetēs* was the sponsor or superintendent of athletic games in ancient Greece, but merely a "warrior" in medieval Latin. Besides Saint Paul's depiction of Christian life as combat (2 Timothy 4), Tertullian *(Ad martyres, PL* 1:624) and Ambrose *(De Elia et ieiunio, PL* 14:714) call Christ our *agonotheta.*

announces the peace: A judicial action is settled, bringing peace *(pax)* to the parties involved.

84.1   *the seven gifts of the Holy Spirit:* The traditional list of the gifts of the Holy Spirit is drawn from Ephesians 4:7–13, Isaiah 11:2–3, and Romans 12:3–8.

saluted the human race: There is a pun on *salutare* (to salute or

greet), from the same root as *salvare* (to save). Christ "greets" the world upon entering it, but also "saves" it.

Depart . . . eternal fire: See Matthew 25:41.

Come . . . the kingdom: See Matthew 25:34, Cantus ID 005350.

85.1   This chapter is a transcription of the preface to Amalar's *Eclogae*.

Moses was a minister . . . New: See Augustine, *Enarrationes in Psalmos* 89.1.

86   *said our Lord's words . . . Lord's Prayer*: The idea that the Mass consisted in the words of institution and the Lord's Prayer can be traced to a letter of Gregory the Great to Bishop John of Syracuse. See Gregory the Great, *Registrum epistolarum* 9.12.

loved the beauty of the Lord's house: Psalms 25:8.

88   *Abbot Notker . . . for these melismas*: The Saint Gall monk Notker prepared a collection of his sequences in 885. In the prooemium he relates that he developed them as a mnemonic device to remember the long melismatic melodies *(neumae)* that Honorius attributes to Gregory the Great. See Calvin M. Bower, *The* Liber Ymnorum *of Notker Balbulus* (London, 2016).

89   *Orate pro me.* The *Orate, fratres* prayer of the current Roman rite existed in a variety of shorter formulas in earlier times, such as simply *Orate,* or *Orate pro me peccatore.*

90.1   *the bishop Martial*: Saint Martial, reputed to be a disciple of Saint Peter, was the first bishop of Limoges (third century). Honorius here furnishes a quasi-apostolic authority for the episcopal blessing.

92   *the inscription on Christ's Cross*: See John 19:20.

93   *the hosts of the heavenly army*: A concluding phrase in many Prefaces.

tower of Eder: Mentioned in Genesis 35:21 and elsewhere as located between Bethlehem and Hebron. Jerome places the tower one mile from Bethlehem.

To pray in spirit and mind: See 1 Corinthians 14.

94   *oration*: There are four proper *orationes* in the Roman Mass: the Collect, the Offertory, the Secret, and the Postcommunion. They are propers, meaning that they change depending on the feast and the season. On the station, see Roger E. Reynolds,

"Stational Liturgies," in *Dictionary of the Middle Ages,* ed. Joseph Strayer (New York, 1982–1989), vol. 7, pp. 623–24.

with those on the right side: See Matthew 25:34.

everything . . . will be given to us: See John 16:23, Matthew 18:19.

95 *we will shine like the sun*: See Matthew 13:43.

96 *from virtue to virtue*: Psalms 83:8.

we will see the Lord's face: See Revelation 22:4.

97 *We say "A continuation of the Gospel" . . . when it is*: The Gospel reading is announced either by *Sequentia sancti Evangelii secundum* ("Continuation of the holy Gospel according to") or by *Initium sancti Evangelii secundum* ("Beginning of the holy Gospel according to").

the Greeks have a prayer: At this point the Greek liturgy has a litany of petitions called the *ektenē,* but the Roman rite goes straight into the offertory.

98 *"Sacrifice" means made holy*: Isidore, *Etymologiae* 6.19.38.

on the millstone of the altar: See Isidore, *Etymologiae* 6.19.31. Immolation was a Roman sacrifice in which milled grain *(mola)* was sprinkled on a victim. This etymology nicely suits the allegory of bread (1.31–32) and is not far off the mark. John Beleth notes that the altar stone covering the relics was known as the *mola; Summa de ecclesiasticis officiis* 1.42b, ed. Heribert Douteil, CCCM 41 (Turnhout, 1976). See also Leviticus 1:3.

A "host" . . . a battle: Medieval orthography often spelled *ostium* ("entrance" or, as here, "beginning") with an initial *h,* creating a link with *hostia* (sacrifice, Eucharistic Host). Thomas Aquinas plays on these associations in his hymn *O salutaris hostia.* Compare Isidore, *Etymologiae* 6.19.33, and Beleth, *Summa* 1.42a. In classical Latin, *ostium belli* means "the commencement of war."

over the cross . . . chrism oil: See 1.162 on the dedication of an altar.

99 *Let there be light*: Genesis 1:3.

These things . . . true witness: Revelation 3:14.

the angelic host . . . to the Lord: A reference to the prayer *Supplices,* where God is asked to send his angel to bear *(perferri)* the offerings to heaven.

100   The first two words of the Preface, *Vere dignum,* often appeared as an elaborate monogram in medieval missals.

103.2   *For it is said . . . struck dead*: Pseudo-Alcuin tells this story in his *De divinis officiis* 40 (*PL* 101:1246), but the story, part of a genre of cautionary tales, is much older.

      Henceforth . . . all these things: This claim presumes a quasi-magical understanding of the sacraments. Honorius is either being facetious to frighten his audience, or his sacramentology differs from the later Catholic dogma that only a validly ordained priest can confect the sacrament.

103.3   *begins with the letter T*: This (fortuitous?) fact created an artistic opportunity, and in most missals the *T* is replaced by a large cross occupying the whole facing page: a fitting symbol identifying the Canon with Christ's sacrifice.

105   *gave testimony*: The apostles, martyrs, and all the orders of saints "gave testimony" because they gave their lives for Christ, whose life and person are contained in the sacrament.

      as Adam was formed: Christ is born on the same day and hour as Adam, since he is the new Adam. Compare Honorius's *De neocosmo* 6 (*PL* 172:266).

      the world was made out of nothing: See *De neocosmo* 3 (*PL* 172:260): "On the sixth day man is created from the clean earth, and in the sixth age Christ is conceived in the Virgin. On the same day God made the animals, and in the sixth age he called believers, his animals, to the pastures of life, and gave them his body to eat." (*Sexta die homo de munda terra formatur, et sexta aetate Christus de Virgine generatur. Ea etiam die Deus animalia fecit, et sexta aetate fideles, animalia sua, ad pascua vitae vocavit, quae pastu corporis sui refecit.*)

106.1   *A mystery . . . Christ*: In reference to the phrase *mysterium fidei* in the institution narrative of the consecration.

      we perceive . . . Body and Blood of Christ. Honorius's explicit statement of Eucharistic doctrine is noteworthy in the wake of the Berengarian controversy, which had occurred a few decades earlier, and heralds his defense of transubstantiation in *Eucharistion* 5 (*PL* 172:1252).

106.2   *king of justice*: See Genesis 14, Hebrews 7.

106.3   *angel of great counsel*: In the Introit *Puer natus,* Cantus ID g00553. See Isaiah 9:6 (Septuagint version).

         is pleased to accept . . . sacrifice of justice: Psalms 50:21.

107   *In former times . . . during the Canon*: Diptychs (*sacrae tabulae, matriculae,* or *libri vivorum et mortuorum*) were notebooks of wood, bone, or ivory on which the names of the living and the dead were written for liturgical commemoration.

         Mark who was also called John: See Acts 12.

108.1   *endorse this sacred oath*: The martyrs (from the Greek word meaning "witness") sign as witnesses of the New Testament (1.106.1). The diptych prayers that flank the Canon are projected into a will-signing ceremony, in which Christ and the saints—stand-ins for all the faithful sufferers of history—sign and endorse the New Testament in their own blood.

109.1   *fatted calf*: See Luke 15:11–32.

         coheirs: See Romans 8:17.

109.2   *from all evils . . . to come*: From the prayer *Libera nos, quaesumus Domine.*

         every word is confirmed by the evidence of two or three witnesses: See Matthew 18:16, 2 Corinthians 13:1, and Deuteronomy 19:15.

111.1   *the Lamb of God who takes away the sins of the world*: See John 1:29.

         must abstain from their wives: Canon law continued the Mosaic proscription (see Exodus 19:15) on intercourse before sacred functions. See Gratian, *Decretum,* part 3 (*De consecratione*), 2.21.

111.2   *The Council of Toledo ordered*: The Fourth Council of Toledo, canon 13.

112   *supplications . . . thanksgivings*: 1 Timothy 2. Commentators were keen to show that the Mass contained every type of prayer mentioned in this key Pauline passage, which was the subject of meditations by Augustine (for example, Letter 149).

113   *Crucify him, crucify him*: Luke 23:21.

114.1   *Pope Leo . . . nine Masses in one day*: As reported by Walafridus Strabo, *De rebus ecclesiasticis* 21 (*PL* 114:943).

         After purifying the chalice . . . grave penance: Receiving the ablutions breaks the priest's fast so that he may not celebrate a

second Mass immediately. Thus, when more than one Mass needed saying, as at Christmas, the ablutions were not done after the first Mass.

115 *at the ninth hour*: Mass was celebrated after Terce on Sundays and major feasts, after Sext on minor feasts and ferial days without fasting, and after None on fast days. The *Gloria in excelsis* is normally said only at those Masses that were said after Terce, but Honorius knows of the two exceptions for the Easter and Pentecost Vigils, and he is trying to account for them.

116 *the Roman authority*: In Rome the Mass of Christmas took place at the church of Saint Anastasia, who was commemorated in a second Collect. This fact puzzled medieval liturgists, but also justified their own additions.

the only thing that the apostles said: See note to 1.86 above.

117.1 *brute beasts*: See Honorius's exegesis of Judges 7 in *Speculum Ecclesiae* (PL 172:841).

117.2 *our bellies ... to the pavement*: See Psalms 43:25 and 118:25.

Abraham, when he fell on his face: See Genesis 17:3.

adoring them: In medieval usage, kings were "adored," given honor and homage.

I bow my knees before the Lord: Ephesians 3:14.

120 *nine prefaces*: The Gelasian sacramentary contains many Prefaces, generally one for each mass, but the Gregorian sacramentary contains only the ten mentioned here.

Qui corporali ieiunio for Sundays in Lent: Other manuscripts read simply "for Lent." Opinions differed about whether the Preface of Lent should be said on Sundays, since it mentions bodily fasting, omitted on Sunday.

none should celebrate Mass without a third person present: See, for example, Gratian, *Decretum,* part 3 *(De consecratione),* 1.61.

121 *Now let us look at ... is celebrated*: On the following sections, see the classic Pugin, *Glossary of Ecclesiastical Ornament,* and Roland Recht, *Believing and Seeing: The Art of Gothic Cathedrals* (Chicago, 2008). There are many parallel passages in Honorius's two sermons for a church dedication in *Speculum Ecclesiae* (PL 172:1103–6).

122	*Ara is Greek*: Actually Greek *ara* (from *araomai*) and Latin *precatio* (from *precor*) both mean "prayer."
123.1	*he showed Moses . . . on this model*: See Exodus 26–30.
123.2	*sent King David a brief*: See 1 Chronicles 28:19, where David claims God wrote the plan in his own hand.
	Solomon . . . on the brief: See 1 Samuel 5.
124.1	*has no abiding city . . . but seeks one to come*: See Hebrews 13:14.
	the living and true God: See the prayer *Memento Domine famulorum,* a commemoration of the whole Church's "sacrifice of praise" *(sacrificium laudis).*
125	*they built a temple*: Bede seems to have been the first Christian author to contrast the two Old Testament houses of God in this way, in his influential *De tabernaculo* 2.1. See also Rabanus Maurus, *In Exodum* (PL 108:136–218).
	temple of glory built out of living stones: See 1 Peter 2.
	will shine like the sun: Matthew 13:43.
	with the garment of salvation . . . justice: See Isaiah 61:10.
126–27	The etymologies in these chapters are largely taken from Isidore, *Etymologiae* 8.
	seven columns . . . house of wisdom: See Proverbs 9.
127	*house of God*: The idea of the *domus Dei* gives rise to the Italian *duomo* and German *Dom* for "cathedral."
	monastery: From Greek *monastērion.*
128	*little churches . . . spiritual alms*: The etymology of "chapel" *(capella)* from "goat skin" is confused, but that from *capenum* is actually correct. See George Cyprian Alston, "Chapel," in *The Catholic Encyclopedia* (New York, 1907–1912), vol. 3, pp. 574–79.
130	*through a glass in a dark manner*: See 1 Corinthians 13:12.
131	*The columns . . . lofty heights*: The columns of a church, which present a narrow, vertical surface, are often decorated with large images or statues of the saints. Thus, Honorius's allegory suggests itself rather obviously to anyone viewing a church interior.
133	*as if by a shield*: Psalms 5:13.
	Oh Lord . . . good will: Psalms 5:13.
	is taken from the Law: See Exodus 25.

divers engravings: See 1 Kings 6:18–35.

a more withdrawn life: That is to say, cloistered monks, hermits, or laymen living secluded from the rest of society.

134   *are hid . . . knowledge*: See Colossians 2:3.

135   *as in a royal city*: Itinerant German kings affixed their regalia in the streets and churches of imperial cities. Regensburg was known especially as *urbs regia*.

crucifying their flesh . . . concupiscences: See Galatians 5:24.

Christ's trophy: For the trophy, see Appendix B.2. Christian imagination celebrated the fact that the beams of the cross resembled the crossed beams of Roman military banners *(vexilla)*. Poets turned the scandal of the Cross on its head by making it a sign of Christ's triumph over death, as in Venantius Fortunatus's hymn *Vexilla regis prodeunt*. The erection of standards over a city signifies subjection.

136   *propitiatory*: A tabernacle for reserving the Eucharist, here likened to the golden lid or "mercy seat" placed over the altar in the holy of holies (Exodus 25 and 27).

137   *tapestries*: Tapestries bearing depictions of Christ and the saints, often decorated very sumptuously with gold and gems, were hung around the Church on solemn feasts. On the design and liturgical function of tapestries, see Laura Weigert, "Setting the Stage," chapter 1 in *Sacred Stories: French Choir Tapestries and the Performance of Clerical Identity* (Ithaca, 2004), 1–16.

life of the perfect: See Matthew 19, Mark 10, Luke 18.

one leaves behind everything: Luke 5:28.

the Catholic Church is our mother: The chief church of a diocese was called the *ecclesia matrix* (mother church), and in many places it was obligatory to be baptized there.

138   *Door*: Christ calls himself the Church's door in John 10:9.

The door . . . through faith: This is in conformity with the duties of the *ostiarius,* or porter, the first grade of minor orders, who according to the Roman Pontifical is to "open God's house at certain hours to the faithful, and always close it to unbelievers" *(certisque horis domum Dei aperiatis fidelibus; et semper claudatis infidelibus)*.

139.1   *ring dance*: The *chorea* was a festive round dance used by laity
        and clergy, especially at Christmas and Easter. See Constant
        Mews, "Liturgists and Dance in the Twelfth Century: The Wit-
        ness of John Beleth and Sicard of Cremona," *Church History* 78,
        no. 3 (2009): 512–48. Here Honorius develops his idea that the
        church, like the tabernacle, is "a likeness of the cosmos" (1.124).
        The Platonic cosmos is painted as a choral dance in Isidore's
        De natura rerum 11, an image Honorius picks up in *Imago mundi*
        1.3. The notion of the celestial *chorea* may also derive from Cal-
        cidius's translation of Plato's *Timaeus* (39b, 40c), where stellar
        motions are called *choreae;* see also in Calicidius's commentary,
        On Plato's Timaeus 124. Macrobius's description of the *hymni de-
        orum* (hymns to the gods) in the *In somnium Scipionis* 2.3.4–6 is
        also relevant. Compare Sicard of Cremona, *Mitrale* 6.15.471–
        99, ed. Gábor Sarback and Lorenz Weinrich, *Sicardi Cremonen-
        sis episcopi Mitralis de officiis,* CCCM 228 (Turnhout, 2008). See
        also Beleth, *Summa* 120, and Botticelli's painting *Mystical Na-
        tivity.*

139.2   *they broke into a ring dance*: See Exodus 15:20–21, wherein Hono-
        rius playfully construes *choreis* (ring dances) instead of the Vul-
        gate's *choris* (choirs).

        they use musical instruments: Perhaps an allusion to contemporary
        Christmas celebrations.

        the heavenly spheres . . . a sweet melody: The "music of the spheres"
        is a constant theme in western cosmology and musical theory.
        Compare Pliny, *Naturalis historia* 2.84, and Isidore, *De natura
        rerum* 13. Compare also Honorius's accounts of heavenly music
        embodied in man as microcosm, in *Imago mundi* 1.80–82 and
        Liber XII quaestionum 2 (PL 172:138–40, 1179). For a history, see
        Andrew Hicks, *Composing the World: Harmony in the Medieval
        Platonic Cosmos* (Oxford, 2017).

140   *The word "choir" . . . form of a crown*: See Isidore, *Etymologiae* 6.19,
        and Sirach 50:13.

        Flavian and Diodorus: See Theodoret of Cyrus, *Historia ecclesias-
        tica* 2.19.

        The stalls: The word *cancellus* (chancel) refers to the reticulated

wooden, iron, or stone barrier separating the sanctuary from the rest of the church, often called a rood screen or chancel screen. Here, it refers to the choir stalls, which often looked like little houses, with overhanging roofs, encircling armrests, and sometimes even a swinging door.

141   *crown chandelier*: A great chandelier, usually located in a church's front nave. It was often designed to look like the heavenly Jerusalem, with the ring made to look like crenellated walls and the candle holders built up like towers *(turres)*. One of the most magnificent examples is found in Charlemagne's Palatine Chapel at Aachen.

   One reason . . . by its candles: As read in a verse inscribed in the corona of the cathedral of Metz: "This crown glitters and shines in the holy temple, / giving light to the people, beauty to the church." *(Cuius in aede sacra rutilans micat ista / corona, ad lumen turbae, vel decus ecclesiae.)*

   crown of life: James 1:12.

142   Compare this chapter to Amalar, *Liber officialis* 3.1.

   their sound . . . of the world: Psalms 18:5.

144   *a cock*: In Christian symbolism, the cock stands for Peter's humiliation, but also the vigilance of Christian pastors, twin associations made in Ambrose's hymn *Aeterne rerum conditor,* traditionally sung at Lauds.

145   *must be placed over the rest*: For Honorius's exalted view of the priesthood and its role in the salvation of the world and Church reform, see his *Summa gloria* and *Offendiculum.*

146.1   *Women do not enter the church after giving birth*: See Leviticus 15.

   and in penance for doing this: In Mosaic law menstruating women were ritually unclean (Leviticus 12), and many Church writers considered intercourse during a period a grave sin. Gregory the Great permitted menstruating women in church, but others, such as the seventh-century archbishop Theodore of Canterbury, forbade it. In parts of medieval Europe, they refrained from entering church or receiving communion.

146.2   *on account of the angels*: Paul's argument in 1 Corinthians 11:10.

   hymns . . . spiritual canticles: See Ephesians 5:19.

147 *crucified to the world*: See Galatians 6:14.

148 *Solomon's portico*: On this notion, see Wayne Dynes, "The Medieval Cloister as Portico of Solomon," in *Gesta* 12, nos. 1/2 (1973): 61–69.

 the multitude . . . unto them: Acts 4:32.

149 *spring of pleasure*: The river or spring of Genesis 2:7, 2:10, often linked with the "torrent of pleasure" in Psalms 35:9.

 tree of life . . . sundry fruit trees: The tree of life features prominently in Honorius's exegesis of Psalms 1 in *Expositio in Psalmos* (PL 172:274). See also his *De vita claustrali* (PL 172:1247).

 the cloister's enclosure: The *secretum* was the place reserved for magistrates in civic buildings and came to refer to the monastic enclosure, the part of the monastery outsiders usually were not permitted to enter.

 fountain of life: Psalms 35:10.

 The multitude . . . possess all things in common: See Acts 4:32.

 God will be all in all: See 1 Corinthians 15:28.

150 *nuptial union*: See Ephesians 5:21–27.

151 The rite of dedication commented by Honorius may be found in *PRG* 1:90–121. For a detailed study of the development of this rite through the ninth century, see Brian Repsher, *The Rite of Church Dedication in the Early Medieval Era* (Lewiston, 1998). On the fully developed medieval rite, see Ruth Horie, *Perceptions of Ecclesia: Church and Soul in Medieval Dedication Sermons* (Turnhout, 2006).

 twelve lit candles: Twelve candles fixed to the walls of the church were lit in anticipation of the ceremony.

 shines and burns: See John 3:35, where Christ calls John the Baptist a lamp.

 Lift up your gates . . . eternal gates: Psalms 23:7.

 threefold power . . . in hell: See Philippians 2:9–11.

 he gave the Church its power . . . on earth: See Matthew 18:18.

 the gates . . . against it: See Matthew 16:18.

 the princes . . . to be raised: See Psalms 23:7.

 the just may enter: See Psalms 117:20.

152.1 *a strong-armed man . . . conquered him*: See Luke 11:21–22.

Peace be with you: See John 20:19, 20:21, 20:26.

one God, one faith, one baptism: See Ephesians 4:5.

155.1   *the queen . . . right hand*: See Psalms 44:10.

a light . . . to the righteous: See Psalms 111:4.

the full number of the gentiles: See Romans 11:25.

155.2   *the Greek language . . . the imperial power*: Latin enjoyed prestige in military, administrative, and legal language during the late antique and Byzantine period. In turn, the Latin language borrowed philosophical terms from Greek. See Augustine, *In Iohannis Evangelium tractatus* 117.4.

156   *voice of exultation*: See Psalms 46:2 and 117:15.

157   *Elisha . . . made clean*: See 2 Kings 2.

159   *God's temple*: See 1 Corinthians 3:16.

In a similar way . . . with the chrism: Honorius refers to the rituals of Christian initiation described in 3.53–68. On the history of baptismal rituals, see Bryan D. Spinks, *Early and Medieval Rituals and Theologies of Baptism: From the New Testament to the Council of Trent* (Routledge, 2017).

160   *is said to be able to penetrate hard stone*: According to Isidore (*Etymologiae* 17.9.39), the roots of the hyssop plant cling to rocks.

sends his angel . . . fear him: See Psalms 33:8.

Exurgat Deus . . . scattered: See Psalm 67.

161   *to compass the church while singing*: They are to sprinkle the outside walls once.

My house: Matthew 21:13, CAO 2428.

Introibo: Psalms 42:4, CAO 3388.

The altar is wiped off . . . Church's tribulation: There is a pun on "linen" *(linteum)* and "outlined" *(delinitur)*.

162   *Erexit . . . in titulum*: See Genesis 28:18, CAO 2665.

oil of gladness: Psalms 44:8.

He became the cornerstone: See Psalms 118:22 and Matthew 21:42–43.

Ecce odor . . . lilies: Responsory, Genesis 27:27, CAO 6601.

163   *Sanctificavit Dominus tabernaculum*: Psalms 45:5, CAO 4748.

Lapides pretiosi . . . gems: CAO 3578.

164   *Confirma hoc . . . confirm in her his work*: Psalms 67:29, CAO 1873.

from your . . . in Jerusalem: Psalms 67:30.

all the fullness . . . corporeally: Colossians 2:9.

165   *Walk, O saints . . . city of God*: CAO 1367.

a new Church . . . built as a city: Psalms 121:3.

the joy . . . Virtues: In medieval use, *tripudium* can mean joy, but also refers to a ritual dance. See note to 1.139.

166   *The saints shall rejoice in glory*: Psalms 149:5, CAO 2812.

168   *Come, ye blessed . . . kingdom*: See Matthew 25:34, Cantus ID 005350.

in the form of a slave: See Philippians 2:7.

they look . . . pierced: John 19:37. See also Zachariah 12:10.

shall see the King . . . in his beauty: Isaiah 33:17.

will blaze . . . like the sun: See Matthew 13:43.

Terribilis . . . iste: Introit, Genesis 28:17, Cantus ID g01401.

will be seen face to face: See 1 Corinthians 13:12.

God will be all in all: See 1 Corinthians 15:28.

169   *in every place of his dominion*: Psalms 102:22.

who has promised . . . gathered in his name: See Matthew 18:19–20.

as if in a praetorium: The pulpit or rood loft was used for public news and announcements, including royal proclamations. Thus, the allegory is germane.

170   *desecrated by a criminal sin*: See note to 3.75.

in the font of tears: After baptism, which may be performed only once, tradition considered tears of repentance a valid way to remove the stain of sin.

Likewise, when the bishop . . . penance and satisfaction: This seems to be Honorius's own opinion.

171   *through the hands . . . heavenly treasury*: See the antiphon *Beatus Laurentius*, CAO 1642.

a house not made . . . in heaven: See 2 Corinthians 5:1.

Nadab and Abihu . . . man from paradise: See Leviticus 10, Numbers 16, 1 Samuel 4, 2 Samuel 6, 1 Kings 2, 2 Chronicles 26, 2 Kings 25, Genesis 37, Exodus 1, Job 2, Jeremiah 38, Daniel 3 and 6, Acts 12, 2 Corinthians 11, Genesis 2, and Isaiah 14.

172   *it remains for us . . . ministers*: For an introduction to ordination in the Middle Ages, see chapters 6 and 7 in Paul Bradshaw, *Rites of*

Ordination: Their History and Theology (Collegeville, 2013), 106–49.

174   *the tithes and offerings*: Diocesan clergy collected tithes from their parishes (usually ten percent of income), and laity could make voluntary offerings of kind or money.

seven orders: There was more than one enumeration of the holy orders, which finally settled on seven only at a late date. See Roger E. Reynolds, "'At Sixes and Sevens'—and Eights and Nines: The Sacred Mathematics of Sacred Orders in the Early Middle Ages," *Speculum* 54 (1979): 669–84.

176   *Asaph and Jeduthun*: See 1 Chronicles 25:1. They were often depicted dancing with David, as in the psalter of Charles the Bald (Paris, Bibliothèque nationale de France, latin 1152).

symmysta: From Greek *symmystēs,* a fellow priest or initiate in a religious brotherhood. Latin Christian writers used it (infrequently) to refer to those in holy orders, to the pope, or simply to a companion. The word is also used in the famous *Hodie cantandus* trope of the Introit of the Third Mass of Christmas, where the prophet Isaiah is called the *presagus et electus symmista Dei* (wise and chosen *symmista* of God).

177   *Exorcist*: From Greek *exorkizō.*

Solomon instructed: Solomon's power as a magician is an extrabiblical tradition, found in the pseudepigraphical *Testament of Solomon.* See also Josephus, *Antiquitates Iudaicae* 8.2.5.

as the priest Sceva's seven sons did: See Acts 19:14.

possessed and obsessed bodies: Possessed bodies are controlled by demons from within, whereas obsessed bodies suffer external demonic attacks.

178   *tenders of the lights*: See Exodus 25:6 and 35:8.

acolytes, or rather candle bearers: As Isidore notes (*Etymologiae* 7.12), the Latins often preferred their own word *ceroferarii,* since carrying the candle was one of the acolyte's main duties, though it is equivalent to the Greek-derived *acolythus.*

paraments and linens: In reference to an altar, the *vestes* are richly embroidered fabrics draped over or hung on the altar, or veils that were hung around the altar, concealing it. The *pallium* or

palla is a linen cloth draped on the altar, over which the corporal is placed.

179   *Nathineans*: Bede links subdeacons with the Nathineans, who helped the Levites in their sacred service. See Bede, *Allegorica expositio in Esdram et Nehemiam* 1.2, and compare Isidore, *Etymologiae* 7.12.23.

180   *Levites . . . lifted up*: Indeed, the Latin *levatus* means "lifted up," but the Hebrew word *levi* means "to belong or adhere to," something closer to the Greek *klēros* (clergy).

permission to leave: They proclaim the dismissal *Ite missa est* at the end of Mass.

must observe perfect chastity: Deacons, unlike inferior ministers, could not marry (though in certain times and places they could be ordained as married men). By the sixth century, subdeacons in the West could no longer marry.

archdeacon: From antiquity archdeacons were an essential part of diocesan administration and the most powerful clerics in the diocese after the bishop. See Adrien Gréa, "*Essai historique sur les archidiacres*," *Bibliothèque de l'École des chartes* 12 (1851): 39–67.

181   *wisdom is gray hair unto man*: Wisdom 4:8.

In the Law . . . through them: See Numbers 16, John 3, Acts 5:34.

shows people the way: See note to 1.145.

ordeals of water and fire: On trials by ordeal, see Evans, *Law and Theology*, 140–43. The liturgical prayers and ceremonies are found in Adolph Franz, *Die kirchlichen Benediktionen im Mittelalter* (Freiburg im Breisgau, 1909), vol. 2, pp. 364–92; the celebration of Mass on the occasion of the ordeal in Adolph Franz, *Die Messe im deutschen Mittelalter* (Darmstadt, 1963), 213–215, and *PRG* 2:246–52, 2:380–414.

182   *An archpriest*: Till now Honorius has discussed the minor and major orders. The following are dignities or prelacies, honorific titles with administrative functions but no corresponding rite of ordination.

chorbishop: A priest assigned certain episcopal functions and privileges. In the High Middle Ages, his role was mostly taken over by the archdeacon.

vidame: The *vicedominus* (or vidame) was a lay officer chosen by the bishop as a protector and advocate for the Church in secular affairs where it was not appropriate for a cleric to act. He lived in a house near the bishop's domains and would, for example, command the bishop's feudal troops, represent him in secular court, or exercise his temporal powers in his domain. See *Encyclopedia Britannica,* 11th ed. (1910–1922), under "vidame."

the seventy men: See Numbers 11.

183   *he is also called a lookout . . . demons and heretics*: There is a play on the words *speculator* (bishop) and *specula* (a high place or a watchtower). *Speculator* is a Latinate equivalent to the Greek *episkopos,* related to *skopein,* which shares a root with Latin *specio* (I see). The pulpits and rood lofts of large churches where bishops preached were also sometimes called watchtowers *(speculae).* See Christine Mohrmann, *"Episcopos-Speculator,"* in *Études sur le Latin des chrétiens* (Rome, 1958–1977), vol. 4, pp. 231–52.

184   *custom demands*: Canon 4 of the Council of Nicaea (325 CE) stipulated that a bishop be ordained by at least three other bishops in his province. For Honorius, the ideal is twelve, since the twelve apostles ordained James, the first bishop.

a king and priest or prophet: Charlemagne was addressed with the sacred title *rex et sacerdos* (king and priest) by the Italian bishops at the Council of Frankfurt in 794; Albertus Werminghoff, *Concilia aevi Karolini,* vol. 1, *MGH Concilia* 2.1 (Hanover, 1906), 142. The Carolingians were styled as Old Testament kings on the model of David.

185   *It is believed that . . . conferred the Holy Spirit*: See Genesis 27, Deuteronomy 31, Matthew 19, and Acts 19:6.

he appointed them rulers: See Exodus 18:25 and Psalms 44:17, and a responsory for feasts of apostles (CAO 6329).

excommunicate rebels: In the twelfth century, those guilty of grave civil crimes automatically incurred the penalty of excommunication, and vice versa anyone guilty of heresy was declared an outlaw and rebel. See Andrew Willard Jones, *Before Church and*

State: A Study of Social Order in the Sacramental Kingdom of St. Louis IX (Steubenville, 2017).

apocrisiarius: See Justinian, *Novellae constitutiones* 6.2.

186   *wreath of victory*: See Appendix B.2.

187.1   *sacred fillet*: Medieval writers sometimes called bishops and abbots *apices,* a reference to the Roman priests of Jupiter who wore a distinctive cap called an *apex.*

The Church declared . . . Mark the Evangelist: This idea originated with Pope Damasus (366–384) and was taken up by his successors, notably Gregory the Great (see ARP 498, no. 268, and Gregory, *Registrum epistolarum* 6.61, 7.37). According to this tradition, Peter was bishop of Antioch before he left for Rome, and the author of the Gospel of Mark, his disciple, was the first bishop of Alexandria. The fact that Peter in one way or another presided over all three regions of the world—Europe, Asia, and Africa—adds weight to the papacy's claim of universal authority.

187.2   *the Antiochene patriarchate was transferred*: This account is a confused attempt to explain the rise of Constantinople to patriarchal status through the Fourth Council of Constantinople in 381. He may also be alluding to the Council of Sardica (343), which established the pope as the highest appellate judge in ecclesiastical cases.

Aquileia: Aquileia was a major see in northern Italy before its destruction by the Huns in 452. On the difference between Eastern and Western understandings of ecclesial jurisdictions and authority, see John Meyendorff, *Imperial Unity and Christian Divisions: The Church 450–680 A.D.* (Yonkers, 2011).

bishop of Carthage . . . transfer: Cyrila, the Arian bishop of Carthage, claimed to be patriarch of Africa in the Vandal Kingdom, and from the fourth century, Carthage was recognized as preeminent by many African bishops. See Victor of Vita, *Historia persecutionis Africanae provinciae* 2.54, and R. A. Markus, "Carthage, Prima Justiniana, Ravenna," *Byzantion* 49 (1979): 277–306.

the decrees of canon law: Originally the *decreta* were imperial judgments on cases of civil or Church law. In the Christian period,
decreta (or *litterae decretales*) referred to papal decrees or to canons of an ecumenical council. Compilations of Latin Church
law were called *Decreta* (as in Gratian's *Decretum*).

188   *the keys . . . were given to Peter*: See Matthew 16:18.

deacons appointed by the apostles: See Acts 6. For a more in-depth
discussion of several points raised in this chapter, see Honorius's comparison of papal and imperial power in *Summa gloria* 4
(*PL* 172:1263).

189   *vicar of Christ*: On the gradual attribution of this title to the
pope, and Honorius's place therein, see Michele Maccarrone,
Vicarius Christi: Storia del titolo papale, Lateranum 18, nos. 1–4
(Rome, 1952), 93–94.

may shine before men: See Matthew 5:16.

walk in newness of life: See Romans 6:4.

190   *rest from all servile labor*: Clergy were not required to do servile
labor, but to collect tithes for their upkeep.

192   *which they had received from the ever-virgin Mary*: According to
tradition, the apostles, once they had joined Jesus, lived in
strict celibacy in imitation of him. Honorius suggests it was
Mary's virginity they were imitating.

192b   *Secular powers . . . Church offices*: This parallel scheme of Church
and state power (hinted at in Amalar, *Liber officialis* 2.13.8)
was developed by Carolingian theologians such as Alcuin and
Walafrid Strabo. See Janet L. Nelson, "Kingship and Empire,"
in *The Cambridge History of Medieval Political Thought,* ed. J.
Burns (Cambridge, 1988), 211–51. This paragraph is a summary,
with minor differences, of Strabo's "Comparatio ecclesiasticorum ordinum et saecularium," in *De rebus ecclesiasticis* (*PL*
114:963–66).

193   On the tonsure, see Julia Barrow, *The Clergy in the Medieval
World* (Cambridge, 2015), 29–34. The chapter is indebted to
Pope Gregory's *Moralia in Iob* 2.82.

serve the Lord in holiness: See Luke 1:74–75.

king and priest: The title *rex et sacerdos* was a sacral title used by Byzantine and Holy Roman emperors. See note to 1.184.

has made us priests and kings for him: See Revelation 1:6.

194   *Christ our king wore a crown of thorns*: On this and the following two chapters, see Bede, *Historia ecclesiastica* 5.21.

of the captivity . . . enemies: Deuteronomy 32:42.

195   See also Gregory of Tours, *Liber miraculorum* 1.28.

196   *Magicians' tonsure*: Honorius is alluding to a defunct Celtic form of tonsure practiced throughout Gaul and England, in which the front part of the head was shaved in a crescent from ear to ear and the back left to grow out.

platta: In Old High German, from Late Latin *plattus* (flattened).

197   *crown or rim*: The "crown," a rim or molding to the edge of the table of the showbread, is described in Exodus 25:24–25. The Vulgate calls this molding *interrasilis,* technically "scraped" or "embossed," but, literally, "shaved in between," perhaps suggesting this allegory. Compare Bede, *De tabernaculo* 1.6.

198   *the sacred vestments*: On the history of Church vestments, see Herbert Norris, *Church Vestments: Their Origin and Development* (New York, 1950), and Maureen Miller, *Clothing the Clergy: Virtue and Power in Medieval Europe c. 800–1200* (Ithaca, 2014).

sealed with the seven orders: Priests have the powers of all the inferior orders.

199   *put on . . . likeness of God*: Ephesians 4:24.

201   *the Law called the ephod*: See Exodus 30.

a watch before our mouth: See Psalms 140:3.

202   *poderes*: Greek *podērēs* (literally, "reaching to the feet").

persevere . . . unto the end: See Matthew 10:22.

his profession: Subdeacons were required to observe perpetual chastity.

203   *The cincture is girded above the loins*: In accordance with Luke 12:35.

204   *At first, it is placed . . . around the neck*: A deacon wears the stole crosswise, then later, when he is ordained a priest, he wears it down his neck.

205 *they have a right to the tree of life*: See Revelation 22:14, which promises the tree of life to those who "wash their robes" *(lavant stolas suas)* in the blood of the Lamb.

Sell me your birthright . . . Esau's stole: Genesis 25:31 and 27:15, where the Septuagint says that Jacob wore Esau's *stolē*. On this verse, Jerome reports a Hebrew tradition to the effect that, as a firstborn son, he had a priestly role and so owned a priestly garment. See Jerome's *Quaestiones Hebraicae in Genesim* on verse 27:15.

206 *the subcingulum*: The subcingulum (in later times worn only by the pope) was in origin probably a double purse hung at the waist. Once no longer employed for this purpose, it retained its symbolic link with almsgiving.

207.2 *the vestment is drawn up onto the arms*: See note on 1.82 above. When the priest draws up the vestment to free his arms, the folds that form are allegorized to refer to the active life.

208 *fano*: See note to 1.229.

209 *from the sandyx plant or from the sandarac color*: Greek *sandyx* refers to a crimson color, and to both the herb and the mineral from which it is obtained. The herb was probably the red sandalwood, the mineral red arsenic sulfate or red lead, both of which were also called *sandaraca*.

Their use is received . . . while preaching: Christ wore sandals (Mark 1:7, Luke 3:16, John 1:27), as did the apostles (Mark 6:9).

210.2 *learn to despise . . . of heaven*: See the Collect *Repleti cibo spiritalis,* CO 5044.

The priests of the Law . . . their nakedness: See Exodus 28:42.

211.2 *under his wings*: Psalms 35 and 52 ask God for protection under his wings. As usual, Honorius strikingly dramatizes the inherited allegory.

212.1 *religion clean . . . spotless*: See James 1:27.

212.2 *fifteen psalms*: The fifteen gradual psalms (Psalms 119–33), which were mystically understood as the steps in Jacob's ladder leading up to heaven (Genesis 28). See, for instance, Jerome's commentary on Psalm 119.

way of charity: In *Speculum Ecclesiae* (PL 172:1087–93), Hono-

rius compares the fifteen paths of charity to the fifteen paths taught by the devil.

tree of life: Christ is the tree of life, the Eucharist its fruit. See Honorius, *Expositio in psalmos* (PL 172:277), and *Eucharistion* (PL 172:1249).

Charity is patient . . . falleth away: 1 Corinthians 13:4–8.

careful and troubled about many things: See Luke 10:41.

the queen . . . right hand: See Psalms 44:10. The psalm was understood to refer allegorically to Mary or the Church.

the good cheer of the giver: See 2 Corinthians 9:7.

213 *The rationale is taken from the Law*: See Exodus 28:15–30 for a description of this ancient pectoral vestment, on which were two purses, called Urim and Thummim, translated as "Doctrine" and "Truth" by Jerome. A handful of bishops, mostly in German lands, wore a humeral garment called the rationale, whose design may have been influenced by the one described in Exodus.

who measures the heavens with his palm: See Isaiah 40:12.

215 *The use of gloves*: On pontifical gloves, see Xavier Barbier de Montault, *Les gants pontificaux* (Tours, 1877).

Take heed . . . seen by them: Matthew 6:1.

So let your light . . . who is in heaven: Matthew 5:16.

seamless: In fact, *inconsutilis* was a medieval name for pontifical gloves.

216 *the prodigal son . . . first robe*: See Luke 15.

It is said . . . ring finger: Compare Isidore, *Etymologiae* 19.32.

love conquers all: See Virgil, *Eclogae* 10.69.

217 On the kinds and history of pastoral staves, see the chapter "The Crosier and Pastoral Staff," in William Wood Seymour, *The Cross in Tradition, History, and Art* (New York, 1898), 236–49.

218 *our Lord commanded . . . to preach*: See Mark 6:8–9.

220 *When . . . mercy*: Habakkuk 3:2.

222.1 *strive lawfully*: See 2 Timothy 2:5.

222.2 *the gold plate . . . Tetragrammaton*: See Exodus 28:36.

223 *a lamp made of tow . . . the ground*: The sense may be that the ministers brush off any burned tow that lands on the pope, as

the rest falls to the ground. Imported from Byzantium, flax-burning ceremonies were used in several sees and eventually incorporated into the papal rite of coronation. See Agostino Paravicini-Bagliani, *The Pope's Body* (Chicago, 2000), 29–39.

227   *the hyacinth tunic*: The tunic or robe of the ephod described in Exodus 28:31–35.

    the conversation . . . in heaven: See Philippians 3:20.

    enter into the joy of the Lord: See Matthew 25:21.

    persevere to the end in holy living: See Tobit 14:17 and Matthew 10:22.

    seventy-two books: According to the Latin Church's reckoning.

228   *longing for the courts . . . unto the ages of ages* See Psalms 83:3, 83:5.

229   *puts on justice like a breastplate*: See Isaiah 59:17.

    serves God in holiness and justice: See Luke 1:75.

    Note, however . . . carries a fano: In certain places, the subdeacon's maniple was larger than the other ministers', perhaps because it originated as a large cloth *(mappula)* for carrying the offerings and sacred vessels. Honorius claims that when the *fano* replaced the *mappula,* the subdeacon retained a relic of the *mappula* in the form of a larger maniple. Nevertheless, the passage is difficult to interpret since he previously claimed that *mappula, fano,* and *sudarium* were all synonymous (see 1.208). Sicard's paraphrase substitutes an allegorical explanation for Honorius's historical one *(Mitrale* 2.8). See Herbert Thurston, "The Vestment of Low Mass: The Maniple," *The Month* 92, no. 412 (October 1898): 397–407.

230   *always to carry . . . his body*: See the Collect for the feast of Saint Luke, *Interveniat,* CO 3180.

    holy religion . . . in the aforementioned steps: See James 1:27, and the steps of charity described in 1.212.2.

231   *Sometimes they take off their chasuble*: Before the Gospel, the deacon leaves the choir to rearrange his chasuble, as explained in note 1.82.

232   This chapter discusses the tunic, the quotidian article of clerical clothing, worn even outside liturgical contexts. It evolved into the surplice and cotta of later centuries. See Joseph Braun, *Die*

liturgische Gewandung im Occident und Orient: Nach Ursprung und Entwicklung, Verwendung und Symbolik (Freiburg im Breisgau, 1907), 63–101, which includes images.

as Solomon and David prescribed: See 2 Chronicles 20.

in holiness and justice: Luke 1:75.

perseverance unto the end: See Tobit 14:17 and Matthew 10:22.

The lace of this tunic: A strip of cloth attached to the head opening, serving to close this passage.

233   *woolen tunics*: The clerical tunic was ordinarily made of linen. Woolen garments were coarser and cheaper, and hence appropriate for penitential seasons.

234   *A priestly frock*: Higher clergy, especially bishops, wore tunics different from those of the lower clergy. The episcopal tunic developed into the rochet, distinguished from the surplice of ordinary clerics by narrower sleeves. The two laces Honorius mentions may have served to close the sleeves of the frock.

  to walk in charity: See Ephesians 5:2; the whole chapter is an exhortation to perfection of life.

235–36   Blessings for arms were included in pontificals with the blessings for vestments and vessels. This partly explains the inclusion of these two chapters here.

238   *Thy rod . . . comforted me*: Psalms 22:4.

  deifying: See the prologue to the *Rule of Saint Benedict*. On deification in the Latin tradition, see Jared Ortiz, *Deification in the Latin Patristic Tradition* (Washington, DC, 2019).

241   *Dinah*: See Genesis 34:26.

Book 2

1.1   *the watches of heaven's citizens*: Romans divided the night (6 p.m. to 6 a.m.) into four watches (*vigiliae*) of three hours. Each watch (*prima vigilia, secunda,* etc.) was divided into three hours counted continuously, from *hora prima* (first hour) to *hora duodecima* (twelfth hour). The night office, or Matins, on Sundays has three nocturns, each containing three elements: psalms, readings, and responsories. The imagery of angelic "watchers"

stems from Nebuchadnezzar's night vision (Daniel 4), which a
gloss relates obliquely to the office, "For angels are always
awake and ready to serve God. We should imitate them by
staying awake through the night frequently" (marginal gloss to
Daniel 4:10 in *Glossa ordinaria,* ed. Martin Morard, CNRS-
Paris, 2017, http://gloss-e.irht.cnrs.fr). Desire for unity with
the angels is expressed in the Matins benediction: "May the
King of the angels bring us into the company of the heavenly
citizens" *(Ad societatem civium supernorum, perducat nos Rex angelorum).*

heavenly Jerusalem . . . kept secure: The background to this image
of the heavenly Jerusalem—borrowed immediately from Amalar *(Liber officialis* 4.3.4 and 4.7; *De ordine antiphonarii* 4)—is
Bede's conjecture *(Allegorica expositio in Esdram et Nehemiam*
3.20, 3.28) that the Divine Office originated with Ezra, who instituted rounds of prayer for the returned Jewish exiles as they
built and defended the walls of Jerusalem (Nehemiah 4:9, 4:16,
9:1–3). Amalar largely follows Bede's moral interpretation of
their plight, while Honorius emphasizes the anagogical.

which is built as a city: Psalms 121:2.

messmates: The *contubernium* was the smallest unit of the Roman
army, composed of eight men and two servants who shared a
tent. On angels as soldiers in God's palace, see Honorius Augustodunensis, *Elucidarium* 6 (*PL* 172:1113b).

1.2   *royal praises*: When the emperor came to a royal city or abbey,
upon his entry he was saluted with hymns (called *laudes regiae*
or *laudes imperiales*), an act that associated him with Christ's
kingship and priesthood (compare 2.30). To draw attention to
this link, we usually translate *laudes* as "lauds," rather than the
more generic "praises." Compare note to 1.6.1.

Domine labia mea aperies: Psalms 50:17.

they keep watch . . . the city: See Psalms 126:1.

Deus in adiutorium meum: Psalms 69:2.

Venite: The Invitatory, Psalm 94.

give honor to the king: The text of Psalm 94 includes an invita-
tion to "adore" God as the "great king" and a genuflection at

the sixth verse. The Invitatory antiphons for saints' feasts often mention a king explicitly, as, for example, "Come let us adore the Lord, king of confessors" *(Regem confessorum Dominum, venite adoremus)*. For his notion of clergy as imperial legates, see Honorius's *Sermo generalis (PL* 172:862c).

2.1   *portrays Abel*: When Honorius picks out one verse from each psalm, he is not "proof texting," but inviting us to put the whole psalm into the mouth of each historical character and in this way to experience the familiar psalms anew through allegory. Honorius states his understanding of the purpose of the psalms as the means of ascent to heaven in his *Expositio in psalmos (PL* 172:271).

brought forth the fruit . . . in due season: See Psalms 1:3 and Genesis 4:1–16.

served the Lord in fear . . . name of the Lord: See Psalms 2:11 and Genesis 4:26.

the Lord protected . . . heaven: See Psalms 3:6 and Genesis 4:21–24.

2.2   *The Lord heard . . . wrath of God*: See Psalms 6:10 and Genesis 5:28–29.

The antiphon . . . psalms are sung: Each psalm begins and ends with an antiphon in one of the musical modes. The mode of the antiphon sets the mode of the psalm. The antiphon's text is usually taken from the psalm itself, sometimes changing depending on the liturgical season or feast. Seasonal or festal antiphons generally draw their texts from sources different from the psalm to which they are attached.

3   *the Lord found just . . . pursuing waters*: See Genesis 6:8–9 and Psalms 7:2.

crowned with glory . . . father's blessing: See Psalms 8:6 and Genesis 9:26.

related all the wonders . . . city of giants: See Psalms 9:2. In Jewish legend, Eber refused to build the Tower of Babel, and so retained the original human language (named "Hebrew" after him). On giants, see Honorius's *Summa gloria (PL* 172:1261) and *Elucidarium* 2.21 *(PL* 172:1151).

trusted in the Lord . . . fire and sulfur: See Psalms 10:2 and 10:7. Je-

rome tells a Jewish tale about how Terah and his family were cast into a fire by the Chaldeans for rejecting idolatry (*Quaestiones Hebraicae in Genesim* 11.28 and 12.4).

4   *Salvum me fac . . . there was no saint*: Psalms 11:2.

Usquequo . . . gave good things: Psalms 12:6.

devoured as bread . . . was glad: See Psalms 13:1, 13:4, 13:6, 13:7.

walked without blemish . . . worked justice: Psalms 14:2.

5   *the choir turns*: When they finish singing the psalms facing one another, the choir turns back toward the altar to sing the versicle.

the lectors' turns: The readings at Matins were performed from a raised ambo or rood loft lectern, which the reader had to travel to from his place in choir. After the verse, the readers mount the lectern in turns to read, first saluting the celebrant in *Iube, domne, benedicere*. After finishing, each reader says, *Tu autem Domine miserere nobis* or *nostri*.

6   *it is said . . . astrology*: A fact related in Josephus, *Antiquitates Iudaicae* 1.8.2, though Honorius substitutes astrology (*mathematica*) for arithmetic (*arithmetica*).

8   *the Lord is their portion and their cup*: See Psalms 15:5.

judgment came forth from the Lord's countenance: See Psalms 16:2.

9   *the Lord made head of the gentiles*: See Psalms 17:44.

10   *justifications . . . songs*: See Psalms 118:54.

11.1 *no speeches . . . all the earth*: See Psalms 18:4–5.

the name of the Lord . . . their sacrifices: See Psalms 19:2, 19:4.

11.2 *rejoiced in . . . strength*: See Psalms 20:2, 20:4.

Sylvester raised the bull from the dead: Several legends about Saint Sylvester's connection with Constantine circulated in the Latin West. In this one, the Jews call a council to debate the truth of Christianity. Sylvester convinces them that the prophets all foretold Christ, and he raised a dead bull to life, which the Jewish representative Zambres could not do. For this and other stories, see the *Legenda aurea*.

rejoiced exceedingly . . . great glory: See Psalms 20:2, 20:4, 20:6.

their king hopeth in the Lord: See Psalms 20:8. Honorius may mean that the peace of Constantine (the cooperation of the

sacred and secular power) was living on in the Latins' own Holy Roman Empire, whose king, following Constantine's example, still professed Christ's name. By at least the next century, the emperor took part in the third nocturn of Christmas Mass (and perhaps at other times), when he read the seventh lesson.

11.3   *will make . . . devour them*: See Psalms 20:10.

the Lord . . . sing his power: See Psalms 20:14.

the melody of the antiphon: The Ratisbon use had only one antiphon for the psalms of the third nocturn on Sundays.

12   *Now to the king . . . Amen*: 1 Timothy 1.

13   *I thank thee . . . thy gates*: From the account of the martyrdom of Saint Laurence in Ado of Vienne's *Martyrology* (PL 123:325), which is the basis of the lessons for the feast.

14.1   *Gregory . . . the musical art*: Pope Gregory the Great, the eponymous compiler of Gregorian chant.

the angels rejoice . . . penance: See Luke 15:7.

14.3   *Note too that . . . hour*: The masculine form *nocturnus* refers to the chanted material (psalms, antiphons, responsories). The feminine *nocturna* designates the name of the night office (Matins, or Nocturns).

15   *at midnight . . . Hebrews*: See Exodus 12.

when the Lord . . . by night: Luke 2:8.

freed those who were keeping watch there: Oblique reference to Psalms 106:10, Isaiah 9:2, and Matthew 4:16.

the Lord will come in judgment . . . place of rejoicing: Compare Luke 12:36–48. Jerome relates the Jewish and early Christian tradition that Christ would come at midnight, as the angel had come at Passover. See Jerome, *Commentarium in Matthaeum* on verse 25:6. See also Lactantius, *Divinarum institutionum* 7.19. Honorius draws his exegesis of Matins and Lauds from a constellation of scriptural allusions all revolving around the *Benedictus* hymn that concludes Lauds: Psalms 106:10, Isaiah 9:2, Matthew 4:16 and 25, Luke 1:78–79 and 12:36–48, Romans 13:12, 1 Corinthians 15. The Christian soul must await the Master's arrival through the night of this life (Luke 12:36–48, Matthew

25) until the dawn, when, like the sun, Christ will shine the morning light of his coming (Luke 1:79) on those living in the darkness of this world or of the old Law (Psalms 106:10, Isaiah 9:2, Matthew 4:16, Romans 13:12) and lead them into the light of the angelic glory. Monks rise at night to witness, to reenact, to experience again, through the stellar motions, this daily accomplishment of Christ's triumph, accompanying his triumphal course with fitting lauds (2.32, 2.44).

will cast out . . . from his city: See Psalms 100:8.

16   *rose at midnight . . . the Lord*: See Psalms 118:62.

    Paul and Silas . . . from heaven: Honorius confounds the "great light" from Peter's liberation in Acts 12 with Paul and Silas's in Acts 16.

17   *In ancient times . . . all the churches*: See Amalar, *Liber officialis* 4.7.9, and Cassiodorus, *Historia ecclesiastica tripartita* 10.9.

18   *laborers in the vineyard*: Christ's weaving of the prophets' vineyard motif (Isaiah 5:1–7, Psalms 80:7–15) into his parable of the vineyard (Matthew 21:33–46) furnishes Honorius yet another dramatic symbolic device for tying together the ages of salvation history. See 1.33 on the mystic winepress.

    the darkness of ignorance. Compare 1 Corinthians 15:34.

20   *meditate on the Law . . . offer up the fruit*: See Psalms 1:2–3.

    serve the Lord . . . against the Lord: See Psalms 2:1, 2:11.

    rise up . . . lifted him up: See Psalms 3:4–7.

    every night . . . in his indignation: See Psalms 6:2, 6:7.

21   *he put his trust . . . was saved*: See Psalms 7:1.

    how admirable . . . of sucklings: See Psalms 8:1, 8:3, 8:6, 8:10.

    sing to the Lord who dwells in Zion: See Psalms 9:12.

    put his trust . . . in his holy temple: See Psalms 10:1, 10:5.

22   *there was no saint*: Psalms 11:2.

    The Lord . . . forget him: Psalms 12:1.

    sing to the Lord . . . good things: Psalms 12:6.

    fool . . . call upon the Lord: Psalms 13:1, 13:5.

    without blemish . . . glorify the Lord: Psalms 14:2, 14:4.

23   *siesta*: From Latin *sexta* (the sixth hour, or about noon), the time of the midday pause and meal. On nonfasting days clerics ate after Sext.

| 24 | *their portion . . . understanding*: See Psalms 15:5, 15:7. |

24   *their portion . . . understanding*: See Psalms 15:5, 15:7.
      judgment . . . cry to the Lord: See Psalms 16:2–3.
      made the head . . . in praise: See Psalms 17:44, 17:4.

25.1   *the justices of the Lord*: See Psalms 18:9.
      to call upon . . . tribulation: See Psalms 19:2, 19:10.
      has not witholden . . . the Lord's power: See Psalms 20:3, 20:14.

25.2   *they had stood . . . marketplace*: See Matthew 20:6.
      receive a penny . . . in the day: See Matthew 20:8–10.
      at the consummation of the world: Matthew 13:40.

26.1   *O God, come to my assistance*: Psalms 69:2.
      Memor fui . . . throughout the night: Psalms 118:55.
      Media nocte surgebam . . . to give praise: Psalms 118:62.
      Exaltare Domine . . . he will also exalt: Psalms 20:14.

26.2   *Exaudi Domine preces servorum tuorum*: A blessing of the reader
      before the lesson. See 2 Chronicles 6.
      Ostende nobis, Domine: Blessing of the reader. See Psalms 84:8.
      Precibus et meritis . . . sanctorum: Blessing of the reader.
      Domne iube: The more common form is *Iube domne,* but *Domne
      iube* is attested, among other forms, in a later ordinal of Saint
      Emmeram (Munich, Bayerische Staatsbibliothek, Clm 14183).
      Tu autem Domine . . . Beatus qui intelligit: Psalms 40:11.

28.1   *was filled with the spirit of all the just*: See Gregory the Great, *Dia-
      logi* 2.8 (PL 66:150). Several epithets given to Benedict in these
      chapters are found in the *Dialogi,* and all are given him by litur-
      gical offices.

28.2   *Deus Deus meus . . . my spirit*: That is, from Psalm 21 to Psalms
      30:6. See Matthew 27:46 and Luke 23:36.

29   *The same man of God . . . join heaven's gladness*: See *Rule of Saint
      Benedict* 11. Scripture gives the epithet "man of God" to Moses,
      Elisha, and other prophets who performed miracles.
      unworthy servants: See Luke 17:10.
      the Rule ordains: The *Rule of Saint Benedict,* in chapter 11.

30   *from the rising . . . to the setting*: See Psalms 49:1.
      The monks show . . . East to West: The monastic bow, made upon
      entering the church, the chapterhouse, and the refectory, is de-
      scribed in Ulrich's Cluniac constitutions (*PL* 149:702), where it
      is called the *ante et retro.* Making a deep bow from the waist

with hands crossed over the legs, the monk moved his body from east to west. Canons performed two bows, east and then west, as described above. Customaries often mention this allegory, which Honorius places here, at Lauds, at sunrise, to accentuate its astrological symbolism.

31   *meaning good*: See Isidore, *Etymologiae* 10.139.

morning Lauds: In modern usage, prayer at daybreak is called Lauds, from *matutinae laudes,* and prayer at midnight is called Matins, which Honorius calls Nocturns (*nocturna,* see 2.14.3).

32   Compare Honorius, *De neocosmo* 1 (*PL* 172:255).

the morning stars . . . loud jubilation: See Job 38:7.

at this hour the angels . . . were created: In his *De Genesi ad litteram* 4.24, Augustine taught that the light created before the world (Genesis 1:3) represents the angels, whose "morning knowledge" is contrasted with our "evening knowledge."

sons of God: Genesis 6:2.

Insofar as we follow . . . general resurrection: That is, our sacrifice of praise on earth draws us after Christ into the company of the angels, who are the first light of Genesis. For Christ the sun, see the *Benedictus* (Luke 1:78) and Malachi 4:2.

33   *It happened . . . Egyptians*: See Exodus 14:24 (read during the Holy Saturday baptismal liturgy).

34   *Christ the victor*: The term alludes to a Christology that sees Christ's work primarily in terms of a victory over the powers of evil, death, and ignorance, as opposed to the atonement Christology of Anselm, among others.

35   *the just shall awaken*: See 1 Corinthians 15:34.

night that comes before . . . light is dawning: See Romans 13:12 (read at Lauds).

shone . . . light: See Preface of the Nativity: "a new light of your glory has shone on the eyes of our mind" *(nova mentis nostrae oculis lux tuae claritatis infulsit),* Cantus ID g02786.

36   *was clothed in beauty . . . marvelous . . . in the beauty*: See Psalms 92:1, 92:4.

37   *the Lord's people . . . served the Lord with gladness*: See Psalms 99:2–4.

38   *in the covert . . . praised him*: See Psalms 62:8, 62:12.

39   *watches for the Lord . . . is stopped*: See Psalms 62:2, 62:7, 62:12.
     Another psalm: Psalm 66.
40   *cast the three children into the furnace of fire*: See Daniel 3:57–75.
41   *through fear . . . God's house*: In the early Church, *lapsi* were those
       who "fell away" from the Church under the Roman persecu-
       tion. Honorius says that those who fall away at the end times
       (see Matthew 24) will be rejoined to the edifice of the Church.
     These three psalms: Psalms 148–50.
43   *Christ's Precursor*: John the Baptist.
     last trumpet: 1 Corinthians 15:52.
     Dominus regnavit . . . reigned: Psalms 92:1.
     In matutinis, Domine: Psalms 62:7–8.
44   *the true light into this world*: See John 1:9.
     Zachary sang it: Luke 1:67–79.
     royal entry: See 1 Thessalonians 4:17. The Greek word *apantēsis*
       (*obviam*, literally, "going out to meet") has sacral-imperial con-
       notations.
     visited his people . . . shadow of death: Psalms 106:10, Isaiah 9:2,
       Matthew 4:16, and Luke 1:68, 79.
     caught up to meet him: See 1 Thessalonians 4:17.
     his brightness . . . the darkness: Luke 1:79.
45   *Come, ye blessed of my Father*: Matthew 25:34.
     the many rooms . . . house: See John 14:2.
     general resurrection: In Catholic doctrine there is both a particu-
       lar judgment and a general one. Each person is judged and re-
       warded once according to his merits at the time of death. At
       the end of the world, all bodies rise for a definitive general
       reckoning of all souls, and the saints, joined to their bodies,
       experience a double joy.
46   *Now as we deplore . . . six nights of the week*: The timeless grand
       theme of Sunday is recapitulated on the weekdays, which stand
       for progress through salvation history.
48   *These six works*: See Matthew 25:35–36.
49   *visited those . . . shadow of death*: See Luke 1:79.
50.1 *stars through baptism*: On this notion, see Daniel's vision in 12:1–3.
     blessing him at all times: See Psalms 33:2.

must eat bread by the sweat of our brow: See Genesis 3:19.

50.2   *If he shall come . . . those servants*: Luke 12:38.

Saint Benedict . . . middle of the night: In the Roman office, the lessons are said after the twelve psalms, whereas in the monastic office, they are said between two groups of six psalms.

51   *Miserere mei, Deus*: Psalm 50.

Verba mea . . . hear my voice: Psalms 5:4–5.

Iudica me . . . Send forth thy light: Psalms 42:3.

Te decet hymnus . . . to be joyful: Psalms 64:9.

Domine refugium . . . with thy mercy: Psalms 89:6, 89:14.

Domine exaudi . . . in the morning: Psalms 142:8.

52   *our soul thirsts . . . right hand receives*: See Psalms 62:2, 62:9.

53.1   *countenance . . . all the nations*: See Psalms 66:2–3.

mercy is better than lives: See Psalms 62:4.

had been angry . . . comforted us: See Isaiah 12:1.

The living . . . this day: See Isaiah 38:19.

My heart . . . gives life: See 1 Samuel 2:1, 2:6.

mortifies the flesh in its vices: See Galatians 5:24.

beams . . . before the Lord's feet: Habakkuk 3:4–5.

rendered vengeance . . . his people: See Deuteronomy 32:43.

53.2   *watch . . . in faith*: See 1 Corinthians 16:13, part of the short chapter read at Monday Lauds in the Regensburg use; see *Breviarium Ratisbonense* (Bamberg, 1495).

We are filled . . . your mercy: Psalms 89:14.

Benedictus . . . our death: See Luke 1:68–79.

53.3   *all things were made new*: See Isaiah 43:19 and Revelation 21:5.

separated the waters . . . below: See Genesis 1:6.

Hannah was cherished . . . defeated: See 1 Samuel 1.

The birds . . . the waters: See hymn for Thursday Vespers, *Magnae Deus potentiae.*

Horns are in his hands: Habbakuk 3:4.

53.4   *scatter . . . humble*: Luke 1:51–52.

Nunc dimittis: Luke 2:29–32.

sing praises . . . seven times a day: See Psalms 118:164.

praise him . . . of ages: See Psalms 83:5.

54   On the hours as ages of life, see Gregory the Great, *Homiliae in*

Evangelia 1.19.2, and Rabanus Maurus, *In Matthaeum* 6.20. Clerical education began at seven years of age. Tonsure and minor orders were conferred during boyhood and adolescence, and the majority of clerics were not ordained to the priesthood. On the ecclesiastical dignities, see 1.182.

in the Law of the Lord: Psalms 118:1.

stood idle . . . all day: See Matthew 20:6.

58 *on Sunday . . . at Prime*: Sunday Prime was therefore called "Long Prime" *(longa Prima)*.

first five psalms: Psalms 21–25.

Deus in nomine: Psalm 53.

Confitemini: Psalm 117.

Beati immaculati: Psalms 118:1–16.

Retribue: Psalms 118:17–32.

Quicumque vult: The Athanasian Creed.

60 *a roaring lion . . . devour*: 1 Peter 5:9.

O God, come to my assistance: Psalms 69:2.

he from harm . . . shall see: Prime hymn, *Iam lucis orto sidere*.

61.1 *Deus in nomine . . . every trouble*: See Psalms 53:3, 53:5, 53:9.

61.2 *Beati immaculati . . . in the Law of the Lord . . . search his testimonies*: See Psalms 118:2.

Retribue . . . wondrous things of God's Law: See Psalms 118:18.

all . . . will be saved: Romans 10:13.

the Son of the living God: See Matthew 16:16.

Exurge Domine: Psalms 43:26.

61.3 *Vivet anima . . . Erravi sicut ovis*: Psalms 118:175–76.

the litany: The Litany of the Saints, usually attached to the liturgical performance of the penitential psalms.

61.4 *chapterhouse*: Chapter is a daily meeting of a monastic or regular community, held after Prime, to hear a chapter from scripture or a religious rule, for the transaction of community business and for the assignment of daily tasks. The room where they meet is called the chapterhouse, and by a conceit, the Capitoline: "Capitoline refers to the chapterhouse, because the senators met there just as the enclosed meet in chapter" *(Capitolium dicitur a Capitulum, quia ibi conveniebant Senatores, sicut in*

Capitulo claustrales; John of Genoa, *Catholicon,* quoted in *Glossarium mediae et infimae latinitatis,* ed. Charles du Cange and others [Niort, 1883–1887], vol. 2, col. 138c, under "4 *capitolium*").

God's animals: The faithful, and Christ, are likened to animals in Honorius Augustodunensis, *Speculum Ecclesiae* (*PL* 172:958, 1060).

Pretiosa: Versicle, Psalms 115:15.

guided and sanctified . . . assigned tasks: Collect at the end of the chapter office, *Dirigere et sanctificare.*

61.5   *Beati immaculati*: The sections of Psalm 118 that Honorius names are: *Beati immaculati,* Psalms 118:1–16; *Retribue,* Psalms 118:17–32; *Legem pone,* Psalms 118:33–48; *Memor esto,* Psalms 118:49–64; *Bonitatem,* Psalms 118:65–80; *Defecit,* Psalms 118:81–96; *Quomodo dilexi,* Psalms 118:97–112; *Iniquos odio,* Psalms 118:113–28; *Mirabilia,* Psalms 118:129–44; *Clamavi,* Psalms 118:145–60; *Principes persecuti,* Psalms 118:161–76.

61.6   *imperial highway*: The *via regia* was a medieval highway linking the most important cities of the Empire, meant to facilitate safe and efficient travel.

In Beati immaculati . . . my meditation: In Psalm 118, verses 1, 19, 34, 51, 57, 72, 85, 97, 113, 136, 153, 163, 174.

62.1   *Let my prayer . . . evening sacrifice*: Psalms 140:2.

62.2   *enter into the joy . . . five virgins*: Matthew 25:21.

souls do magnify . . . endures forever: Luke 1:46, 1:49–50.

62.3   *Vespers of the preceding day*: Feasts in the Roman rite are celebrated with one Vespers the night before (first Vespers) and one on the day of the feast itself (second Vespers).

night has passed: See Romans 13:12.

63   *worthless servants*: Luke 17:10.

man lives not . . . word of God: See Augustine, *Rule* 3.15. The *Rule of Saint Benedict* orders that monks are to read Cassian's *Collationes patrum* on fasting days after the evening meal, later called the collation for this reason.

64.1   *as the apple of his eye*: See Psalms 16:8.

Nunc dimittis: Luke 2:29–32.

64.2   *we begin . . . our daily works*: See the oration *Actiones nostras,* CO 74, said in some places at the end of Prime.

Converte nos . . . from us: Psalms 84:5.

sleep . . . the peace: See Psalms 4:9–10.

64.3   *the terror . . . the dragon*: See Psalms 90:5, 90:13.

in the house of the Lord: See Psalms 133:2.

65   *man full of the spirit of the saints*: Gregory the Great, *Dialogi* 2.8 (PL 66:150).

66.1   *he assigned Beatus vir . . . the others*: Psalms 1, 2, 6.

he chose Dominus Deus meus . . . the others: Psalms 7, 8, 9:1–19.

On Wednesday . . . is understood: Psalms 9:20–39. According to medieval Jewish and Islamic sources, Nimrod (who appears in Genesis 10:8) rebelled against God and directed the construction of the Tower of Babel. Christian tradition associates him with the Antichrist. For more on Nimrod and giants, see Honorius's *Summa gloria* 2 (PL 172:1261), *Elucidarium* 2.21 (PL 172:1151), and *Imago mundi* 1.15 (PL 172:166).

In Domino confido: Psalm 10.

Salvum me fac: Psalm 11.

66.2   *Usquequo Domine along with the rest*: Psalms 12–14.

Conserva me and the rest: Psalms 15, 16, 17:2–25.

Cum sancto sanctus eris: Psalms 17:25–51.

Caeli ennarant: Psalm 18.

Exaudiat: Psalm 19.

66.3   *gradual psalms*: Psalms 119–33. Benedict assigns 119–27 to Terce, Sext, and None. On the ladder of charity, see Honorius Augustodunensis, *Scala coeli minor* (PL 172:1239).

the psalm that signifies God's Law: Psalm 118.

67.1   *like a bridegroom from his bridal chamber*: Psalms 18:6.

Thou art my son . . . begotten thee: Psalms 2:7.

Before the day star I begot thee: Psalms 109:3.

67.2   *The voice of the Lord is upon the waters*: Psalms 28:3.

I will please the Lord: Psalms 114:9.

This is my beloved Son . . . well pleased: Matthew 3:17.

67.3   *Burned offering . . . Behold, I come*: Psalms 39:7–8.

My heart hath uttered a good word: Psalms 44:2.

Let peace be in thy strength: Psalms 121:7.

67.4   *Judas . . . but a wizard*: Likely a reference to Jewish sources that portray Christ as a sorcerer. One popular myth, the *Toledoth*

Yeshu, has Judas face Christ in a magical duel, defeat him, and turn him in to the Temple authorities. Honorius preserves half the story, the part that implicates Judas, and suppresses the rest. See Richard G. Walsh, *Three Versions of Judas* (Abingdon, 2016).

the fool . . . He is not God: Psalms 13:1.

But thou a man . . . together with me: Psalms 54:14–15.

have whetted their tongues . . . bitter thing: Psalms 63:3.

The wicked have wrought upon my back: Psalms 128:3.

67.5   *Men ate the bread of angels*: Psalms 77:25.

God hath forsaken him, pursue and take him: Psalms 70:11.

his eyes . . . tent for God: See Psalms 131:4–5.

67.6   *his enemies have made a noise*: Psalms 82:3.

laid him in the lower pit: Psalms 87:7.

as a man without help . . . dead: Psalms 87:5–6.

sharpened their tongues . . . day of war: Psalms 139:3–4, 139:8.

67.7   *as grass . . . like a pelican*: Psalms 101:5, 101:7, 101:12. According to legend, the pelican feeds its children with its own blood, analogous to Christ's sacrifice on the Cross, when he gave his blood for the salvation of humanity.

like to vanity . . . like a shadow: Psalms 143:4.

67.8   *I have slept . . . hath protected me*: Psalms 3:6.

leave my soul in hell: Psalms 15:17.

he made me the head of the gentiles: Psalms 17:44.

drank of the torrent . . . the head: Psalms 109:7.

68.1   *Lift up your gates . . . shall enter in*: Psalms 23:7.

Who maketh a barren woman . . . children: Psalms 112:9.

68.2   *By the word of the Lord . . . in a vessel*: Psalms 32:5–6.

The Jordan was turned back: Psalms 113:3.

68.3   *The Lord of armies is with us*: Psalms 45:8.

As we have heard . . . thy temple: Psalms 47:9–10.

Of the fruit of thy womb . . . throne: Psalms 131:11.

68.4   *They have thought to cast away my price*: Psalms 61:5.

They that sat in the gate . . . their song: Psalms 68:13.

O daughter of Babylon . . . repay thee: Psalms 136:8.

The Lord will repay for me: Psalms 137:8.